BUSINESS LAW

BUSINESS LAW

Dr. Annamalai Murugan

Assistant Professor
Department of Tourism
Tagore Government Arts and Science College,
Pondicherry

SSDN Publishers & Distributors

New Delhi

Published by

SSDN

SSDN PUBLISHERS & DISTRIBUTORS
5A, Sahni Mansion, Ansari Road
Daryaganj, New Delhi 110002 (India)
Ph: 011- 47520102, 9871115366
E-mail: ssdn.katla@gmail.com, ssdnbooks@gmail.com
www.ssdnbooks.com

Business Law

Paper- Super Sunsine 90 Gsm.
Size- Royal
No. of Pages- 336

Rs. 3200/--

First edition: 2018

ISBN No. 978-81-9375-130-5

PRINTED IN INDIA

Printed at: New Delhi

Preface

Business Law is specially designed for students pursuing the three-year or five-year LLB course in law education institutes and the one-year or two-year LLM course from various universities or institutes. It also caters to students studying business laws in pursuance of CA, CS, MBA, and PGDM programs as well as aspirants of competitive examinations. With its comprehensive and exhaustive coverage of this area of law, it will also serve as a useful reference for teachers and researchers. Beginning with an introduction to business laws, the book goes on to explain the essentials of a valid contract, kinds of special contracts, and the contract of sale of goods etc., Further, it discusses the provisions of the Consumer Protection Act, 1986 and the kinds of negotiable instruments, and explains the concept of Auditing, Memorandum and Companies Act related to Auditing. The text concludes with a thorough and concise explanation of the key legal provisions various Act. All the provisions are explained, wherever necessary, with the help of decided cases and judgments of the High Courts and the Supreme Court of India. We learn the best when we, ourselves, discover ideas, concepts and principles through exploration and application. This makes learning a joy. This book is committed to making the learning of law engaging and interesting. A description of the early chapters on the contract law could serve as an illustration of the method of the book.

Instead of telling students what offer, acceptance and agreement are, and how these constitute the building blocks of the contract law, the opening chapter on a theme presents cases which narrate disputes. The student, in thinking through and settling the disputes, discovers the principles on the theme. The text and commentary in the chapter confirms the principles derived by the student. Further, references to the Indian Contract Act, 1872 serve two purposes. One, it reassures that the law is only expressing what the student has discovered, and two; it informs the student of the provisions in the law book. The student is now ready to take up advanced cases on the theme, which is again done by only narrating a business context, court case or dispute. The reader sharpens his understanding of the legal principles learnt in the previous chapters, by applying them to the cases. The following chapter further elaborates on the theme through a review of landmark judgements, commentaries and illustrations. Thus, the student moves from simple to complex cases, and, at each stage, discovers for himself what the subsequent text confirms, elaborates upon and modifies. This method that of inviting the student to think and engage is followed in the entire book.

Business laws rest on the foundations of contract law. Contract law evolved first. Other business relations, for example, sale of goods, bailment, pledge, guarantee, agency and partnership are specialized forms of contract. The law for these fields developed by working with the principles of contract law. The book follows the sequence in which the laws evolved. The concepts learnt in one chapter are deployed in the following one, leading to a comprehensive understanding of the special forms of contract.

In addition to understanding the legal principles, we are interested in the application of the principles to business practices. Most business organisations have designed or adopted standard conditions of contract. The organisation gets in a contract only on the terms in the stated standard conditions of contract. The clauses in a standard condition of contract are on formation of contract, termination, damages, arbitration, exclusion of liability, quality of goods, delivery and transportation of goods, bank guaranty and modality of payment. The terms are based on the principles of law in the fields of contract, sale of goods, guarantee, bailment and agency. The discovery and discussion of every principle is followed by its implications for the standard contract documents. The principles of contract law and special forms of contract become the basis for the laws regulating business. We take the two which have general application —unfair trade practice and consumer protection. Companies are also entities created through contracts. The core part of the company law derives from the principles governing contracts. However, the modern company law not only embodies the principles but also makes detailed provisions for the working of the companies. The Indian Contract Act , 1872 governs the formation and regulation of contract in India. For facilitating learning of the law on contract act in India, the Contract Act has been edited and abridged for reference. A legal text makes good sense when read with reference to a case or a problem. Towards this, numerous cases are presented for the student to discover and understand the principles of contract law. The exercise also makes the reader familiar with legal provisions. This is strengthened by commentary and review of court cases.

The book has given a comprehensive treatment to the law of contract, sale of goods, negotiable instruments act, auditing, unfair trade practice and consumer protection. In this first edition, the part on contract law has been further expanded by including the themes, quasi-contracts, restitution, termination, anticipatory breach, mistake and alteration of contracts. Writing this book has been an interactive process between the author, students, readers and faculty members. I am thankful for the valuable contributions.

Dr. Annamalai Murugan

Acknowledgements

Several individuals have contributed to prepare the manuscript of this book. The authors gratefully acknowledge contributions of each one of them. I owe much as well to Shri. Satparkash Katla, Managing Director, SSDN Publishers & Distributors, New Delhi who first encouraged me to take on this task and then prodded me to complete it in good time. I appreciate to the entire editorial team at SSDN, without their efforts this edition would not have been in the form in which it is at present.

Dr. Annaṃalai Murugan

Contents

CHAPTER 1

Introduction

PRODUCT LIABILITY IN INDIA

In India, Product liability law, also called "products liability", governs the liability of manufacturers, wholesalers, distributors, and vendors for injury to a person or property caused by dangerous or defective products. The goal of product liability laws is to help protect consumers from dangerous or defective products, while holding manufacturers, distributors, and retailers responsible for putting into the market place products that they knew or should have known were dangerous or defective.

Product liability in India is, essentially, governed by

a) The Consumer Protection Act, 1986
b) The Sales of Goods Act, 1930
c) The Monopolies and Restrictive Trade Practices Act, 1969 (hereinafter referred to as the "MRTP Act")
d) The law of Torts.
e) special statues pertaining to specific goods

In addition, *criminal liability* for injury or damage caused by defective products in India is imposed by virtue of Indian Penal Code and Prevention of Food Adulteration Act 1954 and other special Acts discussed in this Chapter.

CONSUMER PROTECTION ACT 1986 ("CPA")

The Consumer Protection Act, 1986 was enacted for better protection of the interests of consumers. The provisions of the Act came into force with effect from 15-4-87. Consumer Protection Act imposes strict liability on a manufacturer, in case of supply of defective goods by him, and a service provider, in case of deficiency in rendering of its services. The term "defect" and "deficiency", as held in a catena of cases, are to be couched in the widest horizon of there being any kind of fault, imperfection or shortcoming. Furthermore, the standard, which is required to be maintained, in services or goods is not to be restricted to the statutory mandate but shall extend to that claimed by the trader, expressly or impliedly, in any manner whatsoever.

The salient features of the Act are:

(I) it covers all the sectors whether private, public, and cooperative or any person. The provisions of the Act are compensatory as well as preventive and punitive in nature and the Act applies to all goods covered by sale of goods Act and services unless specifically exempted by the Central Government;

(II) It enshrines the following rights of consumers:

(a) right to be protected against the marketing of goods and services which are hazardous to life and property; (b) right to be informed about the quality, quantity, potency, purity, standard and price of goods or services so as to protect the consumers against unfair trade practices; (c) right to be assured, wherever possible, access to a variety of goods and services at competitive prices; (d) right to be heard and to be assured that consumers' interests will receive due consideration at the appropriate fora; (e) right to seek redressal against unfair trade practices or unscrupulous exploitation of consumers; and (f) right to consumer education;

(III) The Act also envisages establishment of Consumer Protection Councils at the central, state and district levels, whose main objectives are to promote and protect the rights of consumers; (v) To provide a simple, speedy and inexpensive redressal of consumer grievances, the Act envisages a three-tier quasi-judicial machinery at the national, state and district levels. These are: National Consumer Disputes Redressal Commission known as National Commission, State Consumer Disputes Redressal Commissions known as State Commissions and District

Consumer Disputes Redressal Forum known as District Forum; and (IV) the provisions of this Act are in addition to and not in derogation of the

provisions of any other law for the time being in force.

Definition of 'Defect' and 'consumer'

Under the CPA, Consumer Forums at the District, State and National level have been specifically constituted to adjudicate claims of consumers for any "*defect*" in goods. A "defect" has been defined in Section 2(1) (f) of the Act as "*any fault, imperfection orshortcoming in the quality, quantity, potency, purity or standard which is required to maintained by or under any law for the time being in force or under any contract, express or implied, or as is claimed by the trader (which includes the manufacturer) in any manner whatsoever in relation to any goods.*"

It is important to mention herein that by virtue of Section 2 (1)(d) persons/entities who had purchased goods for 'commercial purpose' (other than those persons who have purchased goods for using them to earn their livelihood by means of self employment) are excluded from the scope of CPA; they cannot institute proceedings under the CPA even if there is any 'defect' in the goods purchased by them for using the goods for commercial purposes.

Purview of a 'complaint'

According to the CPA, 'Complaint' means any of the following allegations made in writing by a complainant-

i. any unfair trade practice or a restrictive trade practice has been adopted by a trader,
ii. the goods hired or bought suffer from one or more defects
iii. The goods hired or availed of are deficient in any respect
iv. A trader has charged price in excess of price fixed by law or displayed on the goods or any package containing goods

v. Goods which will be hazardous to life and safety when used, are being offered for sale to the public in contravention of the provisions of any law requiring traders to display information in regard to the contents, manner and effect or use of such goods.

Grant of Reliefs under CPA

On arriving at a finding of defect in the goods according to Section 14 CPA, the jurisdictional Consumer Forum may direct one or more of the following: (i) to remove the defect; (ii) to replace the goods with new goods of similar description which shall be free from any defect; (iii) to return to the complainant the price; (iv) to pay such amount as may be awarded as compensation to the consumer for the loss or injury suffered by the consumer due to the negligence of the opposite party; (v) to discontinue the unfair trade practice or the restrictive trade practice or not to repeat them; (vi) to cease and desist manufacture of hazardous goods; (vii) to pay such sums as orders if injury/loss is suffered by a large number of consumers not identifiable conveniently; (viii) to issue corrective advertisement for neutralizing effect of misleading advertisement; (ix) not to offer the hazardous goods for sale; (x) to withdraw the hazardous goods from being offered for sale; (xi) to provide for adequate costs to parties (the Complainant).

There exists no clear pronouncement of the Supreme Court (the apex court in India) till date on whether the liability under the CPA is strict or fault based. However, failure to conform to the standards required under any law, contract or representations of the trader are sufficient to constitute a defect. Furthermore, under Section 14 of the CPA as explained hereinabove, it is only the remedy of compensation that requires the claimant to necessarily prove negligence. In the case of *Abhaya Kumar Panda v. Bajaj Auto* [(1991) 2 CPJ 644], the Orissa State Commission directed repair of the goods, even though there was no intentional defect. Thus, the defence of no negligence may not be accepted by Consumer forums.

Validity of Limitation of liability clauses

Contractual liability has a role to play in product liability claims under the CPA. Courts in India have upheld limitation of liability clauses, which parties have specifically agreed to in the contract as recognized by the Supreme Court in *Bharathi Knitting Company v DHLWorldwide Express Courier* (1996) 4 SCC 704. However, such clauses may be struck down iffound to be unconscionable in nature. In *MarutiUdyog v. Susheel Kumar Gabgotra*, [(2006) 4 SCC 644], the manufacturer of the vehicle had stipulated a warranty clause limiting its liability to merely repair the defects found if any. In view of this clause, the Supreme Court reversed the findings of the National Commission to replace the defective goods and held that the liability of the manufacture was confined to repairing the defect. Compensation was, however, awarded for travel charges to the complainant, which was incurred due to the fault of the car manufacturer.

Applicability of other laws

Section 3 of the CPA provides that the Act is in addition to and not in derogation of any other law. The Supreme Court in *Secretary, Thirumurugan Co-operative Agricultural Credit Society v. M. Lalitha*, [(2004) 1 SCC 305] has interpreted the above provision to mean that the remediesprovided under the CP Act are in addition to the remedies provided under other statutes. Hence, the fact that a remedy is specifically provided for under another statute would not necessarily oust the jurisdiction of the appropriate authority under the CP Act. It has been further held that if forums under one statute and the CP Act are approached, then it is for the appropriate authority to permit the parties to opt between the consumer forum and the other forum, depending on the facts and circumstances of the case.

Establishment of Consumer forums

At present, there are 34 State Commissions, one in each State/UT and 571 district fora besides the National Commission. The state governments are responsible to set up the district fora and the State Commissions. States have been empowered to establish additional District Forum and also additional members in the State Commission to facilitate constituting benches and also for holding circuit benches. The Central Government is empowered to establish the National Commission. It has been empowered to appoint additional members to facilitate creation of more benches and holding of circuit benches. The second bench of the National Commission started functioning from 24 September 2003. The government is monitoring the disposal of cases by the consumer courts through National Commission. As per the current statistics, since its inception and up to 5.9.2008 , 2559451 cases were filed out of which 2327035 cases were disposed of by the District forums in various states of India .

Jurisdiction under Consumer Protection Act 1986

The District Forum has the jurisdiction to entertain complaints where the value of the goods or services and the compensation , if any, claimed, is less than INR 50,000. A State Commission has the jurisdiction to entertain complaints where the value of the goods or services and the compensation , if any, claimed exceeds 500,000 rupees but does not exceed 2 million rupees. It is also appellate forum for orders of the District forum. The National Commisssion has the jurisdiction to entertain complaints where the value of goods and services and the compensation exceeds two million rupees and also hears the appeals against the orders of the State Commission.

Period of limitation

A complaint is only admitted by any of the competent forums under CPA if it is filed within two years from the date on which the cause of action has arisen but it may be entertained after the said period after recording its reasons for condoning such delay , if the complainant satisfies that he had a sufficient cause for not filing the complaint within period of two years.

Procedure to file a complaint

A complaint can be filed in a District Forum or as per pecuniary jurisdiction in another forum within local limits of whose jurisdiction the opposite party or any of the opposite parties resides or carries on business, or has a branch office or personally works for gain.

Class actions

Under CPA Section 2 (1) (b) permits filing of a complaint by a consumer, any voluntary consumer association registered under companies Act 1956 or under any other law, the State government or Central Government, one or more consumers where number of consumers have same interest, incase of death of a consumer , his legal representative may ,make a complaint.

Penalty under Section 27 CPA

According to CPA ,where a trader or the complainant fails to comply with an order made by the relevant consumer forum , such person is liable to a punishment with imprisonment for a term which is not less than one month but which may extend to three years or with fine of not less than two thousand rupees but which may extend to ten thousand rupees or with both

b) THE SALE OF GOODS ACT

Sale of Goods Act, 1930 is one of very early statutes explaining mercantile law in India . Sale of Goods Act repeals and replaces ss76 to 123 of the Contract Act 1872 , which were adequate for their time , but by 1930 it clearly needed a separate legislation due to growing modern commerce. The Act is based upon and largely reproduces , the English sale of goods Act 1893 of the English common law. In principle, the Indian law of sale of goods is same and English authorities on the different interpretations of different sections although not technically binding in India , may usefully be cited.

The provisions of this Act are set against the background of the general law of contract and the personal property and lay down special rules of law which are peculiar to sale of goods. The provisions of the Indian Contract Act unrepealed by the Act , continue to apply to contracts for sale of goods (s3) and any rule of law not inconsistent with this Act is saved. (s.66 (e).) Basic concepts and provisions of Contract Act apply to contract of Sale of Goods also such as offer and acceptance, legally enforceable agreement, mutual consent, parties competent to contract, free consent, lawful object, consideration etc.

Goods covered

Section 2 (7) of the Act defines 'Goods' as every kind of movable property other than actionable claims and money; and includes stock and shares, growing crops, grass, and things attached to or forming part of the land which are agreed to be severed before sale or under the contract of sale.

Contract of sale

A contract of sale of goods is a contract whereby the seller transfers or agrees to transfer the property in goods to the buyer for a price. There may be a contract of sale between one part-owner and another. [section 4(1)]. A contract of sale may be absolute or conditional. [section 4(2)].

Thus, following are essentials of contract of sale – (i). It is contract, i.e. all requirements of 'contract' must be fulfilled (ii). It is of 'goods' (iii) Transfer of property is required (iv) Contract is between buyer and seller (v) Sale should be for 'price' (vi) A part owner can sale his part to another part-owner (vii) Contract may be absolute or conditional (viii) Payment and delivery are concurrent conditions.

Conditions and warranties

According to Section 12 of the Sale of Goods Act, a buyer is conferred with the right to repudiate the contract and sue for damages in case of breach of a condition, whether relating to quantity, quality or description. Breach of warranty, on the other hand, entitles the buyer, to sue for damages but not repudiate the contract. Offer of a thing different from what was contracted for is not a breach of one term , but a total failure to perform the contract. A discussion on this aspect is found in *Anson on Contract* and *Chalmers*,p187-

*'if a man offers to buy peas of another, and he sends him beans, he does not perform his contract but that is not a warranty , there is no warranty that he should sell him peas, the contract is to sell peas and if he sends him anything else instead it is a non performance of it'*1.

1 Lord Abinger CB in *Chanter vHopkins* (1838) 4 M&W ,404, 51 RR 654-655 approved in Ex Ch, *Azemar v Casella* (1867) LR 2 CP 679, *Drummond v Van Ingen* (1887) 12 App Cas 284

By virtue of the wordings of section 12(4) of the Act it would appear that where a stipulation was not a condition , it must necessarily be a warranty.

Although the parties have used no express words that would create a stipulation of a condition or a warranty, the law annexes to sale of goods contracts many conditions, breach of which may be treated by the buyer as avoiding the contract or giving a right to damages. These are called implied conditions and are enforced on the grounds that the law infers from all circumstances of the case that the parties intended to add such a stipulation to their contract but did not put it in express words2

Implied condition as to quality or fitness

Section 16 of the Sale of Goods is most important from the point of view of the present discussion. Section 16 prescribes Implied conditions as to quality or fitness . Section 16(1) requires that the goods shall be reasonably fit for the purpose made known to the seller by the buyer expressly or by implication . Section 16(2) requires only that the goods should be of merchantable quality . Secondly , Section 16 (1) is excluded where the buyer does not rely on seller's skill or judgement , whereas section 16(2) is not so limited, though it doesnot apply when the buyer examines the goods, as regards defects which that examination ought to reveal. Where a defect is revealed to the buyer, not only in section 16(2) excluded, but that fact will normally indicate that it is unreasonable for the buyer then to rely on the seller for the purposes of s. 16(1).

This section reflects the principle of *caveat emptor* . That is, it is for the buyer to satisfy himself that the goods which he is purchasing are of the quality which he requires or if he is buying them for a specific purpose, that they are fit for that purpose. In Section 16, the first exception to the rule of Caveat emptor is that of question of fact whether the buyer did rely on the skill or judgement of the seller, and no presumption is raised against him by reason of the fact that the goods were in esse and he had the opportunity of examining them .Nor is it necessary that he should rely on the sellers skill and judgement only and nothing else.

In *RanbirsinghShankasrsingh Thakur v Hindustan General Electric corp* ltd AIR 1971 Bom97 , where a radio set purchased by a layman from a local distributor on hire purchase basis started giving trouble after two months of purchase, it was held that the article supplied ought to have been reasonably fit for a specific purpose ,and seller's liability in such cases where he knows the purpose to supply goods that are reasonably fit, is an absolute one. It was held that the case fell within the purview of section 16 (1) and 16(2). In the case of sale of an article under its tradename or patent, there is no implied condition as to its fitness for any purpose. Where there is a apparent (as opposed to latent) defect in goods which would have been discovered by reasonable care, the buyer cannot sue the manufacturer in tort or the retailer in contract.

Remedies for breach of warranty

2 *The Moorcock* (1889) 14PD64,68,per Bowen LJ

A breach of warranty does not entitle the buyer to reject the goods and his only remedies would be those provided in Section 59 of the Sale of Goods Act., namely to set up against the seller the breach of warranty in diminution or extinction of the price or to sue the seller for damages for breach of warranty. In *Barium Chemicals ltd v AP Mining Corp ltd* (1980)1 Andh WR 350, the court held that the defence of diminution or extinction of price , by reason of breach of warranty is a statutory defence expressly provided by section 59 and it is not in the nature of a counterclaim or set off .According to Section 13 of the Act, a buyer may treat a breach of condition as a breach of warranty and claim damages instead of rejecting the goods. 3

Measure of damages is governed by Section 73 of the Contract Act, 1872.In the case of warranty of quality, the presumption is that the measure of damages is the difference between what the goods are intrinsically worth at the time of delivery, and what they would have been worth, if they had been according to contract4 , and this must be ascertained by reference to the market price at that time, whether it has fallen or risen since the date of the contract. However, the buyer has a duty to act reasonably in mitigating the loss or damage.

Buyer's right to recover interest

Buyer is only entitled to recover interest when he is entitled to recover the purchase price , when he can sue for the price prepaid as money had and received , by reason of total failure for consideration. He cannot recover interest when his only remedy is to sue for damages, for breach of warranty even though damages may be sufficient to extinguish the price 5.

The Act contains no penal provisions nor does it laydown any special rules of evidence or procedure. Tortious liability, if any, of the parties towards each other or towards third parties is not affected, except as regards questions of property in and the right to possession of the goods which are subject of a contract of sale dealt with by the Act.

Limitation period

According to the Indian limitation Act, 1963 in suits for compensation for breach of any contract,, period of limitation is three years from the time when the contract is broken or where there are successive breaches, when the breach in respect of which the suit is instituted occurs or where the breach is continuing when it ceases. As per Code of Civil procedure, in case of suits for compensation for wrongs to person or movables, suit is to be instituted either where wrong was committed or where defendant resides , or carries on business. Other suits are instituted where defendant resides or where any cause of action wholly or partly arises.

3 *Commissioner of Income tax v prafullakumarmallik* AIR 1969 Orissa 187, B*engalcorppvt ltd v the commissioner of port of Calcutta* AIR 1971 Cal 357.

4 *CW Simson v kokaJagannadha Row Naidu* AIR 1914Mad 633.

5 *Union of India v Rallia Ram* AIR 1963 SC 1685

c) MONOPOLIES AND RESTRICTIVE TRADE PRACTICES ACT, 1969 ("MRTP Act")

In order to promote fair competition in the market and to curb monopolistic and restrictive and unfair trade practices , India enacted the Monopolies and Restrictive trade Practices Act in 1969 .The Monopolies & Restrictive Trade Practices Act, 1969 was the first enactment to deal with competition issues and came into effect on 1st June 1970.

The application and operation of the MRTP Act

The MRTP Act gave new dimensions to the economic legislation of the post Independence era. This enactment imbibed the social and economic philosophy enshrined in the Constitution.

The principle objectives as stated in the Preamble to the Act are:

(i) Prevention of concentration of economic power to the common detriment
(ii) Control of monopolies
(iii) Prohibition of monopolistic trade practices, and
(iv) Prohibition of restrictive trade practices

According to Section 2 (e) of the MRTP Act 'goods' are defined as every kind of moveable property other than actionable claims and money and includes stocks and shares , growing crops , grass and things attached to or forming a part of land which can be severed under an agreement before sale or under contract of sale. This definition also includes products manufactured or processed or mined in India as well as shares and stocks. Goods imported in India also stand included.

In the context of the present discussion Section 36 A of the Act dealing with Unfair Trade practices is of significance. 'Unfair Trade Practice' refers to a trade practice which for the purpose of promoting the sale, use, or supply of any goods or for the provision of any services, adopts any unfair method or unfair or deceptive practice. Any statement whether orally or in writing or by visible representation is considered an unfair trade practice if it falls under nay of the following heads (without need to establish loss or injury to consumers6), interalia,

6 After amendment of this section by MRTP (Amendment) Act,1991,it is no more necessary to prove loss or injury to consumer

- falsely represents that goods are of a particular standard , quality , quantity , grade, composition, style or model,
- falsely represents that the services are of a particular standard , quality or grade,
- falsely represents any second hand goods as new,
- represents that goods or services have sponsorship approval, performance characteristics, accessories, uses or benefits which it does not have

- represents seller has a sponsorship or approval which it does not have,
- makes false or misleading representation concerning need for or usefulness of any goods or services ,
- gives to the public any warranty or guarantee of performance, efficacy or length of life of a product, or any goods not based on any tests
- gives a warranty of a product or a promise to replace, maintain or repair an article which is misleading or given with intention of not fulfilling it
- materially misleads the public concerning price at which a product is ordinarily sold,
- permits the publication of any advertisement for sale or supply a t a bargain price for goods or services not intended to be sold at that price
- permits offering of gifts , prizes with intention of not providing them,
- the conduct of any contest , lottery, game of chance for promotion of its goods
- permits sale of any goods to be used by consumers knowing or having reason to believe that goods donot comply with standards prescribed by competent authority relating to performance ,composition, contents, design, construction, finishing, packaging necessary to prevent or reduce risk of injury to the person using the goods,
- permits the hoarding or destruction of goods , or refuses to sell the goods or to make them available for sale , or to provide any service , if such hoarding, destruction or refusal raises cost of those or other similar goods.

In *Girnar Scooters limited* UTP Enquiry No. 10/1986, order dated 11-6-87, there was false representation about the performance of scooters guaranteeing mileage of 40kms per litre, when factually the performance was not beyond 30kms per litre .The respondents also advertised that a substantial number of customers reported performance in excess of guaranteed mileage. Further, there was suppression of material facts by respondent in not having disclosed the latent defects within their knowledge , in regard to the starting trouble of scooters and stooping during drive , which could not be discovered by the buyer at the time of purchase. The commission accordingly issued a cease and desist order in this case.

In *Proctor and Gamble Home Products Ltd, Hindustan Lever Ltd] (1997) II CPJ 21 MRTP)*, the Commission restrained the company from making false, exaggerated and misleading claims about its "New Ceramides Sun silk extra Treatment Shampoo". In a similar decision, in *Hindustan Oil Co1997 II CPJ 30 MRTPC* case, the claim of the company that its cooking gasunits, by use of kerosene, saved 30 percent against the LPG system was held to be false and misleading and, therefore, advertisement to that effect was restrained by the Commission.

Limitation period

There is no prescribed period of limitation for filing an application under MRTP Act. This is interpreted to mean that the applications for enquiry need to be filed within a reasonable time, which depends on facts and circumstances of each case.

MRTP Act AND CPA

There is an overlapping of jurisdiction of MRTP commission and consumer forums set up under Consumer Protection Act. An aggrieved consumer can thus approach the

MRTP commission or the consumer redressal agencies under CPA for redressal of his grievance. However, a complaint cannot lie in CPA if goods are obtained for commercial purpose and scope of redressal relating to defects in goods is confined to manner and to the extent laid down in section 14 (1) of CPA. Also, MRTP commission has been vested with power to initiate inquiry suomotu in unfair trade practices under section 36 B(d) which consumer forum does not.

The MRTP Act has been comprehensively drafted so as to empower the MRTP Commission to grant temporary injunctions and compensation, for loss and damage, as a result of monopolistic, restrictive practices or unfair trade practises. In a case where the commission concluded there is an unfair trade practice by virtue of Section 36D,it could pass a cease and desist order. However, after MRTP Amendment Act, 1991 , introduction of a new clause © in Section 36 D , the Commission is empowered to order issue of corrective advertisement.7 Also, as per Section 36 E the Commission has been empowered to exercise or perform same powers in relation to unfair trade practices as has been conferred for restrictive trade practice in Section 12 A, 12 B , that is power of commission to grant temporary injunction and power to grant compensation respectively. This power also vests with the consumer courts under Section 13 (3) (B) and 14 of the Consumer protection Act. The cease and desist orders issued by MRTP commission can also be issued by Consumer Courts under Section 14 CPA.

Under Section 13 B MRTP Act , it is empowered to impose punishments for contempt of its orders .Further, Section 48 C of the MRTP Act imposes a penalty for contravention of order made by commission relating to unfair trade practices with an imprisonment for a term not less than 6 months but which may extend to three years and fine which may extend to ten lakhs . In the event of failure of a party to comply with order passed by commission relating to unfair trade practice a formal complaint is required to be filed in court of sessions for trial by that court. In CPA ,where a trader or the complainant fails to comply with an order made by the relevant consumer forum , such person is liable to a punishment with imprisonment for a term which is not less than one month but which may extend to three years or with fine of not less than two thousand rupees but which may extend to ten thousand rupees or with both

7 In the consumer protection Act also after passing of Act 62 of 2002, S.10(wef 15-3-2003) consumer courts have been empowered to order issuance of corrective advertisements.

Class actions under MRTP Act

Class action can be initiated by filing of a complaint for unfair trade practice under Section 36 B of the MRTP Act wherein a complaint could be filed by any trade association, consumer, or registered consumer association or by reference made by central government or state government, upon application made to it by Director General or upon its own knowledge or information.

Advent of Competition Act, 2002

In the context of the new economic policy paradigm, India has chosen to enact a new competition law called the Competition Act, 2002. The MRTP Act has metamorphosed into the new law, Competition Act, 2002. The new law is designed to repeal the extant MRTP Act. As of now, only a few provisions of the new law have been brought into force and the process of constituting the regulatory authority, namely, the Competition Commission of India under the new Act, is underway. The remaining provisions of the new law will be brought into force in a phased manner. For the present, the outgoing law, MRTP Act, 1969 and the new law, Competition Act, 2002 are concurrently in force, though as mentioned above, only some provisions of the new law have been brought into force. Competition Law for India was triggered by Articles 38 and 39 of the Constitution of India. These Articles are a part of the Directive Principles of State Policy. Articles 38 and 39 of the Constitution of India mandate, inter alia, that the State shall strive to promote the welfare of the people by securing and protecting as effectively, as it may, a social order and the State shall, in particular, direct its policy towards securing that the ownership and control of material resources of the community are so distributed as best to subserve the common good; and that the operation of the economic system does not result in the concentration of wealth and means of production to the common detriment.

The Government had appointed a committee in October 1999 to examine the existing MRTP Act for shifting the focus of the law from curbing monopolies to promoting competition and to suggest a modern competition law. Pursuant to the recommendations of this committee, the Competition Act, 2002, was enacted on 13th January 2003. The objectives of the Competition Act are to prevent anti-competitive practices, promote and sustain competition, protect the interests of the consumers and ensure freedom of trade. This Act provides for different notifications for making different provisions of the Act effective including repeal of MRTP Act and dissolution of the MRTP Commission. The objectives of the Act are sought to be achieved through the instrumentality of the Competition Commission of India (CCI) which has been established by the Central Government with effect from 14th October, 2003. The rubric of the Act has essentially four compartments:

1. Anti- Competition Agreements
2. Abuse of Dominance
3. Combination Regulations
4. Competition Advocacy

The Competition Act prohibits anti-competitive agreements and abuse of a dominant position. It also regulates combinations of enterprises and persons. The acquisition of enterprises by persons or the merger or amalgamation of enterprises is considered to be a combination and requires filings with the Competition Commission of India, but only if the thresholds of their assets or turnover exceeds the value stipulated in the Competition Act.

Once the MRTP Act is repealed,the pending Unfair Trade practice cases (except those under (x) of Section 36 A(1)(giving false or misleading facts disparaging the goods) of MRTP Act in the MRTP Commission would be transferred to the concerned consumer courts under the Consumer Protection Act, 1986 i.e National Commission. The pending Monopolistic trade practices and Restrictive trade practices Cases in MRTP Commission shall be taken up for adjudication by the CCI from the stages they are in. Competition Act shall not apply to Unfair trade practice cases. Also, under the consumer protection Act , a complaint would lie if goods, which will be hazardous to life and safety when used , are offered for sale to the public in contravention of any law requiring the traders to display information in regard to the contents , manner and effect of use of such goods (Section 2(1) ©(v). There is no such provision in the Competition Act.

d) LAW OF TORT

In India, a claim under the product liability law shall also lie where the element of negligence, as enunciated in the **Law of Torts**, can be traced. The law of torts, in India is not codified and British precedents are being followed by Courts by altering doctrines for application in the Indian context. 'Tort' may be defined as a civil wrong which is rederessible by an action for unliquidated damages and which is other than a mere breach of contract or breach of trust.

For the Plaintiff to make a successful claim, it must be proved that:-

- Defendant owed a duty to take care
- A breach of such duty
- Plaintiff suffered loss or injury as a result of such breach
- the plaintiff is entitled to damages.

Duty of care depends on reasonable foreseeability of the injury to the plaintiff. For ascertaining the liability of a person for the tort of negligence we compare the conduct of defendant with that of a reasonable man and make him liable only if he fails to perform a duty of care.

While a contractual claim restricts the number of Defendants who are liable to be impleaded in an action, negligence claim allows for inclusion of all those who may have breached distinct duties of care to the ultimate consumer In *Dongoghue v Stevenson* (1842)10 M&W 109, it was held that the consumer could bring an action in tort against the manufacturer even though there was no contract or privity of contract between manufacturer and consumer .

When a person transfers goods to another person under a contract his liability arises not only in contract but also in tort for negligence. In *Clarke v Army and navy Cooperative Society ltd* (1903) 1 K.B 155 , the plaintiff purchased a tin of chlorinated lime from the defendant's store When the plaintiff tried to open it in the usual way by pressing the lid off with a spoon the content flew on to her face and injured her eyes. The defendants knew of this danger but negligently omitted to warn the plaintiff about that . The defendants were held liable in tort towards her.

Liability towards ultimate transferee

Liability towards ultimate transferee can be placed under two heads, Liability for fraud and liability for negligence. In *langridge v levy* (1837) 2 M&W 519, the defendant sold a gun to plaintiff's father for use of the plaintiff and stated that the same had been manufactured by a celebrated manufacturer and was safe. The gun burst when the plaintiff was using it and he was injured. It was held that even though the fraudulent statement was made by defendant to plaintiff's father yet plaintiff was entitled to sue in fraud because the statement made by defendant was intended to be and was communicated to the plaintiff on which he had acted.

Liability for negligence can be placed in three heads –

- Things dangerous per se,
- things not dangerous perse but actually dangerous and known to be so by transferor

- and things neither dangerous per se nor known to be so by the transferor but dangerous infact.

In *Dixon v Bell* (1816)4M&S 198, defendant gave a servant a loaded gun which she fired on plaintiff who was seriously injured. The defendant was held liable for the same.

In case of things not dangerous per se but known to be so, we have seen in *Clarke*' case above that transferor owed a duty to warn about the known dangers not only to immediate transferee but to all persons likely to be endangered by that thing.

For the third category, things neither dangerous per se nor known to be so by the transferor but dangerous infact, application of *Donoghue v Stevenson* principle requires manufacturer to take reasonable care(when thing is to reach ultimate consumer without any possibility of intermediate examination) and is liable for not taking that care despite being no privity of contract. This liability principle has extended to repairers, assemblers, builders and suppliers of products.

Products liability—strict liability in tort

Strict liability in tort is the concept that in certain situations a defendant is liable for plaintiff's damages without any requirement that the plaintiff prove that the defendant was negligent.

In *Greenman v. Yuba Power Products, Inc.* (1963) 59 Cal.2d 57 [13 A.L.R.3d 1049], confronted with injury to an ultimate consumer caused by a defective power tool, the California Supreme Court assigned strict liability to a manufacturer who placed on the market a defective product even though both privity of contract and notice of breach of warranty were lacking. The court rejected both contract and warranty theories, express or implied, as the basis for liability. Strict liability does not rest on a consensual foundation but, rather, on one created by law. The liability was created judicially because of the economic and social need for the protection of consumers in an increasingly complex and mechanized society, and because of the limitations in the negligence and warranty remedies.

Product liability distinguished from negligence

The distinction between products liability and negligence was explained in *Jiminez v. Sears,Roebuck & Co.* (1971) 4 Cal.3d 379, 383 [52 A.L.R.3d 92]: "It is pointed out that in aproducts liability case the plaintiff in order to recover in strict liability in tort must prove that he was injured by a defect in the product and that the product was defective when it left the hands of the retailer or manufacturer; whereas to recover in negligence the plaintiff must prove the same two elements plus an additional element, namely, that the defect in the product was due to negligence (and fault) of the defendant."

Trends in product liability law in India country.

The laws relating to product liability, in India, have been constantly evolving, by way of judicial interpretations and amendments, to become one of the most important socio-economic legislations for the protection of consumers. The legislation, in respect of product liability in India, though was enacted to protect the interest of consumers but the same was, earlier, construed narrowly, thereby frustrating the object sought to be achieved. The trend, however, has changed in the recent times with the Courts adopting a pro-consumer approach. The Courts, in India, have now started awarding compensation and damages which are *more punitive than compensatory* in nature.

In *Wheels World vs. Pradeep Kumar Khurana MANU/CF/0280/2002* the complainant, a doctor by profession, complained to the respondent about deficiency in service in not repairing, free of charge, a technical fault, which occurred during warranty period, in his new Montana car and then not delivering the same for a period of 4 years. A sum of Rs. 30, 000/- with interest

@ 18% per annum from 2/7/1988 to 7/5/1992, was awarded as compensation, in favour of the complainant for his suffering, both professionally and otherwise, on account of non availability of car for a period of 4 years. Further interest, at the same rate for the same period, was also awarded on an amount of Rs. 82, 000/-, being the price of the car as well as an amount of Rs. 55, 00/- towards costs and, last but not the least, an amount of

@ Rs. 50, 000/-, which was deposited by the Respondent on account of stay of imprisonment, was also awarded to the petitioner.

Remedies in tort –Product liability

Generally in tort cases under product liability two remedies are common – one is claim for damages and the other grant of the court has discretion in refusing the latter remedy if grant of damages is sufficient relief injunction. Suits for compensation for wrongs to person or movables is instituted in local limits of jurisdiction where wrong was committed or where defendant resides or carries on business.

Limitation time

In suits relating to tort, for compensation for doing or omitting to do an act alleged to be in pursuance of any enactmernt in force in India , limitation period is one year from the date when act or omission takes place, and for negligence in supply of defective products , generally the limitation periods is three years from the date the right to sue accrues.

PRODUCT LIABILITY INSURANCE

There is no enactment for compulsory insurance to cover supply of defective products in India .It is voluntary on the part of a seller or vendor to take this form of insurance in best interests of his business . The prevalent legislation Public liability Insurance Act, 1991 aims at providing for public liability insurance for the purpose of providing relief to the persons affected by accident occurring while handling any hazardous substance for matters connected therewith .Every owner i.e a person who has control over handling any hazardous substance, has to take insurance policy so that he is insured against liability to give relief incase of death or injury to a person , or damage to any property , arising from an accident occurring while handling any hazardous substance. Further, the Motor vehicles Act, 1988 makes the insurance of motor vehicles against third party risks , compulsory.

CRIMINAL LIABILITY FOR MANUFACTURING OR DISTRIBUTING A DEFECTIVE PRODUCT IN INDIA

The product liability law, in India, apart from the civil liability, also imposes criminal liability in case of non-compliance with the provisions of each of the below mentioned

Acts. The said Acts are in addition to and not in derogation of any other laws in force, which implies that an action imposing penal liability can be simultaneously initiated along with a claim under civil law. Some of these are special Acts pertaining to sale of specific goods such as food, drugs, cosmetics etc.. The provisions of these enactments are preventive in form , though the relief envisaged is an action for breach in civil or criminal court.

- The Foods Adulteration Act, 1954
- The Food Safety and Standards Act, 2006
- The Drug & Cosmetics Act, 1940
- The Indian Penal Code, 1860
- The Standards of Weights and Measures Act, 1956
- The Agricultural Produce (Grading and Marking) Act, 1937 for marking and grading of commodities like vegetables, butter, etc.
- The Indian Standards Institution (Certification Marks) Act , 1952 to formulate a number of standards for different products by ISI
- The Bureau of Indian Standards Act , 1986

Each of the aforesaid Acts provides for imposition of fine and/or imprisonment in case of supply of defective products or adulterated consumables.

The Food Safety and Standards Act, 2006 is the most recent legislation which comprehensively deals with food and safety standards which are to be complied with by manufacturers and producers, non-compliance of which imposes a liability, upon defaulters, of fine, extending uptoRs. Ten Lakhs and/or imprisonment.

The provisions of Indian Penal Code (IPC), on the other hand, in respect of product liability, are attracted when the element of cheating and fraud can be attributed to such defects. For example, in the case of *Smt. Uma Deepak v. MarutiUdyog Ltd Ors (2003) CPJ90(MRTP)* the Complainant alleged that the car sold by the opposite party was not onlyaccidental but the price, for the same, was also overcharged. The Court, in response to the allegations made by the complainant, directed arrest of the Directors as well as the manager of the dealers/agents who sold the said defective car to the complainant and remanded them to judicial custody. Subsequent thereto, the said officers of the opposite party were released on bail and were directed to replace the disputed car with a new car.

Provisions of IPC are also attracted to provide punishment to offenders for false weights and measures , adulteration of goods (food, drugs etc -6 months imprisonment, fine of 1000 rupees or both), and false property marks (one year imprisonment, fine or both). The period of limitation as per Section 468 of the Criminal Procedure Code is 6 months if offence is punishable with fine only , and one year if offence is punishable with upto one year imprisonment and three years if offence is punishable with imprisonment of above one year and upto three years.

The provisions of the Standards of Weights and Measures Act, 1976 are attracted in case of any false packaging, weight or measure which does not conform to the standards established by or under the said Act and breaches the mandatory declaratory requirements on a package. If any mandatory declaration is found missing on the package a fine of upto 2000 rupees shall be levied as per Rule 39 of the Standards of weights and measures packaged commodity rules.

The Drugs and Cosmetic Act, 1940 also provides for criminal liability for manufacturers and producers of medicinal products or cosmetics etc, which do not adhere to the prescribed standards.

Standardisation law in India

The standardization law in India is governed by **a) The Bureau of Indian StandardsAct, 1986** (hereinafter referred to as "BIS"), **b) Agmark Grading and Standardisation** under Agricultural Produce (Grading & Marking) Act, 1937 (in respect of agricultural commodities) and **The Food Safety and Standards Act, 2006**. The mandatory requirement of notifying safety standards is with respect to food items under The Food Safety and Standards Act, 2006 only. There is, however, no mandatory requirement of such notification under the BIS and Agmark, except a few products under mandatory list issued by concerned department, but, if a manufacturer/producer is desirous to grade their commodities under Agmark or BIS, they have to obtain Certificate of Authorisation or Certification Mark, respectively. Since the said certifications acknowledge the safety and health standards in a product, majority of manufacturers/producers, therefore, certify their products under the aforesaid Acts.

The Food Safety and Standards Act, 2006 makes it obligatory for the Food Authority to regulate and monitor the manufacture, processing, distribution, sale and import of food so as to ensure safe and wholesome food. The said Authority clearly sets out standards which are to be maintained with respect to food items and non-adherence of the same makes the defaulter liable to imprisonment and exorbitant fine. A similar legislation, namely the Fruit Products Order, 1955 enacted under the Essential Commodities Act, 1955, supplements the Food and Safety Act and, interalia, sets out quality standards, in relation to fruit products, sweetened aerated water etc., as also sanitary requirements of factory manufacturing fruit products.

The Agmark system, on the other hand, sets out quality standards for agricultural commodities, based on their intrinsic quality. Standards are harmonised with international standards keeping in view the WTO requirements. Certification of agricultural commodities is carried out for the benefit of producer/manufacturer as well as the consumer. While Certification of adulteration prone commodities viz. Butter, Ghee, Vegetable Oils, Ground-Spices, Honey, Wheat Atta etc. is very popular, blended edible vegetable oils and fat spread, on the other hand, are compulsorily required to be certified under Agmark.

Under the BIS Act, such specification which hints at the nature, quality, strength, purity, composition, quantity, dimensions, weight, grade, durability, origin, age, material, mode of manufacture, or other characteristic which distinguishes it from any other article or process, shall be applied to any substance, artificial or natural, or partly artificial or partly natural, whether raw or partly or wholly processed or manufactured. The BIS offers numerous certification schemes, like the product Certification Scheme, whereby manufacturers of products interested in producing their products as per relevant Indian Standards are permitted to use the Standard Mark of the Bureau (the popular ISI mark) on their products after obtaining a licence from the Bureau. The pre-requisites for obtaining a licence require the manufacturer to possess the necessary manufacturing and testing facilities for the product as also follow the quality assurance scheme of the

Bureau, in addition to payment of necessary fees as stipulated. The scheme, though, is voluntary in nature but, the government has made ISI marking compulsory for about 136 products which affect the health and safety of consumers or are products of mass consumption like LPG Cylinders, Food Colours and Additives, Cement, Packaged Drinking Water, etc.. Yet another scheme is the Certification for Indian Importers, wherein, the Government has stipulated compulsory approval, form BIS, for certain category of products before they are imported into India.

The Agmark, on one hand, aims at promotion of Grading and Standardisation of agricultural and allied commodities, and whereas, the BIS provides for standardisation, marking and quality certification of goods, in general. Both the Acts, however, empower the authorities to search and seize goods which, inspite of obtaining certification, do not confirm to the prescribed standards, as well as those for which certification has not been obtained and such marks, as to quality and standard, have been falsely applied. The Acts also provide for imprisonment and/or fine for non-adherence of any of the provisions contained therein.

INDIA AND ITS LEGAL SYSTEM

The main source of law in India is the Constitution which, in turn, gives due recognition to statutes, case law and customary law consistent with its dispensations. Statutes are enacted by Parliament, State Legislatures and Union Territory Legislatures. There is also a vast body of laws known as subordinate legislation in the form of rules, regulations as well as by-laws made by Central and State Governments and local authorities like Municipal Corporations, Municipalities, Gram Panchayats and other local bodies. This subordinate legislation is made under the authority conferred or delegated either by Parliament or State or Union Territory Legislature concerned. The decisions of the Supreme Court are binding on all Courts within the territory of India. As India is a land of diversities, local customs and conventions which are not against statute, morality, etc. are to a limited extent also recognised and taken into account by Courts while administering justice in certain spheres.

Enactment of laws

The Indian Parliament is competent to make laws on matters enumerated in the Union List. State Legislatures are competent to make laws on matters enumerated in the State List. While both the Union and the States have power to legislate on matters enumerated in the Concurrent List, only Parliament has power to make laws on matters not included in the State List or the Concurrent List. In the event of repugnancy, laws made by Parliament shall prevail over law made by State Legislatures, to the extent of the repugnancy. The State law shall be void unless it has received the assent of the President, and in such case, shall prevail in that State.

Applicability of laws

Laws made by Parliament may extend throughout or in any part of the territory of India and those made by State Legislatures may generally apply only within the terrirory of the State concerned. Hence, variations are likely to exist from State to State in provisions of law relating to matters falling in the State and Concurrent Lists.

Judiciary

One of the unique features of the Indian Constitution is that, notwithstanding the adoption of a federal system and existence of Central Acts and State Acts in their respective spheres, it has generally provided for a single integrated system of Courts to administer both Union and State laws. At the apex of the entire judicial system, exists the Supreme Court of India below which are the High Courts in each State or group of States. Below the High Courts lies a hierarchy of Subordinate Courts. Panchayat Courts also function in some States under various names like Nyaya Panchayat, Panchayat Adalat, Gram Kachheri, etc. to decide civil and criminal disputes of petty and local nature. Different State laws provide for different kinds of jurisdiction of courts. Each State is divided into judicial districts presided over by a District and Sessions Judge, which is the principal civil court of original jurisdiction and can try all offences including those punishable with death. The Sessions Judge is the highest judicial authority in a district. Below him, there are Courts of civil jurisdiction, known in different States as Munsifs, Sub-Judges, Civil Judges and the like. Similarly, the criminal judiciary comprises the Chief Judicial Magistrates and Judicial Magistrates of First and Second Class

Class actions for product liability

Class action can be initiated by filing of a complaint for unfair trade practice under Section 36 B of the MRTP Act wherein a complaint could be filed by any trade association, consumer, or registered consumer association or by reference made by central government or state government, upon application made to it by Director General or upon its own knowledge or information.

Under CPA Section 2 (1) (b) permits filing of a complaint by a consumer, any voluntary consumer association registered under companies Act 1956 or under any other law, the State government or Central Government, one or more consumers where number of consumers have same interest, incase of death of a consumer , his legal representative may ,make a complaint.

TAKING OF EVIDENCE ON FOREIGN LAW

In India, according to section 34 and 84 of the Evidence Act ,1872 court may take judicial notice of a publication containing a foreign law if it is issued under authority of foreign government concerned, and may be accepted as set out in the publication, as law in force in particular country at relevant time. What is the whole law of that country may be determined by calling an expert as provided for in Section 45 , Evidence Act

SERVICE OF SUMMONS

According to order 5 rule 9 of Code of civil procedure, where defendant resides within jurisdiction of the court in which the suit is instituted, or has an agent resident within thatjurisdiction who is empowered to accept service of summons, the summons shall, unless the court otherwise directs, be delivered or sent either to proper officer to be served by him or one of his subordinates or to such courier services as are approved by the court. The service of summons may be made by registered post acknowledgement due , fax or by e-mail , courier service provided by high court rules provided plaintiff bears this cost. A defendant who resides outside the jurisdiction of the court in which suit is instituted, summons service may be made by any of the methods mentioned hereinbefore except by registered post acknowledgement due as per rules of high court.

When an acknowledgement receipt is received back declaring defendant refuses to accept the service, the court will declare summons were duly served .Provided summons was properly addressed , prepaid and duly sent by registered post acknowledgement due, such declaration will be made even though summons were lost or mislaid.

If an application is made by plaintiff an order of service of summons personally by plaintiff is also possible served under the sealed cover of the court .

By virtue of Rule 20 of order 5, CPC, an order for substituted service may be made where defendant is deliberately avoiding service of summons, such summons are pasted at last known residence of defendant. Incase where defendant resides out of India, Order 5, rule 25 provides that if such person has no agent in India, summons shall be addressed to defendant at the place where he is residing and sent to him by post, courier, fax or e-mail or other means approved by high court .

RECOGNITION & ENFORCEMENT OF JUDGEMENTS

In case a judgement is passed by Indian court, by virtue of Section 38 Code of civil procedure, a decree may be executed either by court which passed it or by court to which it is sent for execution. According to Section 51, Code of civil procedure, execution order may entail delivery of any property specifically decreed or attachment and sale of any property, ,by arrest and detention in prison, by appointing a receiver, or other manner as the court may deem fit.

RECOGNITION & ENFORCEMENT OF FOREIGN JUDGEMENTS

The Code of civil procedure , in Section 13 of the code lays down the conditions for when foreign judgements are considered not conclusive by Indian courts. It provides that a foreign judgement is conclusive as to any matter directly adjudicated upon between the same parties where it has not been pronounced by a court of competent jurisdiction, where it has not been given on merits of the case, where on the face of it , it appears to be founded on an incorrect view of international law, or refusal to recognize the law of India in cases where such law is applicable.

Further, Section 44 of the Code of civil procedure provides for execution of decrees passed by courts in reciprocating territory. By virtue of this provision, Where a certified copy of adecree of any superior courts of any reciprocating territory has been filed in a district court, the decree may be executed in India as if it had been passed by the District Court. Reciprocating country has been explained to mean any country or territory outside India which central government may, by notification in official gazette declare to be reciprocating territory.

CONCLUSION

India is recognising and realising the imperativeness of strengthening and enforcing a strict Product liability regime to protect the interests of its consumer and general public interest at large. While specific legislations such as Consumer Protection Act, 1986 are in place to protect rights of consumers against supply of defective materials by manufacturers and suppliers, the law of Tort and contract also aid in protecting the interest of consumers. The standardization regimes are shifting from voluntary to mandatory in nature for certain specified products such as packaged drinking water wherein BIS rules makes it a mandatory certification .The judicial framework is hierarchical and well demarcated and rules of evidence to record evidence, summoning of witnesses, and execution and enforcement of judgements are clearly pronounced and are equally effective. Recently, India is witnessing that its exporter community is particularly interested in product liability insurance and certain insurance by strengthening its product liability regime and its future is indeed promising!

CHAPTER 2

What is Law?

Law means a **'set of rules'** which governs our behaviours and relating in a civilized society. So there is **no need of Law in a uncivilized society.**

Why Should One Know Law?

One should know the law to which he is subject because ***ignorance of law is no excuse***

Sources of Mercantile Law in India

- **English Mercantile**
- **Indian Status Law**
- **Judicial Decisions**
- **Customs and Usages**

INDIAN CONTRACT ACT, 1872

Section 1:- **Commencement and applicability:-**

Short Title **Extent and** **commencement**

The Indian Applicable to First day of contract Act whole Indian September 1872 except the state 1872(1st Sept.
of Jammu & 1872) Kashmir

- Prior to this English law of contract was followed in India.
- It has **XI** chapter.
- Law of contract creates jus in **personem** and **not in jus in rem.**
- The Indian Contract Act consists of the following two parts:
  (a) General principals of the Law of Contract.
  (b) Special kinds of contracts.
- The general principals of the Law of Contract are contained in Sections 1 to 75 of the Indian Contract Act. These principles apply to all kinds of contracts irrespective of their nature.

- Special contracts are contained in Sections 124 to 238 of the Indian Contract Act. These special contracts are Indemnity, Guarantee, Bailment, pledge and Agency.

Note: In our discussion on this part of the book, unless otherwise stated, the sections mentioned are those of the Indian Contract Act, 1872.

Contracts as Defined by Eminent Jurists

1. *"Every agreement and promise enforceable at law is a contract." – Pollock*
2. *"A Contract is an agreement between two or more persons which is intended to be enforceable at law and is contracted by the acceptance by one party of an offer made to him by the other party to do or abstain from doing some act." – Halsbury*
3. *"A contract is an agreement creating and defining obligation between the parties" – Salmond*

DEFINITIONS (Sec 2)

1. **Offer(i.e. Proposal) [section 2(a)]:-**When one person signifies to another his willingness to do or to abstain from doing anything, with a view to obtaining the assent of that other person either to such act or abstinence, he is said to make a proposal.
2. **Acceptance 2(b):-** When the person to whom the proposal is made, signifies his assent there to , the proposal is said to be accepted.
3. **Promise 2(b) :-** A Proposal when accepted becomes a promise. In simple words, when an offer is accepted it becomes promise.
4. **Promisor and promise 2(c) :-** When the proposal is accepted, the person making the proposal is called as promisor and the person accepting the proposal is called as promisee.
5. **Consideration 2(d):-** When at the desire of the promisor, the promisee or any other person ***has done or abstained from doing something*** or ***does or abstains from doing something*** or ***promises to do or abstain from doing something***, such act or abstinence or promise is called a consideration for the promise.
   Price paid by the one party for the promise of the other Technical word meaning ***QUIDPRO-QUO*** i.e. ***something in return***.
6. **Agreement 2(e) :-** Every promise and set of promises forming the consideration for each other. In short, agreement = offer + acceptance.
7. **Contract 2(h) :-** An agreement enforceable by Law is a contract.
8. **Void agreement 2(g):-** An agreement not enforceable by law is void.
9. **Voidable contract 2(i):-** An agreement is a voidable contract if it is enforceable by Law at the option of one or more of the parties there to (i.e. the aggrieved party), and it is not enforceable by Law at the option of the other or others.
10. **Void contract :-** A contract which ceases to be enforceable by Law becomes void when it ceases to be enforceable.

ESSENTIALS OF A VALID CONTRACT

"All agreements are contracts, if they are made

- by free consent of the parties, competent to contract,
- for a lawful consideration and
- with a lawful object, and
- not hereby expressly declared to be void." **- Sec.10.**

ESSENTIALS OF VALID CONTRACT

Offer + acceptance = Promise + consideration

= Agreement + enforceability By Law

Contract

1. **Proper offer and proper acceptance with intention to create legal relationship. Cases;-** A and B agree to go to a movie on coming Sunday. A does not turn in resulting in loss of B's time B cannot claim any damages from B since the agreement to watch a movie is a domestic agreement which does not result in a contract.

- In case of social agreement there is no intention to create legal relationship and there the is no contract (Balfour v. Balfour)
- *In case of commercial agreements, the law presume that the parties had the intention to create legal relations.*
- [an agreement of a purely domestic or social nature is not a contract]

2. **Lawful consideration :-** consideration must ***not*** be ***unlawful, immoral or opposed to the public policy.***

3. **Capacity:-** The parties to a contract must have capacity (legal ability) to make valid contract.

Section 11: of the Indian contract Act specify that every person is competent to contract provided.

(i) Is of the age of majority according to the Law which he is subject, and
(ii) Who is of sound mind and
(iii) Is not disqualified from contracting by any law to which he is subject.

- Person of unsound mind can enter into a contract during his lucid interval.
- An alien enemy, foreign sovereigns and accredited representative of a foreign state. Insolvents and convicts are not competent to contract.

4. **Free consent :-** consent of the parties must be genuine consent means agreed upon ***samething in the same sense*** i.e. there should be ***consensus – ad – idem.*** A consent is said to be free when it is not caused by *coercion, undue influence, fraud, misrepresentation or mistake.*
5. **Lawful object**

- The object of agreement should be lawful and legal.
- Two persons cannot enter into an agreement to do a criminal act.

- Consideration or object of an agreement is unlawful if it
(a) is forbidden by law; or
(b) is of such nature that, if permitted, would defeat the provisions of any law; or
(c) is fraudulent; or
(d) Involves or implies, injury to person or property of another; or (e) Court regards it as immoral, or opposed to public policy.

6. **Possibility of performance:**
- The terms of the agreement should be capable of performance.
- An agreements to do act, impossible in itself cannot be enforced.

Example: A agrees to B to discover treasure by magic. The agreement is void because the act in itself is impossible to be performed from the very beginning.

7. **The terms of the agreements are certain or are capable of being made certain [29] Example :** A agreed to pay Rs.5 lakh to B for ultra-modern decoration of his drawing room. The agreement is void because the meaning of the term " ultra – modern" is not certain.
8. **Not declared Void**
- The agreement should be such that it should be capable or being enforced by law.
- Certain agreements have been expressly declared illegal or void by the law.

9. **Necessary legal formalities**
- A contract ***may be oral or in writing.***
- Where a particular type of contract is required by law to be in writing and registered, it must comply with necessary formalities as to writing, registration and attestation.
- If legal formalities are not carried out then the contract is not enforceable by law. **Example :** A promise to pay a time. Barred debt must be in writing.

Agreement is a wider term than contract where as all contracts are agreements. All agreements are not contracts.

All Contracts are Agreements, but all Agreements are not Contracts

The various agreements may be classified into two categories:

Agreement not enforceable by law | **Agreement enforceable by law**

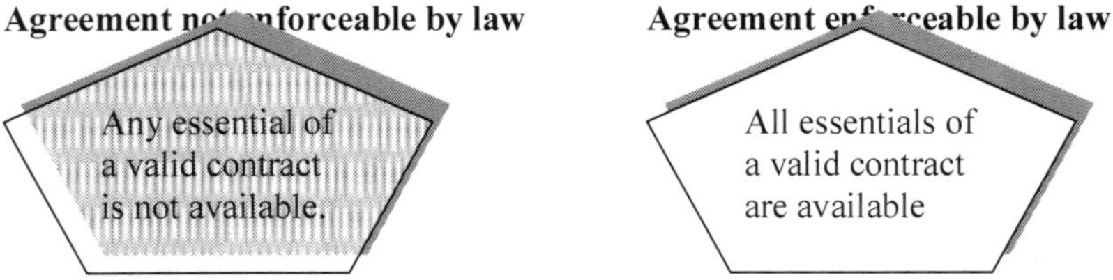

Conclusion:

Thus we see that an agreement may be or may not be enforceable by law, and so ***all agreement are not contract.*** Only those agreements are contracts, which are enforceable by law, In short.

Contracts = Agreement + Enforceability by Law

Hence, we can conclude "All contracts are agreement, but all agreements are not contracts."

Basis	Contract	Agreement
1. Section : 2. Definition : 3. Enforceability : 4. Interrelationship 5. Scope : 6. Validity : 7. Legal : 8. Obligation	Sec. 2(h) A contract is an agreement enforceable by law. Every contract is enforceable A contract includes an agreement. The scope of a contract is limited, as it includes only commercial agreements. Only legal agreements are called contracts. Every contract contains a legal obligation.	Sec. 2(e) Every promise or every set of promises forming consideration for each other is an agreements. Every promise is not enforceable. An agreement does not include a contract. Its scope is relatively wider, as it includes both social agreement and commercial agreements. An agreement may be both legal and illegal. It is not necessary for every agreement to have legal obligation.

Types of contracts

(1) On the Basis creation
- a. Express contract
- b. Implied contract
- c. Tacit contract
- d. Quasi contract
- e. E contract contract
- f. Illegal contract

(2) On the Basis of Validity
- a. Valid contract
- b. Void contract
- c. Voidable contract
- d. Unenforceable

(3) On the Basis of execution
- a. Executed contract
- b. Executed contract
- c. Partly executed and party executory

(4) On the Basis of of Liability
- a. Bilateral contract
- b. Unilateral contract

ON THE BASIC OF CREATION

(a) **Express contract :-** A contract made by word spoken or written. According to **sec 9** in so for as the proposal or acceptance of any promise is made in words, the promise is said to be express.

Example : A says to B 'will you purchase my bike for Rs.20,000?" B says to A "Yes".

(b) **Implied contract:-** A contract inferred by
- The conduct of person or
- The circumstances of the case.

By implies contract means implied by law (i.e.) the law implied a contract through parties never intended. According to **sec 9** in so for as such proposed or acceptance is made otherwise than in words, the promise is said to be implied.

Example:

A stops a taxi by waving his hand and takes his seat. There is an implied contract that A will pay the prescribed fare.

(c) **Tacit contract: -** A contract is said to be tacit when it has to be inferred from the conduct of the parties. **Example** obtaining cash through automatic teller **machine,** sale by fall hammer of an auction sale.

(d) **Quasi Contracts are contracts which are created -** • Neither by word spoken
- Nor written
- Nor by the conduct of the parties.
- But these are created by the law.

Example:

If Mr. A leaves his goods at Mr. B's shop by mistake, then it is for Mr. B to return the goods or to compensate the price. In fact, these contracts depend on the principle that nobody will be allowed to become rich at the expenses of the other.

(e) **e – Contract**: An e – contract is one, which is entered into between two parties via the internet.

On the basis of Validity

(a) **Valid contract:-** An agreement which satisfies all the requirements prescribed by law On the basis of creation

(b) **Void contract (2(j)):-** a contract which ceases to be enforceable by law because void when of ceased to be enforceable

When both parties to an agreement are:-
Under a mistake of facts **[20]**
Consideration or object of an agreement is unlawful **[23]**
Agreement made without consideration **[25]**
Agreement in restrain of marriage **[26]**
Restraint of trade **[27]** Restrain legal proceeding **[28].**
Agreement by wage of wager **[30]**

(c) **Voidable contract 2(i) :-** an agreement which is enforceable by law ***at the option of one or more the parties but not at the option of the other or others is a voidable contract.***

Result of coercion, undue influence, fraud and misrepresentation.

(d) **Unenforceable contract: -** where a contract is good in substance but because of some ***technical defect*** i.e. absence in writing barred by imitation etc one or both the parties cannot sue upon but is described as unenforceable contract. Example: Writing registration or stamping.

Example: An agreement which is required to be stamped will be unenforceable if the same is not stamped at all or is under stamped.

(e) **Illegal contract:-** It is a contract which the law forbids to be made. All illegal agreements are void but all void agreements or contracts are not necessary illegal.

On the basis of execution

Contract that is immoral or opposed to public policy are illegal in nature.

- Unlike illegal agreements there is no punishment to the parties to a void agreement.
- Illegal agreements are void from the very beginning agreements are void from the very beginning but sometimes valid contracts may subsequently becomes void.

(a) **Executed contract :-** A contract in which both the parties have fulfilled their obligations under the contract.
Example: A contracts to buy a car from B by paying cash, B instantly delivers his car.

(b) **Executory contract:-** A contract in which both the parties have still to fulfilled their obligations.
Example : D agrees to buy V's cycle by promising to pay cash on 15th July. V agrees to deliver the cycle on 20th July.

(c) **Partly executed and partly executory:-** A contract in which one of the parties has fulfilled his obligation but the other party is yet to fulfill his obligation.
Example : A sells his car to B and A has delivered the car but B is yet to pay the price. For A, it is excuted contract whereas it is executory contract on the part of B since the price is yet to be paid.

On the basis of liability for performance:-

On the basis of Liability

(a) **Bilateral contract:-** A contract in which both the parties commit to perform their respective promises is called a bilateral contract.
Example : A offers to sell his fiat car to B for Rs.1,00,000 on acceptance of A's offer by B, there is a promise by A to Sell the car and there is a promise by B to purchase the car there are two promise.

(b) **Unilateral contract:-** A unilateral contract is a one sided contract in which only one party has to perform his promise or obligation party has to perform his promise or obligation to do or forbear.
Example :- A wants to get his room painted. He offers Rs.500 to B for this purpose B says to A " if I have spare time on next Sunday I will paint your room". There is a promise by A to pay Rs 500 to B. If B is able to spare time to paint A's room. However there is no promise by B to Paint the house. There is only one promise.

Difference Between Void and Voidable Contract

Matter	Void contract	Voidable contract
Definition	It means contract which cease to be enforceable.	It means an agreement enforceable by law by one or more parties.
Nature	Valid when made subsequently becomes unenforceable.	It remains voidable until cancelled by party.
Rights or remedy	No legal remedy.	Aggrieved party has remedy to cancel the contract.
Performance contract	Party can't demand performance of contract	If aggrieved party does not cancel it within reasonable time, performance
		can be demanded.
Reason	Due to change circumstances	If consent is not obtained freely.
Damages	Not available	Can demand in certain cases.

Difference between Void and illegal Agreement

Matter	Void agreement	Illegal agreement
What	Void agreement is not prohibited by law.	It is prohibited by law.
Effect on collateral transaction	Enforced	Not enforced.
Punishment	No	Yes
Void ab initio	May not be void ab initio	Always void initio

Contract of record:

It is either a judgment of a court of a Recognizance.

A Judgment is an obligation imposed by a Court upon one or more persons in favour of another or others. In real sense, it is not a contract, as it is not based upon any agreement between two parties.

Recognizance is a Bond by which a person undertakes before a Court of Magistrate to observe some condition e.g. to appear on summons.

Contracts of record derive their binding force from the authority of the Court.

Contract under Seal:

(a) A contract under Seal is one which derives its binding force from its form alone.

(b) It is in writing and signed, sealed and delivered by the parties.

(c) It is also called a Deed or a Specialty contract.

OFFER

Offer(i.e. Proposal) [section 2(a)]:-When one person signifies to another his willingness to do or to abstain from doing anything, with a view to obtaining the assent of that other person either to such act or abstinence, he is said to make a proposal.

To form an agreement, there must be at least two elements – one offer and the other acceptance. Thus offer is the foundation of any agreement.

"When one person signifies to another his willingness –

- to do or to abstain from doing anything,
- with a view to obtaining the assent of that other to such act or abstinence, he is said to make a proposal."

The person who makes an offer is called ***"Offeror" or " Promisor"*** and the person to whom the offer is made is called the ***Offeree" or "Promisee***".

Example

Mr. A says to Mr. B, "Will you purchase my car for Rs.1,00,000?" In this case, Mr. A is making an offer to Mr. B. Here A is the offeror and B is the offeree.

Essentials elements of an offer:-

(1) There must be two parties.

(2) The offer must be communicated to the offeree.

(3) The offer must show the willingness of offeror. **Mere telling the plan is not offer**.

(4) The offer must be made with a view to obtaining the assent of the offeree.
(5) A statement made jokingly does not amount to an offer.
(6) An offer may involve a positive act or abstinence by the offeree.
(7) Mere expression of willingness does not constitute an offer.

A tells B' that be desires to marry by the end of 2008, if does not constitute an offer of marriage by A' to B' A further adds will you marry me. Then it become offer.

Legal Rules as to valid offer:

1. ***Offer must be communicated to the offeree:*** The offer is completed only when it has been communicated to the offeree. Until the offer is communicated, it cannot be accepted. *Thus, an offer accepted without its knowledge, does not confer any legal rights on the acceptor.*

   Example:

   A's nephew has absconded from his home. He sent his servant to trace his missing nephew. When he servant had left, A then announced that anybody who discovered the missing boy, would be given the reward of Rs.500. The servant discovered the missing boy without knowing the reward. When the servant came to know about the reward, he brought an action against A to recover the same. But his action failed. It was held that the servant was not entitled to the reward because he did not know about the offer when the discovered the missing boy.

   [Lalman Shukla v. Gauri Datt (1913) All LJ 489]

2. ***The offer must be certain definite and not vague unambiguous and certain.***

   Example: A offered to sell to B. 'a hundred tons of oil'. The offer is uncertain as there is nothing to show what kind of oil is intended to be sold.

3. ***The offer must be capable of creating legal relation. A social invitation is not create legal relation.***

   Example: A invited B to a dinner and B accepted the invitation. It is a mere social invitation. And A will not be liable if he fails to provide dinner to B.

4 ***Offer may be express and implied***

   The offer may be express or implied; An offer may be express as well as implied. An offer which is expressed by words, written or spoken, is called an express offer. The offer which is expressed by conduct, is called an implied offer [Section 9].

5. ***Communication of complete offer***

   Example: A offered to sell his pen to B for Rs.1,000. B replied, "I am ready to pay Rs.950". On A's refusal to sell at this price, B agreed to pay Rs.1,000. held, there was not contract at the acceptance to buy it for Rs.950 was a counter offer, i.e. rejection of the offer of A. Subsequent acceptance to pay Rs.1,000 is a fresh offer from B to which A was not bound go give his acceptance.

6. ***Counter offer*** – *A counter offer amounts to rejection of the original offer*

7. ***Cross offer do not conclude a contract***

8. ***An offer must not thrust the burden of acceptance on the offeree.***

   Example: A made a contract with B and promised that if he was satisfied as a customer he would favorably consider his case for the renewal of the contract. The promise is too vague to create a legal relationship.

- The acceptance cannot be presumed from silence.

Acceptance is valid only if it is communicated to the offeror.

9. ***Offer must be distinguished from invitation to offer.***

   Example: Menu card of restaurant is an invitation to put an offer.

   Example: Price – tags attached with the goods displayed in any showroom or supermarket is also an invitation to proposal. If the salesman or the cashier does not accept the price, the or the cashier does not accept the price, the interested buyer cannot compel him to sell, if he wants to buy it, he must make a proposal.

   Example: Job or tender advertisement inviting applications for a job or inviting tenders is an invitation to an offer.

   Example: An advertisement for auction sale is merely an invitation to make an offer and not an offer for sale. Therefore, an advertisement of an auction can be withdrawn without any notice. The persons going to the auction cannot claim for loss of time and expenses if the advertisement for auction is withdrawn.

10. ***Offeror should have an intention to obtain the consent of the offeree.***
11. An answer to a question is not a offer.

Offer	Invitation to offer
Show his readiness to enter into a contract, it is called as an offer	Person invites offer to make an offer to him.
Purpose of entering contract	Purpose of enter offer
Results in a contract	Results in offer.
Example Application filled in by a prospective applicable to the Institution, a student seeking admission in educational Institution.	**Example** Issue of prospectus by a Company, an education Institution.

KINDS OF OFFER

Express Implied Specific General Cross offer Counter Standing offer offer offer offer offer Open and Continuou s offer

I. **Express offer -** When the offeror expressly communication the offer the offer is said to be an express offer the express communication of the offer may be made by

   Spoken word

   Written word

II. **Implied offer** – when the offer is not communicate expressly. An offer may be implied from:-

   The conduct of the parties or

   The circumstances of the case

III. **Specific:-** It means an offer made in

(a) a particular person or

(b) a group of person: It can be accepted only by that person to whom it is made communication of acceptance is necessary in case of specific offer.

IV. **General offer: -** It means on offer which is made to the public in general.

- General offer can be accepted by anyone.

- If offeree fulfill the term and condition which is given in offer then offer is accepted.
- Communication of acceptance is not necessary is case of general offer

Example

Company advertised that a reward of Rs.100 would be given to any person who would suffer from influenza after using the medicine (Smoke balls) made by the company according to the printed directions.

One lady, Mrs, Carlill, purchased and used the medicine according to the printed directions of the company but suffered from influenza, She filed a suit to recover the reward of Rs.100. The court held that there was a contract as she had accepted a general offer by using the medicine in the prescribed manner and as such as entitled to recover the reward from the company.

Carlill v Carbilic Smoke Ball Co. 1893

V. **Cross offer:-** When two parties exchange identical offers in ignorance at the time of each other's offer the offer's are called cross offer.

Two cross offer does not conclude a contract. Two offer are said to be cross offer if

1. *They are made by the same parties to one another*
2. *Each offer made in ignorance of the offer made by the*
3. *The terms and conditions contained in both the offers' are same.*

Example : A offers by a letter to sell 100 tons of steel at Rs.1,000 per ton. On the same day, B also writes to A offering to buy 100 tons of steel at Rs.1,000 per ton.

When does a contract come into existence: - A contract comes into existence when any of the parties, accept the cross offer made by the other party.

VI Counter offer :- when the offeree give qualified acceptance of the offer subject to modified and variations in the terms of original offer. Counter offer amounts to rejection of the original offer.

Legal effect of counter offer:-

(1) Rejection of original offer
(2) The original offer is lapsed
(3) A counter offer result is a new offer.

In other words an offer made by the offeree in return of the original offer is called as a counter offer.

Example:

A offered to sell his pen to B for Rs.1,000. B replied, " I am ready to pay Rs.950." On A's refusal to sell at this price, B agreed to pay Rs.1,000. Held, there was not contract as the acceptance to buy it for Rs.950 was a counter offer, i.e. rejection of the offer of A. Subsequent acceptance to pay Rs.1,000 is a fresh offer from B to which A was not bound to give his acceptance.

VII Standing, open and continuous offer:- An offer is allowed to ***remain open for acceptance over a period of time*** is known as standing, open or continually offer. Tender for supply of goods is a kind of standing offer.

Example:

When we ask the newspaper vendor to supply the newspaper daily. In such case, we do not repeat our offer daily and the newspaper vendor supplies the newspaper to us daily. The offers of such types are called Standing Offer.

LAPSE OF AN OFFER

An offer should be accepted before it lapses (i.e. comes to an end). An offer may come to an end in any of the following ways stated in Section 6 of the Indian Contract Act:

1. **By communication of notice of revocation:** An offer may come to an end by communication of notice of revocation by the offeror. It may be noted that an offer can be revoked only before its acceptance is complete for the offeror. In other words, an offeror can revoke his offer at any time before he becomes before bound by it. Thus, the communication of revocation of offer should reach the offeree before the acceptance is communicated.
2. **By lapse of time;** Where time is fixed for the acceptance of the offer, and it is not acceptance within the fixed time, the offer comes to an end automatically on the expiry of fixed time. Where no time for acceptance is prescribed, the offer has to be accepted within reasonable time. The offer lapses if it is not accepted within that time. The term 'reasonable time' will depend upon the facts and circumstances of each case.
3. **By failure to accept condition precedent:** Where, the offer requires that some condition must, be fulfilled before the acceptance of the offer, the offer lapses, if it is accepted without fulfilling the condition.
4. **By the death or insanity of the offeror:** Where, the offeror dies or becomes, insane, the offer comes to an end if the fact of his death or insanity comes to the knowledge of the acceptor before he makes his acceptance. But if the offer is accepted in ignorance of the fact of death or insanity of the offeror, the acceptance is valied. This will result in a valid contract, and legal representatives of the deceased offeror shall be bound by the contract. On the death of offeree before acceptance, the offer also comes to an end by operation of law.
5. **By counter – offer by the offeree:** Where, a counter – offer is made by the offeree, and then the original offer automatically comes to an end, as the counter – offer amounts to rejections of the original offer.
6. **By not accepting the offer, according to the prescribed or usual mode:** Where some manner of acceptance is prescribed in the offer, the offeror can revoke the offer if it is not accepted according to the prescribed manner.
7. **By rejection of offer by the offeree:** Where, the offeree rejects the offer, the offer comes to an end. Once the offeree rejects the offer, he cannot revive the offer by subsequently attempting to accept it. The rejection of offer may be express or implied.
8. **By change in law:** Sometimes, there is a change in law which makes the offer illegal or incapable of performance. In such cases also, the offer comes to an end.

ACCEPTANCE

Acceptance 2(b):- When the person to whom the proposal is made, signifies his assent there to , the proposal is said to be accepted.

Legal Rules for the Acceptance

1. **Acceptance must be absolute and unqualified**
   Example: A offers to sell his house to B for Rs. two lakhs. B accepts the offer and promises to pay the price in four installments. This is not pay the acceptance as the acceptance is with variation in the terms of the offer.
2. **Acceptance must be communicated**: Mere mental acceptance is no acceptance, But there is no requirement of communication of acceptance of general offer.
   Example The manager of Railway Company received a draft agreement relating to the supply of coal. The manager marked the draft with the words "Approved" and put the same in the drawer of his table and forgot all about it. Held, there was no contract between the parties as the acceptance was not communicated. It may however, be pointed out that the Court construed a conduct to parties as railway company was accepting the supplies of coal from time to time.
3. **Manner of acceptance**
   General rule say that it must be as per the manner prescribed by offeror. If no mode is prescribed in which it can be accepted, then it must be in some usual and reasonable manner.
4. **If there is deviation in communication of an acceptance of offer**, offeror may reject such acceptance by sending notice within reasonable time. If the offeror doesn't send notice or rejection, he accepted acceptance of offer.
   Example: A offers B and indicates that the acceptance be given by telegram. B sends his acceptance by ordinary post. It is a valid acceptance unless A insists for acceptance in the prescribed manner.
5. **Acceptance of offer must be made by offeror.**
   Example : A applied for the headmastership of a school. He was selected by the appointing authority but the decision was not communicated to him. However, one of members in his individual capacity informed him about the selection. Subsequently, the appointing authority cancelled its decision. A sued the school for breach of contract. The Court rejected the A's action and held that there was no notice of acceptance. "Information by unauthorized person is as insufficient as overhearing from behind the door".
6. **Acceptance must be communicated to offeror**
7. **Time limit for acceptance**

- If the offer prescribes the time limit, it must be accepted within specified time.
- If the offer does not prescribe the time limit, it must be accepted within reasonable time.
  Example : A applied (offered) for shares in a company in early June. The allotment (Acceptance) was made in late November. A refused to take the shares. Held, A was entitled to do so as the reasonable time for acceptance had elapsed.

8. **Acceptance of offer may be** expressly (by words spoken or written); or impliedly (by acceptance of consideration); or by performance of conditions (e.g.in case of a general offer)
9. **Mere silence is not acceptance of the offer**
   Example A offers to B to buy his house for Rs.5 lakhs and writes "If I hear no

more about it within a week, I shall presume the house is mine for Rs.5 lakhs. "B does not respond. Here, no contract is concluded between A and B.

10. **However, following are the two exceptions to the above rule. It means silence amounts as acceptance of offer.**
    - Where offeree agrees that non – refusal by him within specified time shall amount to acceptance of offer.
    - When there is custom or usage of trade which specified that silence shall amount to acceptance.
11. **Acceptance subject to the contract is no acceptance**
    .If the acceptance has been given 'subject to the contract" or subject to approval by certain persons, it has not effect at all. Such an acceptance will not create binding contract until a formal contract is prepared and signed by all the parties.

General Rules as to Communication of Acceptance

1. In case of acceptance by post

Where the acceptance is given by post, the communication of acceptance is complete as against the proposer when the letter of acceptance is posted. Thus, mere posting of letter of acceptance is sufficient to conclude a contract. However, the letter must be properly addressed and stamped.

2. Delayed or no delivery of letter

Where the letter of acceptance is posted by the acceptor but it never reaches the offeror, or it is delayed in transit, it will not affect the validity of acceptance. The offeror is bound by the acceptance.

3. Acceptance by telephones telex or tax

If the communication of an acceptance is made by telephone, tele-printer, telex, fax machines, etc, it completes when the acceptance is received by the offeror. The contract is concluded as soon as the offeror receives not hears the acceptance.

4. The place of Contract

In case of acceptance by the post, the place where the letter is posted is the place of contract. Where the acceptance is given by instantaneous means of communication (telephone, fax, tele-printer, telex etc.), the contract is made at the place where the acceptance is received,

5. The time of Contract

In case of acceptance by post, the time of posting the letter of acceptance to the time of contract. But in case of acceptance by instantaneous means of communication, the time of contract is the time when the offeror gets the communication, the time of contract is the time when offeror gets the communication of acceptance.

6. Communication of acceptance in case of an agent.

Where the offer has been made through an agent, the communication of acceptance is completed when the acceptance is given either to the agent or to the principal. In such a case, if the agent fails to convey the acceptance received from offeree, still the principal is bound by the acceptance.

7. Acceptance on loudspeakers

Acceptance given on loudspeaker is not a valid a acceptance.

1.Who is competent to make a contract:-

Section 11. Every person is competent to contract who is of ***age of majority***

Particulars	Offer	Acceptance
When Communication complete [Sec.4]	• Communication of a proposal is complete when it comes to the knowledge of the person to whom it is made. • **Example :** A proposes by letter, to sell his Tonga to B at Rs.10,000. Communication of the proposal is complete when B receives the letter.	• **As against the offerer/ Proposer**: When it is put in a course of transmission to him so as to be out of the power of the Acceptor. • **As against the Offeree/Acceptor**: When it comes to the knowledge of the Proposer. (See separate question above)
When Revocation can be made [Sec.5]	• Offer/proposal may be revoked at any time before the communication of its acceptance is complete, as against the proposer, but not afterwards. • **Example:** U sends a letter to Y proposing to sell his land. Y sends his acceptance by post. U can revoke the offer at any time before or at the moment when Y posts his letter of acceptance, but not afterwards.	• Acceptance may be revoked at any time before the communication of acceptor, but not afterwards. • **Example:** T sends to S by post, an offer to sell his cycle. S sends his acceptance via post, S could revoke his acceptance, upto any time before or at the moment when he posts his letter of acceptance, but not afterwards.
When communication of revocation is complete [Sec.4]	• **As against the offeror**: When it is put into a course of transmission to the person to whom it is made, so as to be out of the power of the person who makes it. • **Example :** S proposes to H by letter. H sends his acceptance by letter. Suddenly, S sends a telegram revoking his offer. Revocation is complete as against S when the telegram is dispatched; H's revocation of acceptance is complete when S receives such telegram.	• **As against the Offeree**: When it comes to his knowledge. • **Example :** Communication of revocation is complete only when H receives the telegram. • When H revokes his acceptance, it is complete when he dispatches the telegram.

Accepted is lighted match, while offer is a train of gun powder — *Sir willian Anson.*

CAPACITY TO CONTRACT

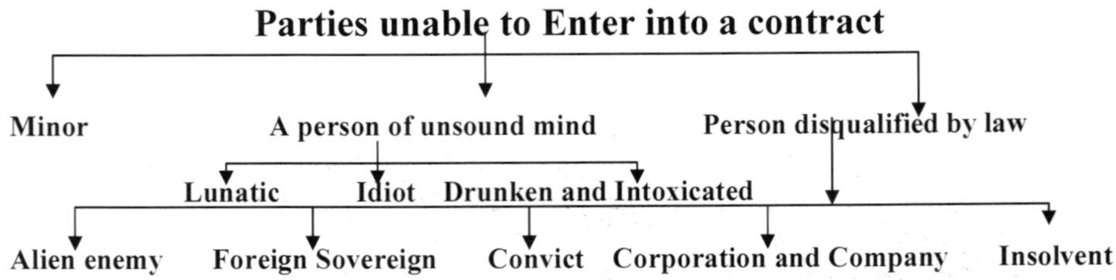

according to the Law to which he is subject, who is of ***sound mind*** and not is ***disqualified from contracting*** by any Law to which he is subject.

Age of majority:- According to ***section 3 of Indian majority Act-1875*** every person domiciled in Indian attains majority on the completion of 18 years of age.

Exception: - ***21 years***- in the following cases.

a. Where a guardian of a minor's person or property is appointed under the Guardian and wards Act, 1890.

b. Where minor's property has passed under the superintendence of the court of words.

Position of Agreements by Minor:-

1. ***Validity: - An agreement with a minor is void-ab-initio Mohoribibee v. [Dharmodas Ghose]***

   Example :

   Mr. D, a minor, mortgaged his house for Rs.20000 to a money – lender, but the mortgagee, i.e. the money – lender, paid him a sum of Rs.8000. Subsequently, the minor sued for setting aside the mortgage. Held that the contract was void, as Mr. D was minor and therefore he is not liable to pay anything to the lender.

2. ***A minor's has received any benefit under a void contract, he cannot be asked to return the same.***
3. ***If a minor has received any benefit under a void contract, he cannot be asked to return the same.***
4. ***Fraudulent representation by a minor- no difference in the status of agreement. The contract remains void.***
5. ***A minor with the consent of all the partners, be admitted to the benefits of an existing partnership.***
6. ***Contracts entered into by minors are void-ab-initio. Hence no specific performance can be enforced for such contracts.***
7. ***Minor's parent/guardians are not liable to a minor's creditor for the breach of contract by the minor.***
8. ***A minor can act as an agent but not personally liable. But he cannot be principal.***
9. ***A minor cannot become shareholder of a the company except when the shares are fully paid up and transfer by share.***

10. ***A minor cannot be adjudicated as insolvent.***

11. ***Can enter into contracts of Apprenticeship, Services, Education, etc:***

(a) A minor can enter into contract of apprenticeship, or for training or instruction in a special art, education, etc.

(b) These are allowed because it generates benefits to the Minor.

12. **Guarantee for and by minor**

A contract of guarantee in favour of a minor is valid. However, a minor cannot be a surety in a contract of guarantee. This is because, the surety is ultimately liable under a contract of guarantee whereas a minor can never be held personally liable.

13. ***Minor as a trade union member***

Any person who has attained the age of fifteen years may be a member for registered trade union, provided the rules of the trade union allow so. Such a member will enjoy all the rights of a member.

EXCEPTION

- ***Contract for the benefit of a minor.***
- ***Contract by Guardian***

Benefit of a minor by his guardian or manager of his estate.

a. within the scope of the authority of the guardian.

b. Is for the benefit of the minor.

- ***Contract for supply of Necessaries.***

Example:

Food, clothes, bed, shelter, shoes, medicines and similar other things required for the maintenance of his life or for the life of his dependents, expenses for instruction in grade or arts; expenses for moral religions or intellectual education, funeral expenses of his deceased family members, marriage expenses of a dependent female member in the family; expenses incurred in the protection of his property or personal liberty, Diwali pooja expenses, etc. have been held by courts to be necessaries of life. ***However, the things like earrings for a male, spectacles for a blind person or a wild animal cannot be considered as necessaries.***

- ***Liability for tort: A minor is liable for a tort, i.e., civil wrong committed by him.***

Example:

A, a 14 – year – old boy drives a car carelessly and injures B. He is liable for the accident i.e., tort.

Person of Unsound Mind

A person of unsound mind

Lunatic | **Idiot** | **Drunken and Intoxicated**

A person who is usually of unsound mind, but occasionally of sound mind can make a contract when he is of sound mind. Similarly, a person who is usually of sound mind, but occasionally of unsound mind, may not make a contract when he is of unsound mind.

- ***At time of entering into a contract, a person must be sound mind.*** Law presumes that every person is of sound mind unless otherwise it is proved before court. An agreement by a person of unsound mind is void. The following are categories of a person considered as person of a unsound mind.
- **An idiot** An idiot is a person who is congenital (by birth) unsound mind. His incapacity is permanent and therefore he can never understand contract and make a rational judgment as to its effects upon his interest. Consequently, the agreement of an idiot is absolutely void ab initio. He is not personally liable even for the payment of necessaries of life supplied to him.
- **Delirious persons** A person delirious from fever is also not capable of understanding the nature and implications of an agreement. Therefore, he cannot enter into a contract so long as delirium lasts.
- **Hypnotized persons** Hypnotism produces temporary incapacity till a person is under the effect of artificial induced sleep.
- **Mental decay** There may be mental decay or senile mind the to old age or poor health. When such person is not capable of understanding the contract and its effect upon his interest, he cannot enter into contract.
- ***Lunatic is not permanently of unsound mined.*** *He can enter into contract during lucid intervals i.e., during period when he is of sound mind.*

Drunken person

Generally of	Occasionally of	Capacity to Contract	Example
Unsound Mind	Sound Mind	Can enter into a Contract when he is of Sound Mind.	A patient in a lunatic asylum, who is at intervals of sound mind, may contract during those intervals.
Sound Mind	Unsound Mind	Cannot make a Contract when he is of Unsound Mind.	A sane man, who is delirious from fever or who is so drunk that he cannot understand terms of a contract or form a judgment, cannot contract
			while such delirium or drunkenness lasts.

An agreement made by intoxicated person is void.

Person Disqualified by Law

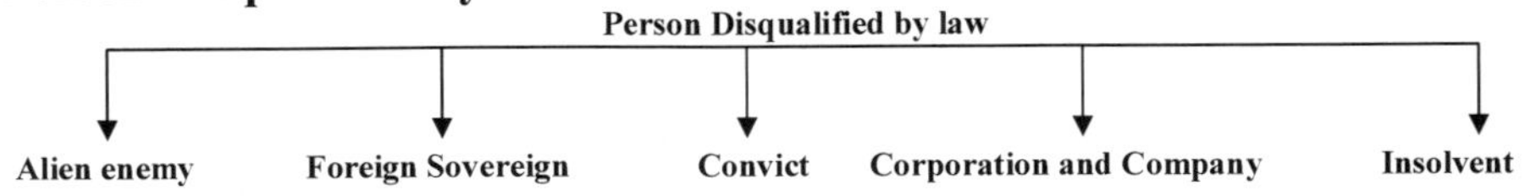

• Body corporate or company or corporation

Contractual capacity of company is determined by object clause of its memorandum of association. Any act done in excess of power given is ultra – virus and hence void.

• Alien enemy

- An 'alien' is a person who is a foreigner to the land. He may be either an 'alien friend' or an 'alien enemy. If the sovereign or state of the alien is at peace with the country of his stay, he is an alien friend. An if a war is declared between the two countries he is termed as an alien enemy.
- During the war, contract can be entered into with alien enemy with the permission of central government.

• **Convict** can't enter into a contract while he is undergoing imprisonment. But he can enter into a contract with permission of central government while undergoing imprisonment. After the imprisonment is over, be becomes capable of entering into contract. Thus the incapacity is only during the period of sentence.

• **Insolvent** When any person is declared as an insolvent, his property vests in receiver and therefore, he can't enter into contract relating to his property. Again he becomes capable to enter into contract when he is discharged by court.

• **Foreign sovereigns, diplomatic staff and representative of foreign staff** can enter into valid contract. However, a suit cannot be filed against them, in the Indian counts without the prior sanction of the central Government.

Third party to a contract cannot sue or a stranger to a contract cannot sue.

Only those persons, who are parties to a contract, can sue and be sued upon the contract.

This Rule is called **"Doctrine of privities of contract." Exception**.

i. **Trust:-** In case of trust a beneficiary can sue upon the contract.

Example:

A transferred certain properties to B to be held by him in trust for the benefit of C. In this case, C although not a party to the trust, can sue for the benefits available to him under the trust.

This exception to the rule of Privity of contract has been recognised in a well known case of khwaja Mohd. Khan v. Hussaini Begum (1910) 32 All 410.

ii. **Family settlement / Marriage contract:-** In case of family settlement members who were not originally party to the contract can also sue upon it.

A female members cone force a provision for marriage expenses made on partition of HUF.

Example:

H sued her father – in – law K to recover Rs.15,000 being arrears of allowance called Pin money payable to her by K under an agreement between K and H's father, consideration being H's marriage to K's son D. Both H and D were minors at the time of marriage. Held, the promise can be made enforceable by H. Provision of marriage expenses of female members of a Joint Hindu Family, entitles the female member to sue for such expenses on a partition between male members.,

Two brothers, on partition of family joint properties, agreed to invest in equal shares for their mother's maintenance. Held, the mother was entitled to require her sons to make the investment.

iii. **Acknowledgement of liability:-** Where a person admits his Liability thereafter if he refused be will be stopped from denying his liability.

Example

X receives money from Y for paying it to Z. X admits the receipt of that amount to Z. Z can recover the amount from X, even though the money is due from Y.

iv. **Assignment of contract.** Assignee (the person to whom benefits of contract are assigned) can enforce upon the contract..

v. Contract entered into through **an agent.**

vi. **Covenants** running with land.

Stranger to consideration:- "*Stranger to contract*" must be distinguished from a stranger to consideration need not necessarily be provided by the promises if may flow from a third party also such a person is ' stranger to consideration,. **(Chinnaya Vs Ramayya).**

CONSIDERATION

MEANING

1. **(a)** Consideration is a **quid pro quo i,e something in return** it may be –
   (i) some benefit right, interest, loss or profit that may accrue to one party or,
   (ii) some forbearance, detriment, loss or responsibility suffered on undertaken by the other party [currie V mussa]

(b) **According to Sir Frederick Pollock,** "consideration is the price for which the promise of the other is bought and the promise thus given for value is enforceable.

2. **Definition [Sec 2(d)]**:- when at the desire of the Promisor, the promise or any other person.

*(a) has done or abstained from doing , or **[Past consideration]***

*(b) does or abstains from doing, or **[Present consideration]***

*(c) promises to do or abstain from doing something **[Future consideration]** such act or abstinence or promise is called a consideration for the promise.*

3. ***Example***

(i) 'P' aggress to sell his car to 'Q' for Rs.50,000 Here 'Q's Promise to pay Rs50,000 is the consideration for P's promise and 'P's promise to sell the car is the consideration for 'Q's promise to pay Rs.50,000.

(ii) 'A' promises his debtor 'B' not to file a suit against him for one year on 'A's agreeing to pay him Rs.10,000 more. Here the abstinence of 'A' is the consideration for 'B's Promise to pay.

Legal Rules for valid consideration

1. Consideration must move at the desire of the promisor.

D constructed a market at the instance of District collector. Occupants of shops promised to pay D a commission on articles sold through their shops. Held, there was no consideration because money was not spent by Plaintiff at the request of the

Defendants, but at instance of a third person viz. the Collector and, thus the contract was void.

Durga Prasad v. Baldeo

2. Consideration may move from the promisee or any other person who is not a party to the contract. ***[Chinnaya's Vs Ramayya]***

A owed Rs.20,000 to B. A persuaded C to sign a Pro Note in favour of B. C promised B that he would pay the amount. On faith of promise by C, B credited the amount to A's account. Held, the discharge of A's account was consideration for C's promise.

National Bank of Upper India v. Bansidhar

3. Consideration may be past, present, Future:

- *Under English law, Past consideration is no consideration.*
- Present consideration :- cash sale
- Future or executory consideration:- A Promises to B to deliver him 100 bags of sugar at a future date . B promise to pay first on delivery.

4. *Consideration should be real and not illusory. Illusory consideration renders the* transaction void consideration is not valid if it is.

(i) Physically impossible (ii) Legally not permissible
(iii) Uncertain (iv) illusory (***fulfillment of a pre existing obligation***)

5. Must be legal:

Consideration must not be unlawful, immoral or opposed to public policy.

6. consideration need not be adequate. A contract is not void merely became of the fact that the consideration is inadequate. The law simply requires that contract should be supported by consideration. So long as consideration exists and it is of some value, courts are not required to consider its adequacy.

Example:

A agreed to sell a watch worth Rs.500 for Rs.20, A's consent to the agreement was freely given. The consideration, though inadequate. Will not affect the validity of the contract. However, the inadequacy of the consideration can be considered in order to know whether the consent of the promisor was free or not . **[Section 25 Explanation II]**

7. The performance of an act what one is legally bound to perform is not consideration for the contract mean's something other than the promisor's existing obligation –

A contract not supported by consideration is void.

Ex. Nudo Pacto non oritur action, i,e, an agreement without consideration is void.

Ex ceptions to the Rule " No consideration . No contract".

1. *Written and registered agreements arising out of love and affection:- [25 (1)]*

- Expressed in writing and registered under law for the time being in force for registration of document
- Natural love and affection
- Between parties standing in a near relation to each other

Example:- An elder brother, on account of natural love and affection, promised to pay the debts of his younger brother. Agreement was put to writing and registered. Held, agreement was valid.

Exception: - ***Rajlukhy Dabee Vs Bhootnath Mukharjee***

Example: A Hindu husband by a registered document, after referring to quarrels and disagreements between himself and his wife, promised to pay his wife a sum of money for her maintenance and separate residence. Held that the promise was unenforceable since natural love and affection was missing.

2. ***Promise to compensate [25(2)]***

- Promise to compensate wholly or in part
- Who has already voluntarily done something for the promisor
- Something which the promisor was legally compellable to do.

Example:- A finds B's purse and give to him. B Promise to give A Rs.500. This is a valid contract.

3. ***Promise to pay a time – barred debt. [Sec 25(3)]***

- A debt barred by limitation con not recovered. Hence, a promise to pay a such a debt is without any consideration.
- Can be enforced only when – in writing and sighed by Debtor or his authorized agent.

Example : A owes B Rs.10,000 but the debt is barred by Limitation Act. A signs a written promise to pay B Rs.8,000 on account of debt. This is a valid contract.

4. **Completed gift-** gift do not require any consideration.
5. **Agency (185)** – According to the Indian contract Act. No consideration is necessary to create an agency.
6. **Bailment (148)-** consideration is not necessary to effect a valid bailment of goods. It is Called Gratuitous Bailment.
7. **Remission (63).**
8. **Charity-** If a person promises to contribute to charity and on this faith the promises undertakes a liability to the extent not exceeding the promised subscription, the contract shall be valid.

FREE CONSENT

According to section 13. Two persons are said to have consented when they agree upon same thing in the same sense.

In English law, this is called **'consensus – ad – idem'**

Effect of absence of consent:

- When there is no consent at all, the agreement is **void – ab – initio'.** It is not enforceable at the option of either party

Example 1:

X have two car one Maruti car and one Honda city car. Y does not know that X has two cars Y offers to buy car at Rs.50,000. Here, there is no identity of mind in respect of the subject matter. Hence there is no consent at all and the agreement is **void – ab – inito**.

Example 2:

An Illiterate woman signed a gift deed thinking that it was a power of attorney – no consent at all and the agreement was void – ab – inito **[Bala Devi V S. Manumdats]**

Free consent

- Consent is said to be free when it is not caused by **[Section 14]**

(a) coercion **[Section 15]**
(b) Undue influence **[Section 16]**
(c) Fraud **[Section 17]**
(d) Misrepresentation **[Section 18]**
(e) Mistake **[Section 20, 21,22]**

Effect of absence of Free Consent :- If consent coercion, undue influence, fraud , Misrepresentation the contract is voidable at the option of party whose consent was not free **[19, 19A]**

Coercion [Section 15]

(a) Committing any act which is forbidden by the **IPC**
(b) Threatening to commit any act which is forbidden by the **IPC.**
(c) Unlawful detaining of any property or
(d) Threatening to detain any property.

Essential elements of coercion

Above four [a – d]

(e) coercion need not necessary proceed from party to contract.
(f) Coercion need not necessary be directed against the other contracting party.
(g) It is immaterial whether the IPC is or is not in force at the time or at the place where the coercion is employed **[Bay of Bengal caption]**

Effect of threat to file a suit:- A threat to file a suit **(whether civil or court)** does not amount to coercion unless the suit is on false charge. Threat to file a suit on false charge is an act forbidden by the **IPC** and thus will amount to an act of coercion.

Effect of Threat to commit suicide:- Threat to commit suicide amounted to coercion and the release deed was example discussed in class. Therefore voidable. **[Chikham Ammiraju v seshama]**

Duress V Coercion

English Law - Duress does not include detaining of property or threat to detain property.

- Duress can be employed only by a party to the contract or his agent.

Effect:- when coercion is employed to obtain the consent of a party the contract is voidable at the option of the party where consent was obtained by coercion.

A threat to strike by employees in support of their demands is not regarded as coercion. This is because the threat to strike is not an offence under the I.P.C. it is a right given under the Industrial Disputes Act.

Detaining property under mortgage: Detention of property by a mortgage until the payment of loan does not amount to coercion.

Undue influence [Section 16]

Meaning of undue influence :- dominating the will of the other person to obtain an unfair advantages over the others.

(a) where the relation subsisting between the parties must be such that one party is in **position to dominate the will** of the other.

(b) The dominant party **use** his position.

(c) Obtain an **unfair advantage** over the other .

Presumption of domination of will

Circumstances	Examples
Where he holds a real or apparent authority over the other	Master and servant, parent and child, Income Tax officer and assesses principal and a Temporary Teacher.
Where he stands in a Trust fiduciary (benefit) relation to the other	Trustee and beneficiary spiritual Guru and his disciples, solicitors and clients. Guardian and wards
Mental Capacity of a person is temporarily or permanent effected by reason of age, illness or mental or bodily distress	Relationship between medical attendant and ward.

Example:-

A Poor Hindu widow agreed to pay interest at 100% P. a because she need the money to established her right of maintenance. It was held that the lender was in position to dominate the will of widow.

No. Presumption of Domination of will:-

- Landlord and Tenant
- Creditor and Debtor
- Husband and wife **(other than Pardanashin)**
- Principal and Agent

Effect of undue Influence:-[Section 19A]

When consent to an agreement is caused by undue influence, the contract is voidable at the option of the party whose consent was so caused.

Burden of Proof:- A contract is presumed to be induced by undue influence if the following two condition:-

- A party has the position to dominate the will of the others
- The transaction is unconscionable (unreasonable)

In such a case dominant party is under the burden to prove the undue influence was not employed.

[Unconscionable transactions:- *if transaction appears to unreasonable the dominant party to prove that there is no undue influence.]*

• **Any other transaction:-** weaker party to prove the influence was employed]

Where some transaction is entered into in the ordinary course of business, but due to certain contingencies, one party is able to make the other party agree to certain terms and conditions then it is not undue influence.

Example:

A applies to a banker for a loan at a time when there is stringency in the money market. The banker declines to make the loan except at an unusually high rate of interest. A accepts the loan on these terms. This is a transaction in the ordinary course of business, and the contract is not induced by undue influence.

Example:

A spiritual guru induced his chela to donate all his property to the ashram and said that in return of it, he will certainly get salvation. The chela did the same. Held, that this is a case, of undue influence so it becomes void.

Contract with Pardanashin woman;-

Induced by undue influence

Burden of Proof – Full disclosure is made to pardanashin women

Pardanashin Women - Understand the contract -

Receipt of competent independent advice .

Rebutting presumption:-

- Dominant party – full disclosure
- Price was adequate
- Receipt of competent independent advice before entering into contract – weaker party.

Undue influence Vs Coercion

Coercion (15)	Undue Influence (16)
Meaning - using or threat to use physical force	- Involves use of moral force (mental pressure)
- obtain the consent of party (intention)	- Obtain an unfair advantage (intention)
- Punishment under IPC	- Not criminally liable
- Parties - Stranger	- Between the parties to the contract
- Relationship - Immaterial	- One party dominate the other party
- Voidable at the option of aggrieved party	- Voidable or court set aside
- Benefit - Back	- Benefit - order of court - Back

Fraud (17)

- The term fraud means a take representation of facts made willfully ***with a view to deceive the other party.***
- **Sec.17-** fraud means any act committed by a party to a contract or with his connivance or by his agent with intent to deceive another party there to or his agent or to induce to enter into contract.

Essentials of fraud :-

(a) By a party to the contract

(b) There must be representation – [an opinion a statement of expression – does not fraud].

(c) The representation must be false.

(d) Before conclusion of contract.

(e) The misrepresentation must be made willfully.

(f) The misrepresentation must be made with a view to deceive the other party.

(g) The other party must have actually been deceived.

(h) The other party have suffered a loss.

Fraud – definition include

- The suggestion, as to fact, of that which is not true by one who does not believe it to be true.
- *The active concealment of a fact by one having knowledge or belief of the fact.*

Ex. A furniture dealer conceals the crakes in furniture by polish work.

- *A promise made without any intention of performing it.*
- *Any other act fitted to deceive.*
- *Any such act or omission as the law specially declared to be fraudulent.*

Ex:- T bought a cannon from H. It was defective, but H had plugged it. T did not examine the cannon, but it burst when he used it. Held as the plug had not deceived T, he was liable to pay for the cannon.

Ex.: Where the representation was true at the time of when it was made but becomes untrue before the contract is entered into and this fact is known to the party who made the representation. If must be corrected. If it is not so corrected it will amount to be fraud.

When the silence amount to fraud:-

(a) **General rule:-** Mere (only) Silence as to facts likely to affect the willingness of a person to enter into a contract is not fraud.

EXCEPTION

where the circumstances of the case are such that regarding being had to them. It is duty of the person keeping silence to speak. Such duty arises in the following two cases.

(1) ***Duty to speak exists where the parties stand in a fiduciary relationship,*** e.g. father and son, guardian and ward, trustee and beneficiary etc. or where contract is a contract of *ubberima fidei (requiring utmost good faith), e.g. contracts of insurance.*

Ex.:- A sells by auction to B a horse which A knows to be unsound. B' is A's daughter and has just come of age. Here the relation between the parties would make it A's duty to tell B is the horse is unsound.

(2) ***When silence itself equivalent to speech.*** B says to A " if you do not deny it I shall assume that the horse is sound". A say nothing – A's silence equivalent to speech. A can held liable to fraud.

*[**Half Truth is worse than a blatant: -** Example – company pay dividend – in class room]*

Effect of Fraud:

Sec. 19: A contract induced by fraud is voidable at the option of the party defrauded. Till the exercise of such option, the Contract is valid.

1. Rescinds of contract
2. Right to insist upon performance
3. Right to claim damages – if he suffered loss.

Exception : The contract is not voidable in the following cases.

- When the party who consent was caused by silence amount to fraud and be has the means of discovering the truth with ordinary diligence. [Ex class room]
- When the party give the consent in ignorance of fraud.
- When the party after become aware of fraud takes a benefit.
- When the parties can't be restored to their original position.
- Where interests of third parties intervene before the contract is avoided.

Misrepresentation (section 18)

Misrepresentation is when a party (person) asserts something which is not true though he believes is to be true. In other words misrepresentation is a falls representation made innocently. An agreement is said to be influenced by misrepresentation if all the following conditions are satisfied.

(a) The party makes a representation of a fact **[The representation by a stranger (By anyone with his connivance or by agent)** to the contract does not affect the validity of the contract.

(b) The misrepresentation was made ***innocently*** i.e. if was not made with a view to deceive the other party.

(c) The other party has actually acted believing the misrepresent to be true.

Misrepresentation include:-

- Unjustified statement of facts – positive assertion – Believe true really not true no basis misrepresentation ¾ Breach of duty.
- Inducing other to make mistake as to qualify or nature of subject matter.

Effect of Misrepresentation:

(1) Right to Rescind contract:-

Can't do

- Discovering the truth with ordinary diligence.
- Give consent in ignorance of misrepresentation
- Become aware of misrepresentation takes a benefit
- Where an innocent third party before the contract is rescinds acquires consideration some interest in the property passing under the contract.
- Where the parties can't be restored to their original position.

(2) Right to insist upon performance.

Ex.:- Unlike Fraud he cannot sue for damage.

Fraud (17)	Misrepresentation (18)
Meaning :- wrongful representation is made Willfully to deceive the party. Knowledge of falsehood. - The person making the wrong statement does not believe it to be true. - Right to claim damage Means of discovering of truth - In case of fraud the contract is voidable even though the aggrieved party had the means of discovering the truth with ordinary diligence. Exception :- Silence	Meaning - innocently without any intention to Deceive the other party. - The person making the wrong statement believes it to be true. - Can't claim damage - In case of misrepresentation the contract is not voidable if the aggrieved party had the means of discovering the truth with ordinary diligence....

MISTAKE

Mistake Erroneous Belief about some facts

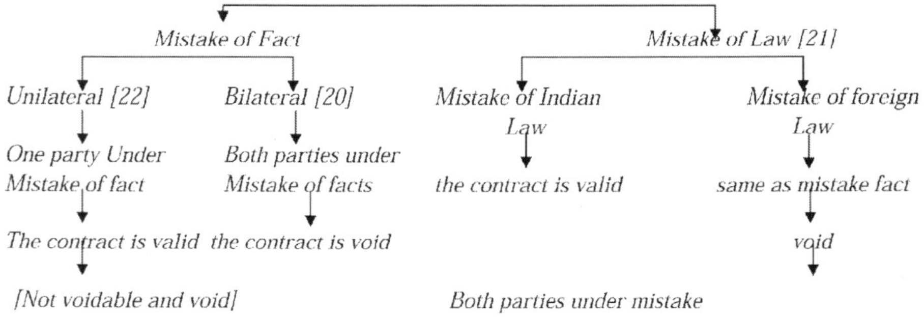

Exception: - Where contract is not valid (void)

1. **Identity of persons contract with**

Ex. :- A woman, falsely misrepresenting herself to be wife of a well known Baron obtained two pearl necklaces from a firm of jewelers on the pretext of showing them to her husband before buying. She pledged them with a broker who took them in good faith. Held that there was no contract between jeweler and woman and even an innocent buyer or a broker did not get a good title. Broker must return necklaces to jeweler. Jeweler intended to deal not with her but with quite a different person, i.e., wife of a Baron.

2. **as the nature of the contract**

Ex.:- illiterate man sign Bill of exchanges by means of false, representation that it was a mere guarantee. It was held that he was not liable for bill of exchange because never intended to sign the bill of exchange

Bilateral Mistakes:-

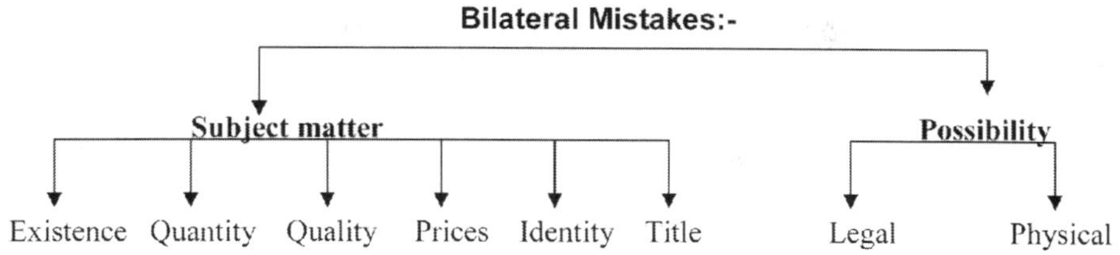

EVERY AGREEMENT OF WHICH THE OBJECT OR CONSIDERATION IS UNLAWFUL IS VOID [SEC 23]

(a) **It is forbidden by law** – law would also include the rules regulations, notifications etc. under or issued under the authority given by a statute.

Ex.:- A sold liquor without license to B. The sale is unlawful as the sale of liquor without license is forbidden by the law, i.e., The Excise Act. Hence, A cannot recover the price.

Ex.:- a Hindu already married and his wife alive entered into a marriage agreement with Y an unmarried girl. The agreement is void because the second marriage is forbidden by Hindu Law.

(b) **If it defeats the Provisions of any Law.**
- not directly prohibited by any Law

Ex.:- A's estate is sold for arrears of revenue under the provision defaulter is prohibited from purchasing the state upon an understanding with A becomes the purchaser and agrees to convey the estate to A . Upon receiving from him the price which B has paid. The agreement is void.

(c) **If it is Fraudulent**

Ex.: Object or consideration of an agreement is fraudulent. An agreement with such an object or consideration is unlawful and void.

(d) **If it involves or Implies injury to a person or property of another.**

Ex. :- Where it create injury to a person or to the property of another. An agreement with such an object or consideration is unlawful and void.

(e) **If the court regards it as immoral.**

- X gave Rs. 10,000 to Y a married woman to obtain a divorce from her husband. X agrees to marry when divorce taken. X would not recover the amt.

1. **Partially unlawful Object or consideration [Sec. 24]:** An Agreement is void if -

(a) any part of a single consideration for one or more objects is unlawful; or

(b) any one or any part of one of several consideration for a single object, is unlawful.

2. **Example:** B is a licensed manufactured of permitted chemicals. A promise B to supervise B's business and combine it with the production of some contraband items together with the permitted items. B promises to pay A, Salary of Rs.10,000 p.m. Agreement is void, object of A's promise and consideration for B's promise being partially unlawful.

3. **Lawful Consideration enforceable:** When there are several distinct promises made for one and the same consideration and one or more of them are of such nature that law will not enforce it, only such of the promises as are unlawful cannot be enforced. Other which are lawful, can be enforced.
4. **Test of Severability:**

(a) If illegal part cannot be severed from legal part of a covenant, contract is altogether void.

(b) If it is possible to severe them, whether the illegality be due to Statute or Common Law, bad part alone may be rejected and good retained.

In case of pre – existing civil liability, the dropping of criminal proceedings need not necessarily be a consideration for the agreement to satisfy that liability.

Union Carbide Corpn. v. UOI

Illegal agreement – Void – ab – intio

- Punishable by the criminal Law of the country or by any special legislation regulation effect of illegal agreement.
- Collateral transactions – illegal
- No action can be taken for the recovery of money paid or property transferred.
- If illegal part **can't be separated** from the legal part.
  Whole agreement is altogether illegal. [Sec.57]
- **If separated**
- Legal part – enforces illegal part – reject.
- Reciprocal promises – In respect of reciprocal promises the agreement as to illegal promise is void.

Agreement opposed to public policy:-

Alternative promises: where in alternative promises one part is illegal, only the legal pent can be enforced. [Sec. 58]

Champerty & Maintenance : (Refer Class Note)

VOID AGREEMENT

2(g)- Void agreement is an agreement which is not enforceable by Law – void – ab – inito.

(1) Agreement by or with person's incompetent to contract **[10, 11]**
(2) Agreement entered into through a mutual mistake **[20]**
(3) Object or consideration – unlawful **[23]**
(4) Consideration or object partially, unlawful **[24]**
(5) Without consideration **[25]**
(6) Restraint of marriage **[26]**
(7) Restraint of trade **[27]**
(8) Legal proceeding **[28]**
(9) Consideration identified **[29]**
(10) Wagering agreement **[30]**
(11) Impossible agreement **[56]**
(12) An agreement to enter into an agreement in the future.

Agreement in Restraint of marriage [26]

Every agreement in restraint of marriage of any person **other than a minor**, is void, Any restraint of marriage whether total or partial is opposed to public policy.

Ex. A promised to marry else except Mr. B, and in default pay her a sum of Rs.1,00,000. A married someone else and B sued A for recovery of the sum. Held, the contract was in restraint of marriage, and as such void.

Ex. The consideration under a Sale Deed was for marriage expenses of a minor girl aged 12. Held the sale was a void transaction being opposed to public policy.

Ex. Two co-widows – agreement – is one of them remarried – she shout forfeit her eight to her share in the deceased husband's property was not void because no restraint was imposed upon either of the two widows from remarrying.

Ex. Wife to divorce herself and to claim maintenance from the husband on his marrying a second wife was not void because no restraint was impose upon husband from marrying a second wife.

Agreement in Restrain of trade [27]

Every agreement by which anyone is restrained from exercised a Lawful profession, trade or business of any kind is void .

Burden for Proof :-

Party supporting the contract:- must show that the restraint is reasonably necessary to protect public interest. Party challenging the contract:- restraints is injurious to the public.

Ex. : In Patna, 29 out of 30 manufacturers of combs agreed with R to supply combs only to him and not to anyone else. Under the agreements R was free to reject the goods if he found no market for them. Held, the agreement amounted to restraint of trade and void.

Exception to Sec. 27

(1) **Sale of goodwill: -** Seller of goodwill of a business may agree with the buyer to restrain from carrying on business.

(a) *Must relate to same business*

(b) *Restriction shall apply within specified Local limits.*

(c) *Restriction shall apply within a reasonable time period*

(d) *The specified local limits – depends on nature of business.*

(a) **Restriction on existing partner [11(2)]**

- Not carry on business other than business of the firm till he is partner.

(b) **Restriction on outgoing partner [36]**

- Not carry on a similar business after retirement
- Local limits + specified period – local limit – nature of business

(c) **Sec. 54:** Upon or in anticipation of dissolution of Firm. Partners may agree that some or all of them will not carry on business similar to that of the Firm within specified periods or local limits.

(d) **Sec. 55(2) :** Partner may agree with due buyers of Goodwill, not to use the Firm name or carry on Firm's business or solicit clients of the Firm.

(e) **Sec. 55(3):** Upon sale of Firm's Goodwill, a partner may agree that he will not carry on any business similar to Firm's within specified periods or local limits.

Exception under judicial interpretations :-

(a) **Trade combination.**

- Traders may from associations among them to regulate the business or to fix prices.
- Such agreement like opening and closing of business venture, licensing of traders, supervision and control of dealers, etc. are valid even if they are in restraint of trade.
- But, a Combination that tends to create monopoly; or when two enter into an agreement to avoid competition, they are against public policy and hence void.

(b) **Sale dealing agreement:** - Agreements to deal in the products of a single manufacturer or to sell the whole produce to a single dealer are valid if their terms are reasonable. Ex.: **.(Discuss in class)**

Agreement – buyer of goods for Delhi market not to sell them in Chennai is valid. - Not to sell any other firm – valid.

(c) **Service agreement.**

- **Agreement:** Employers may enter into agreements with employees – (i) not to engage in other work during the tenure of his employment; or (ii) not to engage in similar work after his termination.
- **During Employment:** The first restraint is always valid, e.g. doctors may be paid non practicing allowances to avoid practicing when they are employed in a hospital.
- **After termination of service**: The second restraint is valid only is it is to protect the trade interests or the employer. It may be imposed to prevent the outgoing employee from using trade secrets he had learnt during his tenure, to the detriment of his previous employer.
- **Valid Agreements :** Requiring employees to serve the organization for a few years after training leaving; or execution of a bond requiring employees leaving the organization to pay compensation to the employer are valid.
- **Use of Personal Skills:** The employer cannot prevent the employees from using his personal skills and knowledge to his benefit; e.g. an employer cannot restrain an employee to act in theatre plays or in perforating an art.

Agreement in Restraint of legal proceedings [28]

- **Agreement restricting enforcement of rights:**
- An agreement by which any party is restricted **absolutely** from enforcing his legal rights under any contract is void.
- Agreements Limiting period of limitation:- An agreement which limits the time within which an action way be brought is void.
- ***A partial restrain is not void, eg.***

Ex. 1: A clause in a contract that any dispute arising between the parties shall be subject to jurisdiction of a court at a particular place only, is valid.

Ex. 2: An agreement is not void merely because if provides that any dispute arising between two or prove person shall be referred to arbitration.

- That has arises.
- Which may arise
- Which has already arisen?

Ex. 3: An agreement not to go in appeal to higher court against the judgment of a lower court not amount to restart of legal proceeding.

An agreement the meaning of which is not certain (Sec 29)

1. An agreement is called an uncertain agreement when the meaning of ***that agreement is not certain or capable of being certain.*** Such agreements are declared ***void*** u/s 29.
2. **Areas of uncertainty**: Uncertainty may relate to – (a) Subject Matter of Contract; or (b) Terms of contract.

(a) Subject Matter: There may be uncertainty as regards – (i) existence; (ii) quantity (iii) quality; (iv) price; or (v) title to the subject matter.

(b) Terms of Contract: There may be uncertainty as regards – (i) existence (ii) quality; (iv) price; or (v) title and other terms in the contract.

Example:

1. A says to B "I shall sell my house; will you buy?" A says, "Yes, I shall buy". Due to uncertainty of price, the agreement is void and unenforceable. There is binding contract.
2. A agreed to pay a certain sum, when he was able to pay. Held, the agreement was void for uncertainty.
3. D agrees to sell his white horse, for Rs.5,000 or Rs.10,000.

WAGERING AGREEMENT [30]

An agreement between two persons under which money or money's worth is payable by one person to another on the happen or non happening of a future uncertain event is called a wagering agreement.

- X promise to pay Rs. 1000 to Y if it is rained on a particular day, and Y promise to pay Rs.1000 to X if it did not.
- Wagering agreement is promise to give money or money's worth upon the determination of uncertain event.- **Sir Willian Anson.**

Essential elements of wagering agreements

(1) The must be a promise to pay money or money's worth

(2) Performance of a promise must depend upon determination of uncertain event. It might have already happened but the parties are not aware about it.

(3) Mutual chancels of Gains or Loss.

(4) Neither party to have control over the events

(5) Neither party should have any other interest in event.

(6) One party is to win and one party is to lose.

Ex. 1:- Agreement to settle the difference between the contract price and market price of certain goods or shares on a particular day.

Ex. 2: A lottery is wagering agreement. Therefore, an agreement to buy and sell lottery tickets is a wagering agreement. Section 294 – A of the Indian Penal Code declares that drawing of lottery is an offence. However, the government may authorize lotteries. The persons authorized to conduct lotteries are exempt from the punishment. But, the lotteries still remain a wagering transaction.

Ex. 3: However, if the crossword puzzle prizes depend upon sameness of the competitor's solution with a previously prepared solution kept with the organizer or newspaper editor, is a lottery and, therefore, a wagering transaction.

Ex. 4: However, when any transaction in any commodity or in shares with an intention of paying or getting difference in price, the agreement is a wager.

Agreement not held as wagers:-

- ***Prize in terms of Prize competition Act, 1955 not exceeding Rs.1000 is not wagering agreement.***
- ***Horse race [500] – An agreement to contribute a plate or prize.***
- ***Contract of insurance utmost in good faith eg. Favour in public policy.***
- ***Share market transaction*** A commercial transaction should always be distinguished from a pure speculative transaction. A commercial transaction is done ***with an intention of delivery of goods (commodity or security)*** and payment of price. Therefore, it is not wagering agreement.
- ***Crossword competition involving skill for its solution.*** If skill plays an important role in the result of a competition and prize depend upon the result, the competition is not Involve applications of skill and prizes are awarded to the participants on the basis of merit of their solutions and not on chance. Therefore, such competitions are valid and are not wagers.
- ***Athletic Competitions also fall in the category of games of skill. Therefore, these are also not wagers.***

Example: A and B, two wrestlers, agreed to enter into a wrestling contest in Ahmedabad on a certain day. They further agreed that a party failing to appear on the fixed day was to forfeit Rs.500 and the winning party will receive a sum of Rs.1,000. Held, it was not a wagering agreement.

Ò! ***Contribution to chit fund is not wager – contributions made by the members are refunded by draw of lots.***

Effects of wagering agreements:-

- Agreement is void.
- No suit can be filled for any recovery of the amount won on any wager.
- It is not illegal. Any agreement collateral to wagering agreement is valid. Ò! However, it is ***illegal in state of Maharashtra and Gujarat.***

ILLEGALAGREEMENT

- Agreement which is prohibited by law is illegal agreement. Example Agreement to commit crime.
- Effects of illegal agreement:
  - It is always void.
  - Any collateral transaction to illegal agreement is also void.
  - No action is allowed on illegal agreement.

	Void Agreement	Illegal agreement
Meaning	Not enforceable by Law	Forbidden by any law
One in another	All void agreement is not illegal	All illegal agreement are void
Reason	10,29,56	Against the provisions of law
Punishment	Not liable to punished	Party are criminally liable
Void – ab – initio	A valid – collateral – is not void	Illegal, collateral – illegal

CONTINGENT CONTRACT

MEANING

A 'contingent contract' is a contract, to do or not to do something. If some event, collateral to such contract does or does not happen

- A contract to pay B Rs.10,000 if B house is burnt.
- A promise to pay B Rs.1,00,000 if a certain, ship does not return within a year.

Essential features of a contingent contract :-

(a) *It is a contract to do or not to do something*

(b) *Dependent on happening or non happening of an event*

(c) *Such on event is a collateral event (i.e. it is collateral) to the contract i.e. the event must not depend upon the mere will of party.*

(d) *The event is uncertain*

Rules regarding contingent contract.

CONTINGENT UPON

Happening of Non – Future Happening of Non – Impossible

Future Event Uncertain Happening of Uncertain conduct of a living Uncertain Event Specified Happening of Specified

Future Event person within Fixed time Uncertain Event within Fixed

Time

[Sec. 32] [Sec. 33] [Sec. 34] [Sec.35] [Sec. 35] [Sec.36]

(1) Contracts contingent upon the happing of an event enforced – such event has happened [32]

Void – such event because impossible [happening of such event]

Ex.:- A contract to pay B a sum of money when B marries e dies without being married to B contract – void

(2) Non happening of a future event:- [33]

Enforced :- when the happening of such events becomes impossible. **Void:-** such event has happened.

Ex.:- A agrees to pay B sum of money if a certain ship does not return. This ship is sunk. The contract can be enforced when the ship sinks.

(3) Happening of an event within a specified time [35]

Enforce :- when such event has happened within the specific time.

Void :- When the happening of such event because impossible before the expiry of specified time.

When such event has not happened within specified time.
A promise to pay B sum of money if a certain ship return within a Year.
Enforce :- ship returns within the year .
Void :- If the ship is burnt within the year / not come within the year.

(4) **Non – happening of an event within a fixed time [35]**
Enforce :- When the happening of such event because impossible before the expiry of specified time.

- When such event has not happened within the specified . .
Void:- When such event has happened within the specified period.

(5) **Future conduct of a living person. [34]**
Enforced:- When such person acts in the manner as desired in the contract.
Void :- When such person does anything which makes the desired future conduct of such person – impossible – dependent upon certain contingency.

- A agrees to pay B a sum of money if B marries C . C married D. The marriage of B to C must now considered impossible, although it is possible that D may die any that C may afterwards marry B.

(6) **Impossible events [36]**

- Such an agreement can not be enforced since it is void whether the impossibility of the event was known to the parties or not is immaterial.
- A agrees to pay B Rs.1,000 if two parallel straight lines should enclose a space. Agreements are void.
- A agrees to pay B Rs.1,000 if B will marry A's daughter C and C was dead at the time of the agreement. Agreement is void.

	Wagering agreement	**Contingent agreement**
1. Defined	Not defined u/s 30	Defined o/s 31
2. Meaning	Promise to give money or money's with upon the determinative of an uncertain event.	To do or not to do something if some event. Collateral to such contract does or does not happen
3. Nature of uncertain event	Contingent nature	Not be a wagering nature
4. Void / valid.	**Void**	**Valid**
5. Interest	No other interest in the subject matter of the agreement except within of loss of wagering amt.	Have real interest outcome of the uncertain gain.
	A wagering agreement is essentially of a contingent nature.	A contingent contract the not be a wagering nature.
	Consists of reciprocal promises futures event is the sole determine factor	Not consist a reciprocal promises future event is fully collateral.

PERFORMANCE

Sec 37:- That the parties to a contract ***must either perform or offer to perform***, their respective promises unless such performance is ***dispensed with or excused*** under the provisions of ***contract Act, or of any other law.***

Performance: - Two types

1. **Actual performance** – actually performed – liability of such a party comes to an end.
2. **Attempted performance or tender of performance refusal to accept offer of performance by promise [38]**

Offer *Doesnot*

3. Promisor ---------- promisee---------attempted performance

of performance accept

Promisor is not responsible for non performance and they can sue the promisee for breach of **contract** – nor he (promisor) thereby lose his rights under the contract.

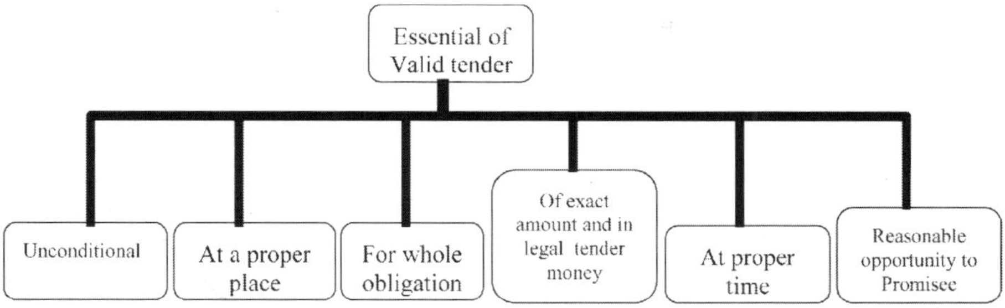

A. Tender or offer of performance to be valid must satisfy the following conditions:-

(i) It must be unconditional
Ex :- 'X' offers to 'Y' the principal amount of the loan. This is not a valid tender since the whole amount of principal and interest is not offered.

(ii) It must be made at a proper time and place.
Ex:- If the promisor wants to deliver the goods at 1 am. This is not a valid tender unless it was so agreed;

(iii) Reasonable opportunity to examine goods.
Ex:- Delivery of something to the promise by the promisor promise must have reasonable opportunity of inspection.

(iv) It must be for the whole obligation :- goods and amount.
Ex:- 'X' a debtor, offer's to pay 'Y' the debt due in installments and tenders the first installment. This is not a valid tender minor deviation – not invalid [Behari lal v ram gulam]

(v) It must be made to the promise or his duty authorized agent.
Ex:- It must be person who is willing to person his part of performance.

(vi) In case of payment of money, tender must be of the exact amount due and it must be in the legal tender.

Type of Tender

™ Tender of goods and services

When a promisor offers to delivery of goods or service to the promise, it is said to be tender of goods or services, if promisee does not accept a valid tender, **It has the following effects:**

(i) The promisor is **not responsible** for non – performance of the contract.

(ii) The promisor is **discharged from his obligation** under the contract. Therefore, he need not offer again.

(iii) **He does not lose his right** under the contract. Therefore, he can sue the promise.

™ Tender of money

Tender of money is an offer to make payment. In case a valid tender of money is not accepted, it will have **the following effects**:

(i) The offeror is not discharged from his obligation to pay the amount.

(ii) The offeror is discharged from his liability for **payment of interest** from the date of the tender of money.

Effect of refusal of party to perform promise Wholly Sec 39.

Promisor – Refuse – Promise – wholly

Promisee can put – can end of the contract or – he can continue the contract if he has given his consent either by words or – by conducts in its continuance.

Result – claim damages. [compensation]

Ex:-

(Refer Class Notes)

Who can demand performance?

1. Promisee – stranger can't demand performance of the contract.
2. Legal Representative – legal representative can demand Exception performance.
   - contrary intention appears from the contract - contract is of a personal nature.
3. Third party – ***Exception to "stranger to a contract"***

Person by whom promise is to be performed Sec 40.

[who will perform the contract]

1. **Promisor himself :-** include personal skill, taste or art work.

Ex:- 'A' promises to paint a picture for 'B' as this promise involves personal skill of 'A'. If must be performed by 'A'.

2. **Promisor or agent :-** [does not involves personal skill]
3. **Legal Representative [does not involve personal skill and taste]**
4. **Third person [Sec 41] :-** Acceptance of promise from the third party:-

If the promisor accepts performance of a contract by a third party, he can't after wards enforce the performance against the promisor although the promisor had neither authorized not ratified the act of the third party.

[In other meaning once the promise accepts the performe from a third person, he cannot compel the promisor the perform the contract again]

Performance of Joint Promises:-

Two or more person make a promise

- **Performed by all the joint promisor [42]**
- All the joint promisor – liable
- Thus in India the liability of joint promisors is joint as well as several.

In England, however the liability of the joint promisors is only joint and not several and accordingly all the joint promisors must be sued jointly.

- **Liability of joint promisor [43]**

1. **Liability** – joint as well as several [unless express A + B + C 900 D. D may compel either A, B or C or any of two of them or all of them.

2. Where a joint promisor has been compelled to perform the whole promise, be may compel every other joint promisor to contribute equally with himself to the performance of the promise (unless a contrary intention appears from the contract).

   C – 9000 – D A + B – C
   3000 3000

3. If any one of the joint promisors make default in such contribution, the remaining joint promisors must bear the loss arising from such default in equal shares

   A + B + C – 9000 (A) – Insolvent

   B + C = 4500 + 4500 = 9000

Sec 44:- ***Release of one joint promisor*** :- where one of the joint promisors is released other joint promisors shall continue to be liable.

[In English law if one joint promisor – discharge then all the joint promisors discharge]

Sec 45:- Rights to claim performance of joint [Devolution of joint rights]

1. During their joint lives – all the joint promisors .
2. After the death of any of them – The representative of such deceased promise jointly with the surging promise
3. With the representatives of all jointly.

   Ex:- 'A' in consideration of Rs 50,000 lent to him by 'B' and ' C' promises 'B' and 'C' jointly to replace them that sum with interest on a day specifies.

- 'B' dies. The right to claim performance rests with 'B' representatives jointly with 'c' during 'C' life.
- And after 'C's death with the representatives of 'B' and 'C' jointly.

Time place and manner of performance [46 – 50]

1. **No time is specified for performance [Sec 46]**
   - Time of performance is not specified + promisor agreed to perform without, a demand from the promise the performance must be made within a reasonable time. Reasonable time – in each particulars case – a **question of fact.**
2. **Time specified but hour not mentioned [47].**

   Time of performance specified + promisor agreed to perform without application by the promisee
   - Performance must perform on the day fixed during the usual business hours and at the place at which the promise ought to be performed.
3. **Where Time is fixed and application to be made [48]**
   - Proper place and within the usual hour of business
   - Promisee to apply for performance
4. **Performance of promise where no place is specified and no application is to be made by the promise [49]**
   - It is the duty of the promisor to apply to the promise to appoint a reasonable place for the performance and perform it at such appointed place.

5. **Performance in manner or at time prescribed or sanctioned by promise [50]**
    - In such prescribed manner and
    - Prescribed time

Ex:- 'A' desires 'B' who owes him Rs 10,000 to send him a promissory note for Rs 10,000 by Post. The debt is discharged as soon as 'B' puts into the post a letter containing the promissory note duly addressed to 'A'.

Performance of reciprocal promises

Reciprocal Promise :- Promises which form the consideration or part of consideration for each other as called reciprocal promises.

1. **Mutual and Independent:-** Such promises all to be performed by each party independently without waiting for the other party to perform his promise can't excuse himself on the ground of non-performance by the default party.

    deliver on Paying

    X *Y* *Y* *6thmay*
    the goods 1*0thmay the price*
    Y – Price – non Payment
    X – goods delivered
2. **Mutual and Dependent:-** Sue damage . The performance of promise by one party depended on the prior performance of the promise by other party.
    [The party at fault becomes liable to pay compensation to the other party may sustain by the non performance of the contract – **[54]**
3. **Mutual and concurrent: -** when reciprocal promises are to be performed simultaneously a promisor need not perform his part unless the promise is ready and willing to perform **[51]**

    deliver *Pay*
    A ---------------- *B*---------------
    the goods *The*Price

Order of performance of reciprocal promises [52]

- Where the order in which reciprocal promises one to be performed is expressly fixed by the contract – they must be performed in that order.
- Order is not expressly fixed – nature of transaction requires

Ex :- 'A' and 'B' contract that 'A' shall build a house for 'B' at a fixed price 'A' promise to build the house must be performed before its promise to pay for it.

Sec 53 :-One party preventing – voidable at the option of the other party so prevented.
- Compensation for loss

Sec 54 :- Legal and illegal

Legal – valid, illegal – void

Sec 58:- alternative promise, one branch being illegal legal branch alone can be enforced.

A – B – 1000 rupees
Deliver – rice + smuggled goods

Time as the essence of the contract (Sec 55)

Where time is essence – the concerned parties must perform their respective promises within the specified time.

Time are fact :- time is specified for the performance of the contract is not by itself sufficient to prove that time is essence of the contract.

- Intention of the parties.

Time is generally considered to be the essence of the contract :-

(a) where the parties have expressly agreed to treat as the essence of the contract.

(b) Delay operates as an injury to the party and

(c) Nature and necessities of the contracts requires it to be performs within the specified time.

- Delivery of the goods – considered – essence of the contract payment of the price – No

[However in case of sale and purchase of an immoral property, the time is presumed to not the essence of the contract]

Time is essence of the contract – party tails to perform

- In time – the contract becomes **voidable** at the option the other party.

Time is not essence – only claim damages for delay in performance

Assignment of contract :-

(a) by – operation of law
- Death
- Insolvency

(b) By an act of parties

Assignment is a made of transferring rights.

tranfer rights

Assignment ----------------- *another person*

and int*erest*

Rules regarding assignment

(a) The liabilities or obligations under a contract can't be assigned

(b) The rights and benefits under a contract which not of a personal nature can be assigned.

(c) ***An actionable claim can always be assigned***

	Succession	Assignment
Meaning	Deceased person	Person – another person
Time	- Legal represent	During the life time of a person
Voluntary Act	On the death of a person	Voluntary
Written document	Not voluntary automatic	Required assignment deed
Scope	operation of law	Rights
	No. required Liability and rights by	

Appropriation of Payments :- [Sec 59 – 61]

- **Appropriation means application of payments** – The question of appropriation of payments arises when a debtor owes several debts to the same creditor and make a payment that is not sufficient to discharge the whole indebtness.

1. Appropriation of Payments

Sometimes, a debtor owes several distinct debts to the same creditor and he makes a payment which is insufficient to satisfy all the debts. In such a case, a question arises as to which particular debt the payment is to be appropriated. Section 59 to 61 of the Act lay down following rules as to appropriation of payments which provide an answer to this question.

• Appropriation as per express instructions

Every debtor who owes several debts to a creditor has a right to instruct his creditor to which particular debt, the payment is to be appropriated or adjusted. Therefore, where the debtor expressly states that the payment is to be applied to the discharge of a particular debt, the payment must be applied accordingly.

Example : A owes B three distinct debts of Rs.2,000, 3,000 and 5,000. A sends Rs.5,000 and instructs B that the payment should be appropriated against the third debt. He is bound to appropriate the payment against the third debt only.

2. Application of payment where debt to be discharge is not indicated [60]

If section 60 is attracted, the creditor shall have the discretion to apply such payment for any lawful debt which is due to him from the person making the payment.

Example: A owes to B, among other debts, the sum of Rs.520. B writes to A and demands payment of this sum. A sends to B Rs.520. This payment is to be applied to the discharge of the debt of which B had demanded payment.

3. Application of payment where neither party appropriates [61]

The payment shall be applied in discharge of the debts in order of time whether they are or are not based by the limitation Act 1963, if the debt are of equal standing (i.e. payable on the same date) the payment shall be applied in discharge of each of these debt proportionately.

• *First interest then principle* • *Director of payer not receiver.* • *Right primary of the debtor*

[whatever is paid, paid according to the intention of paying it]

• ***[Quickquid soivitur, sovitur secundum modem solventies]***

Example: A owes B, the following debts:

Amount of Positions of the debt the debt Rs.2,000 Time barred

Rs.1,000	Time barred
Rs.2,000	Due on 10th June
Rs.3,000	Due on 20th September

A sends Rs. 1,500 in the month of June. He neither expressly intimates nor circumstance of the case imply as to which debt the amount is to be applied. Moreover, B also does not appropriate the payment at his own discretion. Therefore, the payment will be appropriated in order of time. However, here in this case two debts are of equal standing. The payment will, therefore, be appropriated in order of time but to all equal standing debts. In this case, Rs.1,500 will be appropriated towards the first two debts of equal standing proportionately, i.e. in the ratio of 2:1.

DISCHARGE OF A CONTRACT

Discharge of a contract means termination of contractual relation between the parties to a contract in other words a contract is discharged when the rights and obligations created by it are extinguished (i.e. comes to an end).

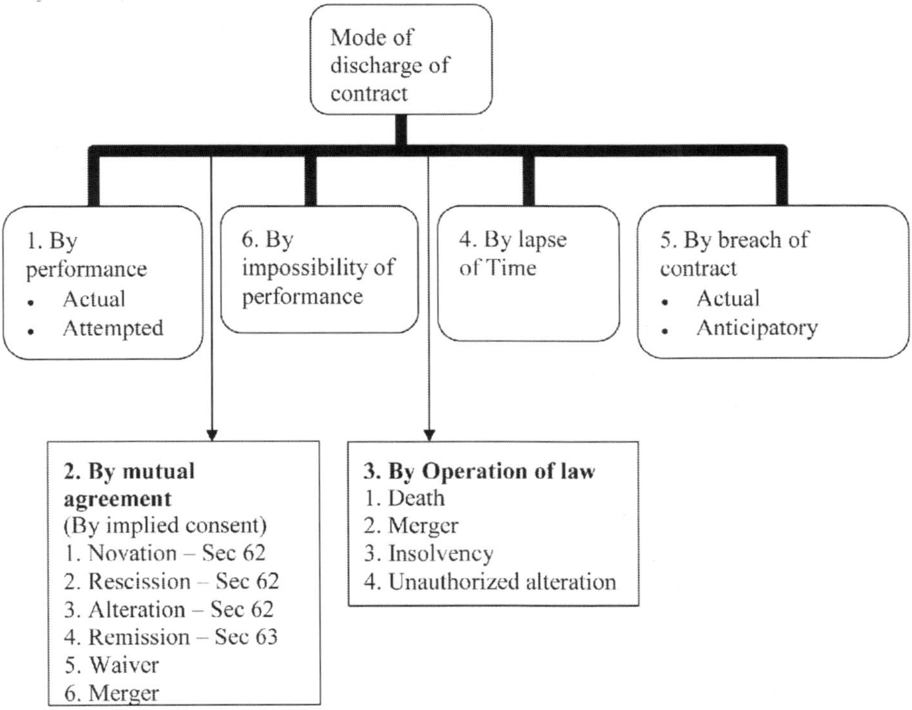

Discharge by performance

fulfillment of obligations by a party to the contract within the time and in the manner prescribed in the contract.

(a) **Actual performance** – no party remains liable under the contract. Both the parties performed.

(b) **Attempted performance or tender.:-** Promisor offers to perform his obligation under the contract but the promise refuses to accept the performance. It is called as attempted performance or tender of performance ¾ But the contract is not discharged.

Discharge by mutual agreement

(a) **Novation [Sec 62]** – Novation means substitution of a new contract in the place of the original contract new contract entered into in consideration of discharge of the old contract. The new contract may be.

- Between the same parties (by change in the terms and condition)
- Between different parties (the term and condition remains same or changed)

Following conditions are satisfied:

(1) **All the parties** must consent **to novation**

(2) The novation must take place before the breach of original contract.

(3) The new contract must be valid and enforceable.

Example: o A owes B Rs.50,000. A enters into an agreements with B and gives B a mortgage of his estate for Rs.40,000 in place of the debt of Rs.50,000. (Between same parties)

- A owes money Rs.50,000 to B under a contract. It is agreed between A, B & C that B shall henceforth accept C as his Debtor instead of A for the same amount. Old debt of A is discharged, and a new debt from C to B is contracted. (Among different parties)

(b) **Rescission [62]:-** Rescission means cancellation of the contract by any party or all the parties to a contract. X promises Y to sell and deliver 100 bales of cotton on 1st oct his go down and Y promises to par for goods on 1st Nov. X does not supply the goods. Y may rescind the contract.

(c) **Alteration [62] :-** Alteration means a change in one or more of the terms of a contracts with mutual consent of parties the parties of new contracts remains the same.

Ex:- X Promises to sell and delivers 100 bales of cotton on 1st oct. and Y promises to pay for goods on 1st Nov. Afterwards X and Y mutually decide that the goods shall be delivered in five equal installments at is godown . Here original contract has been discharged and a new contract has come into effect.

(d) **Remission [63]:-** Remission means accepting a lesser consideration than agreed in the contract. No consideration is necessary for remission. Remission takes place when a Promisee-

(a) *dispense with (wholly or part) the performance of a promise made to him.*

(b) *Extends the time for performance due by the promisors*

(c) *Accept a lesser sum instead of sum due under the contract*

(d) *Accept any other consideration that agreed in the contract*

- A promise to paint a pictured for B. B after words for him to do so. A is no longer bound to perform the promise.

(e) **Waiver:-** Intentional relinquishment of a night under the contract.

(f) **Merger :-** conversion of an inferior right into a superior right is called as merger. (Inferior right end)

Basis	Novation	Alteration
1. Meaning	It is substitution of an existing contract with new one.	It is alteration to some of the terms and conditions of the original Contract.
2. Change in parties	It is made by – (a) change in the terms of the contract or (b) change in the Contracting Parties.	Terms of the contract may be altered by mutual agreements by the same contracting parties. So, there is no change in the parties.
3. New Contract	A New Contract comes into existence in place of the old one.	It is not essential to substitute a new contract in place of the old contract.
4. Performance	Old contract need not be performed New contract must be performed.	Old contract as per the altered terms shall be performed.

Discharge by operation of law

(a) **Death :-** involving the personal skill or ability, knowledge of the deceased party one discharged automatically. In other contract the rights and liability passed to legal represent. **Example :** A promises to perform a dance in B's theatre. A dies. The contract comes to an end.

(b) **Insolvency:-** when a person is declared insolvent. He is discharged from his liability up to the date of insolvency.

Example: A contracts to sell 100 bags of sugar to B. Due to heavy loss by a major fire which leaves nothing to sell, A applies for insolvency and is adjudged insolvent. Contract is discharged.

(c) **By unauthorized material alteration** – without the approval of other party – comes to an end – nature of contract substance or legal effect.

Example : A agrees upon a Promissory Note to pay Rs.5,000 to B. B the amount as Rs.50,000. A is liable to pay only Rs.5,000.

(d) **Merger:** When an inferior right accruing to a party in a contract mergers into a superior right accruing to the same party, ***then the contract conferring inferior right is discharged.***

Example: A took a land on lease from B. Subsequently, A purchases that land. A becomes owner of the land and ownership rights being superior to rights of a lessee, the earlier contract of lease stands terminated.

5. **Rights and liabilities vest in the same person**: Where the rights and liabilities under a Contract vest in the same person, the contract is discharged.

Example: A Bill of Exchange which was accepted by A, reaches A's hands after being negotiated and endorsed through 4 other parties. The contract is discharged.

Discharge by Lapse of time

Where a party fails to take action against the other party within the time prescribe under the **limitation Act, 1963**. All his rights to come end. Recover a debt – **3 Years** recover an immovable property – **12 years**

Ex.:- On 1st July 20X1 X sold goods to Y to Rs 1,00,000 and Y had made no payment till

August 20X4. state the legal position on 1st Aug 20X4

(a) If no. credit period allowed

Ans. (Refer Classroom)

(b) If 2 month credit period allowed.

Discharge by Breach of contract

Failure of a party to perform his part of contract

(a) **Anticipatory Breach of contract :-** Anticipatory breach of contract occurs when the part declares his intention of not performing the contract before the performance is due .

(i) **Express repudiation: -** 5 agrees to supply B 100 tunes of specified category of iron on 15.01.2006 on 31.12.2005. 5 express his unwillingness to supply the iron to B.

(ii) **Party disables himself: -** Implied by conduct.

Ex.:- 5 agrees to sell his fiat car to B on 15.01.2006 on 31.12.05 5 sells his fiat car to T.

(b) **Actual Breach of contract :-** If party fails or neglects or refuses to perform his obligation on the due date of performance or during performance. It is called as actual breach.

During performance – party has performed a part of the contact.

Consequences of Breach of contract:- The aggrieved party (i.e. the party not at face it) is discharged from his obligation and get rights to proceed against the party at fault. The various remedial available to an aggrieved party.

Discharge by Impossibility performance

(a) ***Effect of Initial Impossibility***

(b) ***Effect of supervening. Impossibility***

(a) **Initial Impossibility – at the time of making contract** ¾ Both parties know – put life into deed body – void .

- Both don't know – void.
- One know – compensate to other party

(b) **Effect of super vanity Impossibility:-**

- Where an act becomes impossible after the contract is made – void
- Becomes unlawful, beyond the control of promisor – void
- Promisor alone knows about the Impossibility – compensate loss.
- When an agreement is discovered to be void or where a contract becomes void

Sing

Benefit must refund X--------------*Y. y*

*Ad.*1000

Cases when a contract is discharged on the group of super vent Impossible

(a) Distraction of subject matter - Failure of the ultimate purpose of contract – king coronate process.
(b) Death of personal Incapacity
(c) Declaration of war
(d) change of Law
(e) Non existence or Non occurrence of a particular state of thing necessary for performance.

No Super Impossibility – does not become void

- Difficulty of performance – coal – transport
- Commercial Impossibility
- Default of a third party
- Strikes, knockout and civil disturbance.
- Partial Impossibility – coronation of king and to sailing around the lake by boat.

REMEDIES FOR THE BREACH OF CONTRACT

Remedy means course of action available to an aggrieved party when other party breaches the contract.

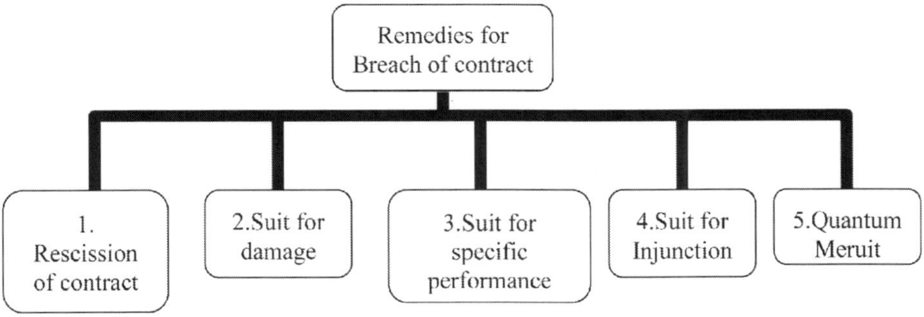

RESCISSION OF CONTRACT – SEC 39

- It means right to party to cancel contract.
- In case of breach of contract, other party may rescind contract.

Effect of Rescission of Contract

- Aggrieved party is not required to perform his part of obligation under contract.
- Aggrieved party claims compensation for any loss.
- Party is liable to restore benefit, if any.

When can Court Grant Rescind Contract?

Court can rescind the contract in the following situation:

- Contract is voidable.
- Contract is unlawful.

SUIT FOR DAMAGES

- It means monetary compensation allowed for loss.
- Purpose is to compensate aggrieved party and ***not to punish party as fault.***
- In India, rules relating to damages are based on English judgment of ***Hadley vs Baxendale.***

The facts of case were – H's mill was stopped due to the breakdown of the shaft. He delivered the shaft to common carrier to repair it and agree to pay certain sum of repair it and agree to pay certain sum of money for doing this work. H has informed to B that delay would result into loss of profit. B delivered the shaft after reasonable time after repair. H filed suit for loss of profit. It was held that B is not liable for loss of profit. The court laid down rule that damage can be recovered if party has breach of contract.

KINDS OF DAMAGES

The following are the different kinds of damages

- **Ordinary damages** These are the damages which are payable for the loss arising naturally and directly as result of breach of contract. It is also known as proximate damage or natural damage.
- **Special damages** These are damages which are payable for loss arising due to some special circumstances. It can be recovered only if special circumstances which result in special loss in case of breach of contract and party have notice of such damage. **Example:** A sends sample of his products for exhibition to an agent of a railway company for carriage to "New Delhi" for an exhibition. The consignment note stated: "Must be at New Delhi, Monday Certain." Due to negligence of the company, the goods reached only after the exhibition was over. Held, the company was liable for the loss caused by late arrival of the products because the company's agent was aware of the special circumstances.
- **Exemplary or punitive or vindictive damages** These damages are allowed not to compensate party ***but as mean of punishment*** to defaulting party. The court may award these damages in the case of:
  - Breach of contract to marry – loss based on mental injury.
  - Wrongful dishonor of cheque – smaller amount, larger the damage.
- **Nominal damages** Where party suffers no loss, the court may allow nominal damages simply to establish that party has proved his case and won. Nominal damage is very small in amount.
- **Damages for inconvenience** If party has suffered physical inconvenience, discomfort for mental agony as result of breach of contract, party can recover the damage for such inconvenience. **Example:** A photographer agreed to take photographs at a wedding ceremony but failed to do so. The bride brought an action for the breach of contract. Held, she was entitled to damages for her injured feelings.
- **Liquidated damages and penalty** Party may specify amount at the time of entering into contract. The amount so specified may be (a) liquidated damage, or (b) penalty.

If specified sum represent, fair and genuine pre – estimate damages likely to result due to breach, it is called ***liquidated damage.***

But if specified sum is ***disproportionate to the damages, it is called as penalty.***

As regard the payment of liquidated damages and penalty court can't' increase amount of damages beyond the amount specified in the contract.

Example : A gives B, a bond for the repayment of Rs.1,000 with interest at 12 per cent, at the end of six months, with a stipulation that, in case of default, the interest shall be payable at the rate of 75 per cent, from the date of default. This is a stipulation by way of penalty, and B is only entitled to recover from A such compensation as the Court considers reasonable.

- **Forfeiture of security deposit** Any clause in contract entitling the aggrieved party to forfeit security deposit in the nature of penalty and court may award reasonable compensation.
- **Payment of interest**
  - It is permissible.
  - If interest is in nature of penalty, court may grant relief.
  - If ***no rate of interest is specified in contract*** party shall be liable to pay ***as per the law in force or as per custom or usage of trade.***
- **Cost of suit or decree** The court has also discretion to award cost of suit for damages in addition to the damages for breach of contract.

Suit for Specific Performance

It means, demanding an order from court that promise agreed in contract shall be carried out.

- **When is specific performance allowed?**
  - Where actual damages arising from breach is not measurable.
  - Where monetary compensation is not adequate remedy.
- **When specific performance is not allowed?**
  - When damages are an adequate remedy.
  - Where performance of contract requires numbers of minute details and therefore not possible for court to supervise.
  - Where contract is of personal in nature.
  - Where contract made by company beyond its power. (ultra – vires)
  - Where one party to contract is minor
  - Where contract is inequitable to either party.

Example : A agree to sell B, an artist painting for Rs.30,000. Later on, he refused to sell it. Here B can file suit against A for specific performance of the contract.

Suit for Injunction

- It means stay order granted by court. ***This order prohibits a person to do particular act.***
- Where there is breach of contract by one party and order, of specific performance is not granted by court, injunction may be granted. Example: Film actress agreed to act exclusively for W for a year and for no one else. During the year she contracted to act for Z.

QUASI CONTRACT

[Contracts implied in law or implied contract]

It means a contract which lacks one or more of the essentials of a contract.

Quasi contract are declared by law as valid contracts on the basis of ***principles of equity*** i.e. *no person shall be allowed to enrich himself at the expense of another the legal obligations of parties remains same.*

Nature of Quasi contracts:

(a) A quasi contract does not arise from any formal agreement but is imposed by law.

(b) Every quasi contract based upon the **principle of equity** and **good conscience.**

(c) A quasi contract is always a right to money and generally though not always to a liquidated sum of money.

(d) A suit for its breach may be filed in the same way as in case of a complete contract.

(e) The right grouted to a party under a quasi contract is not available to him against the whole world but against particular person(s) only.

(f) A suit for breach of a quasi contract may be filed in the same way as in case of an ordinary contract

(g) Although there is no contract between the parties under a quasi contracts, yet they are put in the same position as if he were a contract between them .

Provisions relating to various quasi contracts are contained in section 68 to sec 72 of the contract Act, 1872.

TYPES OF QUASI CONTRACTS

Sec. 68 Supply of Necessaries	**Sec. 69** Reimbursement of money due	**Sec. 70** Obligation to pay for benefit out of non – gratuitous act	**Sec. 71** Responsibility of Finder of Goods	**Sec.72** Person receiving goods are money by mistake

Sec. 68: If a person, incapable of entering into a contract, or anyone whom he is legally bound to support, is supplied by another person, with necessaries suited to his condition in life, the person who has furnished such supplies is entitled to be reimbursed from the property of such incapable person.

1. Meaning of Necessaries:

(a) Necessaries normally include articles required to maintain a particular person in the state, degree and station in life in which he is.

(b) They are essentials to run a life.

(c) An item will not be considered necessary, if a person already has sufficient supply of things of such kind.

(d) Necessaries include Services rendered to a person.

(e) What constitutes necessaries depends on the circumstances of each case.

2. Only property liable: person not liable:

(a) It is only the property (movable and immovable) of the incapable person they shall be liable.

(b) He cannot be held liable personally.

(c) Where he doesn't own any property, nothing shall be payable.

3. **Example:** (i) A supplies B, a lunatic, with necessaries suitable to his condition in life. A is entitled to be reimbursed from B's property. (ii) A who supplies the wife and children of B, a lunatic, with necessaries suitable to their condition in life, is entitled to be reimbursed from B's Property.

Payment By a person who is interested in a transaction [69]

Condition of section [69]

Sec. 69; A person, who is interested in the payment of money and pays such money, which another is bound by low to pay, is entitled to be reimbursed by the other.

(a) one party is legally bound to make a payment
(b) Some other persons make such payment
(c) The person making such payment is not legally bound to make such payment
(d) The person making such payment is interested in paying such amount

Legal effect of sec 69.:- If all the conditions of sec 69 are satisfy the person who is interested in paying such amount shall be entitled to recover the payment made by him.

Ex.:- The goods belonging to A were wrongfully attached in order to realize arrears of Government revenue due by G. A paid the amount to save the goods from sale at was held that A was entitled to recover the amount from G.

Obligation of person enjoying benefit of non-gratuitous act [70]

Conditions of section 70.

Sec.70 : Where a person, lawfully does anything for another person, or delivers anything to him; not intending to do so gratuitously, and such other person enjoys the benefits thereof, then he is bound to make compensation to the other in respect of, or to restore the thing so done or delivered.

(a) A person has lawfully done something for another person or delivered something to another person.
(b) Such person must have acted ***voluntarily and non – gratuitously***.
(c) The other person has enjoyed the benefit of the act done for him or the thing delivered to him.

Legal effect of sec 70.

- If the conditions of sec70 are satisfied, there will be quasi contract between the parties.
- Consequently, the party who has done something or delivered a thing shall be entitled to recover its value from the person who obtained the benefit of the same.

Ex.:- A a trades man leaves goods at B's house by mistake, B treat the goods as his own, He is bound to pay A for them.

- A saves B's property from fire. A is not entitled to compensation from B if the circumstances show that be intended to act gratuitously.

Finder of Goods [71]

A person who finds goods belonging to another and takes them into custody, is subject to the same responsibility as a **Bailee.**

A finder of goods has same rights and duties at that of **bailee.**

- Duty to take reasonable care of the goods ¾ Duty not to use the goods for his own purpose.
- Duty not to mix the goods with own goods

Right to recover expenses, reward, sell the goods

Ex.:- X a guest found a diamond ring at a birthday party of Y. X told Y and other guests about it. He has performed his duty to find the own. If he is not able to find the owner he can retain the ring as bales.

Money paid under a mistake or conversion [72]

Sec. 72: A person to whom money has been paid, or anything delivered by mistake or under coercion, must repay or return it. Conditions of **Sec. 72**

(a) A person has
 (i) paid money to another person or
 (ii) Delivered something to another person

(b) Such person must have acted
 - Under a mistake or under coercion.

Legal effect – quasi contract, recover its value from the person who obtained the benefit of same.

Example: (i) A and B jointly owe Rs.1,000 to C.A alone pays the full amount to C and B not knowing this fact, pays Rs.1,000 again to C.C is bound to repay the amount to B. (ii) A Railway Company refuses to deliver certain goods to the Consignee except upon payment of an illegal charge for carriage. The Consignee pays the sum charged in order to take delivery of goods. He is entitled to recover so much of the charge as was illegally excessive.

(c) A + B . – 100 – A – 100, B – 100, B – return.

Compensation for failure to discharge obligation created by quasi contract [73]

When an obligation created by quasi contract is not discharged the injured party is entitled to reline the same compensation from the party in default as if such person had, contracted to discharge is and broken his contract.

Quantum meruit: - [as much as is earned]

One party preventing the other:- If a party prevents the other party from completing his obligation under the contract the aggrieved party may claim payment on quantum merit for the part of contract already performed by him.

(a) In case of void agreement or contract that becomes

- Any person who has received any advantage under such agreement or contract is bound to restore if or to make compensation for it, to the person from who received it.

Ex.:(1)- A – B – 10000 – to marry c (A's daughter) – C – death of the time of performance of contract – B must repay A Rs 1000.

Ex.(2):- A – B decline 250 quince of rice before the 1st of May. A delivers 130 qu. Only before that day and none after. B retains the 130 qu. after the first of May. He is bound to pay A for them.

Ex(3):-A singer – two nights in every week during the next two month and B any ages to pay her Rs 100 for each night's performance on the sixth night, A willfully absent perfect. B must pay a for the five night on which she had sung.

(b) In case of Act preventing the completing of contract:-

If a party does not complete the contract or prevents the other party to complete the contract the aggrieved party can sue or quantum meruit.

Ex.c:- owner – P write a book to be published as series in his magazine. After a few series were published the publication of the magazine was stopped. It was held that P could claim payment on quantum meruit for the part already published.

(c) In case of divisible contract :-

(1) If the contract is divisible and
(2) If the party not at default has enjoyed benefit of the point performance.
(3) the contract is party performed

If the above condition an satisfied, the party at fault may claim on payment on quantum meruit for the part of contract performed by him be con recover such proportion of the contract price as the work done, by him bears to the work under the contracts.

(d) In case of indivisible contract performed completely but Badly.

- Contract is indivisible
- Lump sum consideration
- Completely performed
- Performed badly

The party at fault may recover the contract price (Lump sum price) less the deduction made for done badly.

Ex.:- X agreed to decorate Y's flat for a lump sum of Rs20,000. X did the complete work but Y complained of faulty work man stop. It costs Y another Rs3000 to remedy the defect. X could recover only Rs 17000 from Y.

(e) In case of Non – gratuitous Act – Three condition

(i) The thing must have been done or delivered lawfully.
(ii) The person who has done or delivered the thing must not have intended to do so gratuitously And
(iii) The person from whom the act is done must have enjoyed the benefit of the act.

Ex.:- A, a tradesman leaves goods at B's shop be mistake B treats the good as his own. He is bound to pay A for them.

Difference between Quasi Contract and Contract

Matter	Quasi – contract	Contract
Intentionally Form	It is not intentionally formed but law imposes upon the parties.	It is intentionally formed by parties.
Essentials of contract	A quasi – contract does not possess all the essential of a valid contract.	A contract possesses all the essentials of a valid contract.
Obligations	Obligations are implied upon by the law.	Obligations are mutually created by the parties.
Foundation	It is founded upon the principle of equity.	It is founded upon general principal of law of contracts.

SPECIAL CONTRACT

Contract of Indemnity

1. INTRODUCTION TO CONTRACT OF INDEMNITY

- **Indemnity Meaning –**
  - To make good the loss incurred by another person
  - To compensate the party who has suffered some loss
  - To protect a party from incurring a loss
- **'Contract of indemnity Definition**
  A contract is called as a 'contract of indemnity' if –
  One party promises to save the other from loss caused to him by the conduct of the promisor himself, or by the conduct of any other person.
- **Modes of contract of indemnity** ***Expressed:*** When a person expressly promises to compensate the other from loss. ***Implied :***
  When the contract is to be inferred from the conduct of the parties or from the circumstances of the case.
- **Essential elements of a contract of indemnity** ***Contract :***

All the essentials of a valid contract must also be present in the contract of indemnity **Example:-** X asks Y to beat Z and promises to indemnify Y against the consequences. Y beats Z and is fined Rs.1,000. Y cannot claim this amount from X because the object of the agreement was unlawful. ***Loss to one party***

A person can indemnify another person only if such other person incurs some loss or it has become certain that he will incur some loss. ***Indemnity by the promisor***

The purpose of contract of indemnity is to protect the indemnity holder from any loss that may be caused to the indemnity holder.

Reason for loss

The contract of indemnity must specify that indemnity holder shall be protected from the ***loss caused due to –***

- Action of the promisor himself; or
- Action of any other person; or
- Any act, event or accident which is not in the control of the parties.

2. RIGHTS OF INDEMNITY HOLDER (Sec. 125)

• Right to recover damages

The indemnity holder has the right to recover all the damages which he is compelled to pay in any suit in respect of any matter covered by the contract of indemnity.

• Right to recover costs

The indemnity holder has the right to recover all the costs which he is compelled to pay in bringing or defending such suit.

Condition:

(a) The indemnifier authorised him to bring or defend the suit; or

(b) The indemnity holder did not contravene the orders of the indemnifier; and The indemnity holder acted as it would have been prudent for him to act in the absence of any contract of indemnity.

• Right to recover sums paid

The indemnity holder has the right to recover all the sums which he has paid under the terms of a compromise of such suit.

(a) The indemnifier authorised him to compromise the suit; or

(b) The indemnifier holder did not contravene the orders of the indemnifier; and the indemnity holder acted as it would have been prudent for him to act in the absence of any contract of indemnity.

Contract of guarantee

3. MEANING OF CERAIN TERMS (Sec. 126)

- **Meaning of 'contract of guarantee'** A 'contract of guarantee' is a contract to –
  - Perform the promise; or
  - Discharge the liability, of a third person in case of his default.
- **Meaning of 'surety'**
  The person who gives the guarantee is called as 'surety'
- **Meaning of 'principal debtor'**
  The person in respect of whose default the guarantee is given is called as 'principal debtor'.
- **Meaning of 'creditor'**
  The person to whom the guarantee is given is called as 'creditor'.

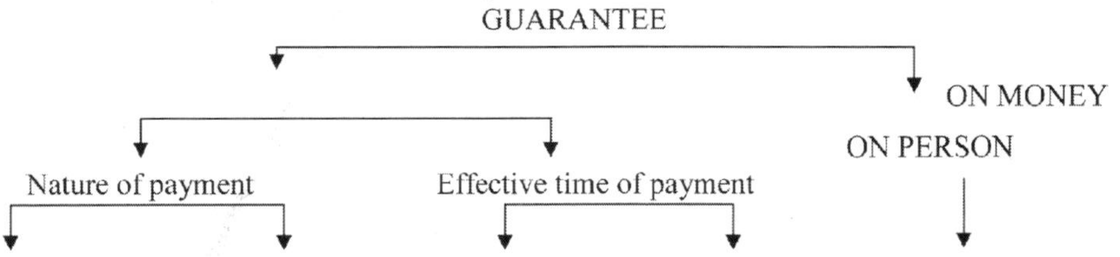

Specific/Simple Guarantee	Continuing Guarantee	Retrospective Guarantee	Prospective Guarantee	Fidelity Guarantee
Guarantee is for a single transaction. It ends when debt is discharged or promise is performed.	Guarantee is for a series of transactions. Liability extends till the revocation of guarantee.	Guarantee is for an existing debt or obligation.	Guarantee is for a future debt or obligation.	Guarantee is on the good conduct or honesty of a person employed in a particular organizations.

4. ESSENTIALS AND LEGAL RULES FOR A VALID CONTRACT OF GUARANTEE

- **Must have all the essentials of a valid contract**
  - All the essentials of a valid contract must be present in the contract of guarantee.
  - Exceptions:

(a) Consideration received by the principal debtor is a sufficient consideration to the surety for giving the guarantee.

(b) Even if principal debtor is incompetent to contract, the guarantee is valid. But, if surety is incompetent to contract, the guarantee is void.

- **Primary liability of some person**
  - The principal debtor must be primarily liable. However, even if the principal debtor is incompetent to contract the guarantee is valid.
  - The debt must be legally enforceable.
  - The debt must not be a time barred debt.
- **The contract must be conditional**
  - The liability of surety is secondary and conditional.
  - The liability of surety arises only if the principal debtor makes a default.
- **No misrepresentation**
  - The creditor should disclose all the facts which are likely to affect the surety's liability.
  - There must not be any concealment of facts.
- **Form of contract**

  A contract of guarantee may be either oral or written.
- **Joining of other co-sureties**

  The guarantee by a surety is not valid if –
  - A condition is imposed by a surety that some other person must also join as a cosurety; but
  - Such other person does not join as a co-surety.

5. NATURE AND EXTENT OF SURETY'S LIABILITY

- **Surety's liability is coextensive with liability of principal debtor**

General rule –

- Surety is liable for all the debts payable by the principal debtor to the creditor.
- Accordingly, interest, damages, costs etc. may also be recovered from the surety.

Exception:-

The contract of guarantee may provide otherwise.

- **Commencement of surety's liability**
  - The liability of surety arises immediately on default by the principal debtor.
  - The creditor is not required to –

(a) first sue the principal debtor; or

(b) first give a notice to the principal debtor.

- **Surety's liability may be limited**

  The surety may fix a limit on his liability up to which the guarantee shall remain effective.

- **Surety's liability may be continuous**
  - The surety may agree to become liable for a series of transactions of continuous nature.
  - However, the surety may fix –
    - a limit on his liability upto which the guarantee shall remain effective; -
    a time period during which the guarantee shall remain effective.

- **Surety's liability may be conditional**

The surety may impose certain conditions in the contract of guarantee. Until those conditions are met, the surety shall not be liable.

6. CONTINUING GUARANTEE

- **Meaning**

A guarantee which extends to a series of transactions is called as continuing guarantee.

- **Revocation (Sec.130)**

Continuing guarantee may be revoked, at anytime, by the surety by giving a notice to the creditor. However, revocations shall be effective only in respect of future transactions (i.e. the liability of the surety with regard to previous transactions remains unaffected)

- **Death of surety (sec. 131)**

Death of the surety operates as a revocation of a continuing guarantee as to future transaction.

7. RIGHTS OF SURETY (Sec.140, 141, 145, 146 and 147)

I. Rights against principal debtor

- **Right of indemnity**
  - There is an implied promise by the principal debtor to indemnity the surety.
  - The surety is entitled to claim from the principal debtor all the sums which he has rightfully paid.
  - The surety cannot recover such sums, which the he has paid wrongfully.

- **Right of subrogation**

On payment of a debt, the surety shall be entitled to all the rights which the creditor could claim against the principal debtor.

II. Rights against the creditor

- **Right of subrogation**
  - The surety can claim all the securities which the creditor had at the time of giving of guarantee

- It is immaterial as to whether the surety had knowledge of such securities or not.
- If the securities are returned by the creditor to the principal debtor the surety is discharged to the extent of value of the securities so returned.

- **Right of set off**
  - Any amount recoverable by the principal debtor may be claimed as deduction.
  - Any amount recoverable by the surety may be claimed as deduction.
- **Rights to share reduction**

If the principal debtor becomes insolvent, the surety may claim proportionate reduction in his liability.

III. Rights against co-sureties

- **Rights to contribution**

General Rule

All the co-sureties shall contribute equally

Exceptions

- Under the contract of guarantee, the co-sureties may fix limits on their respective liabilities. Even in such a case, the co-sureties shall contribute equally, subject to maximum limit fixed by the co-sureties.
- The contract of guarantee may provide that the co-sureties shall contribute in some other proportion.

- **Right to share benefit of securities**

If one co-surety receives any security, all the other co-sureties are entitled to share the benefit of such security.

8. DISTINCTION BETWEEN INDEMNITY AND GUARANTEE

Basis	Contract of indemnity	Contract of guarantee
Meaning	A contract by which one party promises to save the other from loss caused to him is called as a contract of indemnity.	A contract of guarantee is a contract to perform the promise, or discharge the liability of a third person in case of his default.
Parties	There are only two parties, viz, the indemnifier and the indemnity holder.	There are three parties, viz., the principal debtor, creditor and the surety.
Nature of liability	The liability of the indemnifier is primary and independent.	The liability of the surety is secondary and conditional.
Number of contract	In a contract of indemnity there is only one contract.	In the contract of guarantee, there are three contracts; first between principal debtors and creditor, second between creditor and surety, and third between surety and principal debtor.
Nature of contract	The contract of indemnity is for the reimbursement of the loss.	The contract of guarantee is for the security of the creditor.

9. DISCHARGE OF SURETY FROM LIABILITY (Sec.130 to 144)

DISCHARGE OF SURETY

Revocation of contract of Invalidation of contract of Conduct of Creditor guarantee guarantee

- **Notice of revocation by surety**
- ***Specific guarantee***

A specific guarantee can be revoked only if liability of principal debtor has not arisen.

- ***Continuing guarantee***

Acontinuing guarantee can be revoked only in respect of future transactions.

- **Death of surety**

  In case of death of surety, a continuing guarantee is automatically revoked in respect of future transactions.

- **Variance in terms**

If –

- Any variation is made subsequent to formation of contact of guarantee; and
- Such variation is made without the consent of surety;

Then –

- The surety shall be released for such transactions as take place after such variation.

- **Release or discharge of principal debtor**

If –

- The creditor makes a fresh contract with the principal debtor whereby the principal debtor is relieved from his liability; or –
- The creditor does any act or omission resulting in discharge of the principal debtor; **Then –**

The surety is discharged.

- **Composition with principal debtor**

  The surety is discharged if the creditor makes a composition with the principal debtor without obtaining the consent of surety.

- **Giving extension of time to principal debtor**

  The surety is discharged if the creditor extends the time for repayment of the debt by the principal debtor without obtaining the consent of the surety.

- **Loss of security by a creditor**

  The surety is discharged to the extent of security lost by the creditor.

BAILMENT

10. MEANING OF CONTRACT OF BAILMENT (Sec. 148)

A **'bailment'** is the delivery of goods by one person to another for some purpose, upon a contract that they shall, when the purpose is accomplished, be returned or otherwise disposed of according to the directions of the person delivering them.

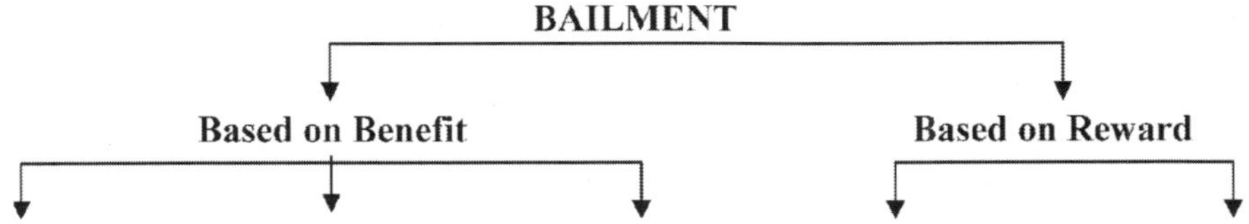

Exclusive benefit of Bailor	Exclusive benefit of Bailee	Mutual Benefit of both	Gratuitous Bailment	Non gratuitous Bailment
J, neighbour of K, agrees to look after K's per while he is out of station. K is benefited.	Z lends a book to Y for reading. Y is benefited.	A hires furniture from B, by payment of hire charges, Both A and B are benefited.	Neither Bailor nor Bailee gets any remuneration, e.g. A lends his book to his are friend.	Bailor or Bailee gets remuneration e.g. G gives his television set for repair to H, a technician. H gets paid for the job.

11. ESSENTIALS OF A VALID CONTRACT OF BAILEMENT (Sec.148)

- **Contract**
  - There must be a contract.
  - The contract may be expressed or implied.
- **Goods**

Bailment can be made of goods only.

- **Delivery**

  There must be delivery of goods by one person to another person.

- **Purpose of delivery**
  - The goods must be delivered for some purpose.
  - The purpose may be expressed or implied.
- **Return or disposal of goods**
  - ***The delivery of goods must be conditional***
  - ***The condition shall be that the goods shall be –***
  - returned (either in original form or in any altered from); or
  - disposed of according to the directions of the bailor, when the purpose is accomplished.

12. MODES OF DELIVERY (Sec.149)

- **Actual delivery**

  Transfer of physical possession of goods from one person to another .

- **Symbolic delivery**
  - Physical possession of goods is not actually transferred.
  - A person does some act resulting in transfer of possession to any other person.

  Examples:

(a) Delivery of keys of a car to a friend

(b) Delivery of a railway receipt.

Constructive delivery

If –

- A person is already in possession of goods of owner.
- Such person contracts to hold the goods as a bailee for a third person.

Then –

Such person becomes the bailee, and the third person becomes the bailor.

13. CLASSIFICATION OF BAILMENT

- **Gratuitous bailment**
- *Bailment without any charges or reward, i.e. –*
  - No hire charges are paid by bailee; and
  - No custody charges are paid by bailor.
- **Non – gratuitous bailment**

Bailment for some charges or reward, i.e.-

- Hire charges are paid by bailee; or
- Custody charges are paid by bailor.

14. DUTIES OF A BAILOR (Sec. 150, 158, 159 and 164)

• Disclose faults in goods [Sec. 150]:

Bailor is bound to disclose to Bailee, faults in the goods bailed, of which he has knowledge. He should also disclose such information which – (a) materially interferes with the use of goods, or (b) expose the Bailee to extraordinary risk.

Liability for Defects in Goods

In case of Gratuitous bailment	In case of Non – Gratuitous Bailment
Bailor is liable only for those losses which arise due to non – disclosed risks.	Bailor is liable for damages whether or not he was aware of the existence of faults.

Example: A owning a motorcycle, allows B, his friend, to take it for a joy ride. A knows that its brakes were not proper but does not disclose it to B. B meets with an accident. A is liable to compensate B for damages. But when A had lent the motorcycle on hire, he is liable to B even if he did not know of the failure of his brakes.

• Bear expenses [Sec.158]

Expenses of Bailment

In case of Gratuitous bailment	In case of Non – Gratuitous Bailment
Bailor shall repay to Bailee, all necessary expenses incurred by him for the purpose of Bailment.	Bailor is liable to repay only extra – ordinary expenses, and not the ordinary expenses.

Example: M lends his car to N and it runs out of petrol. N can recover the amount paid for refueling (ordinary expenses). If in case, the car suffers a breakdown, N can recover such charges as are paid by him in bringing it back to condition (extra – ordinary expenses). He M hired the car to N, he shall be liable only for the repair charges, being extra ordinary expenses.

• Indemnify the bailee for defective title

The bailor shall indemnify the bailee for any loss caused to bailee due to defective title of bailor.

• Indemnify the bailee for premature termination

If –

- the bailment is gratuitous ; and
- for a specific period. **Then –**

(a) the bailor may compel the bailee to return the goods before expiry of the peiod of bailment; but

(b) the bailor shall indemnify the bailee for any loss incurred by the bailee.

• Receive back the goods

- It is the duty of the bailor to receive back the goods, when returned by bailee.

If the bailor wrongfully refuses to receive back the goods, he shall be liable to pay ordinary expenses of custody of goods incurred by the bailee.

15. DUTIES OF A BAILEE (Sec.151 to 157)

- **Take reasonable care**
  - ***The bailee must take such case of goods as a man of ordinary prudence would take*** care of his own goods.
  - ***The bailee shall not be liable for any loss or destruction of goods, if –***

(a) he is not negligent; or

(b) the loss was caused due to an act of God or other unavoidable reasons.

- **Not to make unauthorized use of goods**
  - The bailee must not make any unauthorized use of the goods.
  - If the bailee makes any unauthorized use of goods, then –

(a) the bailment becomes voidable at the option of the bailor; and

(b) the bailee shall be liable for any loss or damage even if such loss is caused due to an act of God or other unavoidable reasons.

- **Not to mix goods**

Goods are mixed with bailor's consent

The parties shall have a proportionate interest in such mixture.

Goods are mixed without bailor's consent, but the goods are separable

- The bailee shall pay the expenses of separation.
- The bailee shall pay damage incurred by the bailor.

Goods are mixed without bailor's consent, and goods are not separable The bailee shall compensate the bailor for any loss caused to him.

- **Return the goods**
  - ***The bailee must return the goods, without waiting for demand from bailor, if –***

(a) the time specified in the contract has expired ; or

(b) the purpose specified in the contract is accomplished.

- ***If the goods are not so returned, then –***

(a) the goods shall be at the risk of the bailee;

(b) the bailee shall be liable for any loss or damage, even if such loss is caused without any fault or negligence of the bailee or due to an act of God or other unavoidable reasons.

- **Return accretion to goods**

The bailee must return to the bailor any accretion (i.e., addition) to the goods bailed.

- **Not to set up an adverse title**

The bailee has no right to allege that the bailor had no authority to bail the goods.

16. RIGHTS OF A BAILOR (Sec. 153, 159, 163, 180, 181)

- **Terminate the bailment**

If –

The bailee does any act inconsistent with the terms and conditions of the contract of bailment.

Then –

The bailment becomes voidable at the option of the bailor.

• **Demand back the goods**

If –

The bailment is gratuitous; and For a specific period.

Then –

(a) the bailor may compel the bailee to return the goods before expiry of the period of bailment; and

(b) the bailor shall indemnify the bailee for any loss incurred by the bailee.

• **File suit against wrongdoer** *The bailor has the right to sue –*

- A third party who does any damages to the goods; or
- A third party who deprives the bailee from using the goods

• **Sue the bailee**

The bailor may sue the bailee to enforce his duties.

17. RIGHTS OF A BAILEE (Sec. 165, 166, 167, 170, 180)

• **Right to compensation**

The bailee has the right to be indemnified by the bailor, if –

- The bailor has no title to the goods; and
- As a consequence, the bailee suffers some loss.

• **Return the goods**

- It is the duty as well as the right of the bailee to return the goods to the bailor.
- In case of joint bailor, the goods may be returned to any of joint bailors.

• **Recover charges incurred** *Extra ordinary expenses*

- The bailor is liable to pay the extraordinary expenses.
- The bailee may recover the extraordinary expenses paid by him.

Ordinary expenses

If the bailment is gratuitous, the bailor is liable to pay the ordinary necessary expenses, i.e., the bailee has the right to recover the ordinary necessary expenses incurred by him.

• **Suit for deciding the title**

The bailee may apply to the Court for deciding the title to goods, if a person other than the bailor claims that the goods belong to him.

• **File suit against wrongdoer** *The bailee has the right to sue –*

- A third party who does any damages to the goods; or
- A third party who deprives the bailee from using the goods.

• **Right of lien**

The bailee has the right to retain the goods delivered to him until the charges due to him are paid by the bailor.

18. DISTINCTION BETWEEN BAILEE'S PARTICULAR AND GENERAL LIEN

Basis of distinction	Bailee's particular lien	Bailee's general lien
1. Natural of right	Particular lien gives right to retain only such goods in respect of which charges due remain unpaid.	General lien gives right to retain any goods belonging to another person for any amount due from him.
2. Condition for exercising lien	Particular lien can be exercised only when some labour or skill has been expended on the goods, resulting in an increase in value of goods.	General lien may be exercised even though no labour or skill has been expended on the goods.
3. Right to whom?	Every bailee is entitled to particular lien.	General lien can be exercised by only such persons as are specified u/s 171. e.g., bankers, factors, wharfingers, Attomeys of High Court, policy brokers. Any other bailee may exercise general lien if there is an agreement to this effect.

19. TERMINATION OF BAILMENT (Sec.153, 159 and 162)

Situation	Explanation	Example
1. Expiry of specified	When bailment is for specific	Z lends a moped to Y for a
period	period, it terminates on the expiry of the specified period.	period of 3 months April – June. The Bailment terminates by the end of June.
2. Accomplishment of specified purpose	Where bailment is for a specified purpose, it terminates when such purpose is accomplished.	G hires tables and chairs, utensils, etc. from H for organizing his son's engagement. G shall return them once the engagement functions are over.
3. Bailee's act inconsistent with conditions	When bailee does some act which is inconsistent with the terms and conditions of bailment, the Bailor may terminate the bailment.	J gives his car to K keeping it in K's garage. K gives it to his son for racing. J can terminate the bailment.
4. Destruction of subject matter	When goods bailed are destroyed, Bailment comes to an end.	K hires a cycle from L. When the cycle is damaged beyond repair in an accident, bailment ends.
5. Gratuitous Bailment	Gratuitous Bailment can be terminated at any time. Also, a Gratuitous Bailment ends by the death of either Bailor or Bailee. **(Sec162)**	**Note:** Where premature termination of bailment by the Bailor, causes loss to the Bailee exceeding the benefits derived by him, the Bailor shall indemnify the Bailee.

20. FINDER OF GOODS (Sec. 71, 168 and 169)

• Finder of lost goods [Sec 71]

A person, who finds goods belonging to another and takes them into his custody, is subject to the same responsibility as a Bailee.

• Implied Agreement

There is an agreement, implied by law between finder and owner of goods.

• Duties of Finder

A finder of lost goods is treated as Bailee of goods found. His duties are –

(a) To take initiative to find the real owner of the goods,

(b) To take reasonable care of the goods found, (c) Not to put the goods found for his personal use, and (d) Not to mix the goods found with his own goods.

• Rights of Finder

Suit for specific reward [Sec.168]	Right of Sale [Sec.169]
Finder of goods is not entitled to sue that owner for compensation for trouble and expenses voluntarily incurred in – (a) preserving the goods, or (b) finding out the owner. However, he is entitled to –	If a thing which is commonly the subject of sale is lost, and Owner cannot be found with reasonable diligence, [or] Owner, if found, does not pay the lawful charges of the Finder.
Lien: Retain the goods against the owner till he receives such compensation Suit: Sue the owner for payment of any specific reward offered by the owner for the return of goods lost, and retains the goods till payment of such reward.	Then, Finder of Goods is entitled to sell the same when – the thing is in danger of perishing, or the thing is in danger of losing the greater part of its value, or The lawful charges of finder, amount to 2/3rd of the value of the thing lost and found.

PLEDGE

21. MEANING OF 'PLEDGE', 'PAWNOR', 'PAWNEE' (Sec.172)

- **'Pledge'**

  The bailment of goods as security for payment of a debt or performance of promise is called 'pledge'.
- **'Pawnor'**

  The bailor in case of a pledge is called as 'pawnor'.
- **'Pawnee'**

  The bailee in case of pledge is called as 'pawnee'.

22. ESSENTIALS A VALID CONTRACT OF PLEDGE (Sec.172)

• Contract

- There must be a contract
- The contract may be expressed or implied.

• Goods

Pledge can be made of goods only.

• Delivery

There must be delivery of goods by one person to another person.

Purpose of delivery

- The goods must be delivered for some purpose.
- The purpose must be to deliver the goods as security for

(a) payment of a debt; or

(b) performance of a promise.

- **Return of goods**
  - The delivery of goods must be conditional
  - The condition shall be that the goods shall be –
  - returned (either in original form or in altered form); or
  - Disposed of according to the directions of the pawnor when the purpose is accomplished.

23. RIGHTS OF PAWNEE (Sec.173 and 176)

- **Right of Retainer [Sec.173]**

Pawnee may retain the goods pledged for –

(a) payment of the debt or the performance of promise,

(b) any interest due on the debt; and

(c) all necessary expenses incurred by him with respect to possession or for preservation of goods pledged.

- **Retainer for subsequent advances [Sec.174]**

(a) Where the Pawnee lends money to the Pawnor subsequently, after the date of pledge, it shall be presumed that the he has a right of retainer over the goods already pledged in respect of the subsequent lending also.

(b) This presumption can be made invalid only by an expenses provision to that effect.

- **Reimbursement of Expenses [Sec.175]**

Where the Pawnee incurs extraordinary expenses to preserve the goods pledged with him, he is entitled to receive such amount from the Pawnor.

- **Rights in case of default by Pawnor [Sec.176]**

(a) **Suit:** Pawnee may institute a suit against Pawnor when there is a default in payment of debt or performance of promise at the stipulated time.

(b) **Retention / Sale of goods:** Pawnee may – (a) retain the goods pledged as collateral security, or (b) sell the goods pledged by giving a reasonable notice to the Pawnor.

(c) **Surplus / Deficit on Sale :** When there is a surplus on sale, Pawnee shall pay the excess to the Pawnor. In case of deficit, Pawnor shall be liable for the balance amount.

(d) **No Notice:** Where the Pawnee does not give a reasonable notice to the Pawnor, the sale is valid, but Pawnee is liable to pay damages to Pawnor.

- **Right against true owner of goods [Sec.178A]**

(a) Where the Pawnor has acquired possession of pledged goods, under a voidable contract u/s 19 or 19A but contract has not been rescinded at the time of pledge, the Pawnee acquires a good title to the goods, against the true owner.

(b) The title of Pawnee is good only where – (a) he had no notice of the Pawnor's defect in title and (b) he acts in good faith.

Reasonable notice u/s 176 means that a notice of intended sale of the security by the Creditor within a certain date, so as to afford an opportunity to the Debtor to pay the amount within the time mentioned in the notice. Notice of sale is essential and a clause in the agreement excluding the requirement of Notice is inconsistent with the Act & is void and unenforceable.	Prabhat Bank Ltd. vs Babu Ram

24. DUTIES OF A PAWNOR (Sec.175)

¾ **Pay the debt**

The pawnor is liable to pay the debt or perform his promise as the case may be.

¾ **Pay deficit on sale**

If the pawnee sells the goods due to default by the pawnor, the pawnor must pay the deficit.

¾ **Pay extra – ordinary expenses**

The pawnor is liable to pay to the pawnee any extraordinary expenses incurred by the pawnee for preservation of goods.

¾ **Disclose faults in goods**

The pawnor is liable to disclose all the faults which –

(a) are material for use of the goods; or **(b)** may put the pawnee to extraordinary risks.

¾ **Indemnify the pawnee**

If loss is caused to the pawnee due to defect in pawnor's title to the goods, the pawnor must indemnify the pawnee.

25. DUTIES OF PAWNEE

• **Not to use the goods**

- The pawnee has no right to use the goods
- However, he may use the goods, if he has been so authorised by the pawnor.

• **Return the goods**

The pawnee must return the goods if the pawnor pays the debt or performs his promise.

¾ **Take reasonable care**

The pawnee must take such care of goods pledged as a man of ordinary prudence would take care of his own goods.

¾ **Not to mix goods**

The pawnee must not mix his own goods with the goods pledged.

¾ **Return increase in goods**

The pawnee must return to the pawnor any accretion to the goods pledged with him.

26. RIGHTS OF A PAWNOR (Sec.177)

¾ **Redeem the goods pledged**

Meaning of redemption

Right to recover back the goods by making payment of the debt or performance of promise.

Time for redemption

Where time of redemption is fixed, the pawnor may exercise redemption – **(a)** within the time so fixed; or

(a) even after expiry of time so fixed, provided –

- the pawnee has not sold the good; and
- the pawnee pays the pawnee all expenses arising on account of his default.

¾ **Enforce pawnee's duties**

The pawnor has the right to enforce the duties of pawnee, if the pawnee fails to fulfill his duties.

¾ **Receive increase in goods**

The pawnor has the right to recover from pawnee any increase in goods pledged.

¾ **Right to receive notice of sale**

In case of default by the pawnor to pay the debt or perform his promise, the pawnee has the right to sell the goods, after giving a reasonable notice to the pawnor. If the pawnee fails to give notice, the pawnor has the right to recover the loss incurred by him.

Basis	Pledge	Bailment
1. Purpose	Pledge is bailment of goods for a specific purpose, i.e. to provide a security for a loan or fulfillment of an obligation.	Bailment may be for purpose other than by way of providing security for a loan or fulfillment of an obligation. It may be for purpose like repairs, safe custody, etc.
2. Sale of Goods	Pawnee, i.e. Pledgee has a right of sale of goods pledged on default of Pawnor. He can do so by giving a notice to the pawnor.	There is no right of sale to the Bailee. Bailee may either – (a) retain goods, or (b) sue the Bailor for non – payment of his dues.
3. Use of Goods	Pledgee has no right of using goods pledged.	Bailee can use the goods bailed as per terms of contract.

AGENCY

27. INTRODUCTION TO CONTRACT OF AGENCY (Sec.182)

¾ **Meaning of 'agent'**

An 'agent' is a person employed to –

- Do any act for another; or
- Represent another in dealings with third persons.

• **Meaning of 'principal'**

'Principal' is the person –

- For whom an act is done by the agent; or
- Who is represented by the agent in respect of dealing with third persons.

• **Test of agency**

Where a person has the capacity to –

- Create contractual relations between the principal and a third party;
- Bind the principal by his own acts, there exists a relationship of agency.

CREATION OF AGENCY

CREATION OF AGENCY

- By Operation of Law
- By Express Agreement
- By Implied Agreement (a) Estoppel, (b) Holding Out, (c) Necessity
- By Ratification of acts

28. SALIENT FEATURES OF AGENCY (Sec. 183, 184, 185 and 226)

- **Principal is liable for the acts of agent**
  - The principal is liable for all the acts of an agent which are lawful and within the scope of agent's authority.
  - The contracts entered into by the agent on behalf of the principal have the same legal consequences as if these contracts were made by the principal himself.
- **Who may employ an agent?** Any person may employ an agent if – • He is of the age of majority; and
  - He is of sound mind.
- **Who can be an agent?**
  - Any person may become an agent.
  - Even a minor or a person of unsound mind can become an agent
- **Liability of agent**
  - Generally an agent is liable to the principal
  - An agent is not liable to the principal if he is a minor or is of unsound mind.
- **Requirement of consideration**

  No consideration is necessary for creating an agency.

29. MODES OF CREATION OF AGANCY (Sec.187, 189, 196, 214 and 237)

- **Express agreement**
  - A person may employ another person as his agent by entering into an express agreement with him.
  - The agreement may be either oral or written.
- **Implied agreement** ***Agency by estoppel***

If –

- a person makes a representation (by his words or conduct) to a third person that a certain person is his agent; and
- the third party believing such representation to be true, enters into a contract with the pretended agent.

Then –

- the person making the representation is prevented from denying the truth of agency. He may be held liable as a principal by such third party.

Agency of holding out

Such an agency comes into existence when a person by his affirmative or positive conduct leads third persons to believe that person doing some act on his behalf is doing with authority.

• **Agency by necessity – Conditions**

(i) There was an actual and definite necessity for acting on behalf of the principal.
(ii) The agent was not in a position to communicate with the principal.
(iii) The act was done for the purpose of protecting the interest of his principal.
(iv) The agent has exercised such reasonable care as a man of ordinary prudence would have exercised in his own case.
(v) The act was done bonafide.

• **Agency by operation of law**

Agency by operation of law arises where the law treats one person as an agent of another.

• **Agency by ratification**

Meaning

If –

- a person (viz., pretended agent) acts on behalf of another person (viz, the principal)
- the pretended agent acts without the knowledge or consent of the principal; and
- Afterwards, the principal accepts such act. **Then –**
- Agency by ratification comes into existence.

Effects of ratification

- The principal is bound by the acts ratified by him as if such acts had been performed by his authority.
- Ratification relates back to the actual date of the act that is ratified and not from the date when the act ratified.

30. ESSENTIALS OF A VALID RATIFICATION (Sec. 197 to 200)

Full knowledge

No valid ratification can be made by a person whose knowledge of the facts of the case is materially defective. In other words, the principal must have full knowledge of all the material facts.

Whole transaction

It must be done for whole transaction in fact; ratification of the part of a transaction operates as a ratification of the whole transaction.

Act on behalf of another person

The acts done by a person (i.e. pretended agent) on behalf of another person (i.e. pretended principal) can only be ratified.

By the principal

Ratification can be made by only such person for whom the act was done.

Existence of principal

The principal must be in existence at the time when the act was done in his name

Contractual capacity

The principal must have contractual capacity both at the time of entering into the contract and at the time of ratification.

Lawful acts.

Only those acts which are lawful can be ratified. Void, illegal, or ultra vires acts cannot be ratified.

Acts within principal's power

Ratification can be made only for such acts which principal had the power to do.

Communication

Ratification must be communicated to the third party so as to bind him

Within reasonable time

Ratification must be made within reasonable time of the act purported to be ratified.

31. KINDS OF AGENTS.

A. Based on Authority

1. Special Agent	2. General Agent	3. Universal Agent
(a) Appointed to perform a particular transaction, e.g. sale of a house property. **(b)** Agent has limited authority **(c)** Agent cannot bind Principal for acts other	**(a)** Appointed to do all acts connected with a particular trade, business or employment. **(b)** Authority is wide and continues till agency is terminated.	**(a)** Appointed to do all acts for the Principal. **(b)** Authority is unlimited **(c)** All acts of Agent bind his Principal provided that his acts are legal and agreeable as per law of land.
than for which he is employed.	**(c)** Principal may limit his authority. **(d)** Principal is bound by all acts unless it is beyond authority of Agent.	

B. Based on Nature of work

1. Commercial or Mercantile Agents	2. Non – Mercantile Agents.
(a) One who is authorised to sell goods or consign goods for the purpose of sale or to buy gods or to raise money on the security of goods. **(b)** Includes Banker, Factor, Auctioneer, Broker, Commission Agent, & Del Credere Agent.	**(a)** Not engaged in business of selling or buying goods, but act in their respective professional capacities. i.e. render professional services for their Principal **(b)** Includes Solicitors, Attorneys, C & F Agents, Insurance Agents, etc.

32. DUTIES OF AN AGENT (Sec. 209 to 218)

1. To conduct the business in accordance with the directions given by the principal
2. To work with reasonable diligence, care and skill.
3. To render proper accounts to the principal on demand.
4. To communicate with his principal in case of difficulty and seek his instructions.
5. Not to deal on his own account unless all the material facts have been disclosed to the principal and consent of the principal has been obtained. If the agent, without the knowledge of the principal, deals in the business of agency on his own account, the principal has the following rights:
   (a) He may repudiate the transaction, if the agent dishonestly conceals any material facts or the dealings of the agent prove to be disadvantageous to him.
   (b) He may claim from the agent the agency business other than the agreed remuneration.
6. Not to make any secret profit out of the agency business other than the agreed remuneration

7. To remit to the principal all the sums received in the principal's accounts in accordance with the terms and conditions of contract of agency.
8. Not to delegate authority or appoint sub – agent.
9. To protect and preserve the interest on behalf of the principal's representative in case of his death or insolvency of the principal.
10. Not to use information obtained in the course of the agency against the princi pal.

33. RIGHTS OF AN AGENT (Sec. 217 to 225)

1. To retain money out of the sums received in agency business for advances made or expenses incurred and remuneration due to him.
2. To receive the agreed remuneration. If the remuneration is not fixed, then he has the right to recover such remuneration as is usual and customary in such business.
3. Right of lien on principal's goods, papers and other property until the amount due to him in respect of the same is paid.
4. An agent has the right to be indemnified by the principal against the consequences of all lawful acts done in exercise of the authority conferred on him.
5. An agent has the right to be indemnified by the principal against consequences of acts done in good faith that caused an injury to third person.
6. To claim compensation for injury caused because of principal's neglect or want of skill.

34. WHEN AN AGENT IS PERSONALLY LIABLE? (Sec. 230 and 231)

General Rule – No personal liability [Sec.230]

In the absence of contract to contrary, an Agent cannot –

(a) personally enforce contracts entered into by him, on behalf of his Principal,

(b) be held personally liable for them.

This is because the Agent merely acts on behalf of his Principal. Thus, he enjoys immunity from being personally sued.

Exceptions, i.e. Agent personally as well as Joint & Severally Liable

The Agent is personally liable in the following cases –

1. **Foreign Principal [Sec.230] :** Where the contract is made by an Agent for the sale or purchase of goods for a merchant resident abroad.
2. **Undisclosed Principal [Sec.230]:** Where the Agent does not disclose the name of his Principal.
3. **Principal cannot be sued [Sec.230]:** Where the Principal, though disclosed, cannot be sued, e.g. Principal becoming of unsound mind, subsequent to appointment of agent.
4. **Acting for a Principal not in existence:** Where the Agent acts for a Principal who is not in existence at the time of making contracts, he shall be personally held liable e.g. contracts entered into by Promoters before incorporation of a Company are made in their personal capacity and hence personally liable.
5. **Agency coupled with interest [Sec.202] :** Where the Agent has an interest in the subject matter of agency.

6. **Agent guilty of Fraud [Sec.238] :** Where an Agent is guilty of fraud or misrepresentation in matters that are outside the scope of his authority, he is personally liable, and do not affect his Principal.
7. **Agent exceeds authority & act not ratified:** Where an Agent acts either without any authority or exceeds his authority, he shall be held personally liable when the principal does not ratify his acts.
8. **Agent receives or pays money:** Where an Agent receives or pays money by mistake or fraud to a third party, he shall be personally liable to such third party. Also ha can personally sue the third party if the fraud or mistake is accountable to such third party.
9. **Express Agreement for personal liability:** Where an Agent expressly aggress to be personally bound.
10. **Execution of Contract in his own name:** Where an Agent executes a contract in his own name, without disclosing that he is acting as Agent for a Principal, he shall be personally liable, e.g. An Agent signs a Negotiable Instrument without making it clear that he is signing it as an Agent only, he shall be held personally liable on the same. He would be personally liable as Maker of P/N, even though he may be described as Agent.
11. **Trade custom or usage:** Where trade usage or custom makes an Agent personally liable.
12. **Agent with special interest:** An Agent with special interest or with a beneficial interest, e.g. a Factor or Auctioneer, can sue and be sued personally. [Subramanya vs Narayana]
13. **Action against Agent or Principal [Sec 233] :** Where the Agent is personally liable, a person dealing with him may hold - (a) either him or (b) his Principal or (c) both of them liable. The liability of Principal and Agent is "joint and several".
14. **Exclusive liability [Sec. 234]**

    Where a person has made a contract with an Agent and –

Where a person has made a contract with an Agent and – • Induces such Agent to act upon it in the belief that only his principal would be held liable, • Induces the principal to act upon it in the belief that only his Agent would be held liable.	Such Third person cannot later on, shift the liability on to – • The Agent, or • The principal, respectively.

35. AGENCY COUPLED WITH INTERST (Sec 202)

- When agency is created for securing some benefit to the agent over and above his remuneration as an agent, it is called as agency coupled with interest.
- The interest should exist at the time of creation of agency. If the interest arises after the creation of agency then it would not be called as agency coupled with interest.
- Agency coupled with interest cannot be terminated to the prejudice of such interest.

- Agency coupled with interest does not terminate even on the death or insanity of the principal.
- Thus, such agency is irrevocable to the extent of such interest.

36. IRREVOCABLE AGENCY (Sec.202 and 204)

Agency coupled with interest

Such agency cannot be terminated to the extend of such interest

Part exercise of authority by the agent

Where the agent has partly exercised the authority, the principle cannot revoke the authority so far as regard such acts and obligation as arise from already done in the agency

Personal liability incurred by agent

Where the agent has incurred personal liability, the agency is irrevocable

37. DELEGATION OF AUTHORITY (Sec.190)

General rule

The general rule is that an agent cannot lawfully employ another act, which he has expressly or impliedly undertaken to perform personally.

Exceptions

(a) There is a custom or usage of trade to that effect.
(b) Where power of the agent to delegate can be inferred from the conduct of the both the principle and the agent.
(c) When the principal is aware of the intention of the agent to appoint sub agent by the does not object to it.
(d) When principle permits appointment of a sub-agent.
(e) If the nature of the agency is such that the sub-agent is necessary.
(f) Where the acts to be done is purely ministerial not involving confidence or use of discretion.
(g) Where unforeseen emergencies arise rendering appointment of a sub-agent necessary.

38. LEGAL RELATIONSHIP BETWEEN THE PRINCIPLE AND SUB-AGENT AND AGENT (Sec.190, 192 and 193)

If sub-agent is properly appointment

(a) Principal is bound to the third parties for the acts of sub-agent.
(b) The agent is responsible to the principal for the acts of sub-agent.
(c) The sub-agent is responsible to the agent for the acts done by him.
(d) The sub – agent is not responsible to the principle, except in case of fraud or willful wrong.

If sub – agent is not properly appointed.

(a) Principal is not bound to the third parties for the acts of sub – agent.
(b) The agent is responsible to the principle and third parties for the acts of sub – agent.

(c) The sub – agent is responsible to the agent for the acts done by him. (d) The sub – agent is not responsible to the principle.

39. LIABILITY OF PRINCIPAL TO THIRD PARTIES FOR THE ACTS OF AGENT (Sec. 226 to 228)

Principal is liable for the acts of agent

- The principal is liable for all the acts of an agent which are lawful and within the scope of agent's authority.
- The contracts entered into by the agent on behalf of the principal have the same legal consequences as if these contracts were made by the principal himself.

When agent exceeds his authority

Whether the acts done within the authority are separable from the acts done beyond authority.

If yes – The principal is not bound for excess acts done by the agent.

If no – The principal is not bound by the transaction and the principal can repudiate the whole transaction.

40. TERMINATION OF AGENCY (Sec.201 to 210)

A. By the acts of parties

By agreement

The principal and the agent may mutually agree to terminate the agency, at anytime.

By revocation

- When the agency is coupled with interest, the principal cannot revoke the agency to the prejudice of such interest.
- The principal can revoke the authority at anytime before, the authority has been exercised so as to bind the principal.
- The principal cannot revoke the authority given to his agent after the authority has been partly exercised.
- When agency if for fixed period, the principal must make compensation to the agent for premature revocation of agency without sufficient cause.
- Revocation may be expressed or implied from the conduct of the principal

By the agent renouncing the business of agency

- Renunciation may be expressed or implied from the conduct of the agent.
- When agency is for fixed period, the agent must make compensation to the principal for premature renunciation of agency without sufficient cause.

B. By operation of law

1. Completion of business of agency
2. Death or insanity of the principal or agent
3. Where the principal or the agent, being a company is dissolved
4. Destruction of subject matter of agency
5. Principal becoming insolvent
6. Expiration of period where agency was for a fixed period.

CHAPTER 3

The Sale of Goods ACT, 1930

SECTION 1:

Commencement and Applicable

APPLICABILITY OF THE ACT

- This act extends to whole of India, ***except the State of Jammu and Kashmir***.
- This act came into force w.e.f. 1 July 1930.
- The 'contract of sale' includes both a sale as sell as an agreement to sell.
- The word Indian was omitted the title of the Act in 1963 (22 sept.)
- This Act does not deal with the sale of immovable property.
- The transaction relating to immovable properties, e.g., the sale, lease, gifts, etc., are governed by a separate Act known as 'Transfer of Property Act, 1882'. This Act is beyond the scope of this book.

DEFINITIONS (Sec. 2)

Buyer – Sec 2 (1)

- A person, who buys or agrees to buy the goods.

Delivery Sec (2) Ò! It means voluntary transfer of possession from one person to another.

Delivery State Sec 2(3)

- Goods are said to be in delivered state, when they are in such state that the ***Buyer would be bound*** to take the delivery of them in accordance with the contract.

Documents of title to Goods 2(4)

- A document of the title to goods may be described as any document used as proof of the possession or control of goods, authorizing or purporting to authorize, either by endorsement or by delivery, the possessor of the document to transfer or receive goods thereby represented.

Section 2(4) of the Sale of Goods Act, 1930 recognizes the following as documents of title to goods:

(i) Bill of lading,

(ii) Dock warrant,

(iii) Warehousekeeper's certificate,
(iv) Wharfinger's certificate,
(v) Railway receipt,
(vi) Multi – modal transport document,
(vii) Warrant or order for the delivery of goods, and
(viii) Any other document used in the ordinary course of business as document of title (as described in the preceding paragraph).

Document of Title v. Document showing the title :

A document of title enables a person named therein to transfer the property by mere endorsement and delivery, whereas a document showing title does not confer any right to transfer by way of endorsement and delivery.

For example, ***a share certificate*** shows that the person named therein is entitled to the shares represented by it, but does not allow transfer of the shares by mere endorsement and delivery of the certificate.

Goods – Sec 2 (7)

- Goods mean every kind of ***movable property.***
- Other than actionable claims and money, and it includes.
- stock and shares, growing crops, grass and things attached to or forming part of land which are agreed to be severed before sale or under the contract of sale.
- You may notice that 'money' and 'actionable claims' have been expressly excluded from the term 'goods'**. 'Money'** ***means the legal tender. 'Money' does not include old coins and foreign currency.*** They can, therefore, be sold or bought as goods. Sale and purchase of foreign currency is, however, also regulated by the foreign Exchange Management Act,
- 'Actionable claims', like debts, are things which a person cannot make use of, but which can be claimed by him by means of a legal action. Actionable claims cannot be sold or purchased like goods, they can only be assigned, as per the provisions of Transfer of property Act.
- Grass, growing crops, trees to be cut and their log wood to be delivered, malba of a building to be demolished, etc. are goods. Similarly, things like goodwill, copyright, trade mark, patents, water, gas electricity are all goods and may be the subject matter of a contract of sale.

Seller – Sec 2 (13)

- A person, who sells or agrees to sell the goods,.

Agreement to sell

- Where transfer of property in goods takes place at future date.

Sale

- Where transfer of property in goods takes place at the time of contract.

ESSENTIAL ELEMENTS OF VALID CONTRACT OF SALES

The following are the essentials of valid contract of sale:

- ***There must be two parties, one seller and other buyer.***
  - Seller and buyer must be different.
  - Part owner can sell goods to another part owner.
  - Partners are not regarded as separate persons for the purpose of sale of the partnership property. They are the joint owners of the goods and as such they

cannot be both sellers and buyers [State of Gujarat v. Ramanlal S & W. (1965)]. But, a partner may buy goods from the firm or sell goods to the firm.

- ***There must be movable goods as subject matter of contract.***
- **There must be a transfer of property in goods. It means general property. (i.e. ownership)**
- **There must be price involved. Price means money consideration for sale of goods.**
  - Exchange of goods for goods is barter.
  - If Exchange is for partly goods and partly for money it is sale.
- **All essential elements of valid contract must be observed.**
- **The contract of sale can be entered into, expressly or impliedly.**

Formation. The contract of sale may provide for any of the following methods.

- *Immediate delivery of goods.*
- *Immediate payment of price but delivery at some future date.*
- *Immediate payment of price and immediate delivery of goods.*
- *Delivery or payment or both made in installments.*
- *Delivery or payment or both will be made at future date.*

TRANSFER OF "PROPERTY IN GOODS"

- Property means general property in goods and not merely special property in goods. It means ownership of goods. ***Special property in goods means possession of goods.***
- Cases where property in goods is not transferred:
  - Bailment
  - Creating charge or pledge

Difference Between Sale and Agreement to Sell

Immediate transfer of ownership to buyer	Ownership remains with the seller
It is executed contract	It is an executory contract
It creates right in rem for buyer	It provides right in personam for buyer and seller
Seller can use for price – if not buyer	Seller can sue for damages
Risk passes to buyer	Risk doesn't passes to buyer
Buyer can get goods even if seller has becomes insolvent	Buyer can get proportionate share in money but can't get goods
Delivery to receiver if buyer becomes insolvent before the payment of price	Delivery can be refused by seller if buyer becomes insolvent.

Difference between Sale and Hire Purchase

Metter	Sale	Hire Purchase
Meaning	Property in goods is transferred from seller to buyer immediately	Agreement where hirer uses goods by paying regular installment and having option to purchase goods on payment of last installment
Applicable Act	Sale of goods Act, 1930	Hire Purchase Act, 1972
Parties	Buyer and seller	Hirer and Hire vendor
How it made?	Orally or in writing	Only in writing – Valid
Transfer of ownership	Immediately buyer becomes owner of goods	When hirer paid last installment
Risk of loss	Risk of loss passes to buyer	Ownership not transferred hire vendor is liable
Return of goods	Buyer can't return goods	Anytime terminate agreement and return
Legal effect of Installment	Buyer remain liable to pay unpaid installment only	Each installment paid is treated as hire charges
Sale tax	Payable immediately	When all installment is paid

Difference between Sale and Bailment

Sale	Bailment
Transfer of property in goods for price	Delivery of goods for specific purpose that it will be returned to bailor or disposed of as per his direction
Property is transferred	It remains with bailor.
Consideration is in form of price, i.e., money	Gratuitous bailment is possible
Goods not returned to seller	Goods returned to bailor purpose of bailment is over

CONTRACT FOR WORK AND SKILL

- Some contract involves use of both service and goods. This type of contract is considered as contract for work and skill.
- This kind of contract involves exercise of skill and labour by one party on some goods or materials supplied by other party or supplied by party who exercise skill and labour for price. It is immaterial who supply material. Alternatively, it can be said that in this kind of contract, main purpose is to exercise work and skill. Supply of own goods is only subsidiary. Intension of parties is to transfer goods only after exercise of some skill and labour.
- As it is not falling within categories of contract for Sale no sales tax is payable.

Example:

(1) A dentist agreed to supply a set of artificial teeth to a patient. The material was wholly found by the dentist. Held, it was a contract for the sale of goods.

(2) An artist was asked to paint a portrait. The material was supplied by the party and not by the painter. It was held to be a contract for work and labour and not of sale.

CLASSIFICATION OF GOODS

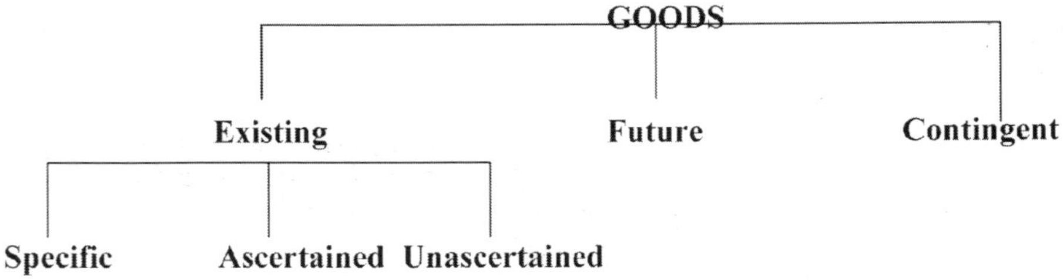

Types of Goods

The goods may be classified into following categories:

Existing goods

- Existing goods are the goods, which are owned and possessed by the seller at the time of sale. Existing goods may be of three types;

(a) Specific Goods:

- The goods, which are identified and agreed upon by the parties at the time of contract of sale.
- It should be noted that the goods must be both identified and agreed upon.

(b) Unascertained Goods:

- These are the goods, are not identified and agreed upon at the time of the contract of sale.
- These goods are merely described by the parties at the time of contract of sale.

(c) Ascertained Goods:

- There are the goods, which are identified after the formation of contract of sale. When the un-ascertained goods are identified and agreed upon by the parties, the goods are known as ascertained goods.

Future Goods

- Future goods are those goods, which do not exist at the time of the contract of sale.
- These goods are to be manufactured or acquired by the seller after the making of the contract of sale.
- Future goods cannot be sold, but there can only be an agreement to sell.

Example:

A, a manufacturer agrees to sell 5 tables and 50 chairs to B at Rs.10,000. B agrees to purchase it. However, tables and chairs are yet to manufactured by A.

Contingent goods

- It is a kind of future goods.
- It is goods, the acquisition of which is contingent upon the happening or non – happening of an uncertain event.

Example:

A agrees to sell the goods loaded on the ship "Titanic", which is coming from London to Bombay. The ship may or may not arrive. So, these goods will be called as contingent goods.

Basis	Futures Goods	Contingent Goods
1. Meaning	Goods that are yet to be manufactured produced or acquired by the Seller after making contract of sale.	Goods, the acquisition of which by the Seller depends upon a contingency, which may or may not happen.
2. Element of uncertainty	Acquisition of Future Goods does not depend upon and uncertainty.	The procurement of Contingent Goods is dependent upon an uncertain event.
3. Scope	Future Goods do not include contingent Goods because of the element of certainty.	They are wider in scope, it includes future Goods.
4. Effect Contract	Where by a contract of Sale, the Seller purports to effect a present sale of future Goods, the contract operates as an "agreement to sell" the Goods[Sec.6(3)]	There may be a "Contract for Sale" of Goods, the acquisition of which by the Seller depends upon a contingency which may or may not happen [Sec.6 (2)]
5. Example	B agrees to buy the entire crop of wheat that would yield in S's farm, at the rate of Rs.1000 per quintal.	A agrees to sell to B a certain painting only if C, its present owner, sells it to him. The sale is contingent upon the sale by C.

Price of Goods – Sec 9 – 10

Price means the money consideration for a sale of a Goods 2(10)
The following are the modes of determining price: [Sec. 9]

- Price is specified under the contract. It is the most common method of determining the price. Here, parties decide the price in advance.
- Price may be determined as per the method specified in contract. ***Example :*** Delivery of rice on 1st December 2008 at the rate prevailing on that day.
- Price may be determined in accordance to custom and usage of trade. This method is applicable if parties regularly trade.
- Where the price is not fixed as above, the buyer shall pay the seller a ***reasonable price.***

  'What is a reasonable price is a question of fact and circumstances.

Fixation of price by third party. (Sec. 10)

If it is so, contract shall specify name of third party.

If third party fails to specify, contract is void but if goods are delivered to buyer and used by him, he is required to pay reasonable price.

If the third party is prevented from fixing price, defaulting party is liable for the damages.

Consequences of Destruction of Specific Goods – Sec 7 – 8

The consequences of destruction of specific goods can be discussed under the following three heads:

- ***If goods perish before making the contract***
  - Contract is void – ab – initio, due to mistake as to existence of subject matter. • It is to be noted that if the seller has knowledge about the destruction of goods,

even then the enters into the contract of sale with buyer, then seller is bound to compensate to the buyer.

- ***Where a part of the goods is perished before making contract***
  - If the goods was divisible, then the contract can be enforced party and if the goods was indivisible, then the contract becomes void – ab – inito.

Example:

A contracted to sell one wagon containing 700 bags of groundnut to B. Unknown to A, 109 bags had been stolen at the time of sale, Therefore, A made a delivery of 591 bags. Held, the sale was void.

If goods perish after the "Agreement to sell; but before' Sale [Sec. 8]

The contract is void if subsequently the goods have perished, and there is no fault on the part of the buyer or seller in perishing the goods.

Example:

A horse was delivered upon trial for 8 days. However, the horse died within 8 days, without the fault of buyer or seller. Held, the seller must bear the loss, as the contract was void.

However, parties to the contract may provide otherwise also.

Section 7 and 8 are applicable only in case of specific goods.

Therefore, if unascertained goods are destroyed either before or after making the agreement, the contract shall not become void. Thus, in an agreement to sell unascertained goods, even if the entire stock of goods is destroyed, the contract that not become void and the seller will have to perform his promise.

Example

'A' agreed to sell to 'B' 100 bags of wheat from his stock of 1,000 bags in his go down. The entire stock was destroyed by fire. 'A' is bound to deliver 100 bags of wheat or else he will be liable for damages.

If the contract does not otherwise provide, then –

- Stipulation as to time of payment is not deemed to be essence of contract.
- Stipulation as to time of delivery is deemed to be essence of contract.

CONDITIONS AND WARRANTIES

- Generally, at the time of sale, the seller makes some representation, statements of stipulations for the praise of his goods. Some of representations are in nature of opinion others are in nature of facts. Representation as to fact which becomes a part of contract of sale is called as stipulation.
- Stipulation may be condition or warranty depends upon its importance in relation to contract.
- Stipulation which is ***essential to the main purpose of contract is known as condition.*** Breach of condition gives the aggrieved party right to terminate the contract.
- Stipulation which is ***collateral to the main purpose of the contract is warranty.*** Breach of warranty gives rise to the aggrieved party right to claim damages but contract cannot be terminated.
- The conditions and warranties ***may be express or implied.***

- Express conditions and warranties are those, which the parties agree expressly, i.e. orally or in writing.
- Implied conditions are those, which are implied by the law in the absence of any agreement to the contrary.

IMPLIED CONDITIONS

The following are the implied conditions which are contained in the Sales of Goods Act:

Conditions as to title – sec 14(a)

- There is an implied condition on the part of the seller that
  - In the case of sale, the seller has a right to sell the goods, and
  - In the agreement to sell, the seller will have a right to sell the goods at the time of passing of ownership in goods.
- If the title of seller out to be defective, the buyer must return the goods to the true owner and recover the price from the seller.

Conditions as to description – Sec 15

- Where the goods are sold by description, there is an implied condition that the goods shall correspond to the description.

Example;

A machine was sold. The buyer has not been the machine, but the seller described it as a new one. However, it was found to be a very old one. Held, the machine was not according to the description.

Sale by sample – Sec 17

- Where the goods are sold by sample, the following are implied conditions.
  - The bulk shall correspond to sample in quality.
  - The buyer shall be given a reasonable opportunity to compare the goods with the sample.
  - The goods shall be free from any defect, rendering them un – merchantable. It is to be noted that this implied condition applies only in the case of latent defects, i.e. those defects which cannot be discovered by ordinary inspection. In fact, such defects are discovered when the goods are put to use or by examination in laboratories. The seller is not liable for apparent or visible defects which can be discovered by examination.

Sale by description as well as sample – Sec 15

- If the sale is by sample as well as description, both conditions shall be satisfied. Goods must correspond with sample as well as description.

Example :

A agreed to sell to C some oil described as "Foreign refined oil" and warranted only equal to sample. The goods supplied were equal to sample, but contained a mixture to hemp oil. Held, C could reject the goods.

Conditions as to quality and fitness for buyer's purpose – Sec 16

- Where the buyer, expressly or impliedly, tells the seller the particular purpose for which he needs the goods and relies on the skill or judgment of the seller, there is an implied condition that the goods shall be reasonably fit for such purpose.
- When the article can be used only for one particular purpose, the buyer need not inform the seller the purpose for which the goods are required.

Example:

A purchased a hot water bottle from a chemist. While the bottle was being used by A's wife, it burst and injured A's wife. Held, the seller was liable for damages as the bottle was not fit for the purpose for which it was meant – Priest vs Last.

Exceptions to the implied condition as to quality or fitness

- The condition as to quality or fitness' well not apply, if the buyer is suffering from an abnormality, which renders the goods unsuitable for a particular purpose and the buyer does not inform the seller about that abnormally.

Example

A purchased a coat. He had abnormally sensitive skin, By wearing the coat, he got skin complaint. Held, there was no breach of condition, as he had not disclosed the abnormally of his skin.

- Where the goods can be used for a number of purposes, the buyer should inform the particular purpose for which such goods were required. If the does not disclose, there is no such conditions of quality or fitness.

Conditions as to merchantability

- Where goods are ***bought by description*** from a seller, who deals in goods of that description, there is an implied conditions that the goods shall be of merchantable quality.
- 'Merchantability' means that there is no defect in the goods, which renders them unfit for sale. Thus, a watch that will not keep time and a pen that will not write cannot be regarded as merchantable. ***Example:*** A radio set was sold to a layman. The set was defective. It did not work in spite of repairs, Held, the buyer could return the set and claim refund.

Condition as to wholesomeness

- In the case of ***eatable and food – stuff,*** there is an implied condition that the goods shall be wholesomeness, i.e., free from any defect which renders them ***unfit for human consumption.***

Example:

A Purchased milk from B, a milk dealer. The milk contained typhoid germs. A's wife on taking the milk got infected and died. Held, A was entitled to get damages – Frost vs Aylesbury Dairy Co. Ltd.

IMPLIED WARRANTIES

The following are the implied warranties which are contained in the Sales of Goods Act:

Warranty as to quiet possession – Sec 14

- In the absence to any contract showing contrary intention, there is an implied warranty that the ***buyer shall have and enjoy quiet possession of the goods***. If the buyer is disturbed in the enjoyment of the goods, he can claim damages from the seller.

Warranty against encumbrances – Sec 14

- Unless the circumstances of the case are such as to show a contrary intension, there is an implied warranty that the ***goods shall be free from any charge or encumbrance*** in favour of any party not declared to the buyer before or at the time contract is made. However, there will not be any such warranty if charge is declared to buyer at the time of sale.

Warranty as to quality and fitness by usage of Trade – Sec 16

- An implied warranty as to quality or fitness for a particular purpose may be annexed by the usage of trade.

Warranty to disclose the dangerous nature of goods

- In case of sale of dangerous goods, the ***seller is under an obligations to warn the buyer about the probable danger.*** Failure to do so will make the seller liable to pay damages.

Example :

A sold a tin of disinfectant to B, knowing that it was likely to be dangerous to the tin, whereupon disinfectant powder went into her eyes, causing her injury. Held, A was liable in damages to B, as he failed to warn B of the probable danger.

Difference between Condition and Warranty

Matter	Condition	Warranty
Stipulation	Essential to main purpose of contract	Collateral (subsidiary) to main purpose of contract.
If breach?	Buyer has right to cancel contract	Buyer has no right to cancel the contract . Can claim damages
Treatment	Breach of condition may be treated as breach of warranty	Breach of warranty can't be treated as breach of condition

DOCTRINE OF CAVEAT EMPTOR

- The doctrine of ***'Caveat Emptor' means "let the buyer beware".***
- ***It means that the buyer while purchasing goods must act with a "third eye and ear", i.e.,***
  - He should be careful to see that the goods purchased will serve his purpose well.

- If the buyer is not careful and he finds later on that the goods do not serve his purpose, he cannot hold the seller liable for it.
- The seller is under no obligation to tell the defects of his articles.

• ***However, in the following exceptions Doctrine of caveat emptor is not applicable:***

- Implied conditions as to quality or fitness. It means when buyer has specified his purpose and relied on skill of seller, the doctrine of caveat emptor is not applicable.
- When goods are sold by description, it should be of merchantable quality. In such case, doctrine of caveat emptor is not applicable.
- In case of edible items, implied condition of wholesomeness is applicable and goods should are not fit for human consumption then buyer is not liable but seller will be liable.
- Usage or custom of trade.

When the consent of buyer is obtained by fraud, the provision of doctrine of caveat emptor is not applicable.

TRANSFER OF OWNERSHIP

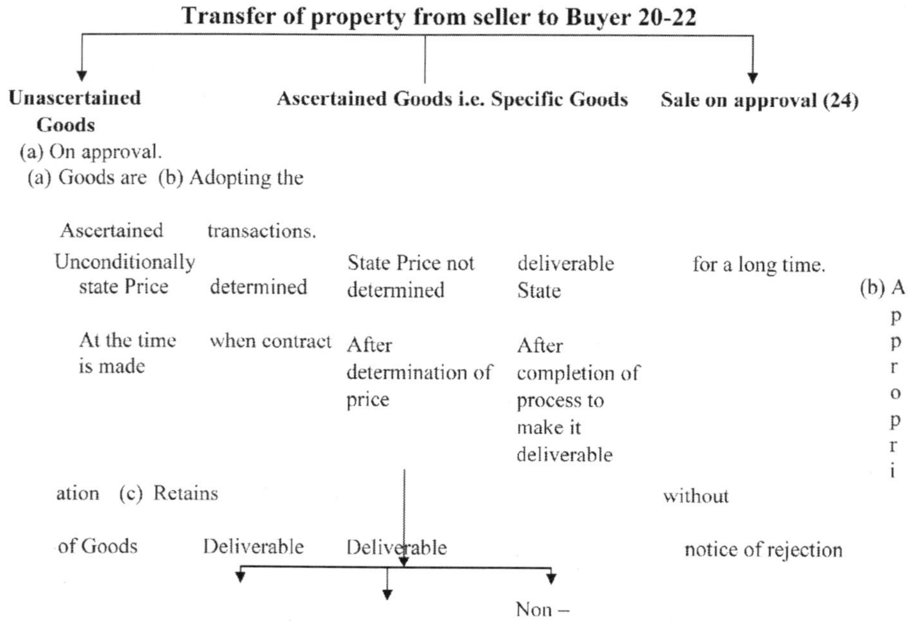

Ownership is transferred immediately at the time of making the contract if all the following conditions are satisfied:

- Contract is for specific goods.
- Goods are in deliverable state.
- Goods are not required to be weighed or measured for determining price.

Example:

A sold to B, 100 bales of cotton lying in his godown. Before the bales could be identified and separated, all bales were destroyed in fire. Here, seller is liable for damage because ownership is not transferred.

Section 21

- If the goods are not ready in deliverable state at the time of making contract of sale, ownership of goods is transferred after formation of contract of sale when following conditions are satisfied;
  - Contract is for specific goods.
  - Goods are put in deliverable state by seller.
  - Fact that the goods are put into deliverable state has come to knowledge to the buyer.

Example:

Certain quantity of oil was purchased by A. The oil was to be filled in tins. B filled up some of the tins and informed A to take the delivery. In the meantime, a fire destroyed the entire quantity of oil. Held, A will bear the loss of the oil which was filed in the tins and the seller must bear the loss of the balances.

Section 22

- If the goods are not weight or measured at the time of making contract of sale, ownership of goods is transferred after the formation of contract of sale when the following conditions are satisfied.
  - Contract is for specific goods
  - At the time of formation, price is not determined. It is determined later by weighed or measurement.
  - Goods are put in deliverable state by the seller.
  - Fact that the goods have been weighed or measured in order to determine price has come to knowledge of buyer.

Example

A sold 10 kg wheat. The wheat was to be weighed. Before the wheat was weighed, it was carried away by the flood. Held, the ownership of the wheat left with the seller and it did not pass to the buyer.

Transfer of ownership in the case of unascertained goods – Sec 18 and 23

- In the case of unascertained goods, when both parties come to know which particular goods shall be delivered, ownership is transferred.
- The following conditions must be satisfied to transfer the ownership:
  - Ascertainment is first step in transfer of ownership. It means process of identification and setting aside goods from a huge mass of goods.
  - Generally, it is made by seller, ***(unilateral act).***

Appropriation

For property to pass ***u/s 23,*** the following conditions must be satisfied –

(a) Goods of the description mentioned in the contract must be produced or obtained.

(b) The must be in a deliverable state, i.e. the Goods are in such state that the Buyer would, under the contract, be bound to take delivery of them.

(c) They must be unconditionally appropriated to the contract, Unconditional appropriation is where, in pursuance of the contract, Seller –

(i) Delivers the Goods to Buyer or a carrier or other bailee for their transmission to Buyer and

(ii) does not reserve the right of disposal. [Sec. 23(2)]

(d) The assent of the parties may be given expressly or impliedly and can be given either before or after the appropriation.

(e) **Example:** A having a quantity of sugar in bulk, more than sufficient to fill 20 bags, contracts to sell to B 20 bags of it. After the contract A fills 20 bags with the sugar, given notice to B that the bags are ready and requires him to take them away. B says he will take them as soon as he can. By this appropriation by A, and assent by B, property in the sugar passes to B.

• Contract to sell unascertained goods is not complete sell, it is agreement to sell.

Example :

20 bags of sugar out of a bulk were agreed to be sold. 4 bags of sugar were filled up and taken away by the buyer. Subsequently, the seller filled up 16 bags and informed the buyer. The buyer replied that he will take delivery as soon as possible. However, before the buyer could take their delivery. Goods were lost. Held, the buyer was responsible as the ownership had passed to the buyer.

Transfer of ownership in Case of Goods Sent on Approval or on sale or Return Basis – Sec. 24

- It means buyer has the option either to return goods. Here, property in goods doesn't pass from seller to buyer:

Case	When ownership transferred
When the buyer given his approval or acceptance. When the buyer does some act of adopting the transaction When the buyer fails to return the goods. (a) If time is fixed for return of goods. (b) If no time is fixed	Approval or acceptance is communicated to seller When act of adoption is done. On expiry of the fixed time On expiry of the reasonable time.

Example

Certain jewellery was delivered to a buyer on sale or return basis. The buyer pledged the jewellery. Held, the buyer had adopted the transaction and as such property had passed and the seller could not recover the jewellery from the Pawnee.

Right to disposal of Goods Sec. 25

- Where the railway receipt or the bill of landing is in the name of the buyer, but is sent through the bank with the instructions that the same is to be delivered against the acceptance of the bill or payment of the price, the property in the goods shall not pass.

Deemed right of reservation Sec. 25

The seller may reserve the right of disposal under the following modes –

Reservation of right of disposal

- **Shipment or Railway delivery**
  - By making the Goods deliverable to the order of the Seller or his agent.
- **Drawing of B/E on buyer**
  - By Seller drawing a bill for the price and making it acceptable by the Buyer.

Passing of Risk Sec. 26

- The general rule is that risk passes with ownership. We can say that risk and ownership and ownership to together. However, express agreement between parties may provide otherwise.
- Possession of goods is immaterial for risk.
- When delivery is delayed because of fault of any party, he is liable for risk.
- Sometime, risk is based upon custom or usage of trade.
- Where the delivery of goods has been delayed due to the fault of buyer/seller, goods are at the risk of the party in fault.

Sale by Non – Owners or Transfer of Title by Non – Owners – Sec 27 – 30

- The general rule is expressed by maxim 'Namodat quod non habet' which means no one can give what he does not himself posses. If seller's title is defective, then buyer's title will be defective.
- Alternatively, we can say that the seller can't give a better title to the buyer than be himself has.

The following are the exceptions to the above general rule:

• Sale of Estoppel [Sec. 27]:

Where the owner by his conduct or by his act leads the buyer to believe that the seller has the authority to sell and induces the buyer to buy the goods, he shall be estopped from denying the fact that seller had no right to sell the goods. ***Example : (Refer Classroom Notes Hira Sweets)***

• *Sale by mercantile agent Sec. 27*

Agent of seller can transfer the title if following conditions are satisfied :

- Agent must be in possession of goods or documents of title.
- Agent has sold goods in ordinary course of business.
- Buyer has acted in good faith.
- Buyer has no knowledge that seller had no authority to sell.

Example

A entrusted his car to a mercantile agent to receive offers and not to sell. A also delivered signed documents to the agent. On the basis of these documents, the agent pretended to the buyer that he had authority to sell the car and thus, the car was sold. Held, the owner was estopped from denying buyers title.

A mercantile agent means an agent having in the customary course of business as such agent authority either to sell goods, or to consign goods for the purpose of sale, or to buy goods, or to raise money on the security of goods ***[Section 2(9)].***

Sale by one of the joint owners – Sec 28

One of the joint owners can sale goods if following condition are satisfied.

- Goods are in sole possession of one of the joint owner.
- Buyer has acted in good faith.
- Buyer has no knowledge that seller had no authority to sell.

Example

A and B Jointly purchased a car. The car was in the possession of A with the consent of B. Later on A sold the car to an innocent purchaser. The purchaser will get a good title.

• *Sale by person in possession under voidable contract*

- Seller must be in possession of goods under contract voidable.
- Goods must have been sold before contract is rescinded.
- Buyer has no knowledge that seller had no authority to sell.

Example

A purchased a watch from B under fraud. A sold the watch to C, who bought it in good faith. C gets goods title.

• *Sale by seller in possession after sale – Sec 30*

- Ownership of goods has been passed to buyer.
- Seller continuous to be in possession of goods even after sale.
- Seller resells goods to new buyer.
- New buyer buys without notice to prior sell.

Example

A sells certain goods to B and promises to deliver the goods the next day. Before the delivery, A sells and delivers the goods to C, who buys them in good faith and without notice of the prior sale to B, C gets a good title to the goods, not with standing that the property had, before he purchased, passed to B.

• *Sale by unpaid seller Sec. 54*

After exercise of his right of lien or right of stoppage goods in transit.

If the owner of goods has declared insolvent and his goods, is sold by official receiver or assignee or liquidator.

• *Sale by finder of goods (Sec.169 of IC Act 1872).*

- The owner can't be found or found but refuse to pay lawful charges to finder.
- The Goods are perishable in nature or in danger. To save goods from loss, finder can sale it.
- Lawful charges of finder amount as 2/3 of its original value.

• *Sale by pawnee or pledge(Sec.176 of IC Act 1872).*

- If there is default on part of payment of price or performance within time. Reasonable notice is given by pawnee or pledge.

PERFORMANCE OF A CONTACT OF SALE

1. ***Meaning Sec.2(2)***: Delivery means voluntary transfer of possession from one person to another.

2. ***Duty of Seller Sec. 31:*** It is the duty of the Seller to deliver the goods and of the buyer to accept and pay for them in accordance with the contract of Sale.
3. ***Mode of delivery : Sec. 33***: Delivery of Goods sold may be made by –

(a) doing anything which the parties agree shall be treated as delivery ; or

(b) which has the effect of putting the Goods in the possession of the Buyer or of any person authorized to hold them on his behalf.

TYPES OF DELIVERY

Actual Delivery

It is a delivery where goods are handed over to the buyer or his authorized agent. It means goods are physically put in possession of the buyer.

Symbolic Delivery

When goods are not physically delivered to the buyer but some symbol of the real possession or control over goods is handed over to buyer.

Example

Delivery of key of the car.

Constructive Delivery

Where the third party who is in possession of goods, acknowledge to hold goods on behalf of the buyer is known as construction delivery.

Example:

A sells 100 bags of cement lying in B's godown. B agrees to hold the 100 bags of cement on behalf of A.

Forward Delivery

Where delivery is to be made in future, and not at the time contract is entered into.

RULES REGARDING DELIVERY

Payment and delivery are concurrent Sec 32.

- General rule suggest that the delivery of goods and payment of price are **concurrent** conditions. However, parties may provide otherwise.

Part Delivery Sec34.

- A delivery of part of goods with an intention of giving the delivery of the whole amounts to the delivery of the whole for the purpose of transfer of ownership of goods but a delivery of part of goods with an intention of separating it from the whole lot does not amount to the delivery of the whole of the goods.

Buyer's duty to Demand the Goods Sec. 35

Ò!It is seller's duty to be ready and willing to deliver the goods to the buyer. But he is not bound to deliver goods unless the buyer makes a demand for delivery of the goods.

Ò!If the buyer fails to demand the delivery of goods, the seller is not liable for breach; Buyer must demand delivery within a reasonable time. However, contract may provide otherwise.

Rules as to Delivery [Sec. 36]

Place of delivery

Situation	Place where goods are to be delivered
If contract specified the place of delivery. Contract does not specify the place of delivery;	At the place specified
In case of sale	At the place at which goods are at the time of sale
In case of agreement of sell	
(i) In respect of existing goods	At the place at which goods are at the time of agreement of sell.
(ii) In respect of future goods	At the place at which goods are manufacture, produce or acquire

Time of Delivery

- If the contract specified time of delivery, goods shall be delivered within such time.
- If no time is specified in contract as to time of delivery of goods, it should be delivered within reasonable time.

Delivery when the Goods in Possession of third party 36(3)

Unless and until such third person acknowledge to the buyer that the holds the goods on his behalf

However this provision shall not affect the operation of the issue or transfer of any documents of the title of the goods.

Time is tender of delivery

Demand or tender of delivery may be treat is reasonable unless made at reasonable hour. That is reasonable hour is a question affects.

Expenses of delivery

- All expenses of making delivery of goods shall be paid by seller
- Buyer shall be the expense for receipt of goods.
- unless otherwise agreed.

Delivery of Wrong quantity Sec 37

- ***If the seller has delivered excess quantity, the buyer has the following options:***
  - To accept the whole of the goods delivered to him.
  - To reject the whole of the goods delivered of him.
  - To accept contracted quantity and reject the excess.
- ***Seller has delivered short quantity, buyer has following options.***
  - To accept the goods delivered to him.
  - To reject whole quantity delivered to him.
- ***Right to reject the goods in excess of the contract does not apply where the variation is*** negligible.
- ***Further, the right to reject the goods is not similar to the right to cancel the contract. If the*** buyer rejects the goods (either because they are less than or in excess of the quantity contracted for), the seller has a right to tender again the contract quantity and the buyer is bound to accept the same.

Delivery of Mixed Quality – Quantity

- The seller is bound to deliver goods of exact quality – quantity otherwise buyer may:
  - Reject the whole.
  - Reject the goods not complying with quality or quantity and accept the rest. ***[Contract is not repudiated] – means subsisting***

Delivery by Installment Sec 38

Delivery by installment is not valid except when the contract provides so or buyer accepts the delivery in installment.

Delivery to Carrier or Wharfinger – Sec 39

- Delivery to carrier or wharfinger amounts as delivery to buyer if the following conditions satisfy:
  - Buyer has made reasonable contract with carrier.
  - Seller is required to give notice to buyer to enable him to insure goods. If not to do then his risk.
- If seller makes valid delivery of goods, buyer has following duties:
  - To accept the goods.
  - To pay the unpaid price.
- Where goods are sent by sea route, seller shall give notice to buyer to insure goods other wise he will be liable for loss.

Risk where goods are delivered at distant place Sec 40

Where the seller agrees to deliver the Goods at his own risk at a place other than at which they are sold, the Buyer shall bear the risk of deterioration necessarily incident to the course of transit, unless otherwise agreed.

Buyer's right to examining goods Sec 41

Delivered to buyer – not previously examined reasonable opportunity.

Seller is bound on request to afforded the buyer a reasonable opportunity of examine the good.

Acceptance of Delivery – Sec 42

Delivery doesn't mean acceptance of goods, Buyer has deemed to have accepted the goods under the following circumstances:

- When he intimates the seller about acceptance of goods.
- After receipt of goods, he does some act of affirmation.
- When he doesn't inform seller about rejection of goods within a reasonable time.

Buyer's not bound to return the rejected good Sec 43.

He is required to intimate the seller about rejection. (Buyer's not bound to return the rejected goods)

Liability of the Buyer for refusal of delivery of goods Sec 44

- If the buyer wrongfully refuses to take delivery of goods, he is liable for damages and expenses like storage cost and transportation cost to the seller.

UNPAID SELLER

Section 45

A seller of goods is deemed to be unpaid in the following cases:

- The price must be due but not paid. (When the ***whole of the price*** has not been paid or tendered)
- A negotiable instrument, like cheque, bill of exchange etc., was received, but the same has been dishonored.
- Seller who has obtained a decree for the price of the goods will also be an unpaid seller, if the decree has not been satisfied.
- When the seller has been paid the large amount but small portion of payment remains to be paid.
- Seller must have an immediate right of action for the price.

Right of an Unpaid Seller

Unpaid seller has the right against goods as well as against the buyer:
Rights of unpaid seller against the goods:

- Where ownership is transferred
  - Right of lien – Sec 47 – 49
  - Right to stoppage in transit – Sec 50 – 52
  - Right to resale of the goods
  - Where ownership is not transferred to the buyer, seller has the right to with hold delivery of goods.

Right of an unpaid seller against the goods Sec 46

The ownership has not been transferred.

Conditions Unpaid Seller + ownership not transferred.

Consequences Lawfully refuse to deliver the goods to the buyer until he is paid the price. Buyer cannot hold the seller liable for now delivery of goods.

Seller's Lien Sec.47

Condition for exercising lien

Condition – Unpaid seller – actual possession

Buyer not paid the price of the good. The unpaid seller can exercise lien even through.

The property is goods has passed to the buyer

He is in the possession of the goods as an agent or bailee for the buyer.

Right of Lien

- It means the right to retain the possession of goods until full price is received.
- Seller can exercise his right of lien on the following two conditions:
  - He must be in possession of the goods.
  - He is the unpaid seller.
- If buyer becomes insolvent, lien can be exercised by unpaid seller.

In the following circumstances, unpaid seller's lien is lost: Sec 49

- When the seller waives his right of lien.
- When the buyer disposes off the goods by sale with consent of seller.

- When the goods are delivered off the buyer or his agent.
- When price is paid by the buyer.
- The right of lien cannot be exercised, where the right of lien has been expressly excluded.
- By delivery of goods to carrier. Without reserving the right of disposal of goods,.
- By Estoppels i.e. where the seller so conducts himself that be leads third parties to believe that the lien does not exist.

Lien is not lost merely become the unpaid seller has obtained a decree for the price of the goods

Part delivery Sec. 48

Part delivery of goods does not disentitle the unpaid seller from exist lien on the remainder goods.

Right of Stoppage in Transit – Sec 50 to 52

Right of stoppage goods in transit Sec 50

- The right of stoppage in transit is an extension of the right of lien.
- The right of lien is a right to retain possession, whereas right of stoppage in transit is a right to regain possession.
- The right of stoppages in transit can be exercised, if the goods are in transit, and the buyer has become insolvent in the meantime.

Conditions : unpaid Seller + possession of goods with carrier (independent) + insolvent buyer

Duration of transit – Sec 51

- Carrier may hold the goods in three capacities:
  - As Seller's Agent : In this case, the seller has lien on the goods, so question of right of stoppage in transit does not arise.
  - As Buyer's Agent: In this case, the seller cannot exercise the right of stoppage in transit.
  - In an Independent Capacity: In this case, sit from the time they are delivered to a carrier for the purpose of transmission to the buyer, until the buyer or his agent takes their delivery.
- Goods are deemed to be in course of transit from the time they are delivered to a carrier for the purpose of transmission to the buyer, until the buyer or his agent takes their delivery.
- The goods are in transit, even if the buyer asks the carrier to take them to some other destination until they are delivered to the buyer at some other destination.
- If the goods are rejected by the buyer and the goods are in the possession of the carrier, the transit is not at an end, even if the seller has refused to take them back.

How Stoppage in transit is effected Sec 52

- Right of Stoppage of Goods in Transit can be exercised either:
  - By taking actual possession of the goods, or
  - By giving notice of his claim to the carrier, who holds the goods

Effect of sub – sale or pledge by the buyer Sec.53

Sub sale of pledge by the buyer	Effect on unpaid seller's right

The unpaid seller's right of lien or stoppage in transit is not affected by any further sale or other disposition of goods by the buyer.

Exception

- When seller has given his assent to such mortgage or other disposition of goods made by the buyer.
- When a document of title has been transferred to the buyer and the buyer transfer the document to a person who has brought the goods in good faith for value.

Distinction Between Lien and Stoppage – in – Transit

	Lien		Stoppage – in – Transit
1.	The goods are in actual possession of the seller.	1.	The goods are in possession of an independent carrier or bailes.
2.	This right can be exercised even when the buyer is solvent but fails or refuses to pay the price.	2.	This right can be exercised only when the buyer becomes insolvent.
3.	This right comes to an end when the seller parts with the goods.	3.	This right commences only when the seller delivers the goods to a carrier.
4.	This is a right to retain possession over the goods.	4.	This is a right to regain possession o the goods.
5.	This right can be exercised by the seller himself.		This right can be exercised by the seller through the carrier or the bailee in whose possession the goods are.

Right of Resale Sec 54

- In case of perishable goods, unpaid seller can resale the goods if following conditions satisfied.
  - Buyer fails to pay the price within reasonable time.
  - Seller is not required to give notice of re – sale.
- In case of other goods (not perishable) unpaid, the seller can resale goods if the following conditions are satisfied:
  - Seller has exercised his right of lien or stoppage of goods in transit.
  - Seller has given notice to buyer to pay the price within reasonable time and buyer fails to pay the price.
- Following will be effect of resale:

Rights	In case of resale after notice	In case of resale without notice
Unpaid seller's right to recover loss on sale	Available	No Available
Original buyers' right to recover profit on goods	Not available	Available
New buyer's right to acquire good title.	Available	Available

Right to Withhold Delivery of Goods

- It means seller refuses to deliver goods to buyer.
- The following conditions must be satisfied to exercise right to withhold delivery of goods:

- Seller is unpaid seller
- Ownership of goods has not been passed.

Right of unpaid seller against buyer:

Suit for price [sec 55]

55 (1) – Property has passed to the buyer
- Buyer wrongfully neglector refuses to pay price of goods

55 (2) - property has not passed to the buyer
- price is payable on a particular date irrespective of delivery.
- Buyer wrongfully neglects or refuses to pay price of goods

Suit for damages for non acceptance (56)

When buyer wrongfully neglects or refuses to accept and pay for the goods, the seller may sue him for damages for non acceptance.

Suit for damages for Breach (60)

Repudiation of contract before due date: Where the contract is repudiated by the buyer before the date of delivery the seller may treat the contract as rescind and sue for damage for the breach.

Suit for interest [61(2) (d)]

Specific agreement between seller and buyer as to interest on price of goods from the date on which payment becomes due the seller may recover the interest from the buyer.

This right is in addition to other remedies available to the seller.

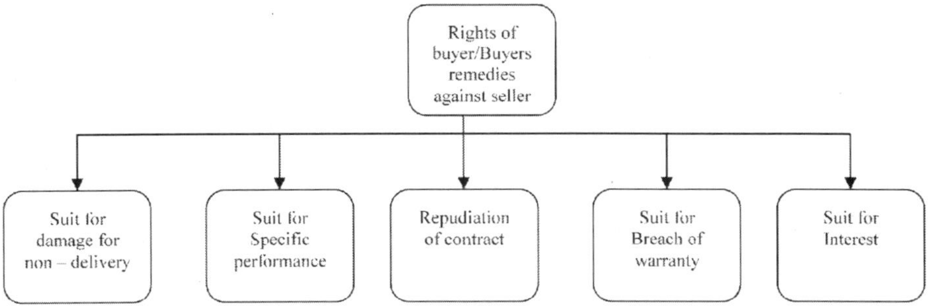

Buyer's right against the seller or remedies against seller

The buyer has following remedies against the seller:

- **Suit for damage for non – delivery Sec 57**
  Buyer is ready and willing the take delivery of goods but seller wrongfully neglects or refuses delivery of goods, buyer may sue seller.
- **Suit for specific performance Sec 58**
  Where seller wrongfully refuses to deliver specific or ascertained goods, court may direct specific performance order.

- **Suit for breach of warranty Sec 59**
  If there is breach of warranty, buyer may claim damages from the seller. Buyer may deduct the amount of damage from price payable if price is not paid. Buyer may recover the damages if price paid.
- **Right to repudiate the contract**
  If the seller declares his intention of non – delivery of goods, buyer may repudiate the contract and immediately sue for damages.
- **Suit for Interest**
- In the absence of any contract to the contrary no interest shall be payable by the buyer on the delay payment. If, there is no such agreement, the seller may give notice to the buyer of his intention to charge interest on delayed payment.

Delivery to Carrier

- It means transporter or bailee to whom goods are delivered by the seller for transportation to buyer.
- When goods are delivered to a carrier, it is deemed delivery of goods to the buyer if following conditions are satisfied:
  - Seller delivers exactly same goods as per contract.
  - The Buyer has informed carrier name, address and goods required to be delivered.
  - The seller delivers goods for the purpose of delivery.

Auction Sale – Sec 64

- It means public sale. The seller invites the interested parties by advertisement to offer the price. (i.e. bid)
- The seller may hire service of auctioneer. An auctioneer is an agent of seller.
- Advertisement of auction sale is not offer but an invitation to make an offer and therefore if an auction sale is not held on appointed day, bidder can't sue auctioneer.
- Every bid amounts as offer and acceptance is given by auctioneer by some usual mode of acceptance e.g., fall of hammer, going – going gone or one – two – three.
- Auction sale starts with placing of bids. Auctioneer accepts the highest bids but he may accept lower bid without giving any reason. When bid accepted, valid contract is formed.
- Bid once made can be withdrawn before fall of hammer even if expressly prohibit.
- Seller can bid at auction sale if bidders are informed of fact. (pretended bidding)
- If the seller makes use of pretended bidding to raise the price, the sale is voidable at the option of the buyer. The bid is said to be pretended when it is made by the seller or some one on his behalf.
- Only one person can be appointed for bidding.(called puffer)
- Auctioneer may set reserve price or upset price. Bid lower that which is invalid.
- 'In the case of Knockout agreement, the buyers joint their hands to eliminate competition among themselves at an raise the bid against each other and only

one of them will bid at the auction. When the profit. Prima facie, a knockout agreement is not illegal. However, if the intention of the parties to the agreement is to defraud a third party, this will be illegal.

Damping is illegal, it includes;

- Pointing out defects in the goods, or
- Misleading the purchaser or doing any other act so that he may not participate in the auction. It empowers the auctioneer to with draw the property from the auction.

Sale in lots :

When the goods are put up for sale in lots, each lot is deemed, prima facie, to be the subject – matter of a separate contract of sale.

Delivery of Goods in Contract by Sea Route

It includes following three categories of contracts:

CIF Contract

- It means 'cost, insurance and freight;
- Here, the price of goods includes the cost of goods, insurance and freight expenses.
- In CIF contract, buyer pays insurance and freight expenses.
- The essential of CIF contract is that seller shall deliver shipping documents to the buyer usually through the bank. If the seller fails to deliver the documents within reasonable time, he is liable for breach of contract.
- Ownership of goods is transferred to the buyer, when he pays the price of goods while receiving shipping documents. If buyer refuses to pay the price, the seller can claim damages for breach of contract.

FOB Contract

- It means free on board. Here, seller is required to put the goods on board of ship at his expense.
- Buyer is liable for all the expenses and risk one goods are loaded on ship.
- The ownership of goods is transferred to the buyer as soon as goods are loaded to ship.

  Ò!

Ex – Ship Contract

- It means contract in which the seller has to deliver the goods to the buyer at the port of destination.
- All the freight charges and risk during voyage for goods remain with seller.
- Ownership of the goods is transferred to the buyer when goods are actually delivered at the port of destination.

CHAPTER 4

Industrial Laws Factories Act, 1948

Introduction

Factories Act is one of the earliest labour welfare legislations. The object of the act is to secure health, safely, welfare, proper working hours, and other benefits to workers. The Act requires that workers should work in healthy and sanitary conditions and for that purposes. It provides that precaution should be taken for safety of workers and prevention of accidents.

Meaning of Factory

Factory means any premises, including the precincts thereof, in any part of which manufacturing process is carried on with or without the aid of power, provided that at least 10 or 20 persons respectively are employed or were employed on any day of the preceding 12 months.

The Act is applicable to all the factories.

Meaning of occupier of factory

Occupier of factory means a person who has ultimate control over affairs of factory. It includes a partner in case of a firm and director in case of a company. It may be noted that if a factory is run by a company, then only the director of the company can be treated as occupier.

The occupier shall ensure, as far as possible health, safety, and welfare of workers while they are working in a factory. The name of the occupier of the factory is required to be informed to the Chief Inspector of Factories. The occupier will be held responsible if the provisions of the Factories Act, 1948 are not complied with.

Facilities and Conveniences

1) Factory should be kept clean.
2) There should be arrangement to dispose off wastes and effluents.
3) Ventilation should be adequate.
4) Reasonable temperature for comfort of employees should be maintained.
5) Dust and fumes should be controlled below permissible limits.
6) Artificial humidification should be at prescribed limits.
7) Over crowding should be avoided.
8) Adequate lighting, drinking water, toilets, and spittoons should be provided.

Additional facilities in case of large factories.

1) Ambulance room, if **500 or more** workers are employed.
2) Canteen, if **250 or more** workers are employed.
3) Rest rooms/ Centers with drinking facility, if **150 or more** workers are employed.
4) Creshes, if **30 or more** women workers are employed.
5) Full time Welfare Officer, **if 500 or more** workers are employed.
6) Safety Officer, if **1000 or more** workers are employed.

Welfare Measures

1) All machines should be properly fenced to protect workers when machinery is in motion.
2) Hoist and lifts should be in good condition and tested periodically.
3) Pressure Plant should be checked as per the rules.
4) Floor, stairs and means of access should be of sound construction and free from obstructions.
5) Safety appliances for eyes, dangerous dust, gas, fumes should be provided.
6) In case of hazardous substance additional safety measures have to be taken.
7) Adequate firefighting equipment should be available.
8) Safety Officer should be appointed if number of workers in factory is 1000 or more.

Working Hours

A worker cannot be employed for more than 48 hours in a week. Weekly holiday is compulsory. If the worker is asked to work on weekly holiday, he should avail the holiday on one of the 3 days immediately after the normal day of holiday. A worker cannot be employed for more than 9 hours in a day. At least ½ hour rest should be provided after every 5 hours. Total period of work including rest interval cannot be more than 10 ½ hours.

Overtime Wages

If a worker works beyond 9 hours a day and 48 hours a week, overtime wages are paid at double the rate of normal wages. However, overtime wages are not payable on tour. Total working hours including overtime should not exceed 60 hours in a week and total overtime hours in a quarter should not exceed 50 hours.

Leave

Worker is entitled in every calendar year annual leave with wages at the rate of 1 day for every 20 days of work performed in the previous calendar year provided that he had worked for 240 days or more in the previous calendar year. Child worker (who is 14 years and above but less than 15 years) is entitled to 1 day leave with wages for every 15 days. While calculating 240 days earned leave, maternity leave up to 12 weeks and lay off days will be considered but leave shall not be earned on those days. Leave can be accumulated up to 30 days in the case of an adult and 40 days in the case of al child.

Leave admissible is exclusive of holidays occurring during or at either end of leave period. Leave cannot be taken for more than 3 times in a year.

It may be noted that above – mentioned benefit are the minimum benefits. Employer can of course provide additional or higher benefits.

Employment of Women

A women worker cannot be employed beyond **6 a.m. to 7 p.m**. State Government can grant exemption to any factory from such provisions but in no case a woman can be permitted to work **during 10 p.m. to 5 a.m**. Shift change can be done only after weekly or other holiday and not in between.

Employment of Children

Children below 14 years of age cannot be employed. A child of age 14 years but below 15 years can be employed for **only 4.5 hours per day**. He should be certified fit by certifying surgeon. He cannot be employed during night from **10 p.m. to 6 a.m.**

A person of 15 years of age but below 18 years of age is termed as **adolescent.** He can be employed as an adult if he certificate of fitness for a full day's work from a certifying surgeon. An adolescent is not permitted to work between 7 p.m. to 6 a.m.

Display on Notice Board.

A Notice containing an abstract of the Factories Act, 1948 and the rules made there under in English and local language shall be displayed by employer.

The name and address of Inspector of factories and Certifying Surgeon shall also be displayed on the Notice Board.

Punishment to Welfare Officer

No punishment can be imposed on Welfare Officer without prior sanction of Chief Commissioner of Factories. However, simple order of termination as per terms of appointment is not punishment and such termination order is valid. [Arun Kumar Bali v. Government, NCT of Delhi]

It means any process for—

Manufacturing process [Sec.2 (k)].

(i) Making, altering, repairing, ornamenting, finishing, packing, online, washing, cleaning. Breaking, up, demolishing, or otherwise treating or adapting any article or substance with a view to its use, sale, transport, delivery or disposal, or

(ii) Pumping oil, water. Sewage, or any other substance, or

(iii) Generating, transforming or transmitting power, or

(iv) composing types for printing, printing by letter press, lithography, photogravure or other similar process or book-binding, or

(v) Constructing, reconstructing, repairing, refitting, finishing, breaking-up ship or "vessels, or

(vi) Preserving or storing any article in cold storage.

Some of the processes which have been held to be manufacturing processes are as follows:

(a) Bidi making [Chintaman Rao v.State of M.P.,(1962) S.C.J.388].

(b) Molding and transformation of raw cinematography films into a finished product [Gemini Studio v. State, (1952-53) 4 F.J.R. 329].

(c) Work done in a salt work which consists of converting sea-water into salt [Ardeshir H. Bhiwandiwala v.State of Bombay, A.I.R. (1962) S.C.29.]
(d) Use of a refrigerator for treating or adapting any article with a view to its sale [New Taj Mahal café Ltd. V. Inspector of Factories, (1956) 1 L.L.J.273].
(e) Work of compositions in printing business [V.K. Press v. Authority, A.I.R. (1955) all. 702].
(f) Use of electric motor for the purpose of lifting or pumping water [Syed Moosa Kazimi v. K.M. Sheriff, A.I.R. (1959) Mad. 542].
(g) Process of moistening, stripping and packing of tobacco leaves [V.P. Gopala Rao v. Public Prosecutor, A.I.R. (1970) S.C. 66].
(h) Activities of a petrol pump [Gateway Auto services v. Regional director, E.S.I. Corpn., (1981) Lab. I.C. 49].

In deciding whether a particular business is a manufacturing process or not, regard must be had to the circumstances of each particular case. To constitute a manufacturing process, there must be some transformation, i.e., the article must become commercially known as something different from which it acquires its existence

General duties of the occupier (Sec. 7-A)

A new Sec. 7-A has been introduced by the Amendment Act of 1987, prescribing the general duties of the occupier in regard to the health, safety and welfare of the workers in his factory. According to it, every occupier shall ensure, so far as is reasonably practicable, the health, safety and welfare of all workers while they are at work in the factory [Sec. 7-A (1)]. Sec. 7-A (2) enumerates the matters in regard to health, safety and welfare of the workers. These matters include—

(a) the provision and maintenance of plant and systems of work in the factory that are safe and without risks to health;
(b) the arrangements in the factory for ensuring safety and absence of risks to health in connection with the use, handling, storage and transport of articles and substances;
(c) the provision of such information, instruction, training and supervision as are necessary to ensure the health and safety of all workers at work;
(d) (i) the maintenance of all places of work in the factory in a condition that is safe and without risks to health, and
(II) the provision and maintenance of such means of access to and egress from such places as are safe and without such risks;
(e) the provision, maintenance or monitoring of such working environment in the factory for the workers that is
(i) safe,
(ii) without risks to health, and
(iii) adequate as regards facilities and arrangements for their welfare at work [Sec. 7A (2)].

In addition to the above duties, every occupier shall also—

(a) prepare, and, as often as may be appropriate, revise, a written statement of his general policy with respect to
(i) the health and safety of the workers at work, and

(ii) the organisation and arrangements for the time being in force for carrying out that policy, and

(b) bring the statement and any revision thereof to the notice of all the workers. In some cases as may be prescribed an occupier may be exempted from this duty [Sec. 7-A (3)].

Powers of inspectors (Sec. 9).

An Inspector may, within the local limits for which he is appointed,—

(a) enter, with assistant who are in the service of the Government or any local or other public authority or with an expert, the premises of a factory;

(b) make examination of the premises, plant, machinery, article or substance;

(c) inquire into any accident or dangerous occurrence, whether resulting in bodily injury, disability or not, and take on the spot or otherwise statements of any person which he may consider necessary for such inquiry;

(d) require the production of any prescribed register or any other document relating to the factory;

(e) seize, or take copies of, any register, record or other document or any portion thereof, as he may consider necessary in respect of any offence under this Act, which he has reason to believe, has been committed:

(f) direct the occupier that any premises or any part thereof, or anything lying therein, shall be left undisputed (whether generally or in particular respects) for so long as in necessary for the purpose of any examination under Clause (b) :

(g) take measurements and photographs and make such recordings as he considers necessary for the purpose of any examination under Clause (b) taking with him any necessary instrument or equipment:

(h) in case of any article or substance found in any premised, being an article or substance which appears to him as having caused or is likely to cause danger to the health or safety of the workers, direct it to be dismantled or subject it to any process of test (but not so as to damage or destroy it unless the same is necessary for carrying out the purposes of the Act.) Further, he may take possession of any such article or substance or a part thereof, and detain it for so long as is necessary for such examination; and (i) Exercise such other powers as may be prescribed.

The above powers of an inspector are subject to any rules which may be made by the State Government in this behalf.

Certifying surgeons (Sec. 10.) Appointment.

- The State Government may appoint qualified medical practitioners to be certifying surgeons for specified local limits or factories [sec. 10 (1)].
- A certifying surgeon may, with the approval of the State Government, authorise any qualified medical practitioner to exercise any of his powers [sec.10. (2)] But no person shall be appointed a certifying surgeon who is or becomes the occupier of a factory or is or becomes directly or indirectly interested therein [sec. 10(3)].
- The State Government may exempt any person or class of persons from the provisions of Sec. 10(3) in respect of any factory or class or description of factories (Proviso to Sec 10(3)].

- The exemption shall however be made by order in writing and subject to such conditions as may be specified in the order.

Duties of certifying surgeons.

The certifying surgeon shall carry out such duties as may be prescribed in connection with—

(a) the examination and certification of young person's ;

(b) the examination of persons engaged in factories in dangerous occupations or processes; and

(c) the exercising of such medical supervision as may be prescribed for any factory where—

(i) cases of illness have occurred which it is reasonable to believe are due to the nature of the manufacturing process carried on, or other conditions of work prevailing, therein;

(ii) by reason of any change in the manufacturing process carried on or in the substances used therein, there is a likelihood of injury to health of worker employed it that manufacturing process;

(iii) young persons are, or about to be, employed in any work which I likely to cause injury to their health [Sec. 10 (4)].

Cleanliness (Sec.11).

(1) ***Factory to be kept clean and fee from effluvia and dirt.***

- Every factory shall be kept clean and fee from effluvia arising from any drain, privy, or other nuisance.
- Accumulation of dirt and refuse shall be removed daily be some effective method.
- The floor of every work-room shall be cleaned at least once in every week by washing, using disinfectants, where necessary, or by some effective method.

(2) ***Effective means of drainage.***

Where a floor is liable to become wet ion the course of any manufacturing process to such an extent as is capable of being drained, effective means of drainage shall be provided.

(3) ***Use of disinfectants, etc., painting and varnishing.***

Use of disinfectants, detergents, painting, repainting and varnishing, revarnishing, whitewashing or colourwashing shall be restored to.

2. **Disposal of wastes and effluents** *(sec.12).*

(1) ***Treatment of wastes and effluents and their disposal.*** Effective arrangements shall be made in every factory for the treatment of wastes and effluents due to the manufacturing process a carried on therein, so as to render them innocuous, and for their disposal [Sec. 12 (1)].

(2) ***Rules by the state Government prescribing arrangements.*** The state government may make rules prescribing the arrangements to be made in this regard. It may also require that such arrangements shall be approved by such authority as may be prescribed [Sec. 12 (2)].

3. **Ventilation and temperature** (Sec. 13.)

(1) ***Maintenance of adequate ventilation and temperature.***

Effective and suitable provision shall be made in every factory for securing and maintaining in every workroom—

(a) Adequate ventilation by the circulation of fresh air, and

(b) Such a temperature as will secure to workers therein reasonable conditions of comfort and prevent injury to health.

(2) ***Process producing high temperature to be separated.***

The walls and roofs shall be of such materials and so designed that the temperature shall not be exceeded but kept as low as practicable. The process which produces high temperatures shall be separated from the workroom, by insulating the hot parts or by other effective means [Sec. 13 (1)].

4. **Dust and fume** (Sec. 14).

(1) *Measures for prevention of inhalation or accumulation of dust and fume.*

- Where dust or fume or impurity of such a nature as is likely to be injurious or offensive to the workers is given off as a result of the manufacturing process being carried on in a factory, effective measures shall be taken in the factory for prevention of inhalation or accumulation of dust and fumes in workrooms.
- If for such a purpose any exhaust appliance is necessary, it shall be applied as near as possible to the point of origin of the dust, fume or other impurity and such point shall be enclosed so far as possible [Sec. 14 (1)].

(2) ***Exhaust for internal combustion engine.***

A stationary internal combustion engine shall not be operated unless the exhaust is conducted into the open air. Other internal combustion engines shall not be operated in any room unless effective measures have been taken to prevent accumulation of fumes therefrom which are injurious [Sec. 14 (2)].

5. Artificial humidification (Sec. 15).

(1) ***Prescription of standards of humidification—ventilation and cooling of air.***

In respect of all factories in which the humidity of the air is artificially increased, the State Government may make rules prescribing standards of humidification. It may also make rules regulating the methods used for artificially increasing the humidity of the air. It may further make rules prescribing methods to be adopted for securing adequate ventilation and cooling of the air in the workrooms [Sec. 15 (1)].

(2) ***Water used for artificial humidification to be clean.***

In any factory in which the humidity of the air is artificially increased, the water used for the purpose shall be taken from a public supply or other source of drinking water, or shall be effectively purified before it is so used [Sec. 15 (2)].

6. Overcrowding (Sec. 16).

(1) ***Overcrowding injurious to health of workers to be avoided.***

There shall not be overcrowding in any room of the factory so as to be injurious to the health of the workers employed therein [Sec. 16 (1)].

(2) ***9.9/14.2 cubic meters of space*** per worker.

- There shall be at least 9.9 cubic meters (for the factories in existence at the time of the commencement of the Act) and 14.2 cubic meters (for the factories built after the commencement of the Act) of space for every worker.

- In calculating the space of 9.9 or 14.2 cubic meters, no account shall be taken of any space which is more than 4.2 meters above the level of the floor of the room [Sec. 16 (2)].

(3) ***Notice of maximum of workers to be employed in a workroom.***

If the Chief Inspector by order in writing so requires, there shall be posted in each workroom of the factory a notice specifying the maximum number of workers who may be employed in the workroom [Sec. 16 (3)].

7. Lighting (Sec. 17).

(1) ***Sufficient and suitable lighting in every part of factory.*** In every part of a factory where workers are working or passing there shall be provided and maintained sufficient and suitable lighting, natural or artificial, or both [Sec. 17 (1)].

(2) ***Glazed windows and skylights to be kept clean.*** All glazed windows and skylights used for the lighting of the workrooms shall be kept clean on both the inner and outer surfaces and free from obstruction [Sec. 17 (2)].

(3) ***Measures for prevention of glare and formation of shadows.*** Effective provision shall also be made for the prevention of (a) glare, either directly from a source of light or by reflection from a smooth or polished surface; and (b) the formation of shadows to such an extent as to cause eye strain or the risk of accident to any worker [Sec. 17 (3)].

(4) ***Prescription of standards of sufficient and suitable lighting.*** The State Government may prescribe standards of sufficient and suitable lighting for factories or for any class or description of factories or for any manufacturing process [Sec. 17 (4)].

8. Drinking water (Sec. 18).

(1) ***Suitable points for wholesome drinking water.*** In every factory, effective arrangements shall be made to provide and maintain at suitable points conveniently situated for all workers employed therein a sufficient supply of wholesome drinking water [sec. 18 (1)].

(2) ***Cooling of drinking water where more than 250 workers employed.*** In every factory wherein more than 250 workers are ordinarily employed, provision shall be made for cooling drinking water during hot weather by effective means and for distribution thereof [Sec. 18(3)].

9. Hoists and lifts (Sec. 28).

- *Hoists and lifts to be of good mechanical construction and to be properly maintained and examined once in every 6 months.* In every factory every hoists and lift shall be of good mechanical construction, sound material, and adequate strength.
- Further it shall be sufficiently protected by enclosures fitted with gates. It shall also be properly maintained and shall be thoroughly examined by a competent person at least once in every 6 months.
- A register containing the prescribed particulars of every such examination shall be kept. The maximum safe working load shall also be plainly marked on every hoist or lift, and no load greater than such load shall be carried thereon.

- The cage of every hoist or lift used for carrying persons shall be fitted with a gate on each side from which access is afforded to a landing.
- The gate shall be fitted with interlocking or other efficient device to secure that the cage cannot be moved unless the gate is closed.

For the purposes of Sec. 28, no lifting machine or appliance shall be deemed to be a hoist or lift unless it has a platform or cage, the direction or movement of which is restricted by a guide or guides (Expl. to Sec. 28 added by the Amendment Act of 1987).

12. Floors, stairs and means of access (Sec. 32). In every factory

(a) all floors, steps, stairs, passages and gangways shall be of sound construction and properly maintained. Further they shall be kept free from obstructions and substances likely to cause persons to skip and handrails shall be provided where necessary;

(b) there shall, so far as is reasonably practicable, be provided and maintained safe means of access to every place at which any person is at any time required to work; and

(c) when any person has to work at a height from where he is likely to fall, provision shall be made, so far as is reasonably practicable, by fencing or otherwise, to ensure the safety of the person so working. This restriction is not applicable if the place provides secure foothold and, where necessary, secure handhold.

13. Safety Officers (Sec. 40-B). In every factory

(i) wherein 1,000 or more workers are ordinarily employed, or

(ii) wherein, in the opinion of the State Government, any manufacturing process or operation is carried on, which process or operation involves any risk of bodily injury, poisoning or disease, or any other hazard to health, to the persons employed in the factory, the occupier shall, if so required by the State Government by notification in the Official *Gazette,* employ such number of Safety Officers as may be specified in that notification [Sec. 40-B) (1)]. The duties, qualifications and conditions of service of Safety Offices shall be such as may be prescribed by the State Government [Sec. 40-B (2)].

WELFARE

Chapter V (Secs. 42 to 50) of the Act deals with facilities for the welfare of workers. The various provisions in this regard are as follows:

1. **Washing facilities** (Sec. 42). In every factory (a) adequate and suitable facilities (separately and adequately screened for the use of male and female workers) shall be provided and maintained for the use of the workers therein; and (b) such facilities shall be conveniently accessibly and shall be kept clean.
2. **Facilities for storing and drying clothing** (Sec. 43). The State Government may make rules requiring the provision of suitable places for keeping clothing of workers not worn during working hours and for the drying of wet clothing in respect of any factory or class of factories.

3. Facilities for sitting (Sec. 44).

(1) ***Provision of sitting arrangement for workers obliged to work in a standing position.*** In every factory, suitable arrangements for sitting shall be provided

and maintained for all workers who are obliged to work in a standing position. This has been done in order that the workers may take advantage of any opportunities for rest which may occur in the course of their work [Sec. 44 (1)].

(2) ***Provision of seating arrangement for workers doing work which can be done in a sitting position.*** If the workers in any factory engaged in a particular manufacturing process or working in a particular room are able to do their work efficiently in a sitting position, the Chief Inspector may require the occupier of the factory to provide such seating arrangements as may be practicable [Sec. 44 (20].

(3) ***Exemption.*** The State Government may, by notification in the Official Gazette, exempt any factory or class of factories or manufacturing process from the application of the provisions of Sec. 44 [Sec. 44 (3)].

4. First-aid appliances (Sec. 45).

(1) ***At least one first-aid box with prescribed contents for every 150 workers.*** There shall in every factory be provided and maintained so as to be readily accessible during all working hours, first-aid boxes or cupboards with the prescribed contents. There shall be at least one such box for every 150 workers ordinarily employed at any one time in the factory [Sec. 45 (1)].

(2) ***First-aid box to have prescribed contents.*** Only the prescribed contents shall be kept in a first-aid box or cupboard [Sec. 45 (2)].

(3) ***First-aid box to be in the charge of responsible person.*** Each first-aid box or cupboard shall be kept in the charge of a separate responsible person who holds a certificate in the first-aid treatment recognized by the State Government. Further, such person shall always be readily available during the working hours of the factory [Sec. 45 (3)].

(4) ***Ambulance room in a factory employing more than 500 workers.*** In every factory wherein more than 500 workers are ordinarily employed there shall be provided and maintained an ambulance room containing the prescribed equipment.

The room shall be in the charge of such medical and nursing staff as may be prescribed and those facilities shall always be made readily available during the working hours of the factory [Sec. 45 (4)].

5. Canteens (Sec. 46)

(1) ***Canteen in factory employing more than 250 workers—the State Government may make rules.***

The State Government may make rules requiring that in any specified factory wherein more than 250 workers are ordinarily employed, a canteen or canteens shall be provided and maintained by the occupier for the use of the workers [Sec. 46 (1)].

(2) ***Provisions in rules.***

The rules made by the State Government as to canteens may provide for

(a) The date by which canteen shall be provided,

(b) The standards in respect of construction, accommodation, furniture and other equipment of the canteen,

(c) The foodstuffs to be served therein and the charges which may be made thereof,

(d) The constitution of a managing committee for the canteen and representation of the workers in the management of the canteen,

(e) The items of expenditure in the running of the canteen which are not to be taken into account in fixing the cost of foodstuffs and which shall be borne by the employer, and

(f) The delegation to the Chief Inspector, subject to such conditions as may be prescribed, of the power to make rules under Clause (c) [Sec. 46 (2)].

6. Shelters, rest rooms and lunch rooms (Sec. 47).

(1) ***Provision for shelters, rest rooms, lunch rooms in factories employing more than 150 workers.***

- In every factory wherein more than150 workers are ordinarily employed, there shall be a provision for shelters, rest rooms and a suitable lunch room where workers can eat meals brought by them with provision for drinking water.
- However, any canteen maintained in accordance with the provisions of Sec. 46 shall be regarded as part of this requirement. Where a lunch room exists, no worker shall eat any food in the workroom [Sec. 47 (1)].

(2) ***Shelters, etc. to be sufficiently lighted, ventilated and cooled.***

The shelters or rest rooms or lunch rooms shall be sufficiently lighted and ventilated and shall be maintained in a cool and clean condition [Sec. 47 (2)].

7. Crèches (Sec. 48).

(1) ***Provision of crèches in factories employing more than 30 women workers.***
In every factory wherein more than 30 women workers are ordinarily employed, there shall be provided and maintained a suitable room or rooms for use of children under the age of 6 years of such women [Sec. 48 (1)].

(2) ***Crèches to be adequately lighted and ventilated and to be under the charge of trained women.***
Rooms for use of children shall provide adequate accommodation, shall be adequately lighted and ventilated. Further they shall be maintained in a clean and sanitary condition and shall be under the charge of women trained in the care of children and infants [Sec. 48 (2)].

(3) ***Prescription of rules by the State Government.***
The State Government may make rules prescribing the location and the standards in respect of construction, accommodation, furniture and other equipment of rooms for use of children. It may also make rules for the provision of additional facilities for the care of children belonging to women workers, including suitable provision of facilities

(a) For washing and changing their clothing,

(b) Of free milk or refreshment or both for the children, and

(c) For the mothers of children to feed them at the necessary intervals. [Sec. 48 (3)].

8. Welfare officers (Sec. 49).

(1) ***Employment of welfare officers in factories employing 500 or more workers.***

In every factory wherein 500 or more workers are ordinarily employed the occupier shall employ in the factory such number of welfare officers as may be prescribed [Sec. 49 (1)].

(2) ***Duties, qualifications and conditions of service to be prescribed by the State Government.***

The State Government may prescribe the duties, qualifications and conditions of service of welfare officers [Sec. 49 (2)].

Even if a factory (say, a sugar factory) employs over 500 workers only for a few months in the year and not continuously, the occupier shall employ the prescribed number of welfare officers [Employers' Assn. of *Northern India v. Secretary of Labour,* A.I.R. (1952) All. 109].

Restriction on double employment (sec. 60)

No adult worker shall be required or allowed to work in any factory on any day on which he has already been working in any other factory save in such circumstances as may be prescribed.

Working hours and notice of periods of work for children (Secs. 71 and 72).

(1) ***Working hours limited to 4-1/2.***

No child shall be employed or permitted to work in any factory—

(a) for more than 4-1/2 hours in any day; (b) during the night [Sec. 71 (1)].

'Night' means a period of at least 12 consecutive hours which shall include the4 interval between 10 P.M. and A.M. [Expl. to Sec. 71 (1)].

(2) ***Period of work of children limited to 2 shifts.***

The period of work of all children employed in a factory shall be limited to 2 shifts. These shifts shall not overlap or spread over more than 5 hours each. Each child shall be employed in only one of the relays which shall not, except with the previous permission in writing of the Chief Inspector, be changed more frequently than once in a period of 30 days [Sec. 71 (2)].

(3) ***Child workers entitled to weekly holidays.***

The provisions of weekly holidays |(Sec. 52) shall apply also to child workers and no exemption from these provisions may be granted in respect of any child [Sec. 71 (3)].

(4) ***Prohibition if the child worker has already been working in another factory.***

No child shall be required or allowed to work in any factory on any day on which he has already been working in another factory [Sec. 71 (4)].

(5) *Female child to work only between 8 A.M. to 7 P.M.*

No female child shall be required or allowed to work in any factory except between 8 A.M. and 7 P.M. [Sec. 71 (5) as introduced by the Amendment Act of 1987].

(6) *Display of notice of work of child-workers.*

There shall be displayed and correctly maintained in every factory in which children are employed a notice of periods of work for children showing clearly for every day the periods during which children may be required or allowed to work [Sec. 72 (1)]. The provisions of Sec. 61(8), (9) and (10) (discussed earlier) also apply to the notice required under Sec. 72 (1) [Sec. 72 (3)].

(7) *Fixation of periods of work beforehand.*

The periods shown in the notice shall be fixed beforehand in accordance with the method laid down for adult workers [Sec. 72 (2)].

5. Restriction on employment of women (Se3c. 66).

A woman shall be required or allowed to work in a factory only between the hours of 6 A.M. and 7 P.M. The State Government may, by notification in the Official *Gazette* in respect of any factory or group or class or description of factories, vary these limits. But no such variation shall authorise the employment of any woman between the hours of 10 P.M. and 5 P.M. Again there shall be no change of shifts in the case of women workers in a factory except after a weekly or any other holiday [Sec. 66 (1)].

The State Government may make rules providing for the exemption from the restrictions imposed by Sec. 66 (1) in case of women working in fish-curing or fish-canning factories, where the employment of women beyond the specified hours is necessary to prevent damage to, or deterioration in, any raw material [Sec. 66 (3)].

Wages during leave period (Sec. 80).

For the leave allowed to a worker he shall be entitled to wages at a rate equal to the daily average of his total full time earnings for the days on which he actually worked during the month immediately preceding his leave. The full time earnings shall be exclusive of any overtime and bonus but inclusive of dearness allowance and the cash equivalent of the advantage accruing through the concessional sale to the worker of foodgrains and other articles [Sec. 80 (1)].

Important Points

1) The Supreme Court held that salt manufacture from sea water by employing different processes is a manufacturing process and the workers engaged in this work are workers within the meaning of Factories Act. [Ardeshir H. Bhiwandiwala v. State of Bombay]
2) The Supreme Court held that sun cured tobacco leaves subjected to processes of moistening, stripping, breaking up, packing with the view to transport them to Company's main Factory for their use in manufacturing Cigarette is a manufacturing process under the Factories Act. [Ardehir H. Bhiwandiwala v. State of Bombay]
3) The cutting of the woods or converting the wood into planks is a part of the manufacturing activity. [Bharati Udyog v. Regional Director ESI Corpn.]
4) Construction of railway, use of materials like sleepers, bolts, loose rails etc, to adaptation their use for ultimately for laying down railways line amounts to manufacturing process. [Lal Mohmd. v. Indian Railway Construction Co. Ltd.]
5) The process undertaken in zonal and sub –stations and electricity generating stations, transforming and transmitting electricity generated at the power station does not fall within the definitions of manufacturing process. [Workmen of Delhi Electric Supply Undertaking v. Management of DESU]
6) Piece – rate workers can be workers within the definition of worker in the Act, but they must be regular workers and not workers who come and work according to their will, [Shankar Balaji Wale v. State of Maharashtra]

7) All persons employed in or in connection with a factory whether or not employed as workers are entitled to the benefits of the Act. [Union of India v. G.M. Kokil]
8) If a factory is being run by a Company, then only a director of that Company can be the occupier for the purpose of the Act.[J.K. Industries Ltd. v. Chief Inspector of Factories]
9) Employees working in canteens in industrial establishment runs by Managing Committee are not employers of the Managing Committee, but are employees of occupier. [Kanpur Suraksha karamchari Union v. Union of India]
10) Preparation of food and beverage and its sale to members of a club is a manufacturing process. [CCI v. ESIC]
11. Receiving products in bulk and packing as per clients requirements amounts to manufacture.
12. A person is said to be employed in the factory if his duties are connected with the business of the factory, no matter whether he stands outside the factory premises or inside it. [Shinde v. Bombay Telephones]
13. It was held the definition of worker includes employees who are entrusted solely with the clerical duties. [Works Manager, Central Rly. Workshop Jhansi v. Vishwanath and others]

Powers of Inspectors

An inspector may exercise any of the following powers within the local limits for which he is appointed:

1. He can enter any place which is used or which, he has reasons to believe, is used as factory.
2. He can make examination of the premises, plant, machinery etc.
3. He can require the production of any prescribed register or any other document relating to the factory.
4. Take measurement and photographs and make such recordings as the considers necessary for the purpose of any examination.

Processes Special Provisions relating to Hazardous

Special provisions relating to hazardous processes have been envisaged under Chapter IV. A of the Factories Act, 1948. This chapter was inserted by the Factories (Amendment) Act, 1987 and Consists of Sections 41 A to 41 H. These sections are as follows:

Constitution of Site Appraisal Committees [Section 41A]: A Committee under the name Site Appraisal Committee shall be constituted by the State Government to advise the Government in the matter of examination of application for establishment of factories involving hazardous processes. The constitution of the site appraisal committee consisting of committee has been specified therein.

The Site Appraisal Committee shall examine an application for the establishment of a factory involving hazardous process and make its recommendation to the State Government within a period of **ninety days in the prescribed from.**

Compulsory disclosure of information by the occupier [Section 41B]: It is compulsory on the part of the occupier of every factory involving a hazardous process to disclose all information regarding dangers, including health hazards to the workers employed in the factory, the Chief Inspector, the local authority within whose jurisdiction the factory is situated and the general public in the vicinity.

Specified responsibility of the occupier in relation to hazardous processes [Section 41C]: Accurate and up to date health records or medical records of the workers of the factory who are exposed to any chemical toxic or any other harmful substances which are manufactured, stored, handled or transported and such records shall be maintained by the occupier of a factory involving any hazardous process.

Inquiry Committee [Section 41D]: In the event of occurrence of an extraordinary situation, the Central Government may appoint an Inquiry Committee to inquire into the standards of health and safety observed in the factory with a view to finding out the causes of any failure or neglect in the adoption of any measures prescribed for the health and safety of the workers or the general public.

Emergency standards [Section 41E]: The director – General of Factory Advice Service and Labour Institutes may be directed by the Central Government to lay down emergency standards in respect of hazardous process.

Permissible limits of exposure of chemical and toxic substances (Section 41F): The second Schedule added to the Act, indicates maximum permissible threshold limits of exposure of chemical and toxic substances in manufacturing processes in any factory.

Workers Participation in safety management (Section 41G): The occupier in every factory shall set up a safety committee consisting of equal number of representatives of workers and management to promote co – operating between the workers and the management in maintaining proper safety and health at work and to review periodically the measure taken in that behalf where hazardous process is involved.

Warning about imminent danger (Section 41H): If there is reasonable apprehension regarding likelihood of imminent danger to the lives or health of the workers employed in a factory, they may bring the same to the notice of the occupier, agent, manager, etc.

CHAPTER 5

Industrial Disputes Act, 1947

Introduction

The object of Industrial Disputes Act, 1947 is to make provisions for investigation and settlement of industrial disputes. The purpose is to bring the conflict between the employer and the employees to an amicable settlement. The Act also provides machinery for settlement of disputes, if dispute cannot be resolved through collective bargaining. In additions to above, the Act also makes other provision in respect of lay – off, retrenchment, strike, lock – out, etc.

Extent of the Act

The act extends to the whole of the India [Sec. 1 (2)]. It applies to all industries whether they are carried on by private owners or by the Government [Western India automobile Assn. v. Industrial Tribunal, Bombay, A.I.R. (1949) F.C.111].

The act has been amended from time to time. The latest amendment to the Act was made in august, 1984.

OBJECTS OF THE ACT

The main objects of the Act are:

To secure industrial peace—

(a) by preventing and settling industrial disputes between the employers and workmen,

(b) by securing and preserving amity and good relations between the employers and workmen through an internal Works committee and

(c) by promoting good relations through an external machinery of conciliation, Courts of inquiry, Labour Courts, Industrial Tribunals and National Tribunals.

(1) To ameliorate the condition of work men in industry—

(a) by redressal of grievances of workmen through a statutory machinery; and

(b) by providing job security [S.N.Rai v. Vishwanath Lal, A.I.R. (1960) Pat. 10.]

What is included in the term 'Industry'? 'Industry' includes—

(a) Any activity of the Dock Labour board established under Sec. 5-A of the Dock workers (regulation of Employment) Act, 1948;

(b) Any activity relating to the promotion of sales or business or both carried on by and establishment.

What is not included in the term 'industry'? 'Industry' does not includes—

(1) Any agriculture operation except where such agricultural operation is carried on in an integrated manner with any other systematic activity and such other activity is the predominant one; or
'Agricultural operation' does not include any activity carried on in a plantation as defined in Sec. 2 (f) of the Plantations Labour Act, 1951.

(2) Hospitals or dispensaries; or

(3) Educational, scientific, research or training institutions; or

(4) Institutions owned or managed by organizations wholly or sub-stantially engaged in any charitable, social or philanthropic service; or

(5) Khadi or village industries; or
According to new clause (kka) as introduced in Sec.2 by the amendment Act of 1982, 'khadi' has the meaning assigned to it in Sec. 2(d0 of the Khadi and Village industries commission Act, 1956.

(6) Any activity of the Government relatable to the sovereign functions of the Government including all the activities carried on by the departments of the Central government dealing with defense research, atomic energy and space; or

(7) Any domestic service; or

(8) Any activity, being a pr4ofession practiced by an individual or body of individuals. If the number of persons employed in relation to such profession is less than 10; or

(9) Any activity, being an activity carried on by a co-operative society or a club or any other like body of individuals, if the number of persons employed in relation to such activity is less than 10.

Employees covered under the Industrial Dispute Act

Every person employed in an establishment for hire or reward, to do any manual, clerical skilled unskilled technical operational or supervisory work is covered under the Act.

1) Persons employed mainly in a managerial or administrative capacity.
2) Person employed in a supervisory capacity and drawing wages exceeding Rs.**1,600/-** p.m. or exercising functions mainly of managerial nature:
3) Persons subject to Army Act, Air force Act, Navy Act or those employed in the police service or as an officer or employee of a prison.

The Act provides for constitution of Works Committee in factories employing 100 or more workers. First of all, the works Committee will try to settle the dispute. If the dispute is not settles it will be referred to the Conciliation Officer. The Conciliation Officer will try to arrive at fair and amicable settlement acceptable to both the parties. If he is unable to do so, he will send the report to the Central Government. The Government may then refer the industrial dispute to the Board of Conciliation. It may be noted that here the employer and the employees can voluntarily refer the matter to arbitration. If no settlement is arrived at then there is arrived that three – tier system of adjudication i.e., Labour Court, Industrial Tribunal and National Tribunal.

Award means an interim or final determination of any industrial dispute or of any question relating thereto by any Labour Court, Industrial Tribunal, or National

Tribunal. The term award also includes arbitration award. The award is required to be published by the Central Government or State Government within 30 days from the date it is made. The award becomes effectives only after 30 days of its publication. Generally the validity period of its publication. Generally the validity period of an award is 1 year.

Settlement means a settlement arrived at in the course of conciliation proceedings. It includes a written agreement between the employer and workman arrived at otherwise than in the course of conciliation proceedings.

The settlement arrived in the course of conciliation and arbitration award and Labour Court award or the Industrial or National Tribunal Award binds all parties to industrial dispute, including present and future workman and all parties who are summoned to appear in the proceedings. If settlement is arrived at otherwise in the course of conciliation proceeding, it binds only those who are actually parties to the agreement; generally, the settlement is valid for 6 months.

Lay off means failure refusal or inability of the employer to give employment to a workman because of any of the following reasons: 1) Shortage of coal, power or raw materials, 2) Accumulation of stock; 3) Breakdown of machinery 4) Natural calamity: 5) Any other similar or analogous reason.

Lay off means not giving employment within 2 hours after reporting to work.. Lay off can be for half day also wherein the worker shall be asked to come in the second half of the shift.

A factory employing 50 or more but less than 100 employees can lay off its workman who have completed 1 year of service by paying compensation equal to 50% of the salary / wages. A factory employing more than 100 employees can lay off its workman with the previous approval of Central Govt, However the approval of Central Govt. is not required in case lay off is done on account of shortage of power or due to natural calamity. Employer can offer him alternate employment if alternate employment does not call for any special skill or previous experience. In such a case lay off compensation will not be payable if the employee refuses to accept the alternate employment.

Retrenchment means the termination of service of a workman by the employer for any reason other than as a punishment inflicted by a disciplinary action. In addition, retrenchment does not include voluntary retirement or retirement on reaching the age of superannuation or termination on account of non – renewal of contract or termination of contract itself or termination due to continued ill – health of workman.

Retrenchment means discharge of surplus labour or staff of the employer. It is not be way of punishment. The retrenchment shall be done on LIFO basis in respect of each category.

A workman who has completed one year of service can be retrenched by giving one month's notice or one month's salary and retrenchment compensation.

Retrenchment compensation is calculated at the rate of 15 days' average wages for every completed year of service or any part thereof in excess of 6 months. Average Wages means average of the wages payable for the proceeding 3 complete calendar months. For the purpose of retrenchment compensation, one day wage shall be calculated by dividing monthly wage by 30.

Strike means a cessation of work by a body of persons, employed in any industry, acting in combination or a concerted refusal, or a refusal under a common understanding of any number of persons who are or have been so employed to continue to work or to accept employment.

1) During pendency of conciliation proceedings and 7 days thereafter;
2) During pendency of proceedings before Labour court or Industrial Tribunal or National Tribunal :
3) During period of arbitration proceedings:
4) During period when settlement or award is in operation in respect of the matters covered by the award or settlement.

In case of public utility services (hospital, railways, ports, docks, telephone, transport etc.), employees have to give at least 14 days' notice for strike. The notice is valid only if strike commences within 6 weeks otherwise fresh notice is required. If such notice is received by any employer, Government authorities should be informed within 5 days of the receipt of notice.

Wages during strike period are payable only if strike is both legal and justified. [Syndicate Bank v. Umesh Naik]

Strike in violation of above provisions is illegal. In Such a case, the workman shall be punishable with fine, which may extend to Rs.50/- per day and with imprisonment, which may extend to 1 month.

Important Points

1) Principals governing Domestic Enquiry

In all such cases, the workmen after taking their seats, refuse to do work.

Go slow does not amount to strike, but it is a serious case of misconduct.

Cessation of work in the support of the demands of workmen belonging to other employer.

Some workers may resort to fast on or near the place of work or residence of the employer.

Since there is no cessation of work, it does not constitute a strike.

Lock out means temporary closing of a place of employment or the suspensions of work or the refusal by the employer to continue to employ any number of persons employed by him.

Employer cannot go for lock – out in the following cases:

1) During pendency of conciliation proceedings and 7 days thereafter.
2) During pendency of proceeding before Labour Court or Industrial Tribunal or National Tribunal:
3) During period of arbitration proceedings:
4) During period when settlement or award is in operation in respect of the matters covered by the award or settlement.

In HAL. Employees Union v. Presiding Officer. It was held that when lock out by employer is legal and justified, workmen are not entitled to compensation and wages for the period during which lock out continue. In case of illegal lock out, the employer can be punished with fine may extend to Rs.1,000/- and with imprisonment, which may extend to 1 month.

1) 1. The enquiry should be conducted by an unbiased person.
2. The enquiry officer should conduct the enquiry in an objective and fair manner.
3. The employee should be given a fair opportunity to defend himself.
4. proper procedure, rules, regulations etc. should be followed white conducting enquiry.

2) It has been held that if on the death of a fellow worker, the workmen acting in combination refuse to resume work, it amounts tostrike. [National Textiles Workers Union v. Meenakshi Mills]
3) Certain gardeners were appointed to look after the bungalow provided to the MD of the Company. The gardeners were supposed to mark their attendance in the Company Register and their salaries were being paid directly by the company. It was held that since the gardeners are working directly under the control of the company, they are workmen under the Industrial Dispute Act. [J.K. Cotton Spinning v. Weaving Mills Co. Ltd.]
4) The Supreme Court held that the teachers employed by the Educational Institutions cannot be considered as workmen within the Industrial Dispute Act, as imparting of education which is the main function of the teacher cannot be considered as skilled or unskilled manual work or supervisory work or technical work. [Sunderambal v. Government of Goa]
5) Unfair Labour Practices means any of the practices specified in the Vth Schedule to the industrial Disputes Act. This Schedule declares certain labour practices as unfair on the part of the employees and their trade unions and on the part of the workmen and their trade unions. Industrial Disputes Act prohibits commission of any unfair labour practice by Employers & Workmen.
6) The Supreme Court held that termination of services of a bus driver on the ground of weak eyesight does not amount to retrenchment under the Industrial Disputes Act because here the employees is being terminated on the ground of continued ill health and not because of surplus labour. [Anand Bihari v. Rajasthan State Road Transport]
7) It was held that a car driver engaged by area manager of a bank for which allowance was given to him was not a workman of the bank under Industrial Dispute Act, eventhough the car was maintained at the bank's expenses, as the control of the driver was not into the hands of the bank. [PNB v. Ghulam Dastagi]
8) An Industrial Dispute exists only when the same has been raised by the workman with the employer. A mere demand to the appropriate government without a dispute being raised by the workman with their employer, cannot become an industrial dispute. [Sindhu Resettlement Corporation ltd. v. Industrial Tribunal]
9) A workmen's case sponsored by a body of workmen either acting through their union or otherwise, would amount to an Industrial Dispute. [Newspaper Ltd., Allahabad v. Industrial Tribunal]
10) The term 'employment or non – employment' is concerned with the employees' failure or refusal to employ a workman. [Western India Automobile Association v. Industrial]
11) A Salesman, whose duties included manual as well as clerical work such as to attend to the customer, prepare cash memos, to assist manager in daily routine is a workman. [Carona Sahu Co. Ltd. v. Labour Court]

12) Refusal to do work which the employer has no right to ask for performance, such a refusal does not constitute a strike. [Northbrooke Jute Co. Ltd. v. Their Workman]
13) Where in pursuance of a common understanding the employees entered the premises of the Bank and refused to take their pens in their hands, it was held to be strike. [Punjab
National Bank Ltd. v. all India Punjab National Bank Employees' Federation]
14) Go – slow does not amount to strike. [Bharat Sugar Mills Ltd. v. Jai Singh]
15) Where the strike was resorted to by using violence or acts of sabotage or for any ulterior purpose, then the strike will be illegal. [Gujarat Steel Tubes Ltd. v. Gujarat Steel Tubes Majdoor Sabha]
16) When the workmen and the management are equally to be blamed for the strike, the Court normally awards half of the wages. [India Marine Service Pvt. Ltd. v. their Workmen]
17) A closure of a place of business for a short duration of 30 days in retaliation to certain acts of workmen was held to be a lockout. [Lord Krishna Sugar Mills Ltd. v. State of U.P]
18) Retrenchment does not include disengagement from service of persons employed for working on daily wages. [U.P. v. Labour court, Haldwani]
19) if the termination of an employees' service is a punishment inflicted by way of disciplinary action, such termination would not amount to retrenchment. [SBI v. Employees of SB]
20) Termination of service of casual workers after their work is over, is not a retrenchment. [Tapan Kumar Jana, v. The General Manager, Calcutta Telephones]
21) Where the services of an employee irregularly appointed were terminated, it was held to be a case of retrenchment. [Prabhudayal Jat v. Alwar Sehkari Bhumi Vikas Bank Ltd]
22) The use of force or violence or acts of sabotage resorted to by the workmen during a strike disentitles them to wages for the strike period. [Crompton Greaves Ltd. v. Workmen, Syndicate Bank v. Umesh Naik]
23) The Government employees have to fundamental right to resort to strike and they cannot take the society at ransom by going on strike, even if there is injustice to some extent. [T.K. Rangarajan v. Govt. of Tamil Nadu & Others]

Under Difference between lock-out and lay-off.

lock-out the employer refuses to give employment because of closing of a place of employment or suspension of work. Under lay-off the employer refuses to give employment because of shortage of coal, power or raw material or the accumulation of stocks or the breakdown of machinery or natural calamity or for any other reason to give employment.

(2) Lock-out is resorted to by the employer to coerce or pressurize the workmen to accept his demands; lay-off is for trade reason beyond the control of the employer.
(3) Lock-out is due to an industrial dispute and continues during the period of dispute; lay-off is not concerned with a dispute with the workmen.

Difference between lock-out and closure. Lock-out and closure of a business are often confused. This is because cessation of work is common to both.

Closure is a fundamental right and if it is not a lock-out, the workers cannot grudge [*J.K. Hosiery Factory v. Labour Appellate Tribunal,* A.I.R. (1956) All. 498]. The State cannot compel an employer to carry on his business because several employees may be thrown out of employment if it is closed. The grounds for closure of a business may be actual loss or apprehended loss. It may also be disinclination to run the risk of running the business [*Indian Metal & Metallurgical Corpn. V. Industrial Tribunal, Madras,* 3 F. J.R. 420 High Court, Madras].

The points of difference between a lock-out and closure are as follows:

(1) In the case of lock-out it is only the place of business which is closed (and not the business itself), while in the case of closure of a business not only the place of business but the business itself is closed [*Express Newspapers (Pvt.) Ltd. V. Their Workmen,*
A.I.R. (1963) S.C. 569]. The closure of a business indicates the final and irrevocable termination of the business itself. Lock-out, on the other hand, indicates the closure of the place of business or the place of employment and not the closure of the business itself.

(2) Lock-out is a weapon of coercion in the hands of employer; closure is generally for trade reasons.

(3) In closure there is severance of employment relationship whereas in lock-out there is no severance but only suspension of such relationship.

(4) A lock-out is caused by the existence or apprehension of an industrial dispute whereas a closure need not be in consequence of an industrial dispute.

National Tribunal [Sec. 2 (n)]. It means— any railway a National Industrial Tribunal constituted under Sec. 7-B.

Public utility service [Sec.2 (n)]. **It means**

(i) Any railway service or any transport service for the carriage of passengers or goods by air;

(ii) Any service in , or in connection with the working of, any major port or dock;

(iii) Any section of an industrial establishment, on the working of which the safety of the establishment or the workmen employed therein depends;

(iv) Any postal, telegraph, or telephone service;

(v) Any industry which supplies power, light or water to the public;

(vi) Any system of public conservancy or sanitation;

(vii) Any industry specified in the First Schedule.

The appropriate Government may, if satisfied that public emergency or interest so requires, by notification in the Official gazette, declare any industry specified in the First Schedule to be public utility service for the purposes of the Industrial disputes Act for such period as may be specified in the notification. The period so specified shall not, in the first instance, exceed 6 month. But it may, by a like notification, be extended from time to time by any period not exceeding 6 month at any time if in the opinion of the appropriate government, public emergency or public interest requires such extension. The first schedule is reproduced below.

Difference between 'retrenchment' and 'closure'. The important points of difference between 'retrenchment' and 'closure' may be enumerated as follows;

(1) Retrenchment is the termination by the employer of the service of the workman for any reason whatsoever, otherwise than as punishment inflicted by way of disciplinary action. It affects only some of the workmen. Closure, on the other hand, means closing down of the business of trade reasons and it affects all the workmen.

(2) In case of retrenchment the services of workmen are terminated on account of surplus labour; while in case of closure it is on account of total closure of work by an employer.

(3) In retrenchment the trade or business remains uninterrupted as it continues; while in closure the business itself is discontinued.

(4) The compensation payable to a workman on retrenchment either on account of surplus labour or closure, shall be equivalent to 15 days' average pay for every completed year of continuous service or any part thereof in excess of 6 months. Retrenchment as a result of bona fide closure of business does not entail any compensation beyond average pay for 3 months.

Difference between lock-out and retrenchment.

(1) Lock-out is temporary; retrenchment is permanent. Retrenchment results in complete severance of industrial relationship between an employer and an employee while lockout keeps this relationship alive even during the cessation of work. The former results in severance of relationship between the employer and employee while the latter amounts to only suspension of the relationship.

(2) Lock-out is with a motive to coerce the workmen to accept the demands of the employer retrenchment is resorted to dispense with surplus labour.

(3) Lock-out is due to and during an industrial dispute; there is no such dispute in case of retrenchment.

CHAPTER 6

Workmen's Compensation Act 1923

Introduction

This Act provides social security to workmen. Under this Act, a workman who dies or suffers disablement, partial or total, due to an accident is entitled to get compensation from his employer.

Applicability of the Act

A workman covered under ESI Act, 1948 is not entitled to get compensation under Workmen's Compensation Act. 1923. Thus, Act is applicable to those factories, mines, transport establishment, construction works, etc. Which are not covered under ESI Act, 1948.

Meaning of Workman

Workman means the following:

(i) Railway servant"
(ii) Crew of ship;
(iii) Crew of aircraft;
(iv) Driver, cleaner, helper or mechanic of motor vehicles;
(v) Workman recruited abroad;
(vi) Person employed in activities like manufacturing process, explosive, mines, shop loading/ unloading, construction, electricity generation and distribution, drivers, horticulture, circus.
(vii) Persons employed in cultivation of land, fishing, rearing of livestock. If the number of persons employed there is more than 25.

Every employee including those employed through contractor who is engaged for the purpose of employer's business is eligible for workman's compensation. However, casuals employees and employees engaged in clerical capacity neither are nor covered.

In case of contract labour, the principle employer is liable to pay compensation in the same manner, as he is liable for his departmental labour, However, he is entitled to be indemnified by the contractor for such compensation. [Managing Director, Orissa State Warehousing Corporation V. Smt, Geetarani]

Employer's Liability for Compensation

An employer is liable to pay compensation if personal injury is caused to a workman ny accident arising out of and in the course of his employment.

However, an employer is not liable in the following.

(1) Injury which results in total or partial disablement of workman up to 3 days;

(2) Injury caused by an accident directly attributable to the following:

(a) Workman working under the influence of drinks or drugs; (b) Willful disobedience of express order of safety; (c) Willful removal of safety guards or devices.

However in a such cases, if the workman does or suffers permanent total disablement the employer will be liable.

Further, an employer is liable to a workman, if a workman contract any specified occupational disease while he is in the service of the employer for at least 6 months.

If may be noted that compensation is payable even when there is no fault of the employer; except the aforesaid cases where the compensation is not payable./ The compensation is payable even if it is found that the employee did not take proper precaution or he was careless or negligible in the performance of his work.

Amount of compensation payable

Compensation is payable to workman in case of partial or total disablement. It is payable to dependants of workman in case of death.

It maybe be noted that compensation is an amount equal to 50% of monthly wages deceased workman multiplied by a factor depending on the age of the workman (more than age, lower the compensation), subject to a minimum compensation of Rs. 80,000/-. In addition to this funeral expenses of Rs. 2,500/- are also paid.

In case of permanent of total disablement, compensation payable is an amount equal to 60% of monthly wages o disabled workman multiplied by a factor depending on the age of the workman (more the age, lo9wer the compensation), subject to a minimum compensation of Rs. 90,000/-

In case of permanent partial disablement, compensation is paid based on percentage of loss of earning capacity.

Accident arising out of and in the course of employment.

Accident arising out of employment: An accident arising out of employment implies a proximate and direct connection between the accidental injury and the employment. In this case, the compensation will be payable if the accident has occurred at the place where the workman was performing his duties.

Accident in the course of employment: An accident in the course of employment implies a casual connection between the accidental injury and the employment. In this case, for the payment of compensation it is not necessary that the accident occurred at the place where the workman was performing his duties, Further, it is also not necessary that the workman must be actually working at the time of his death.

It is well established that there must be some casual connection between the death of the worker and his employment. If the workman dies, as a natural result of the disease from which he was suffering then it will be considered that he has died .of that disease as a wear and tear of his employment and hence no liability would be fixed upon the employer. However, if the employment is contributory cause or has accelerated the death, or if the reason of the death is not only the disease but also the disease coupled with the employment then it could be said that the death arose in the course of the employment and the employer would be liable.

Employer's liability when contractor is engaged

Section 12 makes the employer liable for compensation to such workmen hired by the contractor under following circumstances:

(a) The contractor is engaged to do a work which is part of the trade or business of the employer(called principal);

(b) The workmen were engaged in the course of or for the purpose of his trade or business; and

(c) The accident occurred in or about the premises on which the principal employer has undertaken or undertakes to execute the work concerned.

The amount of compensation shall be calculated with reference to the wages of the workman under the employer by whom he is immediately employed.

Important Points

1) A workman who was on duty had gone to the canteen to take tea where he died. It has been held that the accidental injury arose in the course of employment and the period of recess did not disrupt the continuity of employment. **[Regional Director v. Batul Bibi]**
2) A factory worker suffering from a heart disease while coming out of the factory died inside the factory premises. The stress and strain of work were the accelerating factors to death and therefore the employer was liable to pay the compensation. **[D.N.K Project v. Smt. D. Buchitalli]**
3) A workman .died on duty by heart attack after receiving continuous threats on his life from thieves who he prevented successfully. It has been held that his widow will be entitled to compensation under this Act. **[Smt. A. Seetharamma v. G.M., SouthEastern Railways]**
4) Where an employee was under a contractual obligation to use only a particular means of transport, the area or field of employment would stand extended to the course of the said transport. Accident sustained by transport staff while traveling between depot and residence or vice versa must be treated arising in the course of employment. **[BEST Undertaking v. Mrs. Agnes]**
5) Where the deceased workman was standing in the queue waiting for the bus provided by the employer for reaching the place of work and was run over by the bus by which he was to travel it was held that the workman has died as result of employment injury.
[ESIC v. Sayeeda Khatoon Dannawal]
6) It has been held that an employer will be liable to pay compensation if workman meets with an accident while proceeding to his workplace on a bicycle. **[Indian Rare Earth Ltd. v, Surinder Beevi]**
7) Where a mill worker was stabbed in a communal riot while he was returning home sometime after midnight after the night shift and died just at a short distance from the mill, . it was held that the case clearly falls within the meaning of employment injury. **[Ahmed Khan Pathan v. ESIC]**

8) If a workman suffers as a result of an injury from a physical defect which does not infact reduce his capacity to work but at the same time makes his labour unsaleable in any market. he can establish a right to compensation provided he proves that he had been turned away by a reasonable number of likely employers on account of such defect. **[Sukhai v. Hukam Chand Jute Mills Ltd.]** .
9) If after the accident a worker has become disabled. and cannot do a particular job but the employer offers him another kind of job, the worker is entitled to compensation for partial disablement. **[General Manager, G.I.P. Rly. v. Shankar]**
10) If due to any physical defect, a workman is unable to get any work which a workman of his class ordinarily performs, and has thus lost the power to earn, he is entitled to compensation for total disablement. **[Ball v. William Hunt & Sons Ltd.]**
11) In a case permanent partial disability caused to a workman in accident while working on ship, it was held that workman can be said to have lost his earning capacity even though getting same amount of wages as before. **[Mangru Palji v. Robinsons]**
12) Where a carpenter had amputated his left ann from elbow while working in the factory, it was held to be a case of total disablement. **[Pratap Narain Singh Deo v. Sriniwas Sabata]**
13) Where an electrician who had to go frequently to a heating room from a cooling plant, contracted pneumonia resulting in his death, it was held that the injury caused by an accident is not confined to physical injury and includes nervous shock or break down or mental strain. **[Indian News Chronicle v. Mrs. Lazarus]**
14) Where a workman suffers from heart disease and dies on account of strain of work by keeping continuously standing or working, it was held that the accident arose out of employment. **[Laxmibai Atmaram v. Bomba}' Port Trust]**
15) A workman while returning home after duty was murdered within the premises of the employer. It was held that there was a close and proximate connection between the accident and the employment and hence his wife was entitled to compensation. **[Naima Bibi v. Lodhne Colliery Ltd.]**.
16 Where the workman, a state employee, received injury while performing the electrification work of the town entrusted to state employees by the Municipal Board, it was held that the state and not the board was liable to pay compensation because execution of electrical project was not the ordinary, business of the Municipal Board .
17) Where the cartman engaged by a Rice Mill to carry rice bags from mill to railway station met with an accident on a public road while returning back from railway station resulting in his death, it was held that the Mill Owner was liable to pay compensation.
18) The Supreme Court held that there should be some connection, casual or direct, between the injury/accident and the employment in order to get the compensation under Workmen's Compensation Act. Where a workman has exposed himself to an added peril by his own imprudent act, then the employee will not be eligible for compensation. **[Machenzie v. I.M .. Issak]**

CHAPTER 7

Payment of Wages Act, 1936

Extent of the Act

The Act extends to the whole of India [Sec. 1 (2). It was extended to Jammu and Kashmir by the Central Labour Laws (Extension to Jammu and Kashmir) Act, 1970.

Application of the Act

- The Act applies to the payment of wages to persons employed in any factory, to persons employed (otherwise than in a factory) upon any railway by a railway administration and to an industrial or other establishment specified in Clauses (a) to (g) of Sec. 2 (ii) (which defines industrial or other establishment).
- The persons employed upon a railway by a railway administration may have been employed either directly or through a sub-contractor by a person fulfilling a contract with a railway administration [Sec. 1 (4)].
- The State Government may after giving 3 months' notice extend the provisions of the Act to the payment of wages to any class of persons employed in any industrial establishment or class of establishments specified by the Central Government or a State Government under Clause (h) of Sec. 2 (ii) [Sec. 1 (5)].
- In case of industrial establishments owned by the Central government, such notification can be issued with the concurrence of the Central Government [Proviso to Sec. 1 (5)].

In various States the Act has been extended to shops and establishments also.

The Act does not apply to persons whose wages exceed Rs. 6,500 per month [Sec. 1 (6)]. This limit was raised from Rs. 1,600 to Rs. 6,500 by the Payment of Wages (Amendment) Act, 2005.

Reference to Sections in this Chapter. Reference to Sections in this Chapter, un less otherwise indicated, is to the Payment of Wages Act, 1936.

Industrial or other establishment [Sec. 2 (ii)]. It means any—

(a) Tramway service, or motor transport service engaged in carrying passengers or goods or both by road for hire or reward;

(aa) air transport service other than such service belonging to or exclusively employed in the military, naval or air force of the Union or the Civil Aviation Department of the Government of India;

(b) dock, wharf or jetty;
(c) inland vessel, mechanically propelled;
(d) mine, quarry or oilfield; (e) plantation;
(f) workshop or other establishment in which articles are produced, adapted or manufactured, with a view to their use, transport or sale;
(g) establishment in which any work relating to the construction, development or maintenance of buildings, roads, bridges or canals, or relating to operations connected with navigation, irrigation or supply of water or relating to the transmission or distribution of electricity or any other form of power is being carried on;

Wages [Sec. 2 (vi)].

"*Wages*' means all remuneration (whether by way of salary, allowances or otherwise) expressed in terms of money or capable of being so expressed which would, if the terms of employment, express or implied, were fulfilled, be payable to a person employed in respect of his employment or of work done in such employment. Simply stated, '*wages*' means all remuneration due to any worker or employee if the terms of contract of employment are fulfilled.

The definition of expression '*wages*' is made sufficiently wide by including within the expression:
(a) any remuneration payable under any award or settlement between the parties or order of a Court;
(b) any remuneration to which the person employed is entitled in respect of overtime work or holidays or any leave period:
(c) any additional remuneration payable under the terms of employment (whether called a bonus or by any other name);
(d) any sum which by reason of the termination of employment of the person employed is payable under any law, contract or instrument which provides for the payment of such sum, whether with or without deductions, but does not provide for the time within which the payment is to be made;
(e) any sum to which the person employed is entitled under any scheme framed under any law for the time being in force.

The expression 'wages' does not include:
(1) any bonus (whether under a scheme of profit-sharing or otherwise) which does not form part of the remuneration payable under the terms of employment or which is not payable under any award or settlement between the parties or order of a Court;
(2) the value of any house accommodation, or of the supply of light, water, medical attendance or other amenity or of any service excluded from the computation of wages by a general or special order of the State Government;
(3) any contribution paid by the employer to any pension or provident fund, and the interest which may have accrued thereon;
(4) any travelling allowance or the value of any travelling concession;
(5) any sum paid to the employed person to defray special expenses entailed on him by the nature of his employment; and
(6) any gratuity payable on the termination of employment in cases other than those specified in Clause (d) above.

The definition of the expression 'wages' comprises 3 parts:

The *first* part declares that *'wages'* means all remunerations which would, if the terms of the contract of employment, exp0ress or implied, were fulfilled, be payable to a person employed, in respect of his employment. This clause presents no difficulty whatsoever for it declares in an unambiguous language that an employee is entitled to receive wages in accordance with the terms of his contract.

The *second* part says that the expression *'wages'* shall include any bonus or other remuneration of the nature aforesaid which would be so payable, i.e., payable in accordance with the terms of the contract.

The *third* part declares that the expression *'wages'* shall include 'any sum' payable to such person by reason of the termination of his employment. The language of this clause is wide enough to embrace not only a sum payable to an employee under the terms of a contract but also a sum payable to him under the provisions of any law.

Fixation of wage-periods (Sec. 4)

Every person responsible for the payment of wages under Sec. 3 shall fix periods, known as wage-periods, in respect of which such wages shall be payable [Sec. 4 (1)]. A wage-period shall not exceed one month [Sec. 4 (2)].

Time of payments of wages (Sec. 5)

The rules relating to time of payment of wages are as follows:

Wages to be paid before 7th or 10th day.

- The wages of every person employed upon or in any railway, factory or industrial or other establishment upon or in which less than 1,000 persons are employed, shall be paid before the expiry of 7th day of the following wage-period.
- In case the number of workers exceeds 1,000, the wages shall be paid before the expiry of the 10th day of the following wage-period [Sec. 5 (1)].
- In the case of persons employed on a clock, wharf or jetty or in a mine, the balance of wages due on completion of the final tonnage account of the ship or wagons loaded or unloaded, as the case may be, shall be paid before the expiry of the 7th day from the day of such completion [Proviso to Sec. 5 (1)].

Deductions which may be made from wages (Sec. 7)

Kinds of deductions

1. **Deductions for fines** [Secs. 7 (2) (a) and 8]
2. **Deductions for absence from duty** [Secs. 7 (2) (b) and 9]
3. **Deductions for damage or loss** [Secs. 7 (2) (c), (m), (n) and (o) and 10]
4. **Deductions for services** [Secs. 7 (2) (d), (e) and 11]
5. **Deductions for recovery of advances** [Secs. 7 (2) (f) and 12]
6. **Deductions for recovery of loans** [Secs. 7 (2) (fff) and 12-A)
7. **Deductions for payments to co-operative societies and insurance schemes** [Secs. 7 (2) (i) and (k) and 13]

Other deductions

Deductions made, with the written authorization of the employed person, for contribution to the Prime Minister's National Relief Fund or to such other Fund as may be specified by the appropriate Government [Sec. 7 (2) (p). [This Clause was added by the Payment of Wages (Amendment) Act, 1976]; and

Limit on deductions [Sec. 7 (3)]

- The total amount of deductions which may be made under the above heads [Sec. 7 (2)] in a wage-period from the wages of any employed person shall not exceed 75 per cent of such wages in cases where such deductions are wholly or partly made for payments to co-operative societies under Sec. 7 (2) (i).
- In any other case, they shall not exceed 50 per cent of such wages [Sec. 7 (3)].
- Where the total deductions authorised under Sec. 7 (2) exceed 75 per cent, or as the case may be, 50 per cent of the wages, the excess may be recovered in such manner as may be prescribed [Proviso to Sec. 7 (3|)].

MAINTENANCE OF REGISTERS AND RECORDS

Who may file application? An application for claims arising under the Act may be filed by—

(a) the person employed himself, or
(b) any legal practitioner, or
(c) any official of a registered trade union authorised in writing to act on his behalf, or
(d) any Inspector under the Act, or
(e) any other person acting with the permission of the Authority appointed under Sec. 15 (1) [Sec. 15 (2)].

Application to be filed within 12 months.

- Every application for claims under the Act shall be presented within 12 months from the date on which the deduction from the wages was made or from the date on which the payment of the wages was due to is made [Proviso 1 to Sec. 15 (2)].
- An application may also be admitted after 12 months if the applicant satisfies the Authority that there was a sufficient cause for not making the application within 12 months [Proviso 2 to Sec. 15 (2)].

Procedure

- When any application for claims under the Act is entertained, the Authority shall hear the applicant and the employer or other persons responsible for the payment of wages under Sec. 3, or give them an opportunity of being heard.
- The Authority shall make such further inquiry as may be necessary. It may direct the refund to be made to the employed person of the amount deducted or the payment of the delayed wages, together with such compensation as it may think fit.
- The compensation shall not exceed 10 times the amount improperly deducted, and not exceeding Rs. 3,000 but not less than Rs. 1,500 in case of delayed wages.
- Even where the deducted or delayed wages are paid before the disposal of the application, the Authority may direct the payment of such compensation as it may think fit.

- This amount of compensation shall however not exceeds Rs. 2,000 [Sec. 15 (3)].

Appeal (Sec. 17)

An appeal may be preferred in a Presidency-town before the Court of Small Causes and elsewhere before the District Court against—

(i) an order dismissing either wholly or in part an application made under Sec. 15 (2), or

(ii) a direction made under Sec. 15 (3) by the Authority to refund to the employed person the amount deducted from wages or under Sec. 15 (4) by the Authority for payment of penalty to the employer.

The appeal may be preferred within 30 days of the date on which the order or direction was made [Sec. 17 (1)].

The Court may, if it thinks fit, submit any question of law for the decision of the High Court and, if it so does, shall decide the question in conformity with such decision [Sec. 17 (4)].

CHAPTER 8

Minimum Wages Act, 1948

The object of the Act is to secure the welfare of the workers in a competitive market by 'fixing the minimum rates of wages in certain employments. The Legislature undoubtedly intended to apply the Act to those industries or localities in which, by reason of causes such as unorganized labour or absence of machinery for regulation of wages, wages paid to workers were, in the light of the general level of wages and subsistence level, inadequate [*Bhikusa Yamasa Kshatriya v. Sangammer Akola Taluka, Bidi Kamgar Union,* A.I.R. (1963) S.C. 806].

The Minimum Wages Act was passed in 1948 enabling the Central and State Governments to fix minimum rates of wages payable to employees in a selected number of 'sweated' industries.

The Act applies to the whole of India.

Wages [Sec. 2 (h)].

'Wages' means all remuneration, capable of being expressed in terms of money, which would, if the terms of the contract of employment, express or implied, were fulfilled, be payable to a person employed in respect of his employment or work done in such employment. It includes house rent allowance but does not include—

(i) The value of—
   (a) Any house accommodation, supply of light, water, medical attendance, or
   (b) Any other amenity or any service excluded by general or special order of the appropriate Government;

(ii) Any contribution paid by the employer to any Pension Fund or Provident Fund or under any scheme of social insurance;

(iii) Any travelling allowance or the value of any travelling concession;

(iv) Any sum paid to the person employed to defray special expenses entailed on him by the nature of his employment; or

(v) Any gratuity payable on discharge.

Fixing of minimum rates of wages (Sec. 3)

The responsibility for fixing the minimum rates of wages is that of the appropriate Government. Sec. 3 provides that the appropriate Government—

(a) shall fix the minimum rates of wages payable to employees employed in an employment specified in Part I or part II of the Schedule (reproduced earlier) and in an employment added to either Part by notification in the Official *Gazette* [Sec. 3 (1) (a)];

(b) may, in respect of employees employed in an employment specified in Part II of the Schedule, instead of fixing minimum rates of wages for the whole State, fix such rates for a part of the State or for any specified class or classes of such employment in the whole State or part thereof [Proviso to Sec. 3 (1) (a)];

(c) shall review at such intervals not exceeding 5 years, the minimum rates of wages so fixed and revise the minimum rates if necessary [Sec. 3 (1) (b)].

Minimum number of employees.

- The appropriate Government may refrain from fixing minimum rates of wages in respect of any scheduled employment in which there are in the whole State less than 1,000 employees engaged in such employment.
- But if at any time, the appropriate Government comes to a finding after an inquiry that the number of employees in any scheduled employment has risen to 1,000 or more, it shall fix minimum rates of wages payable as soon as may be after such finding [Sec. 3 (1-A)].

Minimum rates. The appropriate Government may fix—

(a) a minimum rate of wages for time work (referred to as 'a minimum time rate');

(b) a minimum rate of wages for piece work (referred to as 'a minimum piece rate');

(c) a minimum rate of remuneration to apply in the case of such employees employed on piece work for purpose of securing to such employees a minimum rate of wages on a time work basis (referred to as 'a guaranteed time rate');

(d) a minimum rate (whether a time rate or a piece rate) to apply in substitution for the minimum rate which would otherwise be applicable, in respect of overtime work done by employees (referred to as 'overtime rate') [Sec. 3 (2)].

Advisory Board (Sec. 7)

For the purpose of coordinating the work of committees and sub-committees appointed under Sec. 5 and advising the appropriate Government generally in the matter of fixing and revising minimum rates of wages, the appropriate Government shall appoint an Advisory Board (Sec. 7).

No procedure is prescribed in the Act for the Advisory Board to function. It can devise its own procedure *[State of Rajasthan v. Hari Ram Nathwani,* A.I.R. (1976) S.C. 277].

Composition of Committees and Advisory Board (Sec. 9).

Each of the committees, sub-committees and the Advisory Board shall consist of persons to be nominated by the appropriate Government representing employers and employees in the scheduled employments, who shall be equal in number, and independent persons not exceeding 1/3rd of its total number of members. One of the independent persons shall be appointed the Chairman by the appropriate Government.

Wages in kind (Sec. 11)

- Minimum wages payable under the Act shall be paid in cash [Sec. 11 (1)]. But where it has been the custom to pay wages wholly or partly in kind, the appropriate Government may, by notification in the *Official Gazette,* authorise the payment of minimum wages either wholly or partly in kind [Sec. 11 (2)].
- The appropriate Government may also by notification in the Official *Gazette* authorise the provision of the supply of essential commodities at concessional rates [Sec. 11 (3)].
- The cash value of wages in kind [under Sec. 11 (2)] and of concession in respect of supplies of essential commodities at concessional rates authorised under Sec. 11 (2) and (3) shall be estimated in the prescribed manner [Sec. 11 (4)].

Payment of minimum rate of wages (Sec. 12)

- Where in respect of any scheduled employment minimum wages have been fixed, the employer shall pay to every employee wages at a rate not less than the minimum rate of wages fixed for that class of employees in the employment.
- Such wages shall be paid without any deductions except as may be authorised. Where the contract rate of wages is higher, the statutory obligation does not come into play [Sec. 12 (1)].

Sec. 12 does not affect the provisions of the Payment of Wages Act, 1936 [Sec. 12 (2)].

Fixing hours for a normal working day, etc. (Sec. 13)

In regard to any scheduled employment where minimum rates of wages have been fixed, the appropriate Government may—

(a) fix the number of hours of work which constitute a normal working day, inclusive of one or more specified intervals;

(b) provide for a day of rest in every period of 7 days and for payment of remuneration in respect of such day of rest;

(c) provide for payment for work on a day of rest at a rate not less than the overtime rate [Sec. 13 (1)].

Provisions of Sec. 13 (1) to apply subject to conditions.

In relation to the following classes of employees, the provisions of Sec. 13 (1) shall apply only to such extent and subject to such conditions as may be prescribed;

(a) employees engaged on urgent work, or in any emergency which could not have been foreseen or prevented;

(b) employees engaged in work in the nature of preparatory or complementary work which must necessarily be carried on outside the limits laid down for the general working in the employment concerned;

(c) employees whose employment is essentially intermittent;

(d) employees engaged in any work which for technical reasons has to be completed before the duty is over;

(e) employees engaged in work which could not be carried on except at times dependent on the irregular action of natural forces [Sec. 13 (2)].

Intermittent employment.

The employment of an employee is essentially intermittent when it is declared to be so by the appropriate Government. The appropriate Government declares an employment **as intermittent on the ground that the daily** hours of duty of the employee normally include periods of inaction during which the employee may be on duty but is not called upon to display either physical activity or sustained attention [Sec. 13. (3)].

Rates of overtime (Sec. 14)

Where an employee, whose minimum rate of wages is fixed under this Act, by the hour, by the day or by such longer wage-period as may be prescribed, works overtime, the employer shall pay him for every hour or for part of an hour so worked in excess, wages at the rates fixed for overtime work under the Act or under any law of the appropriate Government in force, whichever is higher [Sec. 14 (1)].

The provisions of the minimum Wages Act, 1948 do not prejudice the operation of the provisions of Sec. 59 of the Factories Act, 1948 in any case where those provisions are applicable [sec .14 (2)].

Wages of worker who works for less than normal working day (Sec. 15)

Sometimes an employee whose minimum rate of wages has been fixed by the day may work on any day on which he was employed for as period less than the requisite number of hours constituting a normal working day. In that case he is entitled to receive wages in respect of work done by him on that day as if he had worked for a full normal working day except—

(1) where his failure to work is cause by his unwillingness to work and not by omission of the employer to provide him with work, and

(2) in such other cases and circumstances as may be prescribed.

Wages for two or more classes of work (Sec.16)

Where an employee does two or more classes of work to each of which a different minimum rate of wages is applicable, the employer shall pay to such employee in respect of the time respectively occupied in each such class of work, wages at not less than the minimum rate in force in respect of each such class.

Minimum time rate wages for piece work (Sec.17)

Where an employee is employed on piece work for which minimum time rate and not a minimum piece rate has been fixed under the Act, the employer shall pay to such employee wages at not less than the minimum time rate.

Maintenance of registers and records (Sec. 18)

- Every employer shall maintain registers and records giving particulars of employees employed by him, the work performed by them and such other particulars and in such form as may be prescribed [Sec. 18 (1)].
- He shall also keep exhibited notices in the prescribed form containing prescribed particulars in the prescribed manner in the factory, workshop or place where the employees in the schedule employment may be employed.

- In the case of out-workers, he shall keep these notices exhibited in such factory, workshop or place as may be used for giving out-work to them [sec. 18. (2)].
- The appropriate Government may, by rules made under the Act, provide for the issue of wages books or wage slips to employees employed in any scheduled employment in respect of which minimum rates of wages have been fixed.
- It may also prescribe the manner in which entries shall be made and authenticated in such wage books or wage slips by the employer or his agent [sec. 18 (3)].

ENFORCEMENT OF THE ACT

(Secs. 19 TO 21)

Powers of Inspectors. An Inspector May—

(a) enter at all reasonable hours, with such assistants as he thinks fit, any premises or place where employees are employed or work is given out to out-workers in any scheduled employment in respect of which minimum rate of wages have been fixed, for the purpose of examining any register, record of wages or notices required to be kept or exhibited by or under the Act or rules made there under, and required the production thereof for inspection;

(b) examine any person whom he finds in any such premises or place and who, he has reasonable cause to believe, is an employee employed therein or an employee to whom out-work is given;

(c) require any person giving out-work and any out-workers, to give any information, which is in his power to give, with respect to the names and addresses of the persons to, for and from whom the work is given out or received, and with respect to the payments to be made for the work;

(d) seize or take copies of such register, record of wages or notices as he may consider relevant in respect of an offence under the Act which he has reason to believe has been committed by and employer; and exercise such other powers as may be prescribed [sec. 19

3.6 THE EMPLOYEES' PROVIDENT FUNDS AND MISCELLANEOUS PROVISION ACT, 1952

APPLICABILITY OF PE ACT

[Sec. 1]

- Factory
  1. every establishment which is a factory engaged in any industry specified in schedule I and in which 20 or more persons are employed on any single day, and
  2. any other establishment employing 20 or more persons or class of such establishments which the Central Government may, by notification in the Official Gazette, specify in this behalf.

- **Extension**

The Central Government by notification in the Official Gazette –

(a) add to Schedule I any other industry, where it is of the opinion that a Provident fund scheme should be framed under this Act.[Sec. 4]

(b) may extend the provisions of this act to an establishment employing less than 20 persons after giving not less than 2 months notice of its intention.

- **Voluntary:**

The central PF Commissioner may apply of this Act on an application received from employer and majority of employees by notification in the Office Gazette.

- **Established to include all departments and branches [Sec. 2A]:**

If established consists of different departments of branches, whether situated in the same place or in different places, they shall be treated as part of the same establishment

- **Composite Factories:**

Composite Factories engaged in more than one industry, which may include activities covered in Schedule I as well as other activities. The test for determining the applicability of the Act is whether the activity falling in Schedule I is its primary and domination activity.

NON – APPLICABLE OF PF ACT [Sec. 16]

- **Co-operative Society**

An establishment fulfilling the following conditions:

(a) The establishment has been registered under the Co-operative Societies Act.

(b) It employs less than 50 persons.

(c) It is working without the aid of power

- **Government Undertaking**

Any establishment fulfilling the following conditions:

(a) It belongs to the CG or SG, or is under the control of CG or SG.

(b) The employees of the establishment are entitled to benefit of contributory provident fund or old age pension.

- **Undertaking constituted under an Act**

Any establishment fulfilling the following conditions:

(a) It has been set up under any Central or State or provincial Act.

(b) The employees of the establishment are entitled to benefit of contributory provident fund or old age pension.

- **Power of Central Government to exempt certain Establishments [Sec. 16(2)]**

(a) The Central Government may exempt certain establishments / class of establishments from the applicability of this Act by way of a notification in the Official Gazette.

(b) The exemption is granted taking into consideration –

- the financial position or
- other circumstances of the case and
- on the opinion of the Central Government that is expedient as specified, either prospectively or retrospectively.

DEFINITIONS [Sec. 2]

- **Appropriate Government [Sec. 2(a)]**
- ***AG means CG in the following cases:***

(i) In relation to an establishment belonging to, or under the control of, CG.

(ii) In relation to an establishment connected with a railway company, a major port, a mine or an oil field or a controlled industry.

(iii) In relation to an establishment having departments or branches in more than one State.

- ***In relation to any other establishment, AG means SG.***
- **Authorized officer [Sec. 2(aa)]**
  - Central Provident Fund Commissioner
  - Additional Provident Fund Commissioner
  - Deputy Provident Fund Commissioner
  - Regional Provident Fund Commissioner
  - Such other officer as may be authorized by CG, by notification in Official Gazette.
- **Basic wages [Sec. 2(b)]**
- ***'Basic wages' means –***
  - all emoluments
  - Which are earned by an employee
  - In accordance with the terms of the contract of employment
  - Which are paid or payable in cash to him
  - While

    (a) on duty; or

    (b) while on leave with wages; or (c) while on holidays with wages.
- **'Basic wages' does not include –**

(a) the cash value of any food concession

(b) any dearness allowance (i.e., all cash payments by whatever name called, paid to an employee on account of a rise in the cost of living)

(c) house – rent allowance, overtime allowance

- **Employer [Sec. 2(e)]**
- ***In relation to an establishment which is a factory, employer means-***

(a) the owner or occupier of the factory (Occupier means the person who has ultimate control over the affairs of the factory);

(b) the agent of such owner or occupier,

(c) the legal representative of a deceased owner or occupier (d) Person named as a manager of the factory under the Factories Act.

- ***In relation to any other establishment, employer means –***

(a) the person having the ultimate control over the affairs of the establishment;

(b) the manager or the managing director to whom the affairs of the establishment are entrusted.

- **Employee**
- ***Employee means any person –***
  - who is employed for wages
  - in any kind of work, whether manual or otherwise,

- in or in connection with the work of an establishment
- who gets his wages directly or indirectly from the employer.

•***Employee includes any person –***

(i) employed by or through a contractor in or in connection with the work of establishment

(ii) engaged as an apprentice (not being an apprentice under the Apprentices Act, 1961or under the standing order of the established)

• Factory [Sec.2(g)]

Factory means –

- any premises including the precincts thereof
- in any of which a manufacturing process is being carried on or is ordinary so carried on,
- whether with the aid of power or without the aid of power

• Exempted employee [Sec.2(ff)]

Exempted employee means an employee to whom the Scheme does not apply by reason of exemption granted u/s 17-

• Exempted [Sec. 2(e) M 95, M 07

• In relation to – An establishment which is a Factory

- The owner or occupier of the factory, including agent of such owner or occupier,
- The legal representative of a deceased owner or occupier, and
- Where a person has been named as a manager of the factory u/s 7 of the factories Act, the person so named.

•Any other Establishment

- The person, who, or the Authority which, has the ultimate control over the affairs of the establishment, and
- Where the said affairs are entrusted to a manager, managing director or managing Agent, then such manager, managing director or managing agent.

• Manufacture or manufacturing process [Sec. 2(ic)]

Manufacture or manufacturing process means any process for making, altering repairing ornamenting finishing, packing, oiling, washing cleaning breaking up, demolishing or otherwise treating or adapting any article or substance with a view to its use, sale, transport, delivery or disposal

• Industry [Sec. 2(i)]

Industry means any Industry specified in Schedule I, and includes any other industry added to the Schedule by notification u/s 4.

The following have been held to be "Industries" –

(a) A Company doing business in renewing and reconditioning worn – out machine parts.

(b) A Company carrying on the work of repair and servicing of Motor Cars.

(c) Sugar Factory, Confectionery, and Distillery located within one compound is one Factory.

(d) A Laundry in which mechanical power was used for driving machines used in the aid of the work of washing clothes.

(e) Department of publications and press run by a University.

THE CENTRAL BOARD (Sec. 5A)

Both Central Board of Trustees and Executive Committee under the EPF Act, are constituted by the Central Government by Notification in the Official Gazette. The following are the comparative points of composition etc –

• Administration of fund

- The fund vests in and is administered by Central Board of Trustees, i.e. Board of Trustees or simply the Board.
- The Central Board is formed by CG by notification in the Official Gazette.
- In other words, Central Board shall administer the following funds:
  (a) The Employees Provident Fund
  (b) The Employees Pension Fund
  (c) The Employees Deposit Linked Insurance Fund.

• Board is a body corporate

The Board of Trustees is a body corporate having perpetual succession and common seal.

• Composition of Board

1	Chairman	
1	Vice Chairman	
1	Central Provident fund commissioner	
Maximum officials 5	Representing CG	
Maximum officials 15	Representing SG	
10 persons	Representing employers	- appointed by CG in consultation with association of employers
10 persons	Representing employees	- appointed by CG in consultation with organization of employees.

• Function of Central Board

Rights / Function	Duties
1. Administration of the Fund: Rights to administer the fund subject to Sec. 6A and 6C in such manner as specified in the scheme.	1. Maintenance of Proper Accounts: To maintain proper accounts of Income and expenditure in such from and manner as the Central Government may specify.
2. Performing Other Functions: Perform such other functions as required of it under the Provident Fund Scheme, Family Pension Scheme and Insurance Scheme.	2. Audit of Accounts: To get the accounts audited annually by the C & AG of India.
3. Appointment of Officers: Central Board shall appoint Additional, Deputy,	3. Forwarding Audit Report to Central Government: To forward the audited accounts together with explanations, if any, on any remarks of the Audit Report of the C & AG to the Central Government.

Contd.

Rights / Function	Duties
Regional or Assistant Provident Fund commissioners and other staff as may be considered necessary for efficient administration of the Scheme. 4. Delegation of Functions: Central Board shall delegate in powers and functions to any of its officers as it may deem necessary for efficient administration.	4. Submission of Annual Report: To submit to the Central Government an Annual Report of its work and activities.

EXECUTIVE COMMITTEE (Sec. 5AA)

• Composition of the committee

- Executive Committee is constituted by CG by notification in the Official Gazette.
- Executive committee shall consist of 13 members.
- The members of the Executive Committee are selected out of the members of the Central Board.
- The Executive Committee consists of the following members:

Chairman	- From amongst the members of the Central Board	- appointed by CG.
2 persons	- From amongst the representatives of CG elected to the Central Board	
3 persons	- From amongst the representatives of SG elected to the Central Board	
3 persons	- From amongst the representatives of employers elected to the Central Board	- elected by the Central Board
3 persons	- from amongst the representatives of Employees elected to the Central Board.	
Central Provident Fund Commissioner		

• Purpose of constitution of Executive committee

- The purpose of executive committee is to assist the Central Board in its function.
- The Scheme shall provide for –

(a) Terms and conditions subject to which a member of the Central Board may be appointed or elected to the Executive Committee.

(b) The time, place and procedure of the meetings of the Executive Committee

RECOVERY OF MONEY FROM EMPLOYER (Sec. 8B)

• Issue of certificate to recovery officer

The authorized officer is required to issue a certificate to Recovery Officer specifying the amount due from the employer.

• Which recovery officer

The recovery certificate shall be sent to the Recovery Officer within whose jurisdiction –

(a) the business or profession is situated; or
(b) employer resides; or
(c) Any immovable or movable property of establishment or employer is situated.

- **Mode of recovery**

(a) Attachment and sale of the movable or immovable property of the establishment. If amount so recovered is insufficient for recovering the whole of the amount of arrears specified in the certificate, the movable and immovable property of the employer may also be attached and sold.
(b) Arrest of the employer and his detention in prison.
(c) Appointing a receiver for the management of the movable or immovable properties of the establishment or the employer.

- **Stay of proceeding**
  - The authorised officer may grant time for the payment of the amount, and thereupon the Recovery Officer shall stay the proceeding until the expiry of the time so granted.
  - The stay of proceedings may be granted notwithstanding that a certificate has been issued to the Recovery Officer for the recovery of any amount.

TRANSFER OF ACCOUNTS (Sec.17A)

- **If the new establishment is covered under PF Act**

  If
  - an employer who is a member of PF, leaves an establishment
  - he obtains re-employment in another establishment - the new establishment is also covered under PF Act

  Then
  - the amount standing to his credit will be transferred to his account in the new establishment (i.e. the establishment where he is re – employed)

- **If the new establishment is not covered under PF Act**

  If
  - an employee who is a member of PF, leaves an establishment
  - he obtains re-employment in another establishment
  - the new establishment is not covered under PF Act
  - the new establishment has a Provident Fund of its own
  - the rules of such provident fund permit such transfer ***Then***
  - at the request of employee
  - within such time as be specified CG
  - the amount standing to his credit will be transferred to his account in the new establishment

- **If the old establishment was not covered under PF Act**

  If
  - an employee is employed in an establishment to which the provisions of the PF Act do not apply
  - such establishment has its own Provident Fund

- the rules of such provident fund permit such transfer
- the employee leaves such establishment
- he obtains re – employment in another establishment
- the new establishment is covered under PF Act

Then

- at the request of employee
- the amount standing to his credit will be transferred to his account in the new establishment

PROTECTION AGAINST ATTACHMENT (Sec. 10)

• Nature of protections

The amount standing to the credit of any member in the fund –

(a) shall not in anyway be capable of being assigned or charged:

(b) shall not be liable to attachment under any decree or order of any court in respect of any debt or liability;

(c) shall not be capable of being claimed by the official assignee or the official receiver:

(d) Shall be free from debt or other liability (in the hands of the nominee) incurred by the deceased member.

• No protection

The employee cannot claim any protection in respect of the money which has been withdrawn him from the PF Account.

LIABILITY OF EMPLOYER IN CASE OF TRANSFER OF ESTABLISHMENT (Sec. 17B)

• Contribution due upto the date of transfer

If an employer transfer (whether by way of gift, sale, lease or any other mode) an establishment, he as well as transferee of the establishment shall be jointly and severally responsible for contributions and other sums due upto the date of transfer of establishment.

• Limitation on liability

Liability of transferor

The liability of transferor shall be limited with respect to the period upto the date of transfer.

Liability of transferee

The liability of transferee shall be limited to the assets obtained by him by way of transfer of establishment.

INSPECTORS (Sec. 13)

• Appointment

- AG is empowered to appoint the inspectors for the purpose of EPF Act, EPF Scheme, pension Scheme, and Insurance Scheme. The appointment of inspector shall be made by issue of a notification in the Official Gazette.

- The respective jurisdiction of the inspectors shall be specified by shall Appropriate Government.
- The inspector is a 'public servant' within the meaning of Sec. 21 or IPC.

Powers of inspector

(a) To call such information from the employer or contractor as he considers necessary.

(b) To enter into any establishment and require production of any books, registers and documents.

(c) To examine the employer, his agent or servants.

(d) To make copies and take extracts of any book, register or other document.

(e) To seize the books, registers or other documents as he considers necessary if he has reason to believe that any offence under this Act has been committed by an employer.

(f) To exercise such other powers as may be provided in PF Scheme. Pension Scheme or Insurance Scheme.

17. SCHEMES COVERED UNDER THE ACT

Schemes under EPF Act

Employees Provident Scheme	Employee's Pension Insurance Scheme	Employee's Deposit Linked	Fund Scheme

A. EMPLOYEES PROVIDENT FUND SCHEME

• Quantum of contribution

Employer's contribution - 10% of pay (i.e., basic wages plus dearness allowance plus retaining allowance) – ***Employer's contribution***

- 10% of pay. - Employee may voluntarily contribute a higher amount. ***Rounding off*** The contribution has to be rounded off to nearest rupee. ***'Dearness allowance'*** Dearness allowance includes cash value of any food concession allowed to the employee. ***'Retaining allowance'***

Retaining allowance means an allowance payable to an employee during any period during which the establishment is not working for retaining his services.

• Increase in rate of contribution

- CG is empowered to increase the rate of contribution to 12%.
- The power shall be exercise by way of a notification in the Official Gazette.

• Employee earning more than Rs.6,500

If the pay of an employee exceeds Rs.6,500, the Employer's contribution shall be 10% 12% of Rs.6,500.

• Diversion to Employees' Pension Scheme

Out of employer's contribution of 10%/ 12%, the Employer's contribution of 8.33% shall be diverted to Employees' Pension Scheme.

- **Investment of the contributions**
  - The Board of Trustees is responsible for managing the Fund.
  - The moneys of the Fund shall be invested by the Board of Trustees as per the investment plans approved by the Central Government.
  - Members (i.e. Employees) get interest on the money standing to their credit at a rate recommended by the Government.
- **Advances and withdrawals**

  Employees are allowed to withdraw from their account for specific purposes.

B. EMPLOYEES PENSION SCHEME FROUDED BY (Sec. 6A)

Quantum of contribution

- Employer's contribution of 8.33% shall be diverted to Employer's Pension Scheme.
- CG can contribute to the pension fund, as approved by the parliament.

- **Benefit under the scheme**

(a) Members will get pension –
- on superannuation; or
- on retirement from service; or
- upon permanent total disablement during employment.

(b) Pension, will be available to widow/widower for life or till he/she remarries.

(c) Children will be entitled to pension, upto 25 years of their age. Benefit of pension to children is restricted only for 2 children.

(d) Orphans will be entitled to pension at enhanced rate. Benefit of pension to orphans is restricted only for 2 orphans.

(e) If the person is unmarried or has no family, pension is available to nominee for a specified period.

(f) Funds managed by 6A(4) : Central Board of Trustees constituted u/s 5A.

(g) Scheme provides for 6A(5): All or any of the matters specified in Schedule III.

(h) Period of effect of Scheme 6A(6): Prospectively, or
: Retrospectively from such date as may be specified

C. EMPLOYEE'S DEPOSIT LINKED INSURANCE SCHEME

- **Quantum of contribution**

Employer

The employer is required to pay contribution which cannot be more than 1% of pay of employee. Presently, the rate of contribution is 0.5%. ***Employee*** The employees do not contribute any amount to the scheme.

CG

CG also contributes to the – Insurance Fund at the rate of 0.25% of pay of every employee.

Administration charges

Employer is also required to pay administration charges for the Insurance Scheme, which shall not be more than 0.25% of pay of employee. Presently, the rate of contribution is 0.01% of pay of employee subject to a minimum of Rs.2 per month per member.

- **Exemption from the scheme**
    - Exemption from the scheme can be obtained if LIC Group Gratuity scheme is adopted by employer.
    - If exemption is granted, only inspection charges of 0.005% of pay are payable to PF authorities.

CHAPTER 9

The Payment of Bonus Act, 1965

1. APPLICABILITY OF THE ACT (Sec. 1)

Factories

The Act applies to every factory

Establishment employing 20 or more persons

The Act applies to every establishment in which 20 or more persons are employed on any day of the AY.

Establishment employing less than 20 persons

The Act applies to every other establishment or class of establishments if–

- It employs to 10 or more persons (i.e. it employs persons between 10 and 19 in number);
- The provisions of the Act are made applicable to it by way of a Notification in the Official Gazette by AG; and
- Before issuing such notification, at least 2 months' notice was given to the establishment by AG.

Once applicable forever applicable

- If the Act becomes applicable to an establishment in any AY.
- It shall continue to be applicable to the establishment
- Even if the number of persons employed by it falls below the minimum number of person as required for the applicability of the Act.

2. NON – APPLICABILITY OF THE ACT Sec.32

1. Employees employed by - (a) General insurance companies (b) LIC
2. Seamen as defined under merchant shipping Act, 1958
3. Employees registered under any scheme made under the Dock Workers (Regulation of Employment) Act, 1948 and employed by registered or listed employers.
4. Employees employed by Inland Water Transport Establishments operating on routes passing through any other country.
5. Employees employed by RBI, CG, SG or a local authority.

6. Employees employed by Indian Red Cross Society, universities or other educational institutions, institutions established not for purpose of profit.
7. Employees employed by SFC, NHB, NABARD, IFCI, IDBI, SIDBI, UTI.
8. Any other financial institution notified in the Official Gazette.

3. ACCOUNTING YEAR [(Sec.2(1)]

In relation to a corporation

The year ending on the day on which the books and accounts of the corporation are to be closed and balanced.

In relation to a company The period in respect of which P & L Account of the company is prepared.

In any other case

(a) The year commencing on the 1st April and ending on following 31st March;

(b) However, the employer has an option to close and balance the accounts of the establishment on any day other 31st day of March. In such a case, AY shall end on the day on which the accounts are so closed and balanced.
In other words, the employer may exercise the option to close and balance the accounts on any particular day every year. But such option can be exercised only once.

(c) Further exercise of option shall require the previous permission in writing of the prescribed authority and compliance of conditions as specified by the prescribed authority.

4. MEANING OF ESTABLISHMENT

Any unit, undertaking or place of business in which –

- Any commercial activity or business is carried on; or
- Services are rendered,

Under any form of business organization.

5. ESTABLISHMENTS TO INCLUDE DEPARTMENTS, UNDERTAKINGS, AND BRANCHES (Sec. 3)

General rule

For the purpose of computation of bonus, an establishment shall include department, undertakings, and branches.

Exception

A branch, department or undertaking shall not be treated as part of an establishment if the following 2 conditions are satisfied.

(a) A separate B/S and P & L A/c has been prepared for such branch, department or undertaking.

(b) Such branch, department or undertaking has never been treated as part of the establishment for the purpose of computation of bonus.

6. EMPLOYEE [Sec .2(13)]

Meaning of employee

- any person employed (other than an apprentice)
- on a salary or wage not exceeding Rs.10,000 per month

- in any industry
- to do any work (i.e. skilled, unskilled, manual, supervisory, managerial, administrative, technical or clerical)
- for hire or reward
- Whether the terms of employment are express or implied.

Illustrative list of employees entitled to bonus

- Probationer
- Dismissed employee (provided Sec.9 is not attracted) or suspended employee.
- Retrenched employee
- Temporary employee
- Part time employee
- Employee of a seasonal factory – proportional Bonus according to number of days work.
- Piece rated employee

7. "EMPLOYER" [(Sec. 2(14)]

If establishment is a factory

(a) Owner

(b) Occupier (Occupier means the person who has ultimate control over the affairs of the establishment)

(c) Agent of owner or occupier

(d) Legal representative of deceased owner or occupier

(e) The person named as a manager of the factory under the Factories Act.

If it is any other establishment

(a) The person having ultimate control over the affairs of the establishment

(b) The manager or the managing director to whom the affairs of the establishment are entrusted.

8.'SALARY OR WAGE' [(Sec. 2(21)]

'Salary or wage' means

- remuneration in respect of work done
- which would become payable to an employee
- if the terms of employment (whether expressed or implied) were fulfilled.

'Salary or wage' includes

(a) Dearness allowance (i.e. all cash payments by whatever name called, paid to an employee on account of a rise in the cost of living)

(b) Food allowance or the value of free food given by the employer in lieu of salary)

'Salary or wage' does not include

(a) Allowances

(b) Commission

(c) Bonus (including incentive, production and attendance Bonus)

(d) Traveling concession

(e) Ex-grata payment

(f) Retrenchment compensation, gratuity or other retirement benefits

(g) Any amenity, service, or concessional supply of food grains or other articles

(h) Employer's contribution to PF or pension fund
(i) Remuneration in respect of overtime work.

9. ELIGIBILITY FOR BONUS (Sec. 8)

Every employee is eligible for bonus if he has worked in the establishment e" 30 working days in a AY.

10. DISQUALIFICATION FOR BONUS (Sec. 9)

Conditions for applicability of Sec.9

An employee is disqualified for bonus (and is therefore not eligible to receive bonus) if –

- he has been dismissed from service; and
- the reason for his dismissal was –

(a) fraud; or
(b) riotous or violent behavior while on the premises of the establishment; or
(c) theft, misappropriation or sabotage of any property of the establishment.

Effects of Sec.9

An employee who becomes disqualified u/s 9 shall not be eligible to receive any bonus (whether for current AY or for any previous AY) under the Act.

11. PAYMENT OF MINIMUM BONUS (Sec.10, 11, 12, 13 and 14)

Computation of Allocable surplus (Sec.11)

Amount set on/set off u/s 15 shall be taken into account while computing the allocable surplus for any AY.

Amount of minimum bonus (Sec. 10)

Whether or not the employer has allocable surplus in an AY, every employer is bound to pay to every employee (eligible as per Sec. 8) in respect of every AY, minimum bonus, as follows.

Employee aged ≥ 15 years	Higher of -	8.33% of salary or wage	or Rs.100
Employee aged < 15 years	Higher of -	8.33% of salary or wage	or Rs.60

Proportionate reduction in minimum bonus (Sec. 13)

The minimum bonus of Rs.100/60 shall be proportionately reduced if the employee has not worked on all the working days in the AY.

- **computation of number of working days (Sec. 14)**

It shall be deemed that the employee had worked on the days on which the employee was –

(a) laid off;
(b) on leave with salary or wages;
(c) on maternity leave with salary or wages;
(d) Absent due to temporary disablement caused arising out of and in the course of his employment.

Ceiling on salary or wage (Sec.12)

If the salary or wage of an employee exceeds Rs.3,500 per month, the salary or wage for the purpose of computation of bonus shall be taken as Rs.3,500 per month.

12. PAYMENT OF MAXIMUM BONUS (Sec.11 and 12)

Computation of Allocable surplus (Sec.11)

Amount set on/set off u/s 15 shall be taken into account while computing the allocable surplus for any AY.

Amount of maximum bonus (Sec.11)

If, in an AY, allocable surplus exceeds the amount of minimum bonus, the employer shall pay to every employee, in lieu of minimum bonus, which shall be an amount in proportion to the salary or wage earned by the employee during the AY subject to a maximum of 20% of such salary or wage (Sec.11). Following conclusions may be drawn;

- Sec, 11 applies if, in an AY, allocable surplus exceeds the amount of minimum bonus;
- If Sec, 11 applies, the whole of the allocable surplus shall be divided (i.e. payment shall be made in the form of bonus) amongst the employees in proportion of their salary or wage.
- However, if division of whole of the allocable surplus amongst the employees in proportion of their salary or wage exceeds 20% of salary or wage of the employees, then –
  (a) Such excess shall be carried forward for being set on in the 4 succeeding AY(s);
  (b) Every employee shall be paid bonus equal to 20% of his salary or wage (this payment of maximum of 20% is termed as 'maximum bonus').

Ceiling on salary or wage (Sec. 12)

If the salary or wage of an employee exceeds Rs.3,500 per month, the salary or wage for the purpose of computation of bonus shall be taken as Rs.3,500 per month.

13. SET ON AND SET OFF OF ALLOCABLE SURPLUS (Sec.15)

Allocable surplus > maximum bonus

If, in any AY, allocable surplus (after taking into account the amount set on / set off u/s 15) exceeds maximum bonus, such exceeds (subject to a limit of 20% of salary or wage of the employees) shall be –

- Carried forward
- For being set on in the 4 succeeding AY(s) in the manner illustrated in Fourth Schedule.

Allocable surplus < minimum bonus

If, in any AY, allocable surplus (after taking into account the amount set on/set off u/s 15) is less than the minimum bonus, such deficiency shall be –

- Carried forward
- For being set off in the 4 succeeding AY(s) in the manner illustrated in Fourth Schedule.

Utilization of amount carried forward

- While calculating bonus for any succeeding AY.
- The amount of set off carried forward from the earliest AY.
- Shall first be taken into account.

14. DEDUCTIONS FROM BONUS (Sec. 17 and 18)

Adjustment of bonus (Sec.17)

The employer is entitled to deduct from bonus payable to an employee –

(a) the amount paid as customary bonus (e.g. puja bonus);

(b) the amount paid as interim bonus (i.e. bonus paid before it became payable)

Deductions from bonus (Sec.18)

Conditions

(a) An employee is found guilty of misconduct

(b) Financial loss is actually caused to the employer. **Effects**

- The loss caused to the employer may be recovered from the bonus payable to the employee.
- Such deduction can be made only from the amount of bonus payable in respect of same AY in which the employee has caused financial loss to the employer.

15. TIME LIMIT FOR PAYMENT OF BONUS (Sec. 19)

If there is a dispute regarding payment of bonus

The bonus shall be paid within 1 month of-

- award becoming enforceable ;or - settlement coming into operation

In any other case

Time limit – the bonus shall be paid within 8 months from the end of AY.

Extension of period.

- AG may extent the time limit for payment of bonus.
- Conditions for extension of time are as follows:
  (a) An application shall be made by the employer to AG.
  (b) AG must be satisfied that there are sufficient reasons to grant extension of time for payment of bonus.
  (c) Total period including the period of extension shall not exceed 2 years.

16. PAYMENT OF BONUS LINKED WITH PRODUCTION OR PRODUCTIVITY (Sec.31A)

Applicability of Sec.31A

- Sec. 31A applies only if there is an agreement or settlement between the employer and employers to pay annual bonus linked with production or productivity.
- Sec. 31A overrides the entire Act.

Terms of the agreement

The agreement or settlement may provide that –

- the bonus shall be paid annually to employees;
- such bonus shall be linked production or productivity;.
- Such bonus shall be paid in lieu of bonus based on profits.

Agreement to be void

The agreement or settlement shall be null and void in so far as it purports to deprive an employee of his right to minimum bonus. In other words, every employee shall have a right to receive the minimum bonus even though bonus calculated as per the provision of the agreement or settlement is less than the amount of minimum bonus.

Ceiling on bonus

The bonus linked with production or productivity calculated as per the agreement or settlement shall not exceed 20% of salary or wages earned in the relevant AY.

17. RECOVERY OF BONUS DUE FROM AN EMPLOYER (Sec. 21)

Application by whom?

(a) Employee (including an employee who is no longer in employment) (b) Any person authorized by the employee in writing (c) Legal heirs of the employee.

Time limit

- Application shall be made within 1 year of bonus becoming due for payment
- Time limit for making application may be extended by AG it sufficient cause is shown.

Application to whom?

The application shall be made to AG.

Issue of recovery certificate

If AG is satisfied that bonus is due. It shall issue a recovery certificate.

Recovery by collector

The bonus shall be recovered by the collector in the same manner as if it were arrears of land revenue.

Delegation of powers

The powers u/s 21 may be delegated by AG to such authority as may be specified by AG.

18. SPECIAL PROVISIONS APPLICABLE TO NEW ESTABILISHMENTS (Sec. 16)

First 5 years

(a) Bonus is payable only in respect of an AY in which the employer derives profit.

(b) Bonus shall be calculated in accordance with the provision of the Act.

(c) The Provisions of Sec. 15 (Set on/set off of allocable surplus) shall not apply.

6th year

Set on / set off shall be made

Taking into account the excess/deficiency of the allocable surplus In respect of 5th and 6th AY.

7th year

Set on/set off shall be made

Taking into account the excess / deficiency of the allocable surplus In respect of 5th, 6th, and 7th AY.

8th year onwards

Sec. 15 (set on or set off) shall apply as it applies to any other establishment

Meaning of newly set up establishment

An establishment shall not be deemed to be newly set up merely by reason of a change in its location, management, name or ownership

Meaning of employer deriving profit

An employer shall not be deemed to have derived profit in any AY, unless –

(a) depreciation for such AY has been provided; and

(b) the arrears of depreciation and losses incurred during earlier AY(s) have been fully set off against the profits.

Manner of reckoning first five, 6th, 7th and 8th AY.

First AY means the AY following the AY in which the employer sells the goods manufactured by him or renders services, as the case may be, from such establishment. Similarly, other AY(s) shall be construed.

Meaning of 'sale of goods'

Sale of goods manufactured during the trial running of any factory or of the prospecting stage of any mine or an oil field shall not be taken into consideration.

19. PRESUMPTION ABOUT ACCURACY OF B/S AND P&L A/C OF CORPOR-ATIONS AND COMPANIES (Sec.23)

Applicability of Sec. 23 – Conditions

(a) There is dispute relating to –
- payment of bonus; or
- Applicability of Payment of Bonus Act, 1965.

(b) The dispute is filled with any Court, Tribunal or Arbitrator (hereinafter referred to as the 'said authority').

(c) The employer is a corporation or a company.

(d) During the course of proceedings, the B/S and P & L A/c of such corporation or company are produced before the said authority.

(e) The B/S and P&L A/c have been audited –
- In case of a company • by an auditor qualified u/s 226.
- In case of a corporation • by CAG.

Presumptions about

(a) The said authority may presume that the particulars contained in such B/S and P & L A/c are accurate.

(b) It shall not be necessary for the corporation or company to –
- Prove the accuracy of such B/S and P & L A/c; or
- Produce any affidavit for establishing such accuracy.

20. AUDITED ACCOUNTS OF BANKING COMPANIES NOT TO BE QUESTIONED (Sec. 24)

Applicability of Sec.24 – Conditions

(a) There is a dispute relating to -
- Payment of bonus; or
- Applicability of Payment of Bonus Act. 1965

(c) The dispute is filled with any Court, Tribunal or Arbitrator (hereinafter referred to as the 'said authority').

(d) The employer is a banking company.

(e) During the course of proceedings, the accounts of banking company are produced before the said authority.

(f) The accounts have been duly audited.

Presumptions about the accounts

(a) The said authority may presume that the accounts are accurate.

(b) No trade union or employee shall be allowed to question the correctness of such accounts.

21. AUDIT OF ACCOUNTS OF EMPLOYERS, NOT BEING CORPORATIONS OR COMPANIES (Sec. 25)

Applicability of Sec. 25 – Conditions

(a) There is a dispute relating to
- payment of bonus; or
- applicability of payment of Bonus Act, 1965

(b) The dispute is filled with any court. Tribunal or Arbitrator (hereinafter referred to as the 'said authority').

(c) The employer is any person other than a corporation or a company.

(d) During the course of proceedings, the accounts of such employer are produced before the said authority.

(e) The accounts of the employer have been duly auditor who is duly qualified to act as an auditor of a company (u/s 226 of the companies Act, 1965).

Presumptions about the accounts

(a) The said authority may presume that the accounts are accurate.

(b) It shall not be necessary for the employer to –
- prove the accuracy of such accounts; or
- Produce any affidavit for establishing such accuracy.

Order for audit of accounts

Nature of order

The said authority may order the employer to get his accounts audited – - within such time as may be specified in the order; and - by such auditor as may be specified in the order.

Conditions for making order

The said authority may make such an order, if–

- the accounts of the employer are not audited by an auditor qualified u/s 226;and
- it is of the opinion that audit of accounts is necessary for deciding the dispute.

Consequences of default by employer

If the employer fails to get his accounts audited –

- the said authority may get the accounts audited by such auditor as it thinks fit;
- the remuneration paid to the auditor and other incident expenses shall be paid by the employer.

Presumption of accuracy

The accounts so audited shall be presumed to be accurate.

22. Provisions As To Maintenance Of Records And Registers [Sec.26]

1. **Maintenance of Registers, Records etc. [Sec.26]:** Every Employer shall prepare and maintain such registers, records and other documents in such from and in such manner as may be prescribed.
2. **Duty of Employers:** Maintenance of records and registers is an obligation, and a duty imposed on the Employers for due discharge of their duties regarding payment of Bonus.
3. **Production of Records:** The Employer is legally bound to produce the registers and accounts when called upon by an Inspector.
4. **Offence:** Non – maintenance and non – production of records and registers is an offences.

5. **Registers to be maintained :** Rule 4 of Payment of Bonus Rules, 1965 prescribes the following registers to be maintained by the Employers, viz. –

Register in -	Register to contain –
Form A	Computation of Allocate Surplus referred to in Sec.2(4)
Form B	Set – on and Set – off of Allocable Surplus u/s 15.
Form C	• Details of amount of Bonus due to each of the Employees, • Deductions under Sec.17 and 18, and • Amount Actually disbursed to the Employees.

23. INSPECTORS (Sec. 27)

Manner of appointment

The inspectors shall be appointed by AG by Notification in the Official Gazette.

Numbers and jurisdiction

- Such number of inspectors may be appointed as AG may deem fit.
- AG may define the limits within which the inspectors shall exercise jurisdiction.

Powers of inspector

(a) To call such information from the employer as he considers necessary

(b) To enter into any establishment and require production of any books, registers and documents.

(c) To examine the employer, his agent or servants.

(d) To make copies and take extracts of any book, register or other document (e) To exercise such other powers as may be prescribed.

Purpose of appointment

To ascertain whether or not the provisions of the Act have been complied with by an employer.

Duties of owners etc.

Any person required to produce any accounts, books, register or other documents or to give information by an Inspector shall be legally bound to –

(a) Produce accounts, books, register or other documents required by the Inspector.

(b) Give information required by the Inspector.

24. EXEMPTION FROM PROVISIONS OF THE ACT (Sec. 36)

Grounds for exemption

Before granting exemption, AG shall consider financial position and other relevant circumstances.

Opinion of AG

The exemption shall be given only if AG is satisfied that it is not in public interest to apply all or any of the provisions of this Act to an establishment or class of establishments.

Publication of order

The order of exemption shall be published by way of a notification in the Official Gazette.

Contents of order of exemption

The order of exemption shall specify –

- conditions, subject to which exemption is given, and
- period of exemption

25. ESTABLISHMENT IN PUBLIC SECTOR (Sec. 2(16) and (20)] ¾ Meaning [Sec,. 2(16)]

Establishment in public sector means an establishment owned, controlled or managed by –

(a) a Government company; or as defined u/s 617 of the companies Act, 1965.

(b) a corporation in which 40% or more capital is held by –

- CG, SG, RBI or a corporation owned by CG, SG, or RBI.

Applicability of Act (Sec. 20)

General rule

The Act does not apply to an establishment in public sector. **Exception**

The Act shall apply if the following 2conditions are satisfied;

(a) In an AY, it sells any goods or renders any services, in competition with an establishment in private sector.

(b) The income from such or services or bo is 20% or more of its gross total income of the establishment in public sectors for that accounting year.

26. Procedure for Settlement of Disputes [Sec.22]

1. Area of dispute: Disputes may arise between the employer and employee with respect to –
   (a) Bonus payable under this Act, or
   (b) Applicability of the provisions of this Act to establishment in Public Section
2. Settlement: Any such dispute shall be deemed to be an Industrial Dispute within the meaning of –
   (a) the industrial Dispute Act, or
   (b) Any corresponding law relating to investigation & Settlement of industrial dispute in force in the State.

Hence, the provisions of the Industrial Disputes Act or of such law in force shall apply to the settlement of disputes, unless otherwise expressly provided.

27 Some Other Definitions

1. Appropriate Government [Sec.2(5)

Situation	Appropriate Government
An establishment in respect of which the Appropriate Government under the Industrial Disputes Act, 1947 is the Central Government.	Central Government
Any other Establishment	Government of the State in which the Establishment is situated.

2. Award [Sec.2(7)]: Award means:

(a) An interim or a final determination,

(b) of any industrial dispute or of any question relation thereto,

(c) By – (i) any labour court, Industrial Tribunal or National Tribunal constituted under the Industrial Dispute Act, 1947 or (ii) any other authority constituted under any corresponding law relation to investigation and settlement of industrial dispute in force in the State, and includes an Arbitration Award made u/s 10 A of that Act.

3. Co- Operative Society [Sec.2(10)]: A Society registered or deemed to be registered under the Co – Operative Society Act, 1912, or under any other law for the time being in force in any State relating to Co – operative Societies.

4. Corporation [Sec.2(11)]: Corporation means any Body Corporate established by or under any Central, Provincial or State Act, Corporation does not include a Company or a Co – Operative Society.

5. Company [Sec.2(9)]: Company means as defined u/s 3 of the Companies Act, 1956, and includes a Foreign Company within the meaning of Sec. 591 of that Act.

6. Allocable Surplus [Sec.2(4)]: Most Imp.

In relation to	Allocable surplus
An Employer being a company other than a banking company which has not made the arrangements prescribed under the Income Tax Act, for the declaration and payment within India, of dividends payable out of its profits in accordance with Sec.194 of the said Act	67% of the Available surplus in an Accounting Year.
In any other case	60% of the Available surplus in an Accounting Year.

7. Available Surplus [Sec.2(6)]: RTP, N 83, N 02

Available surplus means the Available Surplus as computed u/s 5.

8. Establishment in Private Sector [Sec.2(15)]:

It means any Establishment other than an establishment in Public Sector

Offences by Companies [Sec.29]

1. **Definitions** : For the purpose of this Section -
   (a) "Company" means any Body Corporate and includes a Firm or other – Association of Individual, and
   (b) "Director", in relation to a Firm, means a Partner in the Firm.
2. **Liability of Company and Person In charge**: Where an offence has been committed by a company, every person who, at any time when the offence was committed, was in charge of and was responsible to, the Company for the conduct of the business of the Company as well as the Company, shall be deemed to be guilty of the offence, and shall be liable to be proceeded against and punishable accordingly.
3. **Due Diligence**: it the person who is liable to any punishment under this Act proves that the offence was committed without his knowledge or that he exercised all due diligence to prevent the commission of such offence, then such person is not liable.
4. **Liability of officers/ Directors etc:** Where an offence has been committed by a Company and it is proved that the offence has been committed with the consent or connivance of, or is attributable to any gross negligence on the part of any Director, Manager, Secretary or other of the Company, such Director, Manager, Secretary or other officer of the company shall also be deemed to be guilty of the offence and shall be liable to be proceeded against and punished accordingly.

SUMMARISED PROCEDURE FOR COMPUTATION OF BONUS

Step 1. Computer gross profit

Step 2. Deduct prior charges from gross profits

Step 3. Compute available surplus **Step 4**. Compute allocable surplus

Step 5. Compute bonus

Step 1. Computation of gross profit

Net profit as shown in P & L Account after making usual and necessary provision

Add:

1. Provision for bonus, depreciation and reserves.
2. Bonus paid to employees in respect of previous accounting years.
3. Gratuity paid or payable to employees in excess of the aggregate of –
   (a) the provision made for approved gratuity fund; and
   (b) the amount actually paid to employees on their retirement or on termination of their employment.
4. Donations in excess of the amount admissible for income tax.
5. Capital expenditure
6. Losses and expenditure of any business situated outside India.
7. Income directly credited to reserves **Less:**
   1. Capital receipts and capital profits.
   2. Profits of any business situated outside India.
   3. Refund of any excess direct tax paid for previous AY.
   4. Cash subsidy received from the Government

Gross profit

Step 2. Deduct prior charges from gross profit **Gross profit Less:**

1. Development Rebate
2. Development Allowance
3. Investment Allowance
4. Depreciation admissible under Income Tax Act.
5. Direct tax which the employer is liable to pay for the AY.
6. Sums referred to in the Third Schedule, viz –

(a) 8.5% of equity share capital (at the beginning of the AY) (b) 6% of Reserve (at the beginning of the AY) (c) Dividend paid on preference shares at actual rate. Gross profit after charges

Step 3. Computation of available surplus [Sec. 2(6) real with Sec. 5] Gross profits after prior charges

Add: Tax saved in respect of bonus paid during the preceding AY [Tax on Gross Profit less Tax on (Gross Profits Bonus paid)

Available surplus

Step 4. Computation of allocable surplus [Sec.2(4)]

(a) If an employer is a company, which has not made prescribed arrangements for declaration and payment of dividend as per Sec.194 of Income Tax Act 1961, then the allocable surplus shall be 67% of the available surplus.

(b) In any other case, the allocable surplus shall be 60% of available surplus.

Step 5. Compute bonus

Bonus shall be calculated as per the provisions contained in Sec.10, 11, 12, 15 and other applicable provision of the Act.

CHAPTER 10

The Payment of Gratuity Act, 1972

1. APPLICABILITY OF THE ACT

Initial Applicability (Sec.1(3)	Continued Applicability [Sec.1(3A)
The Act applies to – (a) Every Factory, Mine, Oilfield, Plantation, Port and Railway Company, (b) Every Shop or Establishment within the meaning of any law for the time being in relation to shops and establishments in a State, in which 10 or more persons are employed, or were employed, on any day of the preceding 12 months, (c) Such other establishments or class of establishments, in which 10 or more employee are employed, or were employed, on any day of the preceding 12 months, as specified by Central Government Notification.	A shop or Establishment to which this Act has become applicable shall continue, to be governed by this Act notwithstanding that the number of persons employed therein at any time after it has become so applicable falls below 10.

Right to receive gratuity

An employee is eligible to receive gratuity under the Act, if -

- He is employed in an establishment to which the Act applies (Sec.1) • He is an employee as per Sec.2(e).
- He has been in continuous service of 5 years – subject to some exceptions.

2. DEFINITIONS (Sec.2)

Appropriate Government [Sec. 2(a)]

• *In relation to any of the following establishment, AG means CG:*

(i) An establishment belonging to, or under the control of, CG.

(ii) An establishment, being a factory, belonging to, or under the control of, CG.

(iii) An establishment connected with a railway company, a major port, a mine or an oil field. (iv) An establishment having branches in more than one state.

• *In relation to any other establishment, AG means SG.*

Family [Sec.2(h)]

In the case of a male employee, means –	In the case of a female employee, family family means-
• The employee himself • The employee herself • Wife of employee • Children of employee (whether married or unmarried) • Dependent parents of employee • Dependent parents of wife of employee • Widow and children of predeceased son of employee	• The employee herself • Husband of employee • Children of employee (whether married or unmarried) • Dependent parents of employee • Dependent parents of husband of employee • Widow and children of predeceased son of employee.

If – the personal law of an employee permits adoption by him/her of a child; and
- the employee lawfully adopts a child

Then – the adopted child shall be deemed to be included in his/her family.

If – any child of the employee is adopted by another person; and
- the personal law of the person making such adoption permits such adoption **Then** – such child shall be deemed to be excluded from his/her family.

Factory [Sec.2(g)]

'Factory' means -	'Factory' does not include -
Any premises including the precincts (adjoining area) thereof – (i) wherein 10 or more workers are working or were working on any day of the preceding 12 months, and in any part of which a manufacturing process is being carried on with the aid of power, or is ordinarily so carried on; or (ii) wherein 20 more workers are working or were working on any day of the preceding 12 months, and in any part of which a manufacturing process is being carried on without the aid of power, or is ordinarily so carried on.	(i) a mine covered under the Mines Act, 1952; (ii) mobile unit belonging to the armed forces of the Union; (iii) a railway running shed; (iv) a hotel, restaurant or eating place.

Employee [Sec. 2(e)]

Employee means –

- Any person (other than an apprentice)
- Employed on wages
- In any establishment, factory, mine, oilfield, plantation, port or railway company or shop
- To do any work (i.e. skilled, unskilled, manual, supervisory, technical or clerical)

- Whether the terms of employment are express or implied
- Whether or not he is employed in a managerial or administrative capacity.

Employee does not include –

- A person who holds a post under CG or SG
- If he is governed by any other Act or by any Rules proving for payment of gratuity:

Employer [Sec.2(f)]

- In relation to any establishment, factory, mine, oilfield, plantation, port or railway company or shop belonging to or under the control of the CG or SG, employer means–

(a) the person or authority appointed by AG for the supervision and control of employers;

(b) head of the Ministry or the Department concerned, in case no person or authority is appointed by AG for the supervision and control of employees.

In relation to any establishment, factory, mine, oilfield, plantation, port or railway company or shop belonging to or under the control of a local authority, employer means –

(a) the person or authority appointed by the local authority for the supervision and control of employees.

(b) The Chief Executive Officer of the local authority, in case no person or authority is appointed by the local authority for the supervision and control of employees.

In any other case, employers means –

(a) the person or the authority having the ultimate control over the affairs of the establishment;

(b) the manager or the managing director (or any other person by whatever name called) to whom the affairs of the establishment are entrusted.

Wages [Sec.2(s)]

•***Wages means***

- all emoluments which are earned by an employee
- while on duty or on leave
- in accordance with the terms and conditions of his employment - Which are paid or payable to him in cash.

•***Wages includes***

- Dearness allowance.

•***Wages does not include –***

- Any bonus, commission, house rent allowance, overtime wages and other allowances.

• **Superannuation [Sec.2(r)]** ***Superannuation means***

- The attainment by the employee of such age.
- as is fixed in the contract or conditions of service
- As the age on attainment of which the employee shall vacate the employment.

•**Retirement [Sec.2(q)]**

Retirement means termination of service of an employee other than on superannuation.

Controlling authority [Sec.2(2) and 3]

- Controlling authority means an authority appointed by AG u/s 3 [Sec.2(d)]
- As per Sec.3, AG may, by notification in the official Gazette, appoint any officer to be a controlling authority, who shall be responsible for the administration of this Act. AG may appoint different controlling authorities for different areas.

Completed year of service [Sec. 2(b)]

Completed year of service means continuous service for one year.

Meaning of Continuous Service [Sec. 2A(1):

Meaning	Permissible interruptions
An employee shall be said to be in continuous service for a period if he has, for that period, been in uninterrupted service, or service with permissible interruptions, whether such uninterrupted or interrupted service was rendered before or after the commencement of this Act.	(a) Sickness, (b) Accident, (c) Leave, (d) Absence from duty without leave (not being absence in respect of which an order treating the absence as break in service has been passed in accordance with, standing orders, rules or regulations governing the employees of the establishment), (e) Lay – off, (f) Strike or Lock – out or cessation of work not due to any fault of the employee.

Deemed Continuous Service: Where an employee is not in continuous service as defined above, he shall be deemed to be in continuous service under the employer, if the following minimum working days conditions are satisfied –

Seasonal Establishments	Other than Seasonal Establishments [Sec.2A(2)]	
[Sec.2A(3)]	For 1 year period	For 6 months period
Not less than 75% of the number of days on which the establishment was in operation during such period.	• 190 days, in the case of any employee employed below, the ground in mine or in an establishment which works for less than 6 days in a week, and 240 days, in any other case, out of 12 calendar months preceding the date of calculation.	• 95 days, in the case of any employee employed below, the ground in mine or in an establishment which work for less than 6 days in a week, and • 120 days, in any other case, out of 6 calendar months preceding the date of calculation.

Inclusion of certain days:

For the purposes of Sec.2A(2), the number of days on which an employee has actually worked under an employer shall include the days on which –

(a) he has been laid –off under an agreement or as permitted by standing order made under the Industrial Employment (Standing Orders) Act, 1946, or under the Industrial Disputes Act, 1947, or under any other law applicable to the establishment,

(b) he has been on leave with full wages, earned in the previous year,

(c) he has been absent due to temporary disablement caused by accident arising out of and in the course of his employment, and

(d) in the case of a female, she has been on maternity leave, however, the total period of such maternity leave does not exceed 12 weeks.

Notification [Sec.2(k)]

- Notification means a Notification published in the Official Gazette.
- The Appropriate Government may by Notification, make Rules for the purpose of carrying the provisions of the Act. [Sec.15]

Prescribed [Sec.2(o)]

Prescribed means prescribed by Rules made under this Act.

Note: (a) An employee who is re – employed without any break in service, (b) a retrenched employee, and (c) an employee resigning from service, will be eligible for Gratuity.

3. DETERMINATION AND PAYMENT OF GRATUITY (Sec.7)

Application for payment of gratuity ***Application by whom?***

- An employee who is eligible for payment of gratuity
- Any person authorised in writing by such employee
- Nominee of the employee (if the deceased employee had made a nomination)
- Legal heir of the employee (if the deceased employee had not made any nomination)1 years

Application to whom?

- Application shall be made to the employee.

Manner of making application

- The application shall be made in writing
- Ordinarily, the application shall be made within 30 days from the date gratuity becomes payable.
- If the date of superannuation or retirement of the employee is known in advance, the employee may apply to the employer before 30 days of date of superannuation or retirement.
- The application shall require the employer to pay the gratuity to the employee.

Determination of amount of gratuity

Determination by employer

- As soon as the gratuity becomes payable, the employer shall determine the amount of gratuity.
- The employer shall give notice to the person to whom gratuity is payable as well as the controlling authority. The notice shall specify the amount of gratuity determined by the employer.
- The employer has to determine the gratuity, and give notice to the person to whom gratuity is payable and controlling authority irrespective of the fact whether an application for payment of gratuity has been made or not.

Payment of gratuity ***Time limit***

Within 30 days of gratuity becoming payable, the employer shall pay the gratuity to the person to whom it is payable.

Consequences of default by employer

- If the employer fails to pay the gratuity within 30 days of gratuity becoming payable, he shall be liable to pay simple interest at such rate as may be notified by CG from time to time.

- The interest shall be paid for the period starting with the due date of payment of gratuity and ending with the actual date of payment of gratuity.

Consequences of default by employee

The employer shall not be liable to pay any interest, if–

- The delay in payment of gratuity is due to the fault of the employee; and
- The employer has obtained permission in writing from the controlling authority for delayed payment on such ground.

Dispute as to gratuity

Nature of disputes

Dispute may arise as to –

- The amount of gratuity payable, or
- The admissibility of any claim of an employee for payment of gratuity: or
- The person entitled to receive the gratuity.

Duty of employer in case of dispute

In case of dispute, the employer shall deposit –

- with the controlling authority
- such amount as he admits to be payable by him.

Inquiry by controlling authority

- The controlling authority shall hold an inquiry. The proceedings before the controlling authority shall be deemed to be judicial proceedings.
- The controlling authority shall give a reasonable opportunity of being heard to the parties concerned.
- Thereafter, the controlling authority determines the gratuity payable. If amount determined by the controlling authority is more than the amount deposited by the employer, the controlling authority shall direct the employer to pay the balance amount.

Powers of controlling authority

For the purpose of concluding an inquiry, the controlling authority shall have the following powers vested in a civil court:

(a) Summoning and enforcing the attendance of any person and examining him on oath.

(b) Requiring the discovery and production of documents.

(c) Receiving evidence on affidavits.

(d) Issuing commission for the examination of witnesses or documents.

Appeal against the order of controlling authority

- Any person aggrieved by an order of the controlling authority may prefer an appeal with AG or such other authority as AG may specify in this behalf (hereinafter called as appellate authority).
- The appeal may be filed within 60 days of receipt of order of the controlling authority. However, if the appellate authority is satisfied that the applicant was prevented by sufficient cause from filling the appeal within the specified period of 60 days, if may admit the appeal within a further period of 60 days.
- Appeal by employer shall not be admitted unless at the time of preferring the appeal, the employer has deposited with the appellate authority a sum equal to the amount of gratuity determined by the controlling authority.

- The appellate authority shall give a reasonable opportunity of being beard to the parties concerned.
- Thereafter, the appellate authority may confirm, modify or reverse the decision of the controlling authority.

4. ELIGIBILITY FOR, AND AMOUNT OF GRATUITY (Sec.4)

Eligibility

Gratuity shall be payable to an employee on the termination of his employment after he has rendered continuous service for not less than 5 years –

(a) On his superannuation, or

(b) On his retirement or resignation, or

(c) On his death or disablement due to accident or disease. [Here, the condition as to 5 years of continuous service is not applicable]

Note: Disablement means such disablement as incapacitates an employee for the work which he was capable of performing service is not applicable]

Payee

Generally, Gratuity is payable to the employee himself, However, Gratuity is payable to the following persons in the situations given below –

Situation	Gratuity Payable to
Death of employee, and nomination has been made.	Nominee(s).
Death of employee, and no nomination has been made.	Heir(s)
Where Nominee(s) or Heir(s) is a Minor	Deposited with controlling Authority, who shall invest the same for the benefit of such Minor in term deposit with SBI or its Subsidiaries or any Nationalized Bank, till such Minor attains majority.

5. REDUCTION AND FORFEITURE OF GRATUITY [Sec.4(6)]

Computation [Sec.4(2)]:

Establishment	Computation of Gratuity Amount
Establishment other than seasonal Establishment i.e. General Rule	15/26 × Last Drawn Salary × No. of completed years of service or part thereof in excess of 6 months. In case of Piece Rate Employee, Daily Wages shall be computed on the average of the total wages of the 3 months preceding the termination of employment (Wages for Overtime work shall not be included)
Seasonal Establishment	• Those who work throughout the year: 15/26 rule as above. • Those who work only during the season: 7 days gratuity for each season.

Maximum [Sec.4(3)]:

The amount of gratuity Payable to an employee shall not exceed Rs.1000000.

Disabled Employee [Sec.4(4)]:

When an employee becomes disabled due to any accident or disease and is not in a position to do the same work and re-employed on reduced wages on some other job, the gratuity will be calculated in 2 parts –

(a) For the period preceding the disablement: on the basis of wages last drawn by the employee at the time of his disablement.

(b) For the period subsequent to the disablement; on the basis of the reduced wages as drawn by him at the time of the termination of services.

Better Terms [Sec.4(5)]:

Sec.4 shall not affect the right of an employee to receive better gratuity under any award or agreement or contract with the employer. However, the maximum statutory limit u/s 4(3) cannot be reduced by mutual settlement or agreement.[Bharat Commerce and Industries vs Ram Prasad]

6. NOMINATION (Sec.6)

In case of termination of service due to death of employee, the gratuity should be paid to his Successors/Heirs. To avoid complications and controversies in such payment, the employee shall make a nomination. The provisions relating to nomination are –

Nomination [Sec.6(1)]

Each employee, who has completed 1 year of service, shall make a nomination for the purpose of the sec.4(1) Second Proviso. Nomination shall be made in From F, in duplicate within 30 days of completion of 1 year of service. If the from is filed after the specified period, but with reasonable grounds of delay, it shall be valid and accepted by the employer.

Multiple Nominees [Sec.6(2)]:

An employee may, in his nomination, distribute the amount of gratuity payable to him under this Act, amongst more than one nominee.

Family [Sec.6(3)]:

If an employee has a family at the time of making a nomination, the nomination shall be made in favour of member(s) of his family. Any nomination made by such employee in favour of a person who is not a member of his family, shall be void. [Sec Note below for "Family"]

Acquiring a Family [Sec.6(4)]:

If at the time of making a nomination, the Employee has no family, the nomination may be made in favour of any person(s), but if the employee subsequently acquires a family, such nomination shall forthwith become invalid and the employee shall make a fresh nomination in favour of member(s) of his family. This fresh nomination should be made in From G, in duplicate, within 90 days of acquiring a family.

Modification [Sec.6(5)]:

A nomination may, subject to Sec.6(3) and 6(4), be modified by an employee at any time, after giving to his employer a written notice of his intention to do so. This modification should be made in From H and be in duplicate.

Death of Nominee [Sec.6(6)]:

If a nominee pre-deceases the employee, the interest of the nominee shall revert back to the employee, who shall file a fresh nomination, in respect of such interest. This modification should be made in From H and be in duplicate.

Custody [Sec.6(7)]:

Every nomination, fresh nomination or alteration of nomination, as the case may be shall be sent by the employee to his employer, who shall keep the same in his safe custody. The Employer shall verify the service particulars of the employee as given in the Nomination Form, and return one copy of the Form to the employee, as acknowledgement.

7. PROTECTION OF GRATUITY (Sec.13)

Nature of protection

- Gratuity payable to an employee shall not be liable to attachment in execution of any decree or order of the Civil or Revenue or Criminal Court.
- It is immaterial as to whether the gratuity is payable to the employee –

(a) Under the Act: or

(b) In an establishment exempted u/s 5.

8. RECOVERY OF GRATUITY (Sec.8)

Recovery certificate

- If the employer fails to pay the gratuity within the prescribed time (i.e. within 30 days of termination of employment), the controlling authority is empowered to issue a certificate to the collector to recover the amount of gratuity.
- Before issue to such certificate, the controlling authority shall give the employer a reasonable opportunity of being heard.

Payment of interest

- The employer shall also be liable to pay compound interest at such rate as may be notified by CG from time to time.
- The interest shall be paid starting from the date of expiry of prescribed period for payment of gratuity and ending with the actual date of payment of gratuity.
- However, the interest payable shall not exceed the amount of gratuity payable.

Recovery by collector

The gratuity shall be recovered by the collector in the same manner as if it were arrears of land revenue. The gratuity so recovered shall be paid to the person entitled to payment of gratuity.

9. COMPULSORY INSURANCE (Sec. 4A)

Compulsory Insurance [Sec.4A(1)]:

Every employer shall obtain insurance for his liability for payment of Gratuity under the Act, from – (a) the LIC, or (b) any other prescribed Insurer. However, the following categories of employers need not obtain such insurance cover –

(a) Employer of an establishment belonging to or under the control of Central / State Government.

(b) Any other Employer, who has established an Approved Gratuity Fund u/s 4A(2).

Approved Gratuity Fund [Sec.4A(2)]:

The Appropriate Government may exempt-

(a) Employers who have already established an Approved Gratuity Fund in respect of his employees and who desires to continue with such arrangement, and

(b) Employers having 500 or more persons, and who establishes and Approved Gratuity Fund in the prescribed manner.

Registration [Sec.4A(3)]:

Every employers shall get his establishment registered with the Controlling Authority. One those employers who have taken an insurance u/s4A(1) or have established an Approved Gratuity Fund u/s 4A(2), shall be registered.

Rules [Sec.4A(4)]:

To give effect to Sec.4A, the Appropriate Government may make Rules including matters such as – (a) composition of Board of Trustees of the Approved Gratuity Fund, and (b) recovery by the Controlling Authority of the amount of gratuity payable to employee, from LIC or any other Insurer with whom an insurance has been taken, or as the case may be, the Board of Trustees of the Approved Gratuity Fund.

Default [Sec.4A(5) & (6)]:

If the employer fails to pay the premium to the Insurer or to contribute to a Gratuity Fund, he shall be liable to pay the amount of gratuity including interest, if any, on delayed payments, to the Controlling Authority, Contravention thereof is punishable with fine upto Rs.10,000 and in case of continuing offence with a further fine of upto Rs.100 per day of default.

10. EXEMPTION FROM PROVISIONS OF THE ACT (Sec.5)

Exemption by whom?

The exemption may be given by AG.

Manner of giving exemption

The exemption can be given only by way of a notification in the Official Gazette.

Terms of exemption

- The exemption shall be subject to such conditions as may be specified in the notification.
- The exemption may be given prospectively or retrospectively.
- The exemption may be given from the operation of all or any of the provisions of any Scheme.

Conditions for giving exemption

The exemption may be given if AG is of the opinion that the employees are in receipt of gratuity not less favourable than the benefits provided under this Act.

11. INSPECTORS (Sec.7A and 7B)

Manner of appointment

- The inspectors shall be appointed by AG by Notification in the Official Gazette.
- Every inspector shall be deemed to be a 'public servant' within the meaning of Sec.21 of IPC.

Number and jurisdiction

- Such number of inspectors may be appointed as AG may deem fit.
- AG may define the area to which the authority of an inspector shall extend.

Where two or more inspectors are appointed for the same area, AG may distribute or allocate work to be performed by them (i.e. AG may define the limits within which the inspectors shall exercise jurisdiction).

Power of inspector

(a) To call such information from the employer as he considers necessary.

(b) To enter into and inspect, at all reasonable times, any premises of any establishment, factory, mine, oilfield, plantation, port or railway company or shop to which this Act applies, any books, registers, records, notices and other documents.

(c) To examine the employer and his servants.

(d) To make copies and take extracts of any books, registers, records, notices and other documents.

(e) To exercise such other powers as may be prescribed.

Purpose of appointment

To ascertain whether or not the provisions of the Act have been complied with by an employer.

Duties of owners etc.

Any person required to produce any accounts, books, register or other documents or to give information by an Inspector shall be legally bound to-

(a) produce accounts, books, register or other documents required by the Inspector; (b) give information required by the Inspector.

CHAPTER 11

Consumer Protection Act, 1986

OBJECT OF THE ACT

According to the preamble, the Act is to provide for better protection of the interests of consumers and for that purpose to make provision to make provision for the establishment of consumer councils and other authorities for the settlement of consumer's disputes and for connected therewith.

It may be noted that Consumer Protection Act (COPRA) is in addition to and not in derogation of any other law. [Section 3]

BASIC RIGHTS OF CONSUMERS [SECTION 6]

The basic rights of consumers that are sought to be promoted and protected are;

a) The right to be protected against marketing of goods and services which are hazardous to life and property:
b) The right to be informed about the quality, quantity, purity, standard and price of goods, or services so as to protect the consumer against unfair trade practices;
c) The right to be assured, wherever possible, access to variety of goods and services at competitive prices;
d) The right to be heard and to be assured that consumers' interest will receive due consideration at appropriate forums;
e) The right to seek redressal against unfair trade practices or restrictive trade practices or unscrupulous exploitation of consumers; and
f) The right to consumer education.

CONSUMER PROTECTION COUNCILS

Introduction

The interest of consumers are sought to promoted and protected under the act inter – alia by establishment of Consumer Protection Councils at the Central, State and District levels.

Central Consumer Protection Council

Section 4 provides that the Central Government shall, by notification, establish a Council to be known as Central Consumer Protection Council, which shall consist of the following members:

(i) The Minister – in – charge of Consumer affairs in the Central Government, who shall be its Chairman; and

(ii) Such number of other official or non – official members representing such interest as may be prescribed.

The Central Council shall consist of 150 members and the term of the Council shall be 3 years. The Central council shall meet as and when necessary, but atleast one meeting shall be held every year.

State Consumer Protection Council

Section 7 provides that the State Government shall, by notification establish a Council to be known as Consumer Protection council for (name of the state), which shall consist of the following members:

(i) The Minister – in – Charge of consumer affairs in the state government, who shall be its chairmans;

(ii) Such number of other or non – official members representing such interest as may be prescribed by the State Government; and

(iii) Such number of other official or non – official members, not exceeding ten, as may be nominated by the Central Government.

The State Council shall meet as and when necessary but not less than two meetings shall be held every year. The procedure to be observed in regard to the transaction of its business at such meeting shall be prescribed by the State Government.

District Consumer Protection Council

Section 8A provides that the State Govt. shall establish for every district, by notification, a council to be known as the District Consumer Protection council, which shall consist of the following members;

(i) The Collector of the district (by whatever name called), who shall be its Chairman; and

(ii) Such number of other official and non –official members representing such interests as may be prescribed by the State Govt.

The District Council shall meet as and when necessary but not less than two meetings shall be held every year.

REDRESSAL MACHINERY UNDER THE ACT

Introduction

The Consumer Protection Act, 1986 provides for a three – tier quasi – judicial redressal machinery at the District, State and National levels for redressal of consumer disputes and grievances. They are known as Consumer disputes Redressal Agencies.

District Consumer Disputes Redressal Forum

The Act provides for the establishment of a District Forum by the State Government in each district of the State by notification. The State Government may establish more than one District Forum in a District if it thinks for to do so.

Section 10 provides that each District Forum shall consist of :

(i) a person who is, or who has been, or is qualified to be, a District Judge, who shall be its President; and

(ii) two other members, one of whom shall be a woman.

The members of District Forum should be persons of ability, integrity and standing and should have experience relating to economics, law, commerce, accountancy, industry, public affairs or administration. They must be graduates and over 35 years of age.

Every member of the District Forum shall hold office for a term of 5 years or up to the age of 65 years, whichever is earlier, and shall be eligible for re – appointment.

Jurisdiction [Sec. 11]: Section 11 provides for the jurisdiction of the District Forum under the following two criteria:

1. Pecuniary limits: The District Forum can entertain complaints where the value of goods or services and the compensation, if any, claimed is up to Rs.20 lakhs.
2. Territorial limits: The District Forum can entertain complaints if any of the opposite party ordinary resides or carries on business or personally works for gain or has a branch office; or the cause of action arises within the local limits of its jurisdiction.

State Consumer Disputes Redressal Commission

The Act provides for the establishment of the State Consumer Disputes Redressal Commission by the State Government in the State by notification.

Section 16 provides that each State Commission shall consist of :

(i) a person who is, or has been a judge of a High Court appointed by the State Government (in consultation with the Chief Justice of the High Court), who shall be its President; and

(ii) not less than two, and not more than such number of members, as may be prescribed, and one of whom shall be a woman.

The members of State Commission should be persons of ability, integrity and standing; and should have experience relating to economics, law, commerce, accountancy, industry, public affairs or administration. They must be graduates and over 35 years of age.

Every member of the State Commission shall hold office for a term of 5 years or up to the age of 67 years, whichever is earlier, and shall be eligible for re – appointment.

Jurisdiction [Sec. 17]: The jurisdiction of the State Commission is as follows:

1. Original Jurisdiction : The State Commission can entertain complains where the value of the goods or services and the compensation, if any, claimed exceeds Rs.20 lakks but does not exceed Rs.1 crore. [Pecuniary Limits]
   The State commission can entertain complaints if any of the opposite party ordinarily resides or carries on business or personally works for gain or has a branch office; or the cause of action arises within the local limits of its jurisdiction. [Territorial Limits]
2. Appellate Jurisdiction: The State Commission also has the jurisdiction to entertain appeals against the orders of any District Forum within the State.

3. Reversionary Jurisdiction : The State commission also has the power to call for the records and pass appropriate orders in any consumer dispute which is pending before or has been decided by any District Forum of the same state.

National Consumer Disputes Redressal Commission

The Act provides for the establishment of the National Consumer Dispute Redressal Commission by the Central Government by notification in the Official Gazette.

Section 20 provides that the National Commission shall consist of :

(i) a person who is or has been a judge of the Supreme Court, to be appointed by the Central Govt. (in consultation with the Chief Justice of India), who shall be its President; and

(ii) not less than four, and not more than such number of members, as may be prescribed, and one of whom shall be a woman.

The members of National Commission should be persons of ability, intergrity and standing; and should have experience relating to economics, law, commerce, accountancy, industry, public affairs or administration. They must be graduates and over 35 years of age.

Every member of the National Commission shall hold office for a term of 5 years or up to the age of 70 years whichever is earlier and shall be eligible for re-appointment.

Jurisdiction [Sec. 21]: The jurisdiction of the National Commission is as follows:

1. **Original Jurisdiction :** The National Commission can entertain complaints where the value of the goods or service and the compensation, if any, claimed exceed Rs.1 crore.
2. **Appellate Jurisdiction** :The National Commission also has the Jurisdiction to entertain appeals against the original orders of any State Commission.
3. **Reversionary Jurisdiction**: The National Commission also has the power to call for the records and pass appropriate orders in any consumer dispute which is pending before or has been decided by any State Commission.

Time limit for filing the Complaint

A complaint must be filed within two years from the date on which the cause of action arose. However, the District Forum, State Commission or National Commission may entertain complaint even after the expiry of two years, if it is satisfied that there was sufficient cause for not filing the complaint within prescribed period of two years.

Time limit for filing the Appeal

An appeal to the:

(i) State Commission against the orders of District Forum:

(ii) National Commission against the original orders of State Commission.

(iii) Supreme Court against the original orders of National Commission.

Must be filed within 30 days from the date of receiving the order or District Forum / State Commission / National Commission. However the State Commission, National Commission Supreme Court may entertain an appeal even after the expiry of said 30 days, if it is satisfied that there was sufficient cause of not filing the appeal within the prescribed period of 30 days.

Further, appellant shall also be required to deposit 50% of the amount required to be paid as per the order of the District Forum/State Commission /National commission or

Rs.25,000/35,000/50,000, respectively, whichever is less.

It may be noted that appeals are allowed only against the original orders passed by the concerned Redressal Agency. Thus, appellate orders passed by the State Commission or National Commission cannot be further appealed against. Similarly, the revisional orders passed by the State Commission or National Commission are also not appealable. However, only the National Commission has the power to review any order made by it when there is an error apparent on the face of the record.

NATURE AND SCOPE OF REMEDIES UNDER THE ACT [SECTION 14]

Where the goods complained against suffer from any of the defects specified in the complaint or any of the allegations contained in the complaint about the services are proved, the District Forum/State Commission / National Commission may pass one or more of the following orders:

a) To remove the defects pointed out by the appropriate laboratory from the goods in question.
b) To replace the goods with new goods of similar description which shall be free from any defect?
c) To return the prices or the charges, as the case may be, to the complainant.
d) To pay the amount of compensation to the consumer for any loss or injury suffered and in addition, punitive damages can be granted:
e) To remove the defects in goods or deficiencies in the services in question.
f) To discontinue the unfair trade practice or the restrictive trade practice.
g) No to offer the hazardous goods for sale;
h) To withdraw the hazardous goods from being offered for sale.
i) To cease manufacture of hazardous goods;
j) To pay such sum as may be determined by it;
k) To issue corrective advertisement; and
l) To provide for adequate costs to parties.

IMPORTANT DEFINITIONSW [SECTION 2]

Complainant [Sec. 2(1) (b)]

Complainant means –

(a) a consumer
(b) any voluntary consumer association registered under any law;
(c) the Central or any State Government
(d) one or more consumers, where there are numerous consumers having the same interest;

or

(e) in case of death of a consumer, his legal heir or representative, **Who or which makes a complaint.**

An association of persons to have locus standi as consumer, it is necessary that all the individuals forming the association must be the consumer having purchased the same goods or hired the same services from the party.

In case the affected consumer is unable to file the complaint due to ignorance, illiteracy or poverty, any recognized consumer association may file the complaint as per the above clause (b). Thus, rule of 'privity of contract' or 'locus standi' , which permits only the aggrieved party to take action, has very rightly been set aside in the spirit of public interest.

Complaint [Sec.2(1)(c)]

Complaint means any allegation in writing made by a complaint that –

(i) an unfair trade practice or a restrictive trade practice has been adopted by any trader;

(ii) the goods bought by him or agreed to be bought by him be suffer from one more defects;

(iii) the services hired or availed of or agreed to be hired or availed of by him suffer from deficiency in any respect;

(iv) the trader has charged a price in excess of the price; (a) fixed under any law; (b) displayed on the goods or any package containing such goods; (c) displayed on the price list exhibited by him; or (d) agreed between the parties.

(v) goods which will be hazardous to life and property when used are being offered for sale to the public;

(vi) services which will be hazardous to life and safety of the public when used, are being offered by the service provider.

With a view to obtain any relief provided by law under this Act.

Consumer [Sec. 2(1) (d)]

Consumer means –

(i) In respect of goods, any person who purchases goods for a consideration but does not include a person who has purchased goods for re – sale or commercial purpose. Such consideration may be paid or promised or partly paid and partly promised or under the system of deferred payments.

(ii) Any person who is using the goods, with the permission of the buyer of such goods as specified in clause (i).

(iii) In respect of service, any person who hires or avails service for a consideration but does not include a person who has availed service for commercial purpose. Such consideration may be paid or promised or partly paid and partly promised or under the system of deferred payment.

(iv) Any person who is beneficiary under the services with the permission of the hirer of such services as specified in clause (iii);

(v) A person who purchases goods or avails services exclusively for the purpose of earnings his livelihood by means of self employment.

Commercial Purpose: A person who has purchased goods for "commercial purpose" shall not be deemed to be a consumer. A purchase of goods could be said to be for a "commercial purpose" only if two conditions are satisfied, namely : (i) the goods must have been purchased for being used in some profit – making activity on a large scale; and (ii) there should be close and direct nexus between the purchase of goods and the profit – making activity.

Thus, a person who buys goods for re – sale or commercial purposes or avails services for commercial purposes is specifically excluded from the definition of 'consumer'. For example, a person buying one truck or tempo or sewing machine or one computer for the purpose of earning his livelihood by self – employment will be eligible to qualify as consumer. However, if a person buys two typewrites, out of which one is used by a person employed by him, he will not be eligible to file a complaint as a consumer because a person buying goods for re – sale or commercial purpose is not a consumer.

For instance, a lawyer purchased a computer and a printer for his office. The printer started giving trouble form the day one. The lawyer lodges a complaint under the Consumer Protection Act. In this case, the printer has not been purchased by the advocate for any commercial purpose treated as consumer and will succeed in his complaint.

[Sanjay Krishana Kant v. M/s Grooy Communication & Others]

Who is a Consumer : Following are some of the important decided cases in this regard:

1. Railway passengers traveling on payment of fare is consumer. [GM, South Eastern Railways v. Anand Prasad Sinha]
2. Beneficiary of bank guarantee is a consumer. [Union Bank v. Seppo Rally]
3. Parents who bring the child to hospital and the child both are consumers. [Spring Meadows Hospital v. Harjot Ahluwalia]
4. Allottees of house by Housing Board are consumers [UP Avas Gram Vikas Parishad v. Garima Shukla]
5. A person obtaining water from a government agency and paying water bills for the water supplied is a consumer. However, only if the water tax is levied, the person availing services will not be a consumer. [Nagrik Parishad v. Garhwal Jal Sansthan]

6 The widow of a deceased policy holder is a consumer, as the term 'consumer' includes any beneficiary of service other than the person who hires the services for consideration. [A Narsamma v. LIC of India]

Who is not a Consumer: following are some of the important decided cases in this regard.

1. A charitable trust is not a consumer if it has purchased machinery for its diagnostic centre, when only 10% patients are provided free services and charges are levied on remaining patients Charitable Trust v. Toshniwal Brothers]
2. Person buying goods for manufacture of another product is not consumer as the goods were intender for commercial purpose. [Rajeev Metal Works' v. MMTC]
3. A tenant is not consumer when landlord has not agreed to render any service to tenant in lease agreement. [Laxmiben Laxmichand Shah v. Sakerben Kanji]
4. A hospital will not be liable, if the hospital happens to be a government hospital where no fee is charged for consultation and treatment, but only a token registration fee is charged. [Indian Medical Assoc. v. V.P. Shanta & others]

Goods [Sec. 2(1) (i)]

Goods means goods as defined in the sale of goods Act, 1930.

As per Sale of Goods Act, goods means every kind of moveable property other than actionable claims and money; and includes stock and shares, growing crops, grass or things attached to or forming part of the land which are agreed to be severed before sale or under the contract of sale.

Therefore, most common products would come within the purview of this definition.

Shares have been specifically included in 'goods'. However, shares before allotment are not goods, as they do not exist before the allotment is made. To constitute a consumer, there must be transaction of goods. Hence, a prospective investor cannot be regarded as a consumer within the meaning of this Act, [Morgan Stanley Mutual Fund v. Kartik Das]

Services [Sec. 2(1) (o)]

Service means services of any description which is made available to potential users and includes, but not limited to the provision of facilities in connection with banking financing, insurance, transport, processing supply of electrical or other energy, board or lodging or both, housing construction entertainment amusement or the purveying of news of other information, but does not include the rendering of any service free of charge or under a contract of personal services.

"Potential Users' mean those who are capable of using the service. [Lucknow Development Authority v. M.K. Gupta]

Contract of Personal Service and Contract for Personal Service: In contract of personal service, the master can order or require what is to be done and how it is to be done. This is out of the purview of COPRA as the master can always dispense with the service of the servant and hence no occasion would arise for him to complain about service of the servant. However, in contract for personal services, the person cannot order what is to be done and how it is to be done. Services rendered in professional category could be treated as contract for personal service and hence covered under COPRA.

Consumer Forum cannot decide disputes arising out of contract of appointment of personal service For instance, Civil Servants and Professors in Universities are appointed under contract of personal service and hence are not covered under COPRA. [Centre for Research & Industrial Development v. Madam Lal Sahni]

What is Service: Following are some of the important decided cases in this regard:

1. Passengers traveling by trains on payment of the stipulated fare charged for the ticket are consumer' and the facility of transportation by rail provided by the railway administration is a 'service' rendered for consideration as defined in the Act. [GM, South Eastern Railways v. Anand Prasad Sinha]
2. Similarly telephone services availed for consideration is a service. [District Manager, Telephones Patna v. Lalit Kr. Baijla]
3. Service rendered to a patient by a medical practitioner (except where the doctor renders service free of charge to every patient) by way of consultation, diagnosis and treatment, both medical and surgical, would fall within the ambit of 'service'. [Indian Medical Association v.V.P. Shanta & Others]

4. Accepting deposits from public agreeing to pay interest is service. If interest and principal is not paid on due dates, it is deficiency of service and consumer forums can issue orders for payment of outstanding dues. [Kalawati v. United Vaish]
5. Education is an activity which comes within the ambit of 'service' because 'service' means service of any description which is made available to potential users under this Act. [The CBSE v. Consumer Disputes Redressal Forum]

What is not service: following are some of the important decided cases in this regard:

1) Conducting examination is not service as a candidate appearing for examination could not be regarded as a person who has hired or availed the services of the University or Board for consideration. Thus, the University or Board in conducting examination is not performed any service. [Chairman, Board of Examination v. Mohideen Abdul Kader]
2. Registration of documents by government is not a service. A person presenting a document for registration is not a consumer. There is no commercialization involved. Officers who are doing the work of registration are doing the statutory duty. [S.P. v. collector of Stamps]
3. Payment of taxes is not hiring of services. No complaint can be lodged against Municipal Corporation for failure to carry out its statutory duty of proper maintenance of drains, as payment of taxes is not hiring of services. [Signet corporation v. Commissioner, MCD, New Delhi]
4. Promotional activities of state and its agencies are not services and complainants are not consumers, as facilities are provided by State and its agencies without any specific consideration. [T.N. Sethuraman v. Goa, Daman and Diu Industrial Development corporation]
5. Even if a litigant pays court fees, he is not hiring services of Court. The Court is exercising sovereign function of dispensation of justice. Thus, complaint against Court for delay in judgment is not maintainable under Consumer Forums.
6. Free Services are not covered under COPRA. The employer (Govt. in this case) deducted insurance premium from salary of employee, but failed to make payment to LIC. When the employee died LIC refused to pay as premium was not paid. It was held that the employer was giving free service and hence he is not liable. [State of Orissa v. LIC]
7. However, if the employer is agent of LIC for the purpose of colleting premium, then general principle of agency as contained in Contract Act shall apply. Employee has no responsibility to intimate LIC about non – remittance of the premium. Hence, LIC has to make payment of compensation if employer has deducted premium from salary of employee. [Delhi Electric Supply v. Basanti Devi]

Consumer Dispute [Sec. 2(1) (e)]

Consumer dispute means dispute where the person against whom a complaint has been made, denies in goods or against any deficiency in services or against charging an exorbitant price.

Defect [Sec. 2(1) (f)]

Defect means any fault, imperfection or shortcoming in the quality, quantity, potency, purity or standard of any goods which is required to be maintained by or under any law for the time being in force or under any contact, express or implied, or as is claimed by the trader in any manner whatsoever in relation to any goods.

In the case of Abhaya Kumar Panda v. Bajaj Auto Ltd. where the motor vehicle sold to the petitioner was found to have major manufacturing defects which could not be removed despite several repairs, it was held to be 'defective'and the vehicle was ordered to be replaced.

Deficiency [sec. 2(1) (g)]

Deficiency means any fault, imperfection, shortcoming or inadequacy in the quality nature and manner of performance of any service which is required to be maintained by or under any law for the time being in force or has been undertaken to be performed by a person in pursuance of a contract or otherwise in relation to any service.

In order to get any loss compensated for deficiency in service, mere loss or injury is not enough. Loss or injury must be coupled with negligence. The term 'negligence' means absence of reasonable care which a prudent person is expected to observe in a given set of circumstances. Thus, no compensation can be claimed even in case of loss or damage. If it was not caused due to negligence of the person. [Consumer Unity and Trust Society v. Bank of Boroda]

For instance, the driver of a bus suddenly, applied the brake to avoid a collision with bullock cart and with result the bus met with an accident resulting in the death of a passenger. The legal heirs of the deceased lodged a complaint with Consumer Forum for compensation on the ground of 'deficiency in service.' In the present case, the accident that occurred had nothing to do with provided to the deceased because the injury sustained has nothing to do with the service provided but due to the direct result of the accident, Further, there was no element of negligence on the part of driver, as he had applied the brakes to avoid a collision. Hence, the heirs of the deceased will not succeed in their complaint against the transport company.

[Chairman, Thiruvallavar Transport Corporation v. Consumer Protection Council]

It may be noted that COPRA does not have any jurisdiction in respect of any matter, if there is some special law dealing with that matter.

What is Deficiency in Service: Following are some of the important decided cases in this regard:

1. Negligence in settlement of Insurance claim, [Div. Manager, LIC of India v. Bhavanam Srinivas Reddy]
2. Ornaments kept in the banks' locker were found lost though the certificate recorded by the custodian of the bank stated all lockers operated during the day had beenm checked and found properly locked. [Punjab National Bank v. K. B. Shetty]
3. Issuing drafts on foreign banks where the bank had no account causing inconvenience to the customer. [Tarun Kumar Kaniyalal Soni v. Punjab National Bank]
4. Honouring forged cheques [Corporation bank v. Filmalaya (P) Ltd.]

6. Debiting cheques to wrong accounts [Corporation Bank v. Filmalaya (P) Ltd.]
7. Failure to give possession of the house after receiving the price and registering the flat in favour of the allottee. [Lucknow development Authority v. Roop Kishore Tandon]
8. Non delivery of letter by a courier company. [Skypack Couries Pvt. Ltd. v. Anupama Bagla]
9. Theft of car from parking of an hotel constitution the deficiency in service. [Atul Virmani. V. Asian Hotels Limited]
10. Delay in issue of units by UTI of about 18 months is deficiency in service. In this case, 15% interest was awared as compensation. [UTI. v. Smt. Bandana Roy]
11. To run a boat club without having necessary equipment and personal trained for meeting an emergency constitutes gross negligence and serious deficiency in service. [Sandhu v. Union of India]
12. Parking vehicle in parking lot on payment of parking charges is bailment. Persons responsible for management of parking area is liable to make good the loss due to theft. [Mahesh Enterprises v. Arun Kumar Gumber]
13. In the case of goods carrier services, the liability of a carrier to whom the goods are entrusted for carriage is that of an insurer and is absolute in terms. So long as the goods are in the custody of the carrier, it is the duty of carrier to take due care as he would have taken of his own goods and he would be liable if any loss or damage was caused to the goods on account of his negligence3 or criminal act or that of his agent and servants. This would be so even if goods are carried 'AT OWNER's RISK ————'. Owners' risk is understood in the sense that the carrier would not be liable for damage or loss to the goods if it was not caused on account of carrier's own negligence or the negligence of his servants and agents. [Nath Brothers v. Best Roadways Ltd.]
14. The transportation of goods through carriers cannot be considered as for commercial purposes and the transporter is liable for any deficiency in service. [Express Goods Service v. Standard Textile Mills]
15. Selling an item at double the price printed on the wrapper is an Unfair Trade Practice. [Kapil Mitra v. Priya Village Roadshow, New Delhi]

What is not Deficiency in Service : Following are some of the important decided cases in this regard:

1. Refusal to give credit to customers on grounds that the unit belonged to a sick Industry or was not economically viable on any other grounds would not fall under deficiency of service as a bank is the sole judge of the credit worthiness of any party. [Asha Sharma v. Union of India]
2. Failure to deliver goods carried by the railways is not covered clause 'deficiency in service rendered' of Consumer Protection Act, But it is covered under Railway claims tribunal Act. 1987 and thus required to be compensated in that Act. [Union of India v. M. Adaikalan]
3. The National Commission held that where the bank has not been accommodating the complainant sufficiency in the matter of grant of adequate mursing facility for small scale industry which consequently became sick, the proper forum

to agitable the said grievance is civil court and not a consumer redressal forum. It further held that the banks have to exercise their discretion and act in accordance with their best judgment after taking into account various relevant factors and hence mere failure to provide financial facility cannot be said to constitute deficiency in service. [Special Machines v. Punjab National Bank]

4. A person or organization engaged in the business of courier services for carriage of mail or parcels falls within the purview of the COPRA, 1986 and delay in delivery of articles or non – delivery will constitute deficiency in service. However the National Commission held that the complainant ought to have insured the documents if they were of great value and as per IATA Regulations, the consignee is bound to declare the nature of the contents and hence did not grant any relief to the complainant. [Air Pack couriers (India) Pvt. Ltd. v. S. Suresh]
5. If the staff gives some information (or leaflet containing some information) which is against the provisions of Statute, the Authority is not liable for deficiency in service. In this case, the postal staff gave incorrect information about rate of interest and maturity period of National Saving Certificate. The Supreme Court held that since the terms are specified by notification of Govt. of India, any information contrary to the notification is not binding on Govt. of India. [Post Master v. Ms. Raja Premeelamma]
6. Disconnection of electric supply for non – payment of charges by consumer is not deficiency in service. Electricity Board has power to discontinue supply. It was also held that electricity board can make supplementary bill for escaped bill. [Swanstic Industries. v. Maharashtra State Electricity Board]
7. Disconnecting power supply for tampering with electric meter is not deficiency in service.[CESC Limited v. Sumitra Pal]
8. In Airline services, delay due to bad weather and poor visibility are unforeseen circumstances and hence there is no deficiency in service. Compensation can be awarded only if there is negligence and loss is suffered by complainant on account of negligence. [Indian Airlines Limited v. Dr. V. J. Philip]

CHAPTER 12

Law Relating to Right to Information

INTRODUCTIONS

Throughout the world, the right to information is seen by many as the Key to strengthening participatory democracy and ensuring more people centered development. In India also, the Government enacted Right to information (RTI) Act in 2005 allowing transparency and autonomy, and access to accountability in public authorities.

In **R.P. Limited Indian Express Newspaper**, the Supreme Court read into Article 21 the right to know. The Supreme Court held that right to know is a necessary ingredient of participatory democracy. Article 21 confers on all persons a right to know which include a right to receive information.

It may be pointed out that the right to impart and receiving information is a species of the right to freedom of speech and expression. Article 19(1) (a) of our Constitution guarantees to all citizens freedom of speech and expression. Right to freedom of speech and expression in Art. 19 (1) (a) carries with it the right to propagate and circulate one's views and opinions subject to reasonable restrictions as mentioned under Article 19(2). The prerequisite for enjoying this right is knowledge and information.

The Right to Information Act, 2005 provides an effective an effective framework the right to information recognized under Article 19 of the Constitution.

DEFINITIONS

Public Authority [Sec. 2(h)]

"Public authority" means any authority or body or institution of self government established or constituted

- By or under the Constitution.
- By any other law made by Parliament.,
- By and other law made by State Legislature.
- By notification issued or order made by the appropriate Govt.

Record [Sec 2(1)]

"Record" includes.

(a) any document, manuscript and file;

(b) any microfilm, microfiche and facsimile copy of a document.

(c) any reproduction of image or images embodied in such microfilm; and
(d) any other material produced by a computer or any other device.

Information [Sec 2(1)]

"Information" means any material in any form including records, documents, memos, e-mails, opinions, advices, press release, circulars, orders, logbooks, contracts, reports, samples, models, data materials held in any electronic form. **Right to Information [Sec. 2(i)]**

"Right to information" means the right to information accessible under this Act with is held by or under the control of any public authority and includes the right to –

(i) taking notes, extracts, or certified copies of documents or records.
(ii) Inspection of work, documents, records.
(iii) Taking certified samples of materials.
(iv) Obtaining information in the form of diskettes, floppies, tapes, video cassettes or in any other electronic mode or through printouts where such information is stored in a computer or in any other device.

OBLIGATIONS OF PUBLIC AUTHORITY

Every public authority under the Act has been entrusted with a duty to maintain records and publish manuals, rules regulations, instructions, etc. in its possession as prescribed under the Act.

As per Sec.4, every public authority has to publish **within 120 days** of the enactment of this Act:

- The particulars of its organization functions and duties.
- The powers and duties of its officers and employees;
- The procedure followed in its decision making process, including channels of supervision and accountability.
- The norms set by it for the discharge of its functions;
- The rules, regulations instruction, manuals and records used by its employees for discharging its functions;
- A statement of the categories of the documents held by it or under its control;
- The particulars of any arrangement that exists for consultation with, or representation by the members of the public in relation to the formulation of policy or implementation thereof;
- A directory of its officers and employees;
- The monthly remuneration received by each of its officers and employees, including the system of compensation as provided in its regulations.
- The budget allocated to each of its agency, including the particulars of all plans, proposed expenditures and reports on disbursements made;
- The manner of execution of subsidy programmes, including the amounts allocated and the details and beneficiaries of such programmes:
- Particulars of recipients of concessions, permits or authorizations granted by it;
- Details of the information available to, or held by it, reduced in an electronic form;
- The particulars of facilities available to citizens for obtaining information, including the working hours of a library or reading room, if maintained for public use;

- The names, designations and other particulars of the public Information Officers,
- Such other information as may be prescribed; and thereafter update the publications every year.

DESIGNATION OF PUBLIC INFORMATION OFFICERS [PIO]

Every public authority has to do the following;

- Designate in all administrative units or officers Central or State Public Information Officers to provide information to persons who have made a request for the information; and
- Designate at each sub – divisional level or sub – district level Central Assistant or State Assistant Public Information Officers to receive the applications for information or appeals or forwarding the same to the Central or State Public Information Officers.

PROCEDURE FOR OBTAINING INFORMATION

PIO shall deal with requests from persons seeking information. If the information requested for is held by another public authority; the PIO shall transfer, within 5 days, the request to that other public authority and inform the applicant immediately.

PIO, on receipt of a request shall as expeditiously as possible and in any case within 30 days of the receipt of the request, provide the information on payment of such fee as may be prescribed. hours of the receipt of the request.

If the PIO fails to give decision on the request Where the information requested for concerns the life or liberty of a person, the same shall be provided within forty eight within the period specified, he shall be deemed to have refused the request.

Where a request has been rejected, the PIO shall communicate the following to the requester:

(i) the reasons for such rejection;

(ii) the period within which an appeal against such rejection may be preferred; and

(iii) the particulars of the Appellate Authority.

EXEMPTION FROM DISCLOSURE

Certain categories of information have been exempted from disclosure under the Act. These are;

- Where disclosure prejudicially affects the sovereignty and integrity of India;
- Information which has been expressly forbidden by any court or tribunal or the disclosure of which may constitute contempt of court:
- Where disclosure would cause a breach of privilege of parliament or the state legislature;
- Information including commercial confidence, trade secrets or intellectual property.
- Information received in confidence from a foreign government;
- Information the disclosure of which endangers life or physical safety of any person or identifies confident source of information or assistance;
- Information that would impede the process of investigation or apprehension or prosecution of offenders;

- Cabinet papers including records of deliberations of the Council of Ministers, Secretaries and other officers before the decisions are taken.

Section 8 provides that personal information which would cause invasion of the privacy unless larger public interest justifies it, shall not disclosed

Section 9 empowers the Public Information Officer to reject a request for information where an infringement of a copyright subsisting in a person would be involved.

It may be noted that as per Section 10 of the RTI Act, only that part of the record, which does not contain any information which is exempt from disclosure and which can reasonably be severed from any part that contains exempt information, may be provided. This is known as partial disclosure.

WHO IS EXCLUDED?

The Act excludes Central Intelligence and Security agencies specified in the Second Schedule like IB, R & AW, Directorate of Revenue Intelligence, Central Economic Intelligence Bureau, Directorate of Enforcement, Narcotics Control Bureaus, Aviation Research Centre, Special Frontier Force, BSF, and Nicobar, the Crime Branch – CID – CB; Dadra and Nagar Haveli and Special Branch, Lakshadweep Police, Agencies specified by the State Governments through a Notification will also be excluded.

The exclusion, however, is not absolute and these organization have an obligation to provide information pertaining to allegations of corruption and human rights violations. Further, information relating to allegations of human rights violation shall be given only with the approval of the Central Information Commission within forty – five days from the date of the receipt of request. [Section 24]

INFORMATION COMMISSIONS

Central Information Commission (CIC)

The Central Information Commission is to be constituted by the Central Government through a Gazette Notification. The Central Information Commission consists of the Chief Central Information Commissioner and Central Information Commission not exceeding 10.

The Chief Information Commissioner and Information Commissioners shall be persons of eminence in public life with wide knowledge and experience in law, science technology, social service, management, journalism, mass media or administration and governance. CIC/IC shall not be a Member of Parliament or Member of the Legislature of any State or Union Territory. He shall not hold – any other office of profit or connected with any political party or carrying on any business or pursuing any prolession.

CIC shall be appointed for a term of 5 years or till he attains the age of 65 years, whichever is earlier. CIC is not eligible for reappointment.

State Information Commission (SIC)

The State Information Commission will be constituted by the state Government through a Gazette notification. The State Information Commission consists of one State. Chief Information Commissioner (SCIC) and not more that 10 State Information Commissioners (SIC). The qualification for appointment as SCIC/SIC shall be the same as that for Central Commissioners.

Powers of Information Commission

The Central Information Commission Information Commission has a duty to receive complaints from any person.

- Who has not been able to submit an information request because a PIO has not been appointed;
- Who has been refused information that was requested.
- Who has received no response to his / her information request within the specified time limits;
- Who thinks the fees charged are unreasonable;
  Who thinks information given is incomplete or false or misleading; and
- Any other matter relating to obtaining information under this law.

If the Commission feels satisfied, an enquiry may be initiated and while initiating an enquiry the Commission has same powers as vested in a Civil Court.

The Central Information Commission or the State Information Commission during the inquiry of any complaint under this Act may examine any record which is under the control of the public authority, and no such record may be withheld from it on any grounds.

APELLATE AUTHORITIES

Any person who does not receive a decision within the specified time or is aggrieved by a decision of the PIO may file an appeal under the Act.

First Appeal

First appeal shall be filed to the officer senior in rank to the PIO in the concerned Public Authority within 30 days, from the expiry of the prescribed time limit for providing the information or from the receipt of the decision. However, the Appellate Authority may entertain the appeal even after the expiry of the aforesaid 30 days, if it is satisfied that the Appellant has been prevented by sufficient cause from filing the appeal within the prescribed period of 30 days.

First Appeal shall be disposed of within 30 days from the date of its receipt or within such extended period not exceeding a total of forty – five days from the date of filing thereof, for reasons to be recorded in writing.

Second Appeal

Second appeal shall be filed to the Central Information Commission or the State Information Commission, as the case may be**, within 90 day**s of the date on which the decision was given or should have been made by the First Appellate Authority. However, the Appellate Authority may entertain the appeal even after the expiry of the aforesaid 90 days, if it is satisfied that the Appellant has been prevented by sufficient cause from filling the appeal within the prescribed period of 90 days.

CHAPTER 13

Competition Act, 2002

INTRODUCTION / REASONS FOR REPEAL OF MRTP ACT, 1969

MRTP Act, 1969 has become obsolete in certain areas in the light to international economic developments relating to competition laws. So the need was felt to shift the focus from curbing monopolies to promoting competition. Hence, the Competition Act, 2002 was enacted, which aims at doing away from the rigidly structured MRTP Act, 1969.

The Competition Act, 2002 is flexible, behavior oriented and also explicitly indicates the parameters which shall be kept in view while deciding the adverse effect on competition, abuse of dominance and prejudicial combinations. The main purpose of the Act is to ensure free and fair competition in the market.

SALIENT/IMPORTANT REATURES OF THE ACT

1) The Competition Act, 2002 has been enacted to prevent practices having an appreciable adverse effect on competition, to promote and sustain competition in the market and to protect the interest of consumers and to ensure freedom of trade.
2) With the enforcement of the Competition Act, 2002 the MRTP Act, 1969 shall stand repeated and the MRTP Commission shall be dissolved.
3) The Competition Act, 2002 seeks to achieve its objectives by prohibiting anti – competitive trade agreements, preventing abuse of dominance, regulating combinations and formulating a policy on competition, creating awareness by imparting training on competition issues.
4) The Competition Act, 2002 provides for the establishment of Competition Commission of India and prescribes its duties, functions and powers.

IMPORTANT DEFINITIONS [SECTION 2]

Agreement

Agreement includes any arrangement or understanding or action in concert –

a) Whether or not, such agreement, understanding or action is formal or in writing or
b) Whether or not, such agreement, understanding or action is intended to be enforceable by legal proceedings.

Cartel

Cartel includes an association of producers, sellers or distributors, traders or service providers who, by agreement amongst themselves, limit, control, or attempt to control the production, distribution, sale or price of goods or services or, trade in goods provision of services.

The Competition Act, 2002 prohibits formation of certain cartels.

Consumer

Consumer means any persons who –

(i) Buys any goods for a consideration which has been paid or promised or partly paid and partly promised, or under my system of deferred payment and includes any person who uses those goods with the approval of the person buying those goods, whether such purchase of goods is for resale or for commercial purpose or for personal use:

(ii) Hires or avails of any services for a consideration which has been paid or promised or partly paid and partly promised, or under any system of deferred payment and includes any person who is the beneficiary of those services with the approval of hirer or avail or of those services, whether such hiring or availing of services is for any commercial purpose or for personal use.

It may be noted that under the competition Act, 2002 even if a person purchases goods or avails of services for commercial purpose. he'll be a consumer, whereas for the purpose of consumer Protection Act, 1986 a person purchasing goods or availing services for commercial purposes is not a consumer and cannot seek relief under that Act.

Enterprise

Enterprise means a person or department of the Government, who or which is, or has been engaged in any activity, relating to the production, storage , supply, distribution, acquisition or control of articles or goods or the provision of services of any kind.

Goods

Goods means goods as defined in the Sale of Goods Act, 1930 and include the following:

(i) Products manufactured processed or mined:

(ii) Debentures, shares and stocks after allotment;

(iii) In relation to 'goods supplied', goods imported in India

Services

Services means service of any description which is made available to potential users and includes the provision of services in connection with business of any industrial or commercial matters such as banking, communication, education, financing, insurance, chit funds, real estate, transport storage material treatment processing, supply of electrical or other energy, boarding, lodging, entertainment, amusement, constructions, repair conveying of news or information and advertising.

It may be noted that under the Competition Act, 2002 the services of industrial or commercial nature also fall within the scope of the Act, whereas under the Consumer Protection Act, 1986 the services of commercial nature or for business or industrial purposes are excluded for interpreting deficiency in the supply of any service.

Relevant Market, Relevant Geographic Market, and Relevant Product Market

The turns Relevant Market, Relevant Geographic Market, and Relevant Product Market have relevance in determination of the agreements being anti – competitive within the meaning, of Section 3 of the Competition Act, 2002.

Relevant Market means the market, which may be determined by the Competition Commission of India with reference to both the markets [Section 2(1)].

Relevant Geographic Market means a market comprising the area in which the conditions of competition for supply of goods or provision of services or demand of goods or services are distinctly homogeneous. Can be distinguished from conditions prevailing in neighboring areas [Section 2(s)]

Relevant Product Market means a market comprising of all those products or services, which are regarded as interchangeable or substitutable by the consumer, by reasons of characteristics of products or services, their prices and intended use [Section 2(1)]

IMPORTANT PROVISIONS

Anti – competitive Agreements

Section 3(1) of the Competition Act, 2002 provides that no enterprise or association of persons shall enter into any agreement in respect of production, supply, distribution, storage, acquisition or control of goods or provision of services, which causes or is likely to cause an appreciable adverse effect on competition. Section 3(2) further provides that any anti competitive agreement within the meaning of section 3(1) shall be void.

Prohibition on Agreements having Appreciable Adverse Effect on Competition

The following agreements shall be deemed to be prohibited under section 3(1), if such agreements cause or are likely to cause an appreciable adverse effect on competition.

a) Tie – in arrangement, i.e. an agreement requiring a purchaser of goods, as a condition of such purchase, to purchase some other goods.

b) Exclusive supply agreement, i.e. an agreement restricting in any manner the purchaser in the course of his trade from acquiring or otherwise dealing in any goods other than those of the seller or any other person.

c) Exclusive distribution agreement i.e. an agreement to limit, restrict or withhold the output or supply of any goods or allocate any area or market for the disposal or sale of the goods.

d) Refusal to deal i..e., an agreement which restricts, or is likely to restrict, by any method the person or classes of persons to whom goods are sold or from whom goods are bought.

e) Resale price maintenance i.e., an agreement to sell goods on condition that the prices to be charged on the resale by the purchaser shall be the prices stipulated by the seller unless it is clearly stated that prices lower than those prices may be charged.

Important Factors while determining whether as agreement has an 'appreciable adverse effect' on competition.

Section 19(3) of the competition Act, 2002 provides that while determining whether as agreement has appreciable adverse effect on competition, the Commission shall give due regard to all or any of the following factors, namely –

a) Creation of barriers to new entrants in the market;
b) Driving existing competitors out of the market;
c) Foreclosure of competition by hindering entry into the market;
d) Accrual of benefit to consumers;
e) Improvements in production or distribution of goods or provision of services; and
f) Promotion of technical, scientific and economic development by means of production or distribution of goods or provision of services. **Regulation of combination**

Regulation of Combination is one of the core provisions of the Competition Act, 2002 Section 5 of the Competition Act, 2002 provides that acquisition of one or more enterprise by one or more persons or merger or amalgamation of enterprise shall be combination of such enterprises and persons or enterprise which are above the certain prescribed size in terms of (a) assets or (b) turnover as provide under section 5.

Section 6 of the Competition Act, 2002 provides that any person or enterprise entering into a combination which causes or is likely to cause an appreciable adverse effect on combination within the relevant market in India and if such a combination is formed, it shall be void.

COMPETITION COMMISSION OF INDIA

Establishment of CCI [Section 7]

Section 7 empowers the Central Government to establish a Commission to be known as "Competition Commission of India." The commission is a body corporate having perpetual succession and common seal.

The Competition Commission has its head office at New Delhi (established w.e.f. 14.10.2003). In addition to this, the Commission can establish its offices at other places in India.

Composition of CCI [Section 8]

The Commission shall consist of a Chairman and other members, which shall not be less than 2 and more than 10. The Chairman and all the members shall be appointed by the Central Government.

Following are the qualification of Chairman and the members:

1) He shall be a person of ability, integrity and standing; and

2) He has been or is qualified to be Judge of a High Court or he has special knowledge and professional experience of not less than 15 years in international trade, economics, business, commerce, law finance, accountancy, management, etc.

Term of Office [Section 10]

The term of office of chairman shall be 5 years or up to the age of 67 years, whichever is earlier and that of other members shall be 5 years or up to the age of 65 years, whichever is earlier. However, they shall be eligible for reappointment.

Removal of Chairperson and other Members [Section 11]

The Chairperson or a Member of CCI may be removed from the office by the Central Government in the following cases:

a) Where he is adjudged as an insolvent:
b) Where he has been engaged in any paid employment;
c) Where he has been convicted of an offence which involved moral turpitude;
d) Where he has acquired such financial or other interest as is likely to affect prejudicially his functions;
e) where he has abused his position and
f) Where he has become physically or mentally incapable.

Restriction on employment of Chairperson and other Members [Section 12]

As per section 12, the Chairperson and other Member shall not, for a period **of two years**, accept and employment connected with the management of administration of any enterprise which has been a party to any proceeding before the Commission under this Act.

However, the said restriction shall not apply where the Chairperson or any Member is offered an employment in a corporation established by or under any Central, State or Provincial Act.

Validity of Acts of Competition Commission of India [Section 15]

Act of Competition Commission of India cannot be challenged on the ground only of any defect in the constitution of competition Commission of India or the existence of any vacancy in the Competition Commission of India. However, acts of Competition Commission of India can be questioned on other acts such as acting mala fide, acting on the basis of untenable evidence, etc.

It may be noted that when an act of Competition Commission of India is called in question on such other grounds, defects in the constitution or the existence of a vacancy in the Competition Commission of India may also be urged as an additional ground.

Powers of CCI

Following are the important powers or CCI.

1) To inquire into anti – competitive agreements and abuse of dominant position.
2) to determine whether an agreement has an appreciable adverse effect on competition:
3) Enquire whether a combination has cause or likely to cause an appreciable adverse effect on competition:

4) To issue 'cease and desist' orders;
5) To grant such interim relief as would be necessary in a particular case;
6) to award compensation;
7) To order division of dominant undertakings:
8) To order demerger:
9) To impose firms;
10) To order cost for frivolous complaints.

Powers of CCI to regulate its own procedure [Section 36]

The CCI has been empowered to lay down its own procedure and regulation and shall not be bound by the procedure laid down by the Code of Civil Procedure, 1908. However, it shall observe the principle of natural justice and shall be subject to the rules made by the Central Government for the procedure to be followed in inquiries.

The CCI shall have the same powers as are vested in the civil court under the Code of Civil

Procedure. 1908 while trying a suit, in respect of the following matters, namely;

i) Summoning and enforcing the attendance of any person and examining them on oath;
ii) Requiring the discovery and production of documents;
iii) Receiving the evidence on affidavits;
iv) Issuing the commission for the examination of witnesses or documents;
v) Requisitioning any public record/document from any office;
vi) Dismissing an application in default or deciding it;
vii) Any other such matter as may be prescribed

Section 36 of the Competition Act, 2002 empowers the Commission to call upon the experts from the fields of economics, commerce, accountancy, international trade or from any other discipline to assist the Commission in the conduct of any inquiry before it.,

DIRECTOR GENERAL

Section 16 empowers the Central Government to appoint a Director General and such number of additional, joint, deputy or assistant Director Generals or other advisers, consultants, or officers. These person shall be appointed from amongst the persons of integrity and outstanding ability and who have experience in investigation and knowledge of accountancy, management, business, public administration, international trade, economics, law etc.

Director General is an important functionary under the Competition Act, 2002. He assists the Commission by furnishing Investigation Report in respect of such matters as are referred to him by the CCI. He also assists the Commission in conducting proceedings of enquiries, which are initiated by the CCI suo moto.

COMPETITION ADVOCACY

Section 49 of the Competition Act, 2002 provides that while formulating a policy on competition including review of laws related to competition, the Central Government may make a reference to the CCI for its opinion on the possible effects of such a policy on competitions.

The Commission shall, *within 60 days of receipt* of such a reference, give its opinion on it to the Central Government. Thereafter the Central Government may formulate such policy as it deems fit. It may be noted that the role of the Commission is advisory and the opinion given by it shall not be binding on the Central Government.

DIFFERENCE BETWEEN MRTP ACT AND COMPETITION ACT

Following are the important differences between the MRTP Act, 1969 and Competition Act, 2002:

1) MRTP Act is based on the pre – liberazation scenario whereas Competition Act is based on the post liberalization scenario.
2) MRTP Act emphasizes on curbing monopolies whereas Competition Act emphasizes on Promoting competition.
3. MRTP Act provides for compulsory registration of agreements relating to restrictive trade practices whereas in Competition Act, there is no such requirement of registration of agreements.
4) Under Competition Act, dominance per se is not bad but only the abuse of dominance is considered bad whereas under the MRTP Act, dominance itself is bad.
5) Combinations are not regulated by MRTP Act whereas they are regulated by Competition Act.
6) MRTP Act does not vest MRTP Commission power to inquire into cartels of foreign origin in a direct manner whereas the Competition Act seeks to regulate them.

CHAPTER **14**

The Negotiable Instruments, Act, 1881

1. INTRODUCTION TO NEGOTIABLE INSTRUMENTS

Definition of Negotiable instrument (Sec.13)

Negotiable instrument means

- a promissory note; or
- bill of exchange; or
- cheque **Payable**
- either to order; or
- to the bearer.

Meaning of Negotiable instrument

- Negotiable instrument means an instrument
- The property in which is acquired by anyone who takes it –
  - Bonafide; and
  - For value
- notwithstanding any defect in the title of any prior party.
- In other words negotiable instrument means an instrument
- Notwithstanding any defect in the title of any prior party.

2. ESSENTIALS OR CHARACTERISTICS OF A NEGOTIABLE INSTRUMENT (Sec.13)

- Freely transferable from one person to another
- Transferable infinitum (i.e. indefinitely).
- HDC gets a good title to negotiable instrument even though the title of transferor is defective.
- A negotiable instrument may more than one payee jointly or alternatively.

3. PRESUMPTIONS AS TO NEGOTIABLE INSTRUMENTS (Sec.118)

Unless the contrary is proved, the following presumptions shall be made –

As to consideration

That every negotiable instrument was made or drawn for consideration and that every such instrument when it has been accepted, endorsed or negotiated has been for consideration.

As to date

That every negotiable instrument bearing a date was made or drawn on such date.

As to time of acceptance

That every accepted bill of exchange was accepted within a reasonable time after its date and before its maturity.

As to time of transfer

That every transfer of a negotiable instrument was made before its maturity.

As to order of endorsements

That the endorsements appearing upon a negotiable instrument were made in the order in which they appear thereon.

As to stamp

That a lost promissory note or bill of exchange was duly stamped.

That holder is a holder;

That the holder of a negotiable instrument is a holder in due course.

As to dishonour

If a suit is filed upon an instrument which has been dishonored, the court shall, on proof of the protest, presume the fact of dishonour.

The above presumptions are rebuttable (debatable) by producing evidence to the contrary. It is the responsibility of the person alleging the non existence of presumptions to prove the same.

The above presumptions are not applicable where an instrument has been obtained by an offence, fraud or for unlawful consideration.

4. MEANING OF PROMISSORY NOTE (Sec.4)

A 'Promissory note' is an instrument in writing (not being a bank – note or a currency – note) containing an unconditional undertaking

Signed by the maker

to pay a certain sum of money only to –

(a) a certain person; or

(b) the order of a certain person.

Rs................ Place.............. Date..............

..... month/days after date. I promise to pay ....or Bearer/Order the sum of Rs...........for value received with interest @.............p.a. with ....rests

.... (Maker)

5. ESSENTIALS CHARACTERISTICS OF A PROMISSORY NOTE (Sec.4)

In writing

An oral promise to pay is not sufficient

Example

A promises to pay Rs.1,000 to 'B', over telephone.

Express promise to pay

There must be express promise to pay.

Mere acknowledgement of indebtedness is not sufficient.

- "I acknowledge myself to be indebted to B in Rs.5,000, to be paid on demand, for value received". The promise to pay is definite and therefore this is a valid promissory note.
- "Mr. B.I.O.U Rs.1,000." There is no promise to pay and therefore this is not a valid promissory note.

Definite and unconditional promise

If a promise to pay is dependent upon an event which is certain to happen, although the time of its happening is uncertain, the promise to pay is unconditional.

- "I promise to pay B Rs.500 seven days after my marriage with C." The promise is conditional since the promise is dependent upon marriage of the promisor with C, which may or not happen.
- "I promise to pay B Rs.500 on D's death, provided D leaves me enough to pay that sum." The promise is conditional since the promise is dependent upon the estate inherited by the promisor.
- "I promise to pay B Rs.500 on D's death." The promise is not conditional, but definite since death of D is certain. Therefore, the promissory not is valid.

Signed by maker

A promissory note must be signed by the maker.

The signatures may be made on any part of the instrument.

Promise to pay a certain sum

- "I promise to pay B Rs.500 and all other sums which shall be due to him." Since the amount payable is not certain, it is not a valid promissory note.
- "I promise to pay B Rs.500 first deducting there from any money which he owes me." Since the amount payable is not certain, it is not a valid promissory note.

Promise to pay money only

"I promise to pay B Rs.500 and to deliver to him my black horse on 1st January next." It is not a valid promissory note since the promisor is required to deliver his black horse also, which is not 'money'.

Payee must be certain

The name of payee must be specified in the promissory note, otherwise it will be invalid.

Stamped

A promissory note must be stamped.

Parties to a promissory note

Maker : The person who makes the promissory note is called as maker. His liability is primary and unconditional.

Payee : The person to whom money is to be paid is named in the promissory note. He is called as payee.

The words **" or to the bearer of the instrument"** is inoperative in view of section 31 of the Reserve Bank of India Act, 1934, which provides that no person in India other than Reserve Bank of India or Central Government can make or issue promissory note payable to bearer of the instrument.

BILL OF EXCHANGE (Sec. 5)

A 'bill of exchange' is an instrument in writing
Containing an unconditional order
Signed by the maker
Directing a certain person

To pay a certain sum of money only to –

(a) a certain person ; or

(b) the order of a certain person; or **(c)** the bearer of the instrument.

Amount: Rs........... Place...............
Date................

.......month/days after date, pay to ....or Bearer/Order the sum of Rupees...........only for value received.

To

....
(Drawer) (Drawee)

Essentials characteristics of a bill of exchange

(a) It must be in writing
(b) It must contain an express order to pay
(c) The order to pay must be definite and unconditional
(d) It must be signed by the drawer
(e) The sum contained in the order must be certain
(f) The order must be to pay money only
(g) Drawer, drawee and payee must be certain (usually, same person is the drawer and payee)
(h) It must be stamped.

Parties to a bill of exchange Drawer

- The person who draws the bill (i.e.the person who makes the bill) is called as drawer.
- His liability is secondary and conditional
- His liability is primary and conditional until the bill is accepted.

Drawee

- The person on whom the bill is drawn is called as drawee.
- On acceptance of the bill

(a) he is called as acceptor;
(b) he becomes liable for the payment of the bill; **(c)** his liability is primary and unconditional.

Payee.

- The person to whom money is to be paid is named in the bill.
- He is called as payee.

The words "or the bearer of the instrument" is inoperative is view of section 31 of the Reserve Bank of India Act, 1934, which provides that no person in India other than Reserve Bank of India or Central Government can make or issue promissory note payable to bearer of the instrument.

Difference between promissory note and bill of exchange.

7. CHEQUE (Sec.6)

A cheque is a bill of exchange drawn on a specified banker and not expressed to be payable otherwise than on demand (i.e. it is always payable on demand) and it includes – - the electronic image of truncated cheque; and - a cheque in electronic from.

Essentials characteristics of a cheque

(a) It must be in writing
(b) It must contain an express order to pay
(c) The order to pay must be definite and unconditional
(d) It must be signed by the drawer
(e) The sum contained in the order must be certain
(f) The order must be to pay money only
(g) Drawer, drawee and payee must be certain
(h) It is always drawn upon a specified banker
(i) It is always payable on demand

- A cheque must contain all the characteristics of a bill of exchange
- A cheque does not require **(a)** stamping ; or **(b)** acceptance.

Parties to a cheque

Drawer

- The person who draws the cheque, i.e., the person who makes the cheque is called as drawer.
- His liability is primary and conditional

Drawee

- The bank on whom the cheque is drawn is called as drawee.
- He makes the payment of the cheque.

Payee

- The person to whom money is to be paid (i.e., the person in whose favour cheque is issued) is named in the cheque. He is called as payee.
- The payee may be the drawer himself or a third party.

Meaning of electronic cheque and truncated cheque

Meaning of truncated cheque

- A truncated cheque means a cheque
- Which is truncated during the course of a clearing cycle
- Either by the clearing house or bank whether paying or receiving payment.
- Immediately on generation of an electronic image.
- For transmission substituting the further physical movement of cheque in writing

Meaning of 'a cheque in electronic form'

- A cheque in electronic form means a cheque
- Which contains the exact mirror image of a paper cheque
- and is generated, written and signed in a secure system ensuring the minimum safety standards with the use of digital signature (with or without biometric signature) and asymmetric crypto system.

Duties of collecting banker

The collecting banker shall verify with due diligence and ordinary care – • The prima facie genuineness of the cheque to be truncated;

- As to whether any fraud, forgery or tampering is apparent on the face of the instrument.

Presentment of truncated cheque

In case of any reasonable suspicion about the genuineness of the electronic image of a truncated cheque (e.g. suspicion as to fraud, forgery, tampering or destruction of the instrument), the paying banker is entitled to –

- Demand any further information regarding the truncated cheque;
- Demand the presentment of truncated cheque itself for verification.

Difference between electronic cheque and truncated cheque

Electronic cheque	Truncated cheque
Paper is not used at any stage in creation of an electronic cheque.	A truncated cheque is nothing but a paper cheque, which is truncated during the clearing cycle.
Digital signatures must be used to create an electronic image of cheque. Thus, an electronic cheque contains digital signature.	The paper cheque, which is afterwards truncated, contains no digital signature. The signatures in ink appear on the truncated cheque.
The original writing of an electronic cheque is in electronic form.	The – original writing of a truncated cheque is on paper duly – signed in ink. After the paper cheque is converted into electronic form, it is truncated and thus, it becomes a truncated cheque.

8. CAPACITY OF A PERSON TO BE A PARTY TO A NEGOTIABLE INSTRUMENT (Sec. 26)

Person must be capable of contracting

A person shall be liable on a negotiable instrument (by reason of making, drawing, accepting endorsing, delivering or negotiating a negotiable instrument) only if he is capable of contracting according to the law to which he is subject.

Liability in case of a minor

- A minor may draw, endorse, deliver and negotiate any negotiable instrument.
- All the parties shall be bound on such negotiable instrument.
- However, the minor shall not be bound on such negotiable instrument.

9. CLASSIFICATION OF NEGOTIABLE INSTRUMENT (Sec. 13, 19 and 21)

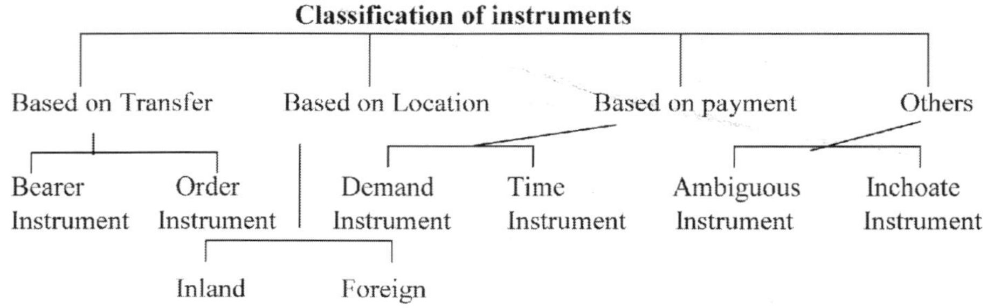

Order Instrument :

An instrument -

- Payable to a particular person or expressed to be payable to a particular person, and
- Does not contain words prohibiting transfer or indicating an intention that it shall not be transferable. ¾ **Bearer Instrument :**

An instrument is payable to bearer of –

(a) it is expressed to be so payable, or

(b) on which the only or last endorsement is an endorsement in blank.

- Promissory note – can not be made payable to bearer
- Bill of exchange can not be made payable to bearer on demand

Demand Instrument:

An instrument which satisfies the following conditions –

(a) Time for payment is not specified.

(b) Expressed to be payable on demand.

(c) Can be presented for payment at any time.

Note: A P/N or B/E, in which no time for payment is specified, and a cheque, are payable on demand. [Sec.19]

Time Instrument :

An instrument in which time for payments is specified and may be payable – (a) After a specified period, or

(b) On a specified day, or

(c) Certain period after, sight, or

(d) On the happening of a certain event.

Inland Instrument [Sec.11]:

A P/N, B/E or cheque is said to be an inland instrument, if any one of the following conditions is satisfied –

(a) Drawn or made in India and made payable in India, or

(b) Drawn or made in India and drawn upon a person resident in India.

Note: Even if an Inland Bill is endorsed to a foreign country, it continues to be an Inland Instrument.

Foreign Instrument [Sec.12]

An instrument which is not an Inland Instrument, is deemed to be a Foreign Instrument.

Ambiguous Instruments [Sec.17]:

(a) Where an instrument may be constructed either as a P/N or as a B/E, the holder may at his option treat it as either, and the instrument shall henceforth be treated accordingly, e.g. a B/E drawn in favour of a fictitious person.

(b) An Ambiguous Instrument treated as a P/N or as a B/E cannot be treated differently afterwards.

Conditions for an inchoate instrument

(a) A person signs a negotiable instrument.

(b) The negotiable instrument is stamped.

(c) The negotiable instrument is either wholly blank or is partially blank.

(d) The person signing such negotiable instrument delivers it to another person.

Legal effect

The holder gets a prima facie authority to make or complete the negotiable instrument.

Liability on an inchoate instrument

Rights of a person to whom an inchoate instrument is delivered He can recover only such amount as he was authorised to fill.

Rights of HDC

He can recover the whole amount stated in the instrument, but not exceeding the amount covered by the stamps.

10. MATURITY OF A NEGOTIABLE INSTRUMENT (Sec.22)

Maturity of a negotiable instrument Days of grace

- It means the date on which the negotiable instrument falls due for payment.
- A negotiable instrument which is payable otherwise than on demand is entitled to 3 days of grace.

11. CALCULATION OF DAYS OF MATURITY (Sec.23 to 25)

Case	Date of maturity
Negotiable instrument payable on a specified day	Specified day + 3rd day
Negotiable instrument payable on a stated number of days after date	Date on which negotiable instrument is drawn + stated number of days + 3rd day
Negotiable instrument payable on stated number of days after sight	Date on which negotiable instrument is presented for4 sight + stated number of days + 3rd day
Negotiable instrument payable on stated number of days after happening of a certain event	Date on which such event happens + stated number of day + 3rd day
Negotiable instrument payable on stated number of months after date	Corresponding day of the relevant month (i.e., date on which negotiable instrument is drawn + stated number of months) + 3rd day

Contd.

Case	Date of maturity
Negotiable instrument payable on stated number of months after sight	Corresponding day of the relevant month* (i.e., Date on which negotiable instrument is presented for sight + stated number of months) + 3rd day
Negotiable instrument payable on stated number of months after happening of a certain event	Corresponding day of the relevant month* (i.e., Date on which such event happens + stated number of months)+ 3rd day
If the day of maturity of negotiable instrument is a public holiday	Immediately preceding business day
If the day of maturity of negotiable instrument is an emergency or unforeseen public holiday	Immediately succeeding business day

12. NEGOTIATION – MEANING AND METHODS (Sec.14)

Meaning of negotiation

Negotiation means transfer of a negotiable instrument to any other person so an to constitute that person the holder of such negotiable instrument.

Methods of negotiation ***Negotiation by delivery***

- A bearer instrument may be negotiated by delivery.
- The delivery must be voluntary

Negotiation by endorsement and delivery

An order instrument can be negotiated only by way of -

(i) endorsement; and (ii) delivery.

13. MEANING OF ENDORSEMENT (Sec. 15)

Endorsement means

Signing

- on the face or back of negotiable instrument; or
- on a slip of paper annexed to the negotiable instrument **By**
- the holder of negotiable instrument **For the purpose of**
- negotiating such negotiable instrument .

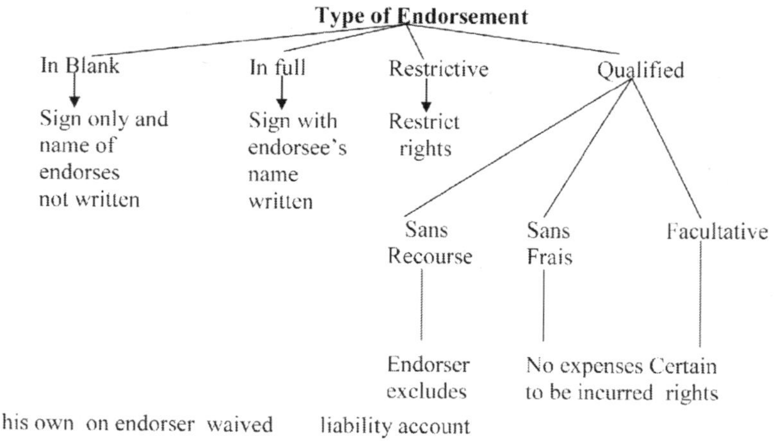

14. ESSENTIAL REQUEREMENTS OF A VALID ENDORSEMENT (Sec.15 and 16)

Writing

The endorsement must be in writing

Signed

The endorsement shall not be valid unless it is signed.

By holder

The endorsement shall be valid only if the negotiable instrument is signed by the holder.

15. KINDS OF ENDORSEMENTS (Sec.16, 50, 52, 56)

General endorsement i.e. endorsement in blank

Meaning

- General endorsement means, an endorsement made by the endorser without writing the name of the endorsee.

Effect

- Order instrument is converted into bearer instrument.

Special endorsement i.e., endorsement in full

Special endorsement means an endorsement made by a holder by –

(a) singing his name, and

(b) adding a direction to pay the amount to a specified person

Restrictive endorsement

An endorsement which restricts the right of further negotiation is called as restrictive endorsement.

Partial endorsement

An endorsement which purports to transfer only a part of the amount of the instrument is called as partial endorsement. Partial endorsement is not valid at law.

Conditional endorsement

(a) **Sans Recourse** – Endorser relieves himself from the liability to all subsequent endorsees.

(b) **Facultative** – Endorser waives any of his rights.

(c) **Contingent** - Endorser makes his liability dependent upon the happening of an event.

16. NEGOTIATION BACK (Sec.90)

Meaning

If –

- a negotiable instrument is negotiated by the holder, but
- the endorser again becomes the holder of such negotiable instrument ***Then*** –
- it is called as negotiation back.

Effect

- The holder cannot enforce payment against an intermediate party to whom he was previously liable.
- The holder can enforce payment against all the parties to whom he was not previously liable.

- However, the holder can sue all the prior parties (including all intermediate parties to whom he was previously liable), if he had made sans recourse endorsement.

17. DISTINCTION BETWEEN NEGOTIATION AND ASSIGNMENT

Basis	Negotiation	Assignment
1. Applicable Act	If a negotiable instrument is transferred by way of negotiation, Negotiable Instrument Act, 1881, applies.	Where any right is transferred by way of assignment, the Transfer of Property Act applies.
2. Meaning	Negotiation means transfer of a negotiable instrument to any other person so as to constitute that person the holder of such negotiable instrument.	Transfer of a right to receive the payment of a debt by one person (viz, assignor) to another document is called as assignment.
3. Scope	Negotiation can be made for transferring negotiable instruments only.	Assignment can be made of any right.
4. Method or manner	A bearer instrument can be negotiated merely by delivery, and an order instrument can be negotiated by endorsement and delivery.	Assignment is valid only if it is made in writing and is signed by the assignor.
5. Notice	Notice of negotiation is not required to be given to any party.	Notice of assignment must be given by the assignee to the debtor.
6. consideration	It is presumed that every negotiable instrument was negotiated for consideration.	There is no such presumption in case of assignment.
7. Burden of proof	The other party has to prove that negotiation was without any consideration.	The assignee has to prove that there was some consideration.
8. Better title	The transferee of a negotiable instrument acquires a title better than that of the transfer, i.e., he becomes a holder in due course.	The assignee does not acquire a title better than that of the assignor.
9. Stamp duty	Negotiation does not require payment of stamp duty.	Assignment requires payment of stamp duty.

MEANING AND PURPOSE OF CROSSING

Meaning of crossing

Crossing means a direction given by the drawer of the cheque to the drawee bank, not to pay the cheque at the counter of the bank, but to pay it to a person who presents it through a banker.

Purpose of crossing

Crossing makes it possible to trace the person to whom the payment has been made. Thus, it makes the cheque safe.

19. TYPES OF CROSSING (Sec. 123 to 131A)

General Crossing ; Sec.123

Where a cheque bears across its face an addition of–

- The words 'and company' or any abbreviations thereof between two parallel transverse lines, or
- Two parallel transverse lines simply.

....
Pay..
.... or bearer
Rupees..
....
....
XYZ Bank
XXXX XXXX

Either with or without the words 'not negotiable', the addition shall be deemed a crossing, and the cheque shall be deemed to be crossed generally.

Where a cheque is crossed generally, the banker on whom it is drawn shall not pay it otherwise than to a banker.

Special Crossing : Sec.124.

Where a cheque bears across its face an addition of the name of a banker, either with or without the words 'not negotiable', that addition shall be deemed a crossing and the cheque shall be deemed to be crossed specially.

....

Pay..

....or bearer

Rupees..

....

XYZ Bank

XXXX XXXX

Two parallel transverse lines are not a must. Where a cheque is crossed specially, the banker on whom it is crossed shall not pay it, otherwise than to the banker to whom it is crossed or his agent for collection.

Difference:

In general crossing the Name of the Bank is not mentioned whereas in special crossing the Name of the Bank is mentioned.

'Not Negotiable' Crossing : Sec.130.

The object of "Not negotiable" crossing is to protect the rights of holder of a cheque.

A person taking a cheque crossed generally or specially, bearing in either cases the words 'not negotiable', shall not have, and shall not be capable of giving a better title to the cheque other than that which the person from whom he took it had.

Ordinarily a person acquiring a cheque in good faith becomes its holder in due course just as in the case of an open document. Such a cheque can be negotiated further.

However, where a cheque is crossed as 'Not Negotiable', either generally or specially, the Holder in due course will not get a better title than the person from whom the received. It maybe noted that though it is mentioned 'Not Negotiable', the cheque can be transferred. The only restriction is with regard to the title passed.

In other words, the principle of nema dat quod non habet (nobody can pass on a title better than what he himself has) will be applicable to a cheque with a 'not negotiable' crossing, even though the cheque is in the hands of a holder in due course.

'Account Payee' Crossing / Restrictive Crossing

The purpose of this crossing bearing the words "A/c Payee" is to obviate the risk of a wrong person obtaining payment on a cheque.

It is a direction to banker to credit the proceeds only to the account of the payee.

The cheque remarks legally negotiable but "A/c payee" crossing hinders the negotiability of the cheque in practice.

20. BOUNCING OR DISHONOUR OF CHEQUES (Sec.31 and 138)

Liability of drawee on dishonour Conditions (Sec.31)

If –

- the drawer has sufficient funds in the account; and
- such funds are properly applicable to payment of the cheque ***Then*** –
- the drawee is duly required to pay the cheque.
- In case of default by drawee (i.e. Banker), the drawee shall compensate the drawer for loss caused to him.

Liability of drawer on dishonour (Sec.138)

Nature of liability

- Imprisonment – 2 years (Maximum); or
- Fine - 2 times the amount of cheque (Maximum); or
- Both

Conditions

- Debt - Cheque was issued to discharge a legally enforceable debt.
- Reason for dishonour – insufficiency of funds
- Presentment of cheque – within 6 months or validity period of the cheque
- Demand made from drawer – within 30 days of dishonour
- Default by drawer to pay - within 15 days of demand made.
- Complaint by holder – within 1 month, with the Court.

21. HOLDER (Sec.8 and 9)

Meaning of 'holder' (Sec.8)

(a) He must be entitled to the possession of negotiable instrument in his own name.

(b) He must be entitled to receive or recover the amount due on negotiable instrument from the parties liable on negotiable instrument.

Holder for value

'Holder for value' means, as regards all parties prior to himself, holder of an instrument for which value has, at any time, been given.

Meaning of 'holder in due course' (Sec.9)

(a) He must be a holder.

(b) He must have become the holder for consideration.

(c) He must have obtained the possession of negotiable instrument before maturity

(d) He must have obtained the negotiable instrument in good faith, i.e. without sufficient cause to believe that any defect existed in the title of the person from whom he derived his title.

Example:-

	Situation	Holder	Holder for Value	Holder in due Course
a.	X steals a cheque	√	×	×
b.	X gets a cheque for consideration but after maturity	√	√	×
c.	X gets a cheque for consideration before maturity.	√	√	√

22. PRIVILEGES OF A HOLDER IN DUE COURSE (Sec.20, 36, 43, 46, 53 and 58)

- Every prior party to a negotiable instrument is liable to a HDC (Sec.36)
- A holder who derives title from HDC has the same rights as that of a HDC (Sec.53)
- No prior party can set up a defense that the negotiable instrument was drawn, made or endorsed by him without any consideration (Sec.43)
- No prior party can set up a defence that the negotiable instrument was lost or was obtained from him by an offence or fraud or for an unlawful consideration. Thus, HDC gets a valid title to the negotiable instrument even though the title of the transferor was defective (Sec.58)
- No Prior party can allege that negotiable instrument was delivered conditionally or for a special purpose only (Sec.46).
- HDC can claim full amount of the negotiable instrument (but not exceeding the amount covered by the stamp) even though such amount is in excess of the amount authorised by the person delivering an inchoate negotiable instrument (Sec.20).

23. DIFFERNCE BETWEEN HOLDER AND HDC

24. PAYMENT IN DUE COURSE. (Sec.10)

- Payment is made as per apparent tenor.
- Payment is made in good faith- ™ Payment is made without negligence
- Payment is made to holder of negotiable instrument
- Payment is made in money only

25. PROTECTION TO PAYING BANKER (Sec.85)

Cheque payable to order • Payment is made in due course.

- The protection shall be available notwithstanding that any endorsement subsequently turns out to be a forgery.

Cheque originally payable to bearer

- Payment is made in due course
- Payment is made to the bearer of the cheque

Basis	Holder	HDC
1. consideration	A person becomes a holder even if he obtains the negotiable instrument without any consideration.	A person becomes a HDC only if he obtains the negotiable instrument for consideration.
2. Before Maturity	A person becomes a holder even is he obtains the negotiable instrument after the maturity of the negotiable instrument.	A person becomes a HDC only if he obtains the negotiable instrument before its maturity.
3. Good Faith, i.e., bonafide	A person becomes a holder, even if he does not obtain the negotiable instrument in good faith.	For being a HDC, a person must obtain the negotiable instrument in good faith.
4. Privileges	A holder is not entitled to the privileges, which are available for HDC.	A HDC is entitled to various privileges as specified under the Negotiable Instruments Act, 1881.
5. Right to sue	A holder cannot sue all the prior parties.	A HDC can sue all the prior parties.

- The protection shall be available notwithstanding that any endorsement appears on the cheque

Cheques crossed generally

- Payment is made in due course.
- Payment is made to any banker.

Cheques crossed specially

- Payment is made in due course
- Payment is made to the banker to whom the cheque is crossed.

BANKER MUST REFUSE TO HONOUR A CUSTOMER'S CHEQUE

- Stop payment
- Garnishee order
- Death of customer
- Insolvency of customer
- Insanity or customer
- Assignment of funds by customer
- Defect in title of holder
- Loss of cheque
- Materially altered cheque, mutilated cheque, cheque of doubtful validity, incomplete cheque
- Different signatures
- Receipt of application for closure of account
- Irregular endorsement
- Stale cheque, i.e., outdated cheque
- Post dated cheque

Undated cheque

28. BANKER MAY REFUSE TO HONOUR A CUSTOMER'S CHEQUE

- Insufficient funds
- Funds not applicable
- Presentment at different branch

Presentment after banking hours

EFFECT OF NON – PRESENTMENT OF CHEQUE WITHIN REASONABLE TIME (Sec.84)

No liability of drawer if bank fails Conditions

(a) The drawer has sufficient balance when he issue the cheque, and when the cheque ought to be presented for payment.

(b) The holder fails to present the cheque within a reasonable time of issue of the cheque.

(c) Meanwhile (i.e. after issue of the cheque but before presentation of the cheque by the holder) the bank fails, and consequently the drawer suffers actual damages.

30. MATERIAL ALTERATION (Sec.20, 49, 87 and 125)

Meaning

An alteration is called as material alteration if it alters –

- the character or operation (i.e. the legal effect) of a negotiable instrument; or
- the rights and liabilities of any of the parties to a negotiable instrument.

Material alterations authorised by Act

(a) Filling blanks of an inchoate instrument (Sec.20)

(b) Conversion of a blank endorsement into an endorsement in full (Sec.49) (c) Crossing of cheques (Sec.125)

(d) Conversion of general crossing into special crossing or not negotiable crossing or A/c Payee Crossing (but not vice – versa)

(e) Conversion of a bearer instrument into an order instrument by deleting the word 'Bearer'.

Effects of material alteration (87)

All the parties to negotiable not consenting to the material alteration are discharged.

31. ACCEPTANCE (Sec.7 and 86)

Meaning of acceptance (Sec.7)

(a) The drawee signs the bill; and

(b) The drawee delivers it to the holder of the bill; or

Effect (Sec.7)

The drawee becomes the acceptor.

Essentials of a valid acceptance (Sec.7)

(a) Writing (whether on the face or back of the bill)

(b) Signed (Signature without the word 'accepted' is also valid)

(c) Signing on the bill

(d) Delivery or intimation to the holder that the bill has been accepted.

Types of acceptance (Sec.86)

(a) **General** – Acceptance of bill without any qualification.

(b) **Qualified** – Acceptance of bill subject to some qualification (e.g. accepting the bill subject to the condition that the payment of bill shall be made only on happening of an event specified therein).

Effect of qualified acceptance (Sec. 86)

(a) The holder may object to the qualified acceptance. In such a case, it shall be treated that the bill is dishonoured due to non – acceptance.

(b) He may give his consent to the qualified acceptance. In such a case, all the previous parties, not consenting to it, are discharged.

32. DISHONOUR BY NON – ACCEPTANCE (Sec.91)

Meaning

A bill is dishonoured by non – acceptance if it is duly presented for acceptance, but the drawee refuses to accept the bill.

Cases in which a bill is dishonoured by non – acceptance

(a) Where a bill is not accepted by the drawee within 48 hours of presentment of bill. If the holder allows to the drawee more than 48 hours for acceptance, all the prior parties not consenting to the same are discharged from liability to such holder.

(b) In case there are two or more drawees who are not partners, if the bill is not accepted by all the drawees.

(c) Where the drawee is a fictitious person

(d) When the drawee cannot be found even after a reasonable search.

(e) When the drawee is incompetent to contract.

(f) Where the drawee gives a conditional acceptance, and the holder does not give his consent to the conditional acceptance.

Effects

- The holders gets an immediate right to sue all the prior parties.
- He need not wait till the maturity of the bill for it to be dishonoured on presentment for payment.

Non – applicability

A promissory note or a cheque cannot be dishonoured by non – acceptance since a promissory note or a cheque does not require any acceptance.

33. ACCEPTANCE FOR HONOUR (Sec.108 to 112)

Meaning

The person who accepts the bill for the honour of any other person is called as an acceptor for honour;

Conditions for 'acceptance for honour'

- The bill must have been noted for non – acceptance
- The acceptance is given –
  - for the honour of any party already liable under the bill.
  - By any person who is already not liable under the bill.
  - With the consent of the holder of the bill.
- The acceptance must be made in writing on the bill.

Liability of acceptor for honour

- He is liable to pay the amount of the bill, if the drawee does not pay.
- He is liable only to the parties subsequent to the party for whose honour the bill is accepted.

Rights of acceptor for honour

He is entitled to recover the amount paid by him from the party for whose honour the bill was accepted, and from all the parties prior to such party.

34. PAYMENT FOR HONOUR (Sec.113 and 114)

Meaning of 'payer for honour'

A person who pays a bill for honour of any other person is called as 'payer for honour'

Conditions for 'payment for honour'

- The bill must have been noted for non – payment.
- Payment for honour is made –

- for the honour of any party already liable under the bill.
- By any person (whether or not he is already liable under the bill). - With the consent of the holder of the public.
- The payment must be recorded by Notary Public.

Rights of payer for honour

- The payer for honour is entitled to all the rights of a holder.
- He can recover all the sums paid by him form – (a) the party for whose honour he pays; and (b) all the parties prior to such party.

35. DISHONOUR BY NON – PAYMENT (Sec.92)

Kinds of negotiable A negotiable instrument shall be dishonoured by non – payment instrument if default in payment is made by the following parties	
Promissory note	Maker
Bill	Acceptor (Drawee, in case the bill does not require acceptance
Cheque	Drawee

36. NOTICE OF DISHONOUR (Sec.93 to 98)

Notice by whom?

Notice may be given by the holder or any party liable on the negotiable instrument.

Notice to whom?

Notice must be given to all the parties to whom the holder seeks to make liable

Contents of notice

Notice must disclose the fact of dishonour of negotiable instrument

Effects of default

A party (other than the party primarily liable on the negotiable instrument) to whom notice of dishonour is not given is discharged from liability on the negotiable instrument.

When notice of dishonour is unnecessary or excused (Sec.98)

(a) When notice of dishonour is dispensed with by a party.

(b) Where the drawer of the cheque has countermanded payment, notice to drawer is not required to be given.

(c) When the party entitled cannot be found even after due search.

(d) Where the party bound to give notice is unable to give notice without any fault of his own.

37. NOTING AND PROTESTING (Sec.99 to 103)

Meaning of noting

Recording the fact of dishonour of a negotiable instrument on the negotiable instrument.

Procedure and contents of noting

- The dishonoured bill is handed over to a Notary Public.
- Notary Public presents it again for acceptance/payment.
- If the drawee/acceptor refuses to accept or pay the bill, the Notary Public records the fact of dishonour on the bill.

Noting is optional

It is net mandatory to get the fact of dishonour noted.

Meaning of protest

A certificate issued by Notary Public stating the fact of dishonour.

38. DRAWEE IN CASE OF NEED (Sec.7 and 115)

- The name of any person may be given in a bill as 'drawee in case of need'.
- His liability arises on the bill only when the bill is not accepted by the drawee named in the bill.
- The bill is not dishonoured until it has been dishonoured by drawee in case of need.

39. DISCHARGE OF A NEGOTIABLE INSTRUMENT

The Negotiable Instrument is deemed to be discharged in the following cases –

Payment [Sec.78]:

- When the party primarily liable on the instrument i.e. Maker of P/N, Acceptor of B/E or Drawee Bank, makes the payment in due course to the Holder at or after maturity.
- Payment by a party who is secondarily liable does not discharge the instrument because the payer holds it to enforce it against prior indorsers and the principle Debtor.

Cancellation of N/I [Sec.82]:

When the holder cancels an instrument with intention to release the party primarily liable thereon from liability, the instrument is discharged and ceases to be negotiable.

Express Waiver of Rights by Holder:

The N/I is discharged when the Holder, at or after its maturity absolucly and unconditionally renounces in writing , his rights against all the parties to the instrument.

Lapse of time :

An instrument becomes discharged by lapse of time making the debt time barred under the limitation Act.

Insolvency of party primarily liable:

When the party primarily liable becomes insolvent, the instrument is discharged and the holder cannot make any other prior party liable thereon.

Material Alteration to Instrument ;

The instrument stands discharged when it is rendered void by a material alteration to the Instrument.

Negotiation to Acceptor [Sec. 90];

When a B/E which has been negotiated is, at or after maturity, held by the Acceptor in his own right, all rights of action thereon are extinguished, i.e. the B/E is discharged.

40. DISCHARGE OF A PARTY (Sec.82 to 90)

Discharge by	Causal Factor	Discharge of ....
Cancellation	Holder deliberately cancels the name of Acceptor / Indorser (by striking off the name) with an intent to discharge him from liability.	Maker, Acceptor or Indorser of N/I is discharged from liability to such Holder and to all parties claiming under such Holder.
	Note: Cancellation done under of the Holder would be inopera party.	a mistake or without authority tive and will and discharge any
Release	Holder discharges the Maker/Acceptor / Indorser by any method other than cancellation of names, e.g. separate agreement of waiver, release, or remission etc.	Maker, Acceptor or Indorser of N/I is discharged from liability to such Holder and to all parties claiming under such Holder.
Payment	Party primarily liable on the N/I makes payment in due course to the Holder at or after maturity.	All the parties to the instrument stand discharged, as the instrument is also discharged by such payment.
Allowing Drawee more than 48 hours to accept	Holder of a B/E allows the Drawee more than 48 hours, exclusive of public holidays, to consider whether he will accept the same.	All previous parties not consenting to such allowance are thereby discharged from liability to such holder.
Cheque not duly presented	Cheque is not presented for payment within a reasonable time, and Drawer suffers actual damage as a result of the delay by the bankers.	Drawer is discharged as against the Holder to the extent of the actual damage suffered by him.
	Note: Holder of the cheque as t dischared shall be a Creditors t such damage and entitled to rec	which such Drawer is the Banker to the extent of over the amount from him.
Payment of Cheque payable to order	Cheque payable to order purpose to be endorsed by or on behalf of the payee is paid in due course.	The Drawee i.e. the Paying Banker is discharged from liability.
Cheque originally expressed payable to Bearer	Bank makes a payment in due course to a Bearer.	The Drawee, i.e. the paying Banker is discharged from liability notwithstanding any indorsement (full or blank or restrictive) thereon.
Payment of Drafts	A Draft drawn by one Bank upon another office of the same Bank for a sum of money payable to order on demand is paid in due course.	The Bank is discharged from liability.
Taking Qualified or Limited Acceptance	Holder of B/E agrees to acceptance – Which is qualified, or Limited to part of money due, or Which substitutes a different time or place for payment or Not signed by all Drawees who are not partners.	All prior parties whose consent is not obtained to such an acceptance are discharged from liability to the Holder and those claiming under such Holder.

Material alteration	Any material alteration without the consent of any party thereto.	N/I is void as against anyone who is a party at the time of making such alteration.
Material alteration	Any material alteration made by the indorsee.	Indorser is discharged from all liability to the Indorsee in
		respect of consideration thereof.
Payment of altered instrument	Payment in due course is made in respect of – A P/N, B/E or cheque has been materially altered but does not appear to be so altered, and A cheque presented for payment which at the time of presentment does not appear to have an obliterated crossing	The person or Banker making such payment in due course is discharged from all liability thereon.
Non – presentment of a bill for acceptance	Where B/E payable after a certain period after sight, is not presented for acceptance by the Holder within a reasonable time.	Drawer and all Indorsers who were liable towards such a Holder are discharged from their liability.
No notice dishonour	When the Holder does not send any notice of dishonour.	Any party to a N/I (other than party primarily liable) to whom notice of dishonour is not sent is discharged from liability as against the holder.

Note : The parties to a N/I are also discharged by operation of law, in the following cases

- Upon Order of Insolvency Court, the Insolvent is discharged.
- When a judgment is obtained against the Acceptor, Maker or Indorser, debt under the bill is merged into Judgment Debt.
- By lapse of time, when the remedy becomes time – barred.

41. MEANING OF HUNDI

A. TYPE OF HUNDIS

Shah jog hundi

- Three parties – Drawer, Drawee and financier (Shah)
- Payable to shah
- Shah presents the hundi when it falls due for payment to drawee on behalf of holder

Jokhmi hundi

- Documentary bill drawn by consignor on consignee in respect of goods shipped by consignor.
- Name of the vessel by which goods are shipped is mentioned in the hundi.
- Consignee is required to pay only on goods reaching destination.

Nam Jog Hundi

- Hundi payable to party named or to his order.
- Party has right to endorse as in the case of Bill of Exchange.

Jawabee Hundi

- Instrument for remitting money
- Form – Ordinary letter advising parties that he may collect money from banker.
- Remitter hands over hundi to banker
- Banker endorses hundi to a correspondent residing in the town in which payee is resident
- Correspondent forwards hundi to payee.
- Payee on presenting letter collects amount from correspondent.

Dhani Jog Hundi

- Hundi payable to owner, i.e., person who owns it

Firman Hundi

- Hundi payable at sight

Dharshani Hundi

- Hundi payable at sight
- Transferable by endorsement
- Similar to bill of exchange payable on demand.

Maidi Hundi

- Known in Bengal as MUDDATI HUNDI
- Hundi payment after a time
- Usually, the interest for the period upto the due date is deducted in advance.

B. OTHER TERMS

Zikri Chit

- Issued by some party liable thereon to the holder of hundi
- Letter of protection addressed to a merchant in town where hundi is payable requesting acceptance of the hundi in case of dishonour.
- Intended to be used by holder if hundi is dishonoured by non – acceptance. ¾
  Peth
- Duplicate copy of hundi issued on loss of original hundi.
- The holder at the time when bill is lost before it is overdue may apply to the drawer to give him another bill of the same tenor (Sec.45). The holder may give security, if required to indemnify him against all persons in case the bill alleged to have been lost is found again. If the drawer refuses to give a duplicate bill on request, he may be compelled to do so.

Perpeth

- Triplicate copy of hundi given on loss of duplicate hundi

Khoka

A hundi paid and cancelled.

CHAPTER 15

Auditing

The concept of audit is a very old Phenomenon. The word "audit" is taken from the Latin word "Auditus"- act of hearing. An ancient time, the owners of the business verify their accounts by expert accountants or book-keepers to detect errors and frauds. Even the king and Amenders used to listen from the accountants regarding receipts and payments of their kingdom.

At the end of fifteenth century due to renaissance in Italy there was a rapid growth in industry, trade and commerce. The principle of doubled entry system was introduced by Luca Pacioli, a famous Italian mathematician. Besides cash transaction accounting system also records credit transactions and as a result complexity of accounts was increased.

As a result of industrial revolution in England in the 18th century there was a subs trial increase in the volume of business. A rapid increase in commercial activity, emergence of banking, insurance and joint stock companies, Separation of ownership from management of the business, growing activities in the government sector led the need for audit of accounts.

A rapid change in socio-economic business environment scenario, requirement of the globalization of business, complex regarding true accounts, necessity of the government to get audited accounts for different purposes have influenced auditing to be used a fact-finding tool have caused a greater responsibility in the technique, scope, reporting standard, professional, legal, moral and ethical responsibilities from the auditors.

AUDITING- DEFINITION, SCOPE AND FEATURE.

Auditing" In modern concept, auditing is the scientific and systematic examination of the books, accounts, vouchers and other financial records that will help the auditor to give opinion regarding true and fair view of the state of affairs of the business and to verify that profit and loss account reflects a true and fair view of profit or loss for the financial year.

In the words of Spicer and Pegler, "Audit is such an examination of the books, accounts and vouchers of a business, as will enable the auditor to satisfy himself that the balance sheet is properly drawn up, so as to give a trued and fair view of the state of affairs of the business, and whether the Profit and Loss account gives a true and fair view of profit or loss for the for the financial period, according to the best of his information and the explanations given to his and as shown by the books; and if not, in what respect he is not satisfied."

According to F.R.M. De Paula., "An audit denotes the examination of a Balance Sheet and Profit and Loss Account prepared by others together with the books, accounts and vouchers relating thereto in such a manner that the auditor may be able to satisfy himself and honestly report that, in his opinion, such Balance Sheet is properly drawn up so as to exhibit a true and correct view of the state of affairs of the particular concern according to the information and explanations given to him and as shown by books."

Prof. Montgomerty "Auditing is a systematic examination of the books and records of business or other organization in order to ascertain or verify and to report upon the facts regarding its financial operations and the result thereof.

M.L. Shandilya "Auditing may be defined as inspecting comparing, checking reviewing, vouching ascertaining, scrutinizing, examining and verifying the books of accounts of a business concern with a view to have a correct and true idea of its financial state of affairs.

According to the **Institute of Charted Accountants of India** auditing is "a systematic and independent (Financial and otherwise) of an enterprise for a stated purpose. In any auditing situation the auditor perceives and recognizes the propositions before him for examination, collects evidence, evaluates the same and on this basis formulates his judgment which is communicated through his audit report."

The meaning of an Audit contains

- An intelligent and critical examination of the books of accounts of business.
- It is done by an independent qualified person.
- It is done with the help of vouchers, documents, information and explanations received from the clients.
- The auditor satisfied himself with the authenticity of the financial accounts prepared for a particular period.
- The auditor reports that
    - The balance Sheet exhibits a true and fair view of the state of affairs of the concern.
    - The Profit and Loss account reveals the true and fair view of the profit or loss for the financial period.
    - The accounts have been prepared in conformity with the concerned law.
    - If he is not satisfied then reports in what respect he is not satisfied.

Benefits of Business: Business may get many advantages of conducting audit by a qualified auditor. The advantages are discussed below:

(a) **True and Fair view:** With the help of audit of accounts, it is possible get a true and fair view of the financial position of the business.

(b) **Detection of errors and frauds:** If books of accounts are audited, errors and frauds can be detected and necessary action can be taken to prevent it.

(c) **Moral pressure on the employees:** If audit is conducted by the organization, employees should be cautions and there should be a moral pressure on them. As a result, chances of errors and frauds will be minimized.

(d) **Proper accounting control:** A system of regular audit helps the organization to maintain proper books of accounts regularly and books of accounts are kept up to date.

(e) **Acceptable evidence:** Audited accounts are very strong financial document acceptable to many interested parties e.g. taking loan from financial institution, determination of income tax, sales tax, amalgamation of companies, determination of purchase consideration, admission, retirement, death of a partner etc.

(f) **Helps to determine future policy:** By comparing the audited accounts with past year the trend of financial activities can be determined. On the basis of this review, weaknesses are found out and future policy is determined.

(g) **Valuable suggestions given by the auditor:** If there is a system of continues audit in the organization the auditor can give his valuable advice for the improvement of the business.

(h) **Increase in goodwill:** Audit of business on a regular basis increases confidence to the interested parties and general public. As a result goodwill of the business increases.

(ii) **To the Owner:** The owners of the business are also interested to know the financial position of the business. There are discussed below:

(a) **Benefit to the sole proprietor:** In case of large business, the proprietor can get a true and fair view of the accounts maintained by his employees and also able to know the state of affairs and profit made by him. The proprietor is also benefited for getting loan from financial institutions, to pay income tax etc.

(b) **Benefits to the partners:** Shareholders are the owners of a company. With the help of audited accounts help to the partners to settle their unsettled disputed, for taking loan from financial institutions, to get off the books of accounts maintained by the employees etc.

(c) **Benefits to the shareholders:** Shareholders are the owners of a company. With the help of audited accounts they get a real picture of the financial position of The company and they can assure that business is running efficiently.

(d) **Benefit to the non-profit seeking organizations:** There are different non-profit seeking organizations e.g., charitable institution, club, religious institute, school, college etc. This organization run with public money. Whether public money is properly utilized or not can be revealed from the audited accounts.

(iii) **To the third parties:** Besides business and the owners, there are different outside interested parties who required audited accounts for different purposes: These are:

(a) Government may be interested to get the audited accounts to show the deficiency of the business for giving grant and subsidy.

(b) Financial institutions sections loan to the organization on the basis of verification of financial soundness form the audited accounts.

(c) Tax authorities may depend on audited accounts for determination of income tax, sales tax, excise duty etc.

(d) Prospective buyers who want to invest money in shares and debentures of a company may rely on audited accounts.

(e) Creditors who supply goods to the business may asses the solvency and liquidity position of the business on the basis of audited accounts.

(f) For settlement of insurance claim, insurance companies can barely on audited accounts.

From the above discussion, it is clear that both accounting and auditing are not contradictory but complementary to each other,

To achieve the primary objective, an auditor has to verify that:

(i) All the transactions are properly recorded in the books of accounts.

(ii) All the transactions are for the current financial year.

(iii) To verify that all the assets and liabilities are properly shown in the balance Sheet.

(iv) All materials facts have been considered while preparing financial statements.

Objective Of audit

- **Primary**
  - Reflects true and fair view of the books Accounts and certify it to the appointing Authority
- **Secondary**
  - 1. Detection of errors and frauds.
  - 2. Prevention of errors and frauds.
  - 3. Necessary steps to rectify the above

(1) **Errors**: Errors means careless representation of books of accounts or mistake in the process of keeping accounting records by the employees' who maintain the books of accounts. There are different types of errors founds in the books of accounts while conducting audit by an auditor. Errors may be of two type's i.e., intentional errors and unintentional errors. Intentional errors are conducted by the dishonest employees to falsify the books of accounts for their personal interest. Unintentional errors are made due to the be shown diagrammatically which are as follows:

Error

- Clerical Errors
- Errors of Principle

- Errors of Omission
- Errors of Commission
- Errors of Duplication
- Compensating Errors

Frauds- Detection and Measures for Remedy

Frauds are the international misrepresentation of transactions in the books of accounts by the dishonest employees to deceive another. Fraud may be of two types i.e. (a) Misappropriation of cash and goods and (b) Falsification or manipulation of accounts. The different type of frauds can be shown diagrammatically which are as follows:

Frauds

- Misappropriation Of cash and Goods
- Falsification or manipulation of Accounts

DEFERENCE BETWEEN ERROR AND FRAUDS

Errors	Frauds
1. Errors means careless representation of books of account or mistake in the process of keeping accounting records by the employees' who maintain the books of accounts	1. Frauds are the intentional misrepresentation of transactions in the books of accounts by the dishonest employees to deceive another. Fraud may be of tow types i.e., (i) Misappropriation of cash and goods and (ii) Falsification or manipulation of accounts
2. Errors may be international or unintentional	2. Fraud is always intentional and is committed to deceive the organization.
3. Generally employees of the accounting department commit errors whether intentional or unintentional	3. Generally frauds of cash and goods are done by the higher level of management staff
4. Unintentional errors are comparatively easier to detect. Intentional errors can also be finding out by the auditor if proper attention is given.	4. It is comparatively through to detect frauds because this is always intentional.

DISTINCTION BETWEEN ACCOUNTANCY AND AUDITING

Accountancy: Accountancy and auditing is not a similar thing Accountancy is related with maintaining books of accounts and to prepare financial statements. i.e., Profit and loss Account and Balance Sheet in such a way that will reflect the financial position and supplies the information relating to financial position to the interested parties. For this, it has to collect, classify summaries and present the financial date in such a manner that is acceptable to the different users.

Audit: In modern concept, audit is the scientific and systematic examination of the books, accounts vouchers and other financial records that will help the auditor to give opinion and other financial regarding true and fair view of the state of affairs of The business and to verify that profit and loss account reflects a true and fair of profit or loss for the financial year.

Therefore, where the works of an accountants ends, the work of auditor starts. The different between accountancy and auditing are given below:

Accountancy	Auditing
1. Accountancy is related with maintaining books of accounts and to prepare financial statements i.e. profit and Loss account and Balances Sheet in such a way that will reflect the financial position and supplies the information relating to financial position to the interested parties.	1. Auditing is the scientific and systematic examination of the books, accounts, vouchers and other financial records that will help the auditor to given opinion regarding true and fair view of he state of affairs of the business and to verify that profit and loss account reflects a true and fair view of profit or loss for the financial year.

Contd.

Accountancy	Auditing
2. To reflect the financial position to the business at the end of the financial year and its presentation to the different interested parties are the main object of accountancy	2. The main objective of audit of a business is to show that the books of accounts are prepared with recognized accounting principles and reflects the true and fair view of the financial position of the organization and to give opinion regarding true and fair view of the state of affairs of the business and to verify the at profit and loss account reflects a true and fair view of profit or loss for the financial year.
3. The accounting job is done by an a accountant i.e. he may not be a professionally qualified person i.e. Charted Accountant. The accountant is a paid employee of the organization.	3. Generally the audit works is done by an independent professionally qualified person i.e. a Charted Accountant. The auditor is not an employee of the organization. He works on the basis of audit if required.
4. The accounting work is done throughout the accounting year.	4. Generally audit is conducted at the end of the financial year except in case of big organizations, there may be continuous audit if required.
5. An accountant does not require a special skill and expertise for doing accounting work	5. A social knowledge, skill and expertise are require for doing auditing work.
6. An accountant may not have an idea regarding audit	6. The auditor must have a sound knowledge in accountancy. Otherwise auditing works is not possible
7. The work of accounting begins first with the past financial transactions	7. The work of audit starts when the tasks of financial accounts are completed.
8. There are some generally accepted accounting principles followed by all the organizations while preparing books of accounts.	8. In India the work of audit controlled by the Company's act, 1956 and the standard auditing practices (SAP) framed by the Institutes of Character Accountant of India.
9. If there is may errors and frauds the employees are accountable of the management of the company.	9. If there are any undisclosed errors or frauds due to the negligence of the auditor, he will be liable as per civil, criminal and professional misconduct of the country.
10. After completion of accounting work the accountant gives his report to the management of the company	10. After completion of audit work the auditor gives his audit report to the shareholders (in case of a company) and in other cases to the appointing authority.

3. MAJOR INFLUENCES OF AUDITING

- Industrial Revolution
- Ownership
- Professional Management
- Statutory Provisions
- Case Laws
- Information Technology

6. ROLE OF EVIDNCE IN AUDITING

Meaning and Importance

- Evaluation of the proposition in terms of materiality or significance. • Collection of evidence within given Limits of time and costs
- Evaluation of evidence obtained as valid or not valid.
- Formation of judgment as to the propositions at issue.

Types of Audit Evidence

Meaning

Audit Evidence refers to any information obtained by the auditor so that he can draw conclusions & express opinion on financial statements.

Analytical evidence

These evidences consist of journals, subsidiary books allocation sheets reconciliation statements or any other records which supports the data appearing in the books of accounts.

Corroborative Evidence

This evidence consist of invoices, confirmations cancelled cheques or similar documents.

- Physical examination by the auditor of the thing represented in the accounts.
- Written of oral statement by independent third parties.
- Authoritative documents prepared inside or outside the enterprise.
- Formal or informal statement by officers and employees of the enterprise.
- Calculations performed by the auditor.
- Satisfactory internal control procedure.
- Subsequent actions by the enterprise and by others
- Subsidiary or detailed records with no significant indications of irregularities.
- Interrelationship within the data examined.

Obtaining Audit Evidence

- Inspection
- Observation
- Inquiry and Confirmation
- Computation
- Analytical Review

7. AUDIT TECHNIQUES AND PRACTICES

Audit Techniques:

- Physical Examination
- Confirmation
- Comparing Documents with The Records (Vouching)
- Computation
- Re tracking Book – keeping
- Scanning
- Inquiry
- Examining Subsidiary Records
- Co – relation With The Related Information
- Observation of Pertinent Activities.

Professional Pronouncements

Contained in your module as per page B – 7, 8, 9.

International Financial Reporting Standards (IFRS)

The international federation of accounts had issued following international financial reporting standards. Actually these standards are pronounced by the International Accounting Standard Board (IASB) constituted in place of old International Accounting Standards Committee (IASC) in 2001, this pronunciation has amended certain IAS by IFRS. These IFRS apply to the general purpose of financial statements and other financial reporting by profit oriented entities. These IFRS apply to individual company and consolidated financial statements. The ICA of India has decided to fully converge with IFRS from the accounting period commencing on or after 1st April 2011.

IFRS 1 – First time adoption of International Financial Reporting Standards.
IFRS 2 – Share based payments
IFRS 3 – Business combinations
IFRS 4 – Insurance contracts
IFRS 5 – Noncurrent assets held for sale and discontinued operations
IFRS 6 – Exploration for and evaluation of mineral assets
IFRS 7 – Financial instruments disclosures
IFRS 8 – Operating segments

Guidance Note

The ICA of India issued a number of guidance notes on matters raised by its members relating to auditing. These notes are recommendatory in nature, cost accountant should ordinarily follow recommendations to an auditing matter but this guidance notes will be superseded by the accounting standard coming in force (after guidance note).

The ICWA of India issued no. of guidance notes as for the benefit of cost accounts, which includes. (i) Guidance note on valuation audit under (centre excise law). (ii) Guidance on central excise – MODVAT audit (iii) guidelines on cost audit (iv) guidelines on inventory valuation (v) total cost management in the manufacturing process (vi) guidelines on transfer pricing (vii) guidelines on CENVAT audit under central excise. (viii) Environmental audit.

8. GENERALLY ACCEPTED AUDITING STANDARDS PRINCIPLES (GAAS/GAAP)

General Standards –

- Independence – The auditor, in all matters relating to the assignments, should follow an independent attitude.
- Due Care – In exercising the work of audit, the auditor should exercise due care.

Field Work Standards –

- Planning and Supervision – Before the beginning of an audit, the audit work should be properly planned and the work assigned to assistants be carefully supervised.
- Internal Control – The internal controls existing in the enterprise be studied and evaluated beforehand.

- Evidential Matter – While auditing, auditor should collect the evidential documents to afford a reasonable basis for forming an opinion on the financial statements.

Reporting Standards –

- **Financial Statements** – Auditor should make a mention whether the financial statements are prepared according to the Generally Accepted Auditing Standards Principles or not-
- **Consistency** – He should make a mention whether these Principles / Standards are consistently are taken as reasonably adequate.
- **Obligation** – Auditor should submit his report, when the work is finished, stating clearly his opinion or if not possible make a mention there in that "optioning cannot be expressed" and in such a case support it with reasons.

These formal standards / principles are framed in the context of statutory auditing but the AICPA suggest that while following these GAAP/GAAS, due consideration be given to materiality and "audit risk".

The International Federation of Accountants had issued following nine broad GAAP i.e.

Basic Principle governing an audit:

- Integrity, Objective and Independence
- Confidentially
- Skills and Competence
- Work Performed by Others
- Documentation
- Planning
- Audit Evidence
- Accounting System and Internal Control
- Audit Conclusions and Reporting

US – GAAP

The features of US-GAAP and Indian Accounting Standards are clear from their differences. They are as follows:-

India	USA
1. **Financial Statement** Prepared in accordance with the presentation requirements of Schedule VI to the Companies. Act, 1956 (Schedule VI).	1. **Financial Statements** Not required to be prepared under any specify format as long a they comply with the disclosure requirements of US Accounting Standards.
2. **Fixed Assets & Depreciation** Revaluation of assets permitted. Depreciation is based (usually) on rates set out in Schedule XIV to the Companies Act, 1956.	2. **Fixed Assets & Depreciation** Revaluation of assets not permitted except in cases of quasi-re-organisations. Depreciation is over the useful economic lives of assets. Depreciation and profit / loss on sale is based on historic cost.
3. **Investment in own shares** Expressly prohibited except in cases	3. **Investment in own shares** Permitted, and is shown as a reductions form

Contd.

India	USA
of buy back of own securities.	shareholder's equity
4. **R & D** Costs can be capitalized subject to the conditions of the criteria of technical feasibility of the production resource availability and existence of market, etc. (AS – 8, Research & Development, issued by the Institute of Chartered Accountants of India)	4. **R & D** Costs are expenses as incurred except for plant and depreciation if they have alternative future uses or expenses as incurred if they have no alternative future uses.
5. **Goodwill** Purchased goodwill is capitalized and amortized over the expected period of benefit or charged against available capital reserves. No, standard except for brief references is AS – 10, Fixed Assets and AS – 14, Accounting for Amalgamations Goodwill arising from amalgamations can be written off over 5 years.	5. **Goodwill** Treated as any other intangible asset, and is capitalized and amortized. The maximum carry forward and period is 40 years.
6. **Pre – operative Expenses** All direct and indirect expenses incurred prior to commencement of business are treated capitalized to the cost of fixed cost of assets. These are also allowed to be deferred and written off over a period of 3 – 5 years or 10 years.	6. **Pre – operative Expenses** Concept does not exist. They are expenses unless they are capital is nature.
7. **Assets and Liabilities** No mandatory disclosure of current and long term components.	7. **Assets and Liabilities** Mandatory disclosures about current and long term components separately. Current component normally refers to one year of the operation cycle.
8. **Foreign Currency Transactions** Gains and losses resulting from the translation of financial statements into a reporting currency should be recognized as income or expenses for the period.	8. **Foreign Currency Transactions** Exchange gain/loss is taken to the income statement. The concept of capitalization of exchange fluctuations arising from foreign currency liabilities incurred for acquiring fixed assets does not exist.
9. **Foreign Currency Transactions** Gains and losses resulting from the transaction of financial statements into a reporting currency should be recognized as income or expenses for the period.	9. **Foreign Currency Transaction** Gains and losses resulting from the transaction of Financial Statements into a reporting currency are reported of a separate component of shareholder's equity in the balance sheet.
10. **Related Party Transaction** No specific disclosures required. Auditors have a duty to report certain transactions entered into by related parties as defined under the companies Act, 1956: AS – 18 is issued w.e.f. 01.04.2001	10. **Related Party Transactions** Disclosures are stringent and require descriptions of nature of relations and control, transactions, amounts involved, and amounts due.

9. CONCEPT OF MATERIALITY IN AUDITING

According to AAS 13, "information is material if its misstatement (i.e. omission or erroneous statement) could influence the economic decision of user taken on basic of the financial information. Materiality depends on the size and nature of the item, judged in the particular circumstances of its misstatement.

The following are some of the specific requirements in the form of Balance Sheet based materiality consideration implicit in the very process of prescribing the format in Part I of schedule VI.

- Loans from directors to be shown separately.
- Nature of interest if any of any director with the bankers or other officers of the company at any time during the year should be disclosed by way of a note.

The maximum due by directors or other officers of the company at any time during the year should be disclosed by way of a note.

Further whenever there is any change in the basis of accounting the effect thereof must be disclosed.

AAS 13 on ' Audit Materiality' requires that the auditor should consider materiality and is relationship with audit risk when conducting an Audit.

Circumstance of Materiality

According to the ICFAI the circumstance of materiality are as under –

- Mistake discovered like valuation of stock calculation of depreciations calculation of interest estimation of liability etc.
- Non – disclosure of abnormal and unusual items or non recurring or expenditure etc.
- Non – disclosure of items violating the statutory provision. etc.

Materiality and Audit Risk

Risk of Providing inappropriate opinion

Inherent Risk (I.R)	Control Risk (CR)	Detection Risk (D.R.)
Risk that Material Misstatement may occur	Risk that I.C. fail to operate as desired.	Risk that auditor's substantive procedures will not detect a material Misstatement
Arises at level of management	Arises at level of management	Arises at auditor's level.
Auditor can only assess this risk	Auditor can only assess this risk.	Auditor can frame this risk.
Risk of system of management	Risk of I.C. system of management	Risk of substantive procedure adopted by auditor.
This is generally high, However certain factors may be present due to which it can be less than high.	This is evaluated in stages (See chart below)	DR should be inversely proportionate to combined assessment of I R & C R DR $\propto 1/(IR + CR)$ If IR & CR are high, DR should be kept at low level.

- **Internal Risk** – Risk that material error will remain.
- **Control Risk** – Risk that client's internal control system cannot prevent or make up for such error.
- **Detection Risk** – Risk that material errors though they are there will not be detected.

AUDIT MEMORANDUM- ITS CONTENTS

Accounts of the Company

LOCATION OF BOOKS OF ACCOUNT [Sec.209(1) and (2)]

1. **Registered office :** All the books of account shall be kept at the registered office.
2. **Any other place *Place in India***
   All or any of the books may be kept at any other place in India.

Board resolution

The Board must pass a resolution according approval to keep the books at such other place.

Requirements of Board resolution

The Board resolution must specify –

(i) the nature of books of be kept at such other place; and

(ii) the full address of such other place. ***Notice of registrar***

- The company shall give a notice to the registrar.
- The notice shall be given within 7 days of passing the Board resolution.

3. Branch office

Nature of books

All the books of account in respect of branch office may be kept at such branch office.

Duties of the company

(a) The branch office shall prepare up – to – date summarized return.

(b) The interval between preparation of any two summarized returns shall not exceed 3 months.

(c) The summarized returns shall be sent to be company (at the registered office or at such other place where the books are kept) within a reasonable time of compilation of the returns.

CONTENTS OF BOOKS OF ACCOUNT [Sec.209(1)]

Nature of books to be kept

Every company shall keep books of account with respect to –

(a) receipts and expenditures (b) sale and purchase of goods.

(c) Assets and liabilities.

(d) Prescribed particulars relating to cost incurred on materials, labour and other items if –

   (i) the company is engaged in production or processing or manufacturing or mining, and

   (ii) an order for maintenance of cost records in made by CG.

PROPER BOOKS OF ACCOUNT [Sec. 209(3) and 541(2)

Conditions prescribed u/s 209(3) ***True and fair view***

- The books must not suppress any transaction.
- The books must not contain any fictitious transaction.

Accrual basis Cash basis and Hybrid system of maintenance of books is prohibited. ***Double entry***

Single entry system of maintenance of books is prohibited.

Conditions prescribed u/s 541(2) ***Explain financial position*** The books must be such as fully explain the financial position and transaction of the company. ***Disclosure relating to goods***

The books must sufficiently disclose –

(a) the details of annual stock takings.

(b) All purchase and sale of goods.

(c) The particulars of buyers and sellers, except where goods are sold by way of ordinary retail trade.

PRESERVATION OF BOOKS OF ACCOUNT [Sec. 209(4A)]

- Books of account for 8 years immediately preceding the current year shall be preserved.
- The relevant vouchers shall also be preserved.

RESPONSIBILITY FOR MAINTENANCE OF BOOKS OF ACCOUNT [Sec.209(5) and (6)]

Persons responsible u/s 209(6)

(a) MD or manager

(b) Every director, if the company has neither employed MD nor manager

(c) All officers and employees of the company.

Charging a competent person with duty of maintenance of books [Sec.209(5)] ***Duty charged to whom?*** Any competent and reliable person ***Duty charged by whom?*** By the manager or MD or Board

Effect – Defense for persons responsible u/s 209(6)

The persons responsible u/s 209(6) may put a defense that the person charged with the duty of maintenance of books of account was competent, reliable and was in a position to discharge such duty.

ANNUAL ACCOUNTS – LEGAL REQUIREMENTS [Sec.210 and 211]

Laying of annual accounts at an AGM ***Duty of laying of annual accounts*** It is the duty of the Board of directors to lay the annual accounts at every AGM. ***Meaning of annual accounts***

(i) B/S

(ii) P&L A/c

Requirements of B/S and P & L A/c

B/S

(i) The B/S shall be in the same form as set out in Part I of Schedule VI.

(ii) The B/S must comply with the "Notes" given at the end of Part I of Schedule VI.

P&L A/c

(i) No form has been prescribed for P & L A/c.

(ii) P &L A/c must comply with the requirements of Part II of Schedule VI.

B/S and P&L A/c

B/S and P&L A/c must give a true and fair view.

'Financial year' ***Meaning of FY***

- The period for which P&L A/c is prepared is called as FY.
- It may be more or less than a calendar year.

Maximum period of FY

- FY shall not exceed a period of 15 months.
- But, it may exceed upto 18 months with the special permission of registrar.

Change of FY from year to year

- The Board is empowered to decide the period covered in a FY.
- The period covered in a FY may be different from the period covered in the preceding FY(s).

Responsibility

Same persons are responsible for preparation of B/S and P&L A/c as are responsible for maintenance of books of account.

ACCOUNTING STANDARDS (Sec.211. 217 and 227)

Meaning of accounting standards

- AS means the standards of accounting recommended by ICAI, as may be prescribed by CG after consultation with National Advisory Committee on Accounting Standards.
- Until AS are prescribed by CG, the standards of accounting specified by the ICAI shall be AS.

Duties of the company regarding AS (Sec. 211)

Compliance with AS Every company shall comply with AS.

Disclosure in case of non – compliance

- Deviation from AS.
- Reasons for deviation
- Financial effect due to deviation.

Duties of the auditor regarding AS (Sec.227)

- The auditor shall state as to whether the P&L A/c and B/S comply with AS.
- If the P&L A/c or B/S does not comply with AS, the auditor shall qualify the audit report.

Duties of the directors regarding AS [Sec. 217(2AA)]

(a) Director's Responsibility Statement must be included in Board's report.

(b) Following disclosures must be given in the Directors' Responsibility Statement;

- Whether applicable AS have been followed
- In case of material departures, proper explanation therefore must be given.

CONTENTS OF BOARDS' REPORT [Sec.217]

Contents specified u/s 217(1)

(a) The state of the company's affairs

(b) Profits proposed to be transferred to reserves.

(c) Dividend recommended by the Board (d) Material changes subsequent to close of FY.

Disclosure relating to conservation of energy etc.

Conservation of energy

(a) Energy conservation measures taken
(b) Additional investment and proposals being implemented for reduction of consumption of energy.
(c) Impact of measures on reduction of energy consumption and cost of production.
(d) Total energy consumption and energy consumption per unit of production.

Technology absorption Efforts made in technology absorption.

Foreign exchange earnings and outgo

(a) Activities relating to exports
(b) Initiatives taken to increase the exports, development of new export markets and export plans.
(c) Total foreign exchange used and earned.

Changes during the financial year Nature of disclosure required. ***Change in –***

(a) nature of the company's business.
(b) Company's subsidiaries.
(c) Nature of business carried on by subsidiaries of the company
(d) Generally, in the classes of business in which company has an interest.

When is disclosure required?

- Disclosure is required if it would result in better understanding of state of affairs of the company.
- Disclosure is not required if such disclosure will be harmful to the business of the company or its subsidiaries.

Disclosure of particulars of certain employees

When is disclosure required?

(a) An employee who received a remuneration of Rs.24 lakhs or more during the FY.
(b) An employee who received a remuneration of Rs.2 lakhs per month or more for any part of FY.
(c) An employee satisfying the following 2 conditions.
(i) He has received remuneration at a rate which, in the aggregate, is in excess of remuneration drawn by MD or WTD or manager.
(ii) He holds 2% or more of the equity share capital.

Nature of disclosure required

Designation, Remuneration, Nature of duties, Qualifications and experience, Age, Last employment, Nature of employment, Other terms and conditions, Percentage of equity shares held, Whether the employee is a relative of any director or manager.

Disclosures in Director's Responsibility Statement [Sec.217(2AA)] ***Accounting standards***

- The directors shall state as to whether they have complied with the AS.
- In case of material departures, the directors shall give proper explanation for the same.

Accounting policies

The directors shall state as to whether the accounting policies – • Have been consistently applied ; and

- Used by them are reasonable.

Judgments and estimates

The directors shall state as to whether the judgments and estimators made by them are –

- Reasonable and prudent; and
- Give a true and fair view;

Proper and sufficient care

The directors shall state as to whether they has taken proper and sufficient care for –

- The maintenance of adequate accounting records in accordance with the provision of this Act;
- Safeguarding and assets of the company; and
- Preventing and detecting fraud and other irregularities.

Going concern Assumption

The directors shall state as to whether they have adopted the assumptions of going concern while preparing annual accounts.

Reasons for non – completion of buyback

- Every buy – back should be completed within 12 months from the date of passing the resolution for buy – back (whether SR or a resolution at a BM only).
- If a buy – back could not be completed within the specified period of 12 months, the Board shall disclose the reasons for the same.

Comments on auditors' report

The Board shall give fullest information and explanation in respect of every reservation, qualification or averse remark contained in the auditors' report.

SIGNING OF BOARD'S REPORT AND ANNUAL ACCOUNTS (Sec.215 and 217)

Signing of Boards' report (Sec.217)

Case (a)

The chairman of the Board is authoridsed by the Board to sign the Board's report The Board's report shall be signed y the chairman of the Board. ***Case (b)***

In any other case

- The Board's report shall be signed by 2 directors (one of whom shall be MD, if there is one).
- The Boards' report shall be signed by 1 director, if only I director is for the time being in India.

Signing of annual accounts (Sec.215)

Case (a)

If only I director is for the time being the India

The annual accounts shall be signed y – (a) the manager or secretary; and (b) I director.

Case (b)

Any other case

The annual accounts shall be signed by –

(a) the manager or secretary; and

(b) 2 directors (one of whom shall be MD, if there is one)

Approval of annual accounts

B/S and P&L A/c shall be approved by the Board before –

- they are signed on behalf of the Board; and
- they are submitted to the auditors for their report thereon.

CIRCULATION OF ANNUAL ACCOUNTS, ETC. [Sec.219]

Nature of documents requiring circulation

(a) Balance sheet

(b) Profit and loss account

(c) Auditors' report

(d) Every other document required to be annexed or attached to B/S

The above documents have been referred to as' annual accounts etc.' u/s 219 and 270.

Persons entitled to receive annual accounts, etc.

(a) Every member

(b) Every debenture trustee

(c) All persons who are entitled to receive the notice of GM, e.g. the auditors

Supplying of annual accounts, etc. on demand

Who can demand the annual accounts, etc.

(a) A member (b) A debenture holder (c) Any depositor.

Duties of the company

The company shall supply the annual accounts, etc.

- free of cost
- within 7 days of demand.

Consequences of default

CLB may direct the company to furnish the annual accounts, etc. Time limit for circulation of annual accounts, etc. ***General rule***

The annual accounts, etc. shall be sent at least 21 days before the date of GM.

Exception

The annual accounts, etc. may be sent less than 21 days before the date of GM, if so agreed by all the members entitled to vote at the GM.

Circulation of annual accounts, etc. in case of a listed company

Option 1

The company may send the annual accounts, etc. in full.

Option 2

The company shall comply with the following 2 conditions

(a) The company shall send the abridged version of the annual accounts etc.

(b) The unabridged version of the annual accounts etc. shall be made available for inspection at the registered office during working hours for a period of 21 days before the date of AGM.

FILING OF ANNUAL ACCOUNTS WITH THE REGISTRAR (Sec.220)

Where thirty five days from the date of presenting before annual general meeting three copies of the balance sheet and the profit and loss account signed by the managing director, Manager or secretary of the co. be filed with the Registrar. In case of default the company and every officer by the company who is in default shall be liable to like punishment as is provided by section 162 for a default in complying with the provisions of section 159, 160 or 161.

Teeming and Lading – A process of Misappropriating Cash- Auditors Duty in this respect. Teeming and lading is a process of misappropriating cash from an organization by the dishonest employees. In this process, collection from credit customers are misappropriated and collection from subsequent customers are recorded in the accounts of previous customers and this process is goes on until the dishonest employees leave the organization or absconded.

i. **Auditor's Duty:** This type of fraud is very hard to detect. The auditor should carefully detect the following points.
ii. **Internal check system**: The auditor should verify the internal check system and its effectiveness regarding cash received from customers and the amount deposited into bank.
iii. **Checking Debtors account:** Verify all the debtors account and the amount due from them with the statement sent by them and also check how much delay is made by them, confirm the debtors balance if any.
iv. **Verify Bank Pass Book**: Check the bank pass book to show that all receipts are deposited in to bank and prepare bank reconciliation statement if required.
v. **Checking of Receipt:** The auditor should verify the counterfoils of receipts with the cash book and confirm that all receipts are properly recorded in the cash book.
vi. **Confirmation from Debtors:** If any suspicion arises during the course of audit regarding collection from credit customers, the auditor may take help direct confirmation with the debtors and may meet with them is situation arises.

CHAPTER 16

Companies Act Prvisions Relating to Audits

DISQUALIFICATIONS FROM APPOINTMENT AS AN AUDITOR [Sec.226 (3)]

1. A body corporate
2. An officer or employee of the company
3. A person who is a partner / employee of either an officer / employee of the company.
4. A person who –
   a) Is Indebted to the company for amount exceeding Rs.1000
   b) Has given any guarantee / provided any security in connection with any third person for an amount exceeding Rs.1,000.
5. A person holding any security (means an instrument carrying voting rights) of the company.
6. A person disqualified from acting as auditor of the company's subsidiary or holding company or of any other subsidiary of the same holding company.[Sec.226(4)]
7. A partnership firm, wherein any partner is disqualified because of any of the aforesaid Provisions.

VACATION OF OFFICE [Sec.226 (5)]

If after being appointed as an auditor, he attracts any of the disqualifications in Sec.226 (3) or (4) above, he shall be deemed to have vacated his office.

APPOINTMENT OFAUDITOR
FIRST AUDITORS [Sec.224 (5)]

(a) Appointed by	- Board of Directors
(b) Time limit of appointment	- Within 1 month of date of
(c) Tenure of Office	- Until conclusion of 1st AGM.
(d) Failure to appoint within 1 Month of registration.	- Appointment by shareholders at General Meeting, by passing Ordinary resolution.
(e) First Auditor's name included in Articles	- Articles to be void. Only by procedure in Sec.224 (5) above.
(f) Notice appointment	- NOT required. Neither by company to 1st Auditor, Nor by the First Auditor to the Registrar.

2. SUBSEQUENT AUDITORS

A) Appointment at an AGM	Nature of meeting	At every AGM, the auditor are appointed or reappointed by the company
	Nature of regulation	Ordinary resolution
	Nature of business	Ordinary business
B) Tenure of office	The auditors hold office from the conclusion of the meeting in which they are appointed to the conclusion of the next AGM.	
C) Notice of appointment	Notice by the company	The company shall give notice of appointment reappointment to the auditor. Such notice shall be given within 7 days of the appointment or reappointment
	Notice by auditor	The auditor shall give notice to the register Such notice shall be given within 30 days of receipt of notice of appointment or reappointment from the company. The notice shall state to whether he has accepted or refused the appointment.

REAPPOINTMENT OF RETIRING AUDITOR

a) Reappointment of retiring auditor	- At an AGM, - the retiring auditor, by whatsoever authority appointed, - shall retire and he shall be reappointed.
b) Exception	The retiring auditor shall not be reappointed in the following cases: (i) Where he is not qualified or is disqualified for reappointment. (ii) Where he has expressed his unwillingness in writing to be reappointment. (iii) Where a resolution has been passed at the AGM appointing somebody instead of him or providing expressly that he shall not be reappointed. (iv) Where notice has been given of an indented resolution to appoint some person in the place of a retiring auditor, and by reason of the death, incapacity or disqualification of the person, the resolution cannot be proceeded with.
c) AGM not held within time whether auditor vacates his office?	• The auditors hold office from the conclusion of the meeting in which they are appointed to the conclusion of the next AGM. As such the appointment of auditors is made in terms of this period and not for any FY. • Therefore, an auditor shall continue in his office even if AGM is not held within the time limits specified u/s 166 and 210.

APPOINTMENT OF AUDITORS BY CG.

a) Notice to CG	Notice by whom?	The company shall give notice to CG.
	When is notice required?	If no auditors are appointed or reappointed at an AGM.
	Time limit for giving notice	The notice shall be given by the company within 7 days of conclusion of AGM.
b) Appointment by CG	On receipt of notice from the company, CG shall fill the vacancy.	
c) No auditor is appointed examples	(i) Where the appointment of a person appointed as an auditor in an auditor in an AGM is void ab initio. (ii) where OR is passed, but the appointment of auditors requires SR.	

REMUNERATION OF AUDITOR

a) Right to remuneration fix	If appointment made by member	(i) The remuneration shall be fixed by the members is GM. (ii) Alternatively, the GM may determine the manner in which the remuneration shall be fixed.
	If appointment is made by board	The remuneration shall be fixed by the Board.
	If appointment is made by CG	The remuneration shall be fixed by CG.
	If appointment is made by CAG	(i) The remuneration shall be fixed by the member in GM. (ii) Alternatively, the GM may determine the manner in which the remuneration shall be fixed.
b) Meaning of remuneration	• Any sum paid by the company in respect of the auditors, expenses shall be deemed to be included in the expression remuneration. • Out – of – pocket – expenses of the auditors shall be included in the remuneration unless the resolution fixing the remuneration specifically provides that such expenses shall be paid separately. • Remuneration for other services is permissible without sanction of shareholders. However, disclosure in P & L A/c is required.	

REMOVAL OF AUDITORS

a) Removal of first auditor before expire of his term (i.e. before the 1st term AGM) (sec.224(5)]	(i) OR shall be passed at a GM. (ii) No special notice is required for such removal. (iii) Procedure prescribed u/s 225(2) and (3) shall be followed. (iv) Any other person may be appointment in his place.
b) Removal of subsequent auditor before expire of his term (i.e. before the AGM) [Sec.224(7)]	(i) Previous approval of GC is required, (ii) OR shall be passed at a GM. (iii) No special notice is required for such removal. (iv) Procedure prescribed u/s 225(2) and (3) shall be followed.
c) Removal of auditor (whether first auditor subsequent auditor) at an AGM (sec.225)	(i) Previous approval of CG is not required. (ii) OR shall be passed at a GM. (iii) Special notice is required for such removal. (iv) Procedure prescribed u/s 225(2) and (3) shall be followed. Special notice may require that – (i) the retiring auditor shall not be reappointed; or (ii) some person, other than retiring auditor, shall be appointed, as an auditor.

Contd.

d) Removal by CG	When can CG exercise its power u/s 408?	Where appointment of nominee directors is made u/s 408 to end the oppression or mismanagement.
	Nature of power of CG	• Amongst other power, CG has power to give directions to the company u/s 408. • The directions may include a direction to remove the existing auditor. • The directions given by CG shall come into effect as if all the provision of the Act, in this behalf has been compiled with.
	Effect of direction of CG	a) The existing auditor shall vacate office without requiring any action for his removal.

Procedure prescribed u/s 225 (2) and (3).

a) Notice to auditor		The company shell sends the notice of removal to the auditor.
b) Right of the auditor	(i)	Right to be heard orally at the meeting.
	(ii)	Right to make a representation in writing to the company.
	(iii)	Right to get his representation circulated amongst the member.
c) Duties of company	(i)	To send a copy of the representation to every member of the company.
	(ii)	To state the fact of the representation heaving been made in the notice given to the member.
d) Reading of representation		If a copy of not sent by the company to the member, the auditor may require that the representation shall be read out at the meeting.

e) Intervention CLB/CLT by	Application to whom?		An application may be made to CLB/ NCLT.
	Application by whom?	•	The company, or
		•	Any other aggrieved person.
	Satisfaction of CLB/NCLT		The right to make a representation is being abused by the auditor to secure needless publicity for defamatory matter.
	Order by CLB / NCLT	(i)	Copy of representation not be sent to the members.
		(ii)	The representation need not be read out at the meeting.
		(iii)	Cost on such an application shall be paid by the auditor.

AUDIT OF ACCOUNTS OF BRANCH OFFICE

Meaning of branch office	(i) Any establishment described as a branch by the company (ii) Any establishment carrying on either the same or substantially the same activity as that carried on by the head office. (iii) Any establishment engaged in any production, processing or manufacture [Sec.2(9)]
b) Qualifications of branch auditor	(i) The company's auditor as appointed as an auditor u/s 224. (ii) Any person qualified to be appointed as an auditor u/s 226. (iii) Where the branch office is situated in a foreign country, any person duly qualified to act as auditor in such foreign country may also be appointed as an auditor.
c) Appointments of branch auditor	(i) Appointment may be made by the member in GM. (ii) Alternatively, the shareholders may authorize the Board to make the appointment of branch auditor in consultation with company's auditor.
d) Power and duties of branch auditor	A branch auditor has the same powers and duties as that of company's auditor.
e) Right of company's auditor	Where the accounts of any branch office are audited by a person other than the company's auditor, the company's auditor has the following rights; (i) Right to visit the branch office, if he deems it necessary to do so for the performance of his duties and auditor. (ii) Right of access at all times to the books, accounts and vouchers to the company maintained at the branch office.
f) Remuneration of branch auditor	(i) The remuneration shall be fixed by the members in GM. (ii) Alternatively the GM may authorize the Board to fix the remuneration.
g) Report of branch auditor	• Report shall be prepared in accordance with sec.227. • Report shall be prepared in accordance with CARO. • Report shall be forwarded to the company's auditor. • The company's auditor, while preparing his report, shall deal with the report of the branch auditor in such manner as he deems fit.

EXEMPTION FROM BRANCH AUDIT

(a)

(i) Any manufacturing processing or treading activity is carried on at the branch office.

(ii) The exemption is available only if the amount calculated in step 2 is not more then amount calculating in Step 3. Step 1. Calculate 'quantum of activity'.

The quantum of activity means the highest of the following:

(i) Aggregate value of goods produced or manufactured or processed at the branch office.

(ii) Aggregate value of goods sold any services rendered by the branch office.

(iii) Aggregate value of expenditure, whether of revenue or capital nature, incurred by the branch office.

Step 2. Calculate average of ' quantum of activity' by taking average of the quantum of activity during 3 FYs immediately preceding the relevant FY.

Step 3. Calculate the higher of the following two limits:

(i) Rs.2 lakhs;or

(ii) 2% of the average of the total turnover of the company including all its branch offices, earnings from services rendered and earnings from any other source.

b) Exemption in other cases - Conditions for claiming exemption;

Discretion of CG	Exemption may be given for specified period and subject to conditions.
Withdrawal of exemption by CG	CG may withdraw the exemption if the term and conditions of exemption are not complied with.
Submission of a copy of exemption order	A copy of exemption order shall be submitted to the company auditor.
Reading of exemption order	It shall be the duty of the auditor to read the exemption order at the GM.
Ground for exemption	Additional conditions for claiming exemption
(a) Company has made sufficient arrangements for scrutiny and check of account of branch office	• Company is not carrying on manufacturing processing or trading activities; and • Scrutiny and check shall be made by a responsible person. Such person is competent to scrutinize and check the accounts.
(b) A branch auditor is not likely to be available at a reasonable cost	CG shall pay regard to the nature quantum of activity carried on at the branch office.
(c) Company has made arrangements for the audit of accounts of branch office	Audit shall be done by a person otherwise qualified for appointment as a branch auditor, except that he is an employee of the company.
(d) For any other person	CG is satisfied that exemption should be granted.

SPECIAL AUDIT

a) Circumstances in which special audit may be ordered	CG is of an opinion that – (i) The affairs of the company are not being managed in accordance with sound business principles or prudent commercial practices; or (ii) The company is being managed in a manner likely to cause serious injury or damage to the interests of the trade, industry or business to which it pertains; or (iii) The financial position of the company is such as to endanger its solvency.	
b) Period of special audit	Special audit shall be conducted for such period as may be specified in the order of CG.	
c) Appointment of special auditor	⌚ Special auditor shall be appointed by CG. ⌚ The person appointed to conduct the special audit shall be –(i) Company's auditors; or (ii) Any other CA (whether or not he is in practice.)	
d) Powers and duties	Special auditor shall have same powers and duties as that of a company's auditor.	
e) Directions by CG.	CG may direct any person to furnish to the special auditor such information as may be required by him.	
f) Report of special auditor	Submission of report	The special auditor shall submit his report to CG
	Action by CG	On receipt of report, CG may take such action, as it deems fit.
g) Remuneration special auditor	⌚ Remuneration shall be determined by CG. ⌚ Such determination shall be final.	

COST AUDIT

a) Cost audit – when required?	(i) The company is compulsorily required to maintain cost records as per Sec.209 (1) (d); and (ii) CG has issued a direction to the company to conduct a cost audit.	
b) Qualifications of cost auditor	(i) Cost accountant; or (ii) CA, possessing the prescribed qualifications, if CG is of the opinion that – sufficient number of cost accountants are not available for conducting the cost audit; and a notification is issued to this effect.	
c) Disqualification of a cost auditor	(i) A person disqualified to act as a statutory auditor u/s 226. (ii) The statutory auditor of the company .	
d) Vacation of office	The cost auditor shall vacate his office if after appointment; any of the disqualifications are attracted to him.	
e) Appointment of cost auditor	The cost auditor shall be appointed by the Board. The appointment of cost auditor requires previous of CG.	
f) Ceiling on number of audits	Timing of certificate giving	The auditor shall, before appointment, give a certificate of his eligibility to appointed as cost auditor.
	Requirement certificate of	The certificate shall state that the appointment, if made, will be within the
		ceiling on number of audits as specified u/s 224(1B).
g) Powers And Duties of cost auditor	The cost auditor shall have same power and duties as that of a company's auditor (given u/s227).	
h) Cost Audit Report	Submission of report	The cost auditor shall submit a report to CG and the company. The report shall be submitted within 180 days of close FY.
	Reply by the company	The company shall furnish to CG full information and explanations on every reservation or qualification contained in cost audit report. The reply shall be submitted within 30 days from the date of receipt of cost audit report.
	Calling of further information	CG may call further information from the company. The company shall furnish the information required by CG within the time specified by CG.
	Action by CG	CG may take such action as it deems fit.
i) Duties of the company	(i) Give all facilities and assistance to the cost auditor. (ii) Submit cost records to the cost auditor within 30 days of the close of FY.	

Types of audit report

Standard unqualified report

It is issued when the following conditions are met:

(a) all financial statements give a true and fair view in accordance with the financial reporting framework used for the preparation and presentation of the financial statements.

(b) the financial statements have been prepared in accordance with the generally accepted accounting principle.

(c) the financial statements comply with relevant statutory requirements and regulations; and

(d) disclosure are adequate and statutory requirements with regard to them have been adhered to;

In case of a limited company, thus if the auditor makes various statutory affirmations contained in section 227 without any reservation, he is said to have issued an unqualified audit report or clean report.

Modified reports

SA 700, The Auditor' Report on Financial Statements, states. An auditors' report is considered to be modified when it includes.

(a) Matters that do not affect the auditor's opinion

- Emphasis of matter

(b) Matters that do affect the auditors' opinion

- Qualified opinion
- Disclaimer of opinion
- Adverse opinion

(i) Unqualified report with an 'emphasis of matter' paragraph

(a) Auditor may attach paragraph to an unqualified opinion to put emphasis on a matter regarding financial statements due to its importance.

(b) Such a matter is, generally, included in a note to the financial statements which discusses it in greater details.

(c) 'Emphasis of matter' paragraph does not change the nature of the audit report as it relates to a matter that does not affect the auditor's opinion.

(d) Examples of situation in which an auditor's introduces 'emphasis of matter' paragraph are given below;

- Going concern doubt
- Significant uncertainty

(ii) Qualified audit report

(a) Qualified audit report is a report wherein the auditor has expressed a qualified opinion, that is to say, an opinion subject to certain reservations.

(b) Important aspects in relation to qualification in an audit report are mentioned below

- The auditor shall give a qualified opinion when the subject matter of qualification is not highly material and pervasive and he believes that he overall financial statements give a true and fair view.
- A qualification should be preceded by the words 'subject to' or 'except that' to make it clear that the matter is of exceptional nature.
- The audit report should quantity the effect of individual qualifications also the total effect of all qualification on the financial statements.
- The auditor shall the reasons for his qualification.
- In case of a limited company, if any of the statutory affirmations in section 227(2) and section 227(3) are answered in negative or with qualification by the auditor, the audit report would be termed as a 'qualified audit report'.
- Qualification which deal with matters, which have an adverse effect on the functioning of the company should be thick type o in italics.

(c) A qualified report can result from:

- Scope limitation
- Disagreement with management with regard to departure from generally accepted accounting principles or adequacy of disclosure.

(iii) Disclaimer of opinion

(a) The auditor issues a declaimer of opinion if the subject matter involved is material pervasive and he I unable to obtain sufficient appropriate evidence to express an opinion on it.

(b) A disclaimer an result because material and pervasive uncertainties could not be resolved, there is going concern doubt or there is a material limitation on the scope of the audit.

(iv) Adverse report

(a) When the auditor is of the opinion that the effect of disagreement with the management is material and pervasive to the financial statement, he gives an adverse report.

(b) The auditor must, categorically state that the financial statements do not give a true and fair view.

AUDIT REPORTS UNDER COMPANIES ACT, 1956.

Report on specific enquiries Section 227(IA)

Section 227(IA) requires the auditor to make specific enquiries during the conduct of his audit. He is however, not required to report on these matters unless he has any special comments to make. It should be understood that the auditor should only enquire on the specific matters and is not to investigate into them. It requires reporting on following.

(i) Whether loans and advances made by the company on the basis of security have been property secured and whether the terms on which they have been made are not prejudicial to the interests of the company or its members.

(ii) Whether book entries are prejudicial to the interests of the company.

(iii) Whether the sale price of the shares, debentures and other securities held by the company is less than their purchase price.

(iv) Whether loans and advances made by the company have been shown as deposits.

(v) Whether personal expenses have been charged to revenue account.

(vi) Where it is stated in the books and papers of the company that any shares have been allotted for cash, whether cash has actually been received in respect of such allotment, and if no cash has actually been so received, whether the position as stated in the accounts books and the balance sheet is correct, regular and not misleading.

Report on true and fair view Section 227(2)

The auditor shall state whether, in his opinion and to the best of his information and according to the explanations given to him, the Balance sheet and Profit & loss account give –

(i) the information required by the Act, and
(ii) a true and fair view of state of affairs of the company.

Report on principal assertions Section 227(3)

1. Whether he has obtained all the information and explanations; 2. Whether in his opinion, proper books of account have been kept.
3. Whether the report of branch auditor has been forwarded to him and how he has dealt with the same in preparing his audit report.
4. Whether the B/S and P& L account are in agreement with the books of account and returns ;
5. Whether AS have been complied with:
6. The observations or comments of the auditors which have any adverse effect on the functioning of the company in thick type or in italics;
7. Whether any director is disqualified from being appointed as a director u/s 274(1)(g).
8. Whether cess payable by the company has been so paid.

(NOTE: The companies (Second Amendment) Act, 2002 provides for section 441A which states as follows:

- A cess on companies will be levied for purpose of rehabilitation or revival of sick industrial Co.
- These provisions are made in sections 441 A to 441 F.
- The amount to be collected must be in a range of 0.005% to 0.1% on value of annual turnover/annual gross receipts (whichever is more) as the Central Government may notify from time to time is official gazette.
- The company shall pay the amount to Central Government within 3 months from close of every financial year).

Report on CARO Section 227 (4A) The auditor has to report on all the matters specified in CARO.

CHAPTER 17

Review and Audit of Internal Control System

Brief description of different types of the following

(i) **Statutory audit:** Statutory audit is a compulsory audit for the companies conducted by the qualified independent auditor as per company's act, 1956.

(ii) **Non-statutory audit**: The audit which is not compulsory under the statute and depends on need of the organization is known as non-statutory audit: E.G. audit of soleproprietorship and partnership firm.

(iii) **Government audit**: When audit of government departments are made by the employees of the government department under the supervision of Comptrollers and Auditor General of India is known as government audit.

(iv) **Complete Audit**: When audit start after completing books of accounts and after the close of the financial year is known as complete audit.

(v) **Partial audit:** When audit is conducted for some particular work out of various matters is known as partial audit e.g. Verification of assets.

(vi) **Balance sheet Audit**: A balance Sheet audit is an audit relating to verification of assets and liabilities appearing in the balance sheet. In this audit the auditor starts audit work from the balance sheet and proceeds backwards.

(vii) **Continuous audit:** Continuous audit is a system of audit where the auditor and his staff examines all the transactions and books of accounts in details continuously throughout the year at regular intervals i.e., weekly or fortnightly or monthly etc.

(viii) **Periodical audit:** Periodical audit is an audit which is conducted at the end middle of the year to pay interim dividend or to get half yearly financial statements for different purposes of the management.

(ix) **Interim audit**: Interim audit is an audit, which is generally conducted at the middle of the year to pay interim dividend or the get half yearly financial statements for different purposes of the management.

(x) **Cost Audit:** Cost audit means examining by the company and to verify the audit of costing records maintained by the company and to verify each element of cost to give a true and fair view of cost of production so that cost efficiency can be achieved.

(xi) Management audit: Management audit is a method of independent and systematic evaluation of the management activities at all levels of management to ascertain the functions, efficiency and achievement of the management (i.e. policies) as compared to standards set by the company.

(xii) Social Audit: Business is a part of society, so it has some social obligation towards the society, Social audit is a process of audit of organizations of a country to evaluate the benefit the entity has received from the country and its contribution to the welfare of the society.

(xiii) System audit: A system audit is a technique of certification of effectiveness of system of accounting internal control and internal check instead of checking all transactions in detail. This audit is applicable in large organization where there are numerous transactions.

(xiv) Property audit: Property audit is a method of audit which verifies the reasonableness of expenditure incurred by an organization and is not detrimental to public interest. This audit is generally applicable to the government organizations.

(xv) Performance audit: Performance audit is a special type of audit which determines the overall performance of the organization and efficiency and economy of utilizing resources as compared to predetermined standards. It seeks to identify possibilities for economy, efficiency and effectiveness.

(xvi) Tax audit: Tax audit is a special type of audit directed by the tax department in case of needs and complexities of the business e.g. tax audit is compulsory in case of solepartnership and partnership firm if turnover exceed Rs. 40,00000.

(xvii) Special Audit: When audit is done by the special auditors as per section 223A of the company's act, by order of the central government regarding the affairs, management and financial position of the company is known as special audit.

(xviii) Human resource audit: When the audit is conducted to evaluate and review of the performance and contribution of the organization's employees towards the overall achievement of the entity's goal is known as human resource audit.

(xix) Financial audit: Financial audit is the scientific and systematic examination of the books, accounts, vouchers and other financial records that will help the auditor to give opinion regarding true and fair view of the state of affairs of the business and to verify that profit and loss account reflects a true and fair view of profit or loss for the financial year.

CONTINUOUS AUDIT

Continuous audit: Continuous audit is a system of audit where the auditor and his staff

Examines all the transactions and books of accounts in details continuously throughout the year at regular intervals i.e. weekly or fortnightly or monthly etc.

According to Spicer and Pegler, "a continuous audit is one where the auditor's staff is occupied continuously on the accounts the whole year round, or where the auditor attends at intervals, fixed or otherwise, during the currency of the financial year and performs an interim audit; such audits are adopted where the work involved is considerable and have many points in their favour although they are subject to certain disadvantages."

Where this audit is applicable: In the following cases continuous audit is applicable.

(i) Where there are enormous transactions in a big organizations and continuous monitoring of accounts are required.

(ii) If there is no internal check system in the organization or the system is not very much effective.

(iii) When the company wants to declare interim dividend and for this purpose interim accounts are to be prepared.

(iv) In case of financial institutional and insurance companies, where it is necessary to get the final accounts just after the end of the financial year.

(v) If the management of the company are to get statement of accounts at a regular intervals.

Advantages of continuous audit: Following are the advantage of continuous audit in an organization. These are discussed below.

(i) Extensive checking: As the auditor regularly visits the client's office, he should get time for extensive checking of small transactions and the audit work can ne smoothly conducted.

(ii) Early detection of errors and frauds: As continuous audit is conducted throughout the whole year, errors and frauds can be quickly detected. The accounting staff should not get sufficient time to manipulate accounts.

(iii) Early Preparation of Final accounts: AS this audit is conducted throughout the whole year, it is possible to prepare final accounts i.e. Profit and Loss account and Balance Sheet just at the end of the financial year. The management and the owners can know the financial results without delay.

(iv) Deceleration of interim dividend: Those companies who want to declare interim dividend at the middle of the year is to prepare interim accounts. Continuous audit helps to get interim account in time.

(v) More reliability on audited accounts: If continuous audit is done throughout the year, all the interested parties can rely much on the audited accounts.

(vi) Moral check: As a result of continuous audit employees should feel a moral pressure and the chances of errors and frauds are minimized.

(vii) Early declaration of dividend: With the help of continuous audit final accounts are prepared just at the end of the financial year and the shareholder get dividend without delay.

(viii) Early submission of report: As continuous audit is conducted throughout the year the auditor can complete final accounts audited just at the end of the financial year and can submit his audit report to the shareholders as early as possible.

(ix) Increase in efficiency: As audit is conducted on continuous basis, all the transactions are correctly recorded in the books of accounts and overall efficiency in according work can be made.

Disadvantage of continuous audit: The following are the disadvantages of continuous audit:

(i) **High Cost:** As continuous audit is conducted throughout the year the organization has to give huge remuneration to the auditor. Therefore, a small concern cannot afford the high cost of conducting such audit.

(ii) **Difficulties in accounting work.** As a result of frequent visits of the auditor often it is seen that the books of accounts are checked by the audit staff and for this audit work is hampered.

(iii) **Change of figures**: It may so happen that the portion of accounts which have already examined by the auditor may alter the figures by the dishonest employees to achieve some personal interest.

(iv) **Loss of continuity of work:** As continuous audit is conducted at regular intervals, the auditor may left unchecked same audit work which was pending during his last audit work.

(v) **Adverse effect on employees morale:**

(vi) monotony in Work

(vii) Chances of collusion between organization's staff and auditor's staff

How disadvantage many overcome:

(i) No work unfelt:

(ii) Prepare fixed audit programme

(iii) Rotation of Work

(iv) Frequent visit:

(v) Use of special mark:

(vi) Use of ink for writing of castings

(vii) Keep important notes:

(viii) Preparation of effective audit programme

(ix) Pending of checking impersonal and general ledger:

(x) A revise of the past work

DISTINCTION BETWEEN STATUTORY AUDIT AND INTERNAL AUDIT

Statutory Audit	Internal Audit
1. Statutory audit is a compulsory audit for the companies conducted by the qualified independent auditor as per company's Act, 1956. The primary duty of a Statutory auditor is to give opinion in his report that profit and loss account and balance sheet of the company have been drawn up as per law and whether the accounts shows a true and fair view of the state of affairs of the company of not.	1. Internal audit being a part of internal control system is a detailed review of the books of accounts throughout the accounting year by a specialist group of employed auditors independently within an organization to assure management that proper accounts has been maintained, adequate safeguards to maintain revenue and protect misappropriation of assets and evaluated the effectiveness of policies given by the management.
2. Statutory audit is compulsory for every company as per company Act, 1956.	2. Internal audit is not compulsory for i.e. it is optional i.e. non-stationary and is conducted in case of necessity.
3. Statutory audit is conducted by independent external auditor	3. Internal audit is an audit conducted by the employees of the company.

Contd.

Statutory Audit	Internal Audit
4. Statutory auditors are generally appointed by the shareholders in the annual general meeting of the company.	4. Internal audit is an audit conducted by the employees of the company.
5. A Statutory auditor must have prescribed qualifications under section 226 of the company's Act, 1956.	5. No statutory qualifications are prescribed in the company's act for Internal auditor.
6. Generally statutory audit is done after the preparation of final accounts and at the end of the financial year.	6. Internal audit is done on a continuous basis and for the whole year.
7. The scope, nature, rights and duties of Statutory auditors are determined by the company's Act, 1956.	7. The scope nature, rights and duties of work is determined by the management.
8. Statutory auditor has to give his report to the shareholders	8. Internal auditor has to submit his report to the management.
9. Only shareholders of the Company can remove the statutory auditor in the annual general meeting.	9. Internal auditor can be removed by the management.
10. Remuneration of statutory audit is fixed by the shareholders in the annual general meeting	10. Remuneration of internal auditor is fixed by the management.
11. Statutory auditor is not an advisor except specifically requested.	11. Internal auditor gives suggestion to the management regarding efficiency of business and how to prevent errors and frauds.
12. Statutory auditor while auditing may take help of test checking	12. Each and every transaction is checked by internal auditor.
13. Statutory auditors has a right to attend Annual general meeting of the company	13. Internal auditor has no right to attend in the annual general meeting of the company.
14. Statutory audit is compulsory for the companies. Hence, internal audit is optional and conducted according to the needs of the company.	14. Internal audit is not a substitute\e of statutory audit. In additional to internal audit statutory audit is required.
15. In statutory audit, right, duties, nature and scope of an auditor is determined by the companies Act, 1956.	15. The option and suggestion given by an internal auditor is highly includes by the top management i.e., freedom of work of the internal auditor is restricted.

CARO, 2003

i) Fixed Assets:

a) Whether the company is maintaining proper records showing full particulars, including quantitative details and situation of fixed assets;

b) Whether these fixed assets have been physically verified by the management at reasonable intervals; whether any material discrepancies were noticed on such verification and if so, whether the same have been properly dealt with in the books of account;

c) If a substantial part of fixed assets have been disposed off during the year, whether it has affected the going concern.

(ii)Inventory:

a) Whether physical verification of inventory has been conducted at reasonable intervals by the management;

b) Are the procedures of the physical verification of inventory followed by the management reasonable and adequate in relation to the size of the company and the nature of its business? If not, the inadequacies in such procedures should be reported.

c) Whether the company is maintaining proper records of inventory and whether any material discrepancies were noticed on physical verification and if so, whether the same have been properly dealt with in the books of account.

iii)Loan Given or Taken:

a) Has the company granted any loans, secured or unsecured to companies, firms or other parties covered in the register maintained under Section 301 of the Act. If so, give the number of parties and amount involved in the transactions:

b) Whether the rate of interest and other terms & conditions of loans given by the company, secured or unsecured, are prima – facie prejudicial to the interest of the company;

c) Whether the receipts of the principal amount and interest are also regular;

d) If overdue amount is more than one lakh, whether reasonable steps have been taken by the company for recover of the principal and interest.

iv) Internal Control:

Is there an adequate internal control system commensurate with the size of the company and the nature of its business, for the purchase of inventory and fixed assets and for the sale of goods and services? Whether there is a continuing failure to correct major weaknesses in internal control system.

v) Section 301:

a) Whether the particulars or arrangements referred to in Section 301 of the Act have been entered in the register required to be maintained under the section:

b) Whether transactions made in pursuance of such contracts or arrangements have been made at prices which are reasonable having regard to the prevailing market prices at the relevant time.

[This information is required only in case of transaction exceeding the value of five lakh rupees in respect of any party and in any one financial year]

vi) Deposits from the public;

In case the company has accepted deposits from the public, whether the directives issued by the Reserves Bank of India (RBI) and the provisions of Section 58 A and 58AA or any other relevant provision of the Act and the rules framed there under, whether applicable, have been complied with. If not the nature of contraventions should be stated ; if an order has been passed by Company Law Board (CLB) or National Company Law Tribunal (NCLT) or Reserve Bank of India (RBI) or any court or any other Tribunal whether the same has been complied with or not?

viii) Internal Audit System:

In the case of listed companies and / or other companies having a paid – up capital and reserves exceeding Rs. 50 lakhs as at the commencement of the financial year concerned, or having an average annual turnover exceeding five crores rupees for a period of three consecutive financial years immediately preceding the financial year concerned, whether the company has an internal audit system commensurate with its size and nature of its business.

vii) Cost Records:

Where maintenance of cost records have been prescribed by the Central Government under section 209 of the Act, whether such accounts and records have been made and maintained.

ix) Statutory Dues:

a) Is the company regular in depositing undisputed statutory dues including Provident fund, Investor, Education and Protection Fund, Employee's State Insurance, Income Tax, Sales – Tax, VAT, Service Tax, Wealth Tax, Custom Duty, Excise Duty, Cess & any other statutory dues with the appropriate authorities and if not, the extent of the arrears of outstanding statutory dues as at the last day of financial year concerned for a period of more than six months from the date they become payable, shall be indicated by the auditor:

b) In case dues of Income Tax/ Sales Tax/ Wealth Tax Service Tax/ Custom Tax / Excise Duty / Cess have not been deposited on account of any dispute, the amounts involved and the forum where dispute is pending shall be mentioned.

x) Company Registered for more than 5 years;

Whether in case of a company which has been registered for a period not less than five years, its accumulated losses at the end of the financial year are not less than fifty percent of its net worth and whether is has incurred cash losses in such financial year and in the immediately preceding financial year.

xi) Default in payment of dues of Financial Institutions or Debenture holders;

Whether the company has defaulted in repayment of dues to a financial institution or bank or debenture holders? If yes, the period of amount of default to be reported.

xii) Loan / Advance Secured:

Whether adequate documents & records are maintained in cases where the company has granted loans and advances on the basis of security by way of pledge of shares, debentures and others securities ; if not, the deficiencies of be pointed out.

xiii) Special Statutes to Chit Fund:

Whether the provisions of any special statute applicable to chit fund have been duly complied with?

a) Whether the net owned fund to deposit liability ratio is more than 1:20 as on the date of balance sheet;

b) Whether the company has complied with the prudential norms on income recognition and provisioning against substandard / doubtful / loss assets;

c) Whether the company has adequate procedures for appraisal of credit. Proposals/ request , assessment of credit needs and repayment capacity of the borrowers;

d) Whether the repayment schedule of various loans granted by the Nidhi is based on the repayment capacity of the borrower.

xiv) Company Trading or Dealing in Shares / Securities, etc;

If the company is dealing or trading in shares, securities, debentures and other investments, whether proper records have been maintained of the transaction and contracts and whether timely entries have been made therein; also whether the shares, securities, debentures and other investments have been held by the company, in its own name except to the extent of the exemption, if any granted under Section 49 of the Act.

xv) Guarantee to Bank / Financial Institution;

Whether the company has given any guarantee for loans taken by others, from bank or financial institutions, the terms and conditions whereof are prejudicial to the interest of the company.

xvi) Term Loans;

Whether the term loans were applied for the purpose for which the loans were obtained.

xvii) Short Term Funds;

Whether the funds raised on short term basis have been used for long term investment. If yes, the nature and amount is to be indicated.

xviii) Preferential allotment to parties covered under registered maintained under Section 301:

Whether the company has made any Preferential allotment of shares to parties and companies covered in the Registered maintained under Section 301 of the Act, and if so whether the price at which shares have been issued is prejudicial to the interest of the company.

xix) Security/ Charge created for debentures issued:

Whether securities or change has been created in respect of debentures issued?

xx) End Use;

Whether the management has disclosed the end use of money raised by public issues and the same has been verified.

xxi) Fraud on / by company reported:

Whether any fraud on or by the company has been noticed or reported during the year, if yes, the nature and the amount involved is to be indicated.

Summary of CARO, 2003

Non – applicability to:

(a) Banking Companies

(b) Insurance Companies

(c) Companies registered under Sec. 25 of Companies Act.

(d) Pvt. Ltd. Company at all times during the year whose –

- (i) Paid up capital + Reserves $\leq$ 50 lakhs; and
- (ii) Loans outstanding $\leq$ 25 lakhs; and
- (iii) Turnover $\leq$ 5 crores

'Turnover'

- Includes both sale of goods & rendering of services.
- Commission to 3rd parties should not be deducted.
- Following shall be deducted;
    - Trade discounts
    - Sales Tax/ Excise duty, if credited separately to such A/cs
    - Sales Returns (even if relating to prior years)

'Reserves'

[(Capital Reserve + Revaluation Reserve) + (Revenue Reserve – Debit Bal. of P & L A/cs)

(Upto the extent of revenue reserve only)

'Loan outstanding'

- Both long term & short term shall be taken.
- Aggregate of loans from both banks & financial institutions shall be taken.
- Loan taken from a company shall not be considered.

1.Fixed Assets

- Proper records (situation wise and quantity wise)
- Physical verification and discrepancies
- If disposed off '! whether affecting going concern

2.Inventories

- Physical verification
- Procedure reasonable (inadequacy to be pointed out)
- Proper records and discrepancy.

3. Loan to parties covered under register u/s.301

Given	Taken
1. If yes, number of parties and amount	1. If yes, number of parties and amount
2. Interest, term & conditions prejudicial	2. Interest, term & conditions prejudicial
4. 3. Receipt regular **Interest Control**	3. Payment regular

4. If overdue amount > 1 lakh, reasonable steps.

- Purchase of inventory and Fixed assets
- Sale of goods and services
- Is failure to correct weaknesses?

5. **Transaction with parties covered under register u/s. 301**

- Particulars of contract / arrangements entered in register
- Transaction at reasonable prices (for transaction > 5 lakh for each party for each F.Y.)

6. **Companies accepting public deposit**

- RBI/Companies Act/any other act complied.
- Order by CLB / RBI/ NCLT complied.

7. **Internal Audit**

Listed Company or **Other Company**

(i) Paid up capital + reserves > 50 lakh at starting of year or

(ii) Average annual turnover > 5 crore Rs. For F.Y. immediately preceding this year.

8. **Cost Record:** Whether maintained, if prescribed.
9. **Statutory Dues**
   - Regular in depositing undisputed statutory dues. If not, extent of arrears as at balance date exceeding 6 months to be reported.
   - If dispute, amount and forum.
10. **Company registered e" 5 years**
    - Accumulated losses at end e" 50% of net worth, and
    - Cash loss in this / immediately preceding F.Y.
11. **Defaulted:** Default in payment of dues of Financial Institutions or Debenture holders – Yes, then amount.
12. **Loan / Advance (secured):** Proper records/Documents (deficiency)
13. **Special Statutes to Chit Fund:**
    - Net owned fund/deposit liability > 1/20 as at Balance sheet.
    - Companies complied with prudential norms.
    - Adequate procedure for credit appraisal.
    - Repayment schedule based on repayment capacity.
14. **Company trading / dealing in Share / securities, etc.**
    - Proper records of transfer and contracts
    - Timely entries
    - Investment in own name (except u/s 49)
15. **Guarantee to Bank / Financial Institution:** Terms and conditions prejudicial
16. **Term Loans:** Applied for purpose for which obtained.
17. **Short term funds** – Used for long term (amount and nature);
18. **Preferential allotment to parties covered under register maintained u/s. 301**
    - Whether made.
    - Price (whether prejudicial)
19. **Security / charge** – created for debenture issued.
20. **End use**: Whether management disclosed end use of money raised by public issue and same verified.
21. **Fraud:** on / by company reported. If yes, then, nature and amount.

AUDIT PROGRAMME- ITS FEATURES AND OBJECTIVES

Audit programme: Audit programme means a written plan made by the auditor before doing actual audit work. It is a detailed plan and procedure to be followed for audit work.

In the opinion of professor W.B. Meigs, "An audit programme is a detailed plan of auditing work to be performed, specifying the procedures to be followed in verification of each item in the financial statements and giving the estimated time required."

Features or principles of Audit Programme:

Every audit programme has some common features. These are discussed below:

(i) Cover all aspect of audit: Audit programme cover all areas of auditor work so that no matters left unchecked.

(ii) Techniques and procedures: All important techniques and procedures of audit works are to be given in details so that audit programme can be constructive.

(iii) Time bound: Any audit programme should consider the time

(iv) Logical: The techniques and procedures to be followed by the audit staff should be based on logic and not haphazard.

(v) Flexibility: Audit programme should not be rigid rather it will be flexible enough and may be changed according to the need or situation.

(vi) Covers only important matters: Planning of audit programme should be such that only important matter which requires examination is to be considered

OBJECTIVE OF AUDIT PROGRAMME

An audit programme has a great importance to an auditor. Audit programme is guideline or roadmap through which an auditor conducts audit works in a smooth way. The objectives for which an audit programme is prepared are discussed below:

(i) Proper distribution of work:

(ii) No work unleft:

(iii) Finished within scheduled time

(iv) Evidence for future reference

(v) Systematic procedure can be maintained:

Steps for preparing Audit programme and its Contents:

Before preparing audit programme an auditor has to consider the following steps:

(i) Purpose and scope of audit:

(ii) Nature of the organization

(iii) Effectiveness of internal control and internal check system:

(iv) Procedure of accounting

(v) Books of accounts

(vi) Important documents

(vii) Verification of last year audited accounts

Contents of generally audit programme: The matters which are generally included in an audit programme are given below:

(i) Name and address of the organization.

(ii) The objects and the nature of the business

(iii) Time scheduled for completing audit work.

(iv) Date of commencement of audit work.

(v) Details of audit work to be done as per importance and sequence e.g. examination of cash and bank account, checking of purchase and sales day book, verification if different transaction, valuation of assets and liabilities etc.

(vi) Opinion given by the previous auditor in his report.

(vii) Procedures and methods of accounting followed by the organization

(viii) List of importance documents etc.

Advantages of a fixed audit programme:

An audit programme has many advantages which are discussed below:

(i) Proper distribution of work
(ii) Help to know the portion of work completed:
(iii) Responsibility and accountability:
(iv) No pending of work
(v) No loss of time
(vi) Continuity of work
(vii) Evidence for future disputes
(viii) Monitoring and controlling of work
(ix) Increase in performance of the audit staff
(x) Helps to prepare futures audit programme

Disadvantage of a fixed audit programme

Though audit programme has many advantages still it is not free from limitations. The limitations are:

(i) Lack of flexibility:
(ii) Monotony in work
(iii) Not suitable for small organizations
(iv) Difficulties for inefficient staff
(v) Problems to cover all items:

Steps to be taken to remove the drawbacks of fixed audit programme:

The problems or difficulties arise for preparing fixed audit programme can be removed in the following way:

(i) Flexible audit programme
(ii) Modification of programme
(iii) Encourage to the audit assistances
(iv) Effectiveness of internal control system
(v) Participation of the audit staff
(vi) Checking without notice
(vii) Change of audit programme after some years

Audit Note Book and Its Contents

Audit note book: During the course of audit work the auditor and his staff may have to face different queries and problems relating to various matters. These queries and matters which require explanations and solutions are noted in a bound book is known as audit note book.

Contents of audit note book: The audit note book records the following general points.

(i) Objectives and nature of the business, organization structure relating to administration and accounts.
(ii) The manes of the management staff and their functions, power and responsibilities.
(iii) Important points of Memorandum of association, Articles of Association, minutes in case of companies, and partnership deed in case of partnership business which may be required in future.

(iv) important contracts made by the client with the third parties.
(v) List of missing vouchers and duplicate found if any.
(vi) List of all important documents.
(vii) Suggestions given by the audit staff.
(viii) Methods of according and efficiency of internal control system.
(ix) List of queries for which further explanations are required.
(x) List of all important correspondence.
(xi) Date's and information for future reference.
(xii) Submission and balances of important ledger accounts.
(xiii) List of matters for which detailed investigation is required.
(ix) Matters of opinion which is to be given in the audit report.
(x) Portion of audit work already completed.
(xi) A list of errors and frauds detected in the books of accounts while conducting audit work.

Advantages of Audit Note Book:

Audit note book is a very important document to an auditor, by maintaining audit note book and auditor gets many advantages. These are discussed below:

(i) **A storehouse of important information:** The auditor and his staff keep important information in the audit note book which will be required for audit work. For any future reference these information helps the auditor.
(ii) **Minimization of errors and frauds:** As all the important information is recorded in the audit note book chances of errors and frauds are minimized.
(iii) **Effectiveness of work:** With the help of audit note book the auditor can evaluate the progress of work done by the audit staff and can also judge their knowledge and efficiency.
(iv) **Continuity of work:** If all the important matters are accurately recorded in the audit note book, there is no chance of dislocation of work if any new staff joined for audit work or if any existing audit staff transferred for other work.
(v) **Evidence for future reference**: Audit note book is a very important document to the auditor. He can defend himself against the charges made by the company or by the third parties for negligence and misfeasance if audit note book is properly maintained by him.
(vi) **Helps for future audit programme:** On the basis of important information and records in the audit note book future audit programme is prepared.

ROUTINE CHECKING AND ITS OBJECTIVES

Routine checking: Routine checking is a checking of books of original entry and ledgers as a matter of routine work to determine the arithmetical accuracy and to detect errors and frauds and ensures the reliability of final accounts.

Objective of routine checking: The objectives of routine checking are discussed below:

(i) Checking of primary books
(ii) Examining arithmetical accuracy
(iii) Examination of pointing

(iv) Helps to detect errors and frauds
(v) Prevent to alter errors and frauds
(vi) Accuracy of Trail Balance
(vii) Reliability of Final Accounts

Advantage or importance of Routine Checking:

There are many advantages of routine checking. These are discusses below:
(i) Examination of arithmetical accuracy
(ii) Through checking of books of accounts
(iii) Detection and prevention of frauds
(iv) Reliability of final accounts
(v) Prevent to alter figures
(vi) Easy examination

Disadvantages or Limitations of Routines Checking.

The following are the limitations of routine checking.
(i) All errors can not be detected
(ii) All frauds can not be detected
(iii) Highly mechanical

Audit Working Paper and its Objectives

Audit working papers: Audit working papers are the permanent financial evidences obtained during the course of audit and is required to give audit conclusions and for future references.

According to Mautz, "Audit work papers are the specific device used to accumulate the evidence needed by an auditor to support his opinion."

Examples of audit working papers: The following are the examples of audit working papers generally kept for future reference:
(i) Documents regarding audit programme and audit note book.
(ii) Statement of reconciliation between cash book and bank pass book.
(iii) Copy of correspondence between the auditors and debtors creditors, bank, income tax authority and with the other third parties.
(iv) Important points of minutes of board meetings and shareholder's meetings.
(v) Copy of previous audit report.
(vi) List of all fixed assets, debtors, creditors, investment etc.
(vii) Copies of certificates received from the management regarding valuation of closing stock, outstanding expenses, accrued income etc.

Objective or purposes or importance of preserving audit working papers:

Audit working papers have a great importance to the auditor. This is an documents of audit work already made because all important documents are kept as working papers during the audit period.
(i) **Evidence of work performed:** Audit working papers acts as written documents of audit work already made because all importance documents are kept as working papers during the audit period.
(ii) **Documentary evidence for future reference:** if any charges are made against the auditor for negligence and misfeasance of work, he can defend himself with the help of working papers.

(iii) **Measurement of efficiency:** On the basis of preparation of working papers, the auditor can evaluate the efficiencies of audit staff.

(iv) **Report can be made within short time:** If the working papers prepared by the audit staff are available within the time schedule, the auditor can prepare his audit report within a short time.

(v) **Continuity of work:** If all the working papers are readily available there will be no dislocation of work, if any new staff joined for audit work or if any existing audit staff transferred for other work.

(vi) **Helps for preparing futures working papers:** Present working papers acts as a guide to the auditor for preparing future working papers. If there are nay weaknesses in the present working papers the auditor can rectify it at the time of preparing future working papers.

(vii) **Giving advice to the management:** If there is weakness in the system of internal control and internal check and in the system of maintaining accounts, the auditor cab give valuable advice to the top management on the basis of his working papers.

(viii) **Acts as a good control system:** With the help of audit working papers, the auditor can monitor and control the total work distributed among the audit staff. As a result cooperation between the employees increases.

Features/Principles/ characteristics/ essentials/ scope of maintaining goods working papers:

Successful audit work depends on maintaining and preserving of good working papers. For this purpose, some common principles are to be followed. These are discussed below:

(i) **Relevance:** Only working papers which are materials for the purpose of audit are to be preserved. Irrelevant working papers should not be kept.

(ii) **Completer information:** The working papers prepared by the audit staff should be complete and accurate in all respect so that necessary information can be obtained when the situation demands. The data's and figures should be arithmetically correct.

(iii) **Arrangement of working papers:** Working papers should be arranged according to the need and priority of audit work. Besides that audit staff should mention the date on which it was prepared. He should also sign on the face of the working paper.

(iv) **Changeability:** Working papers should not be rigid. This should be prepared according to the need of the audit work and changes are to be made if required.

(v) Safe custody: Working papers should be kept secret and protected in such a way that no one can access these without authorization.

(vi) **Correctness in presentation:** The working papers should contain such information's which is correct and not misleading. Goods presentation of information should not create any problems at the time of using of working papers.

OWNERSHIP OF WORKING PAPER:

There is great controversy regarding the perspective or ownership of working papers i.e. who is the owner of the working papers. Both the auditor and his client demand these working papers to be kept with them. The logic of the owner is that the auditor has prepared audit working papers on behalf of the company in the capacity of agent. Moreover, the auditor contracted with the third parties of the company has collected information which has been recorded in the audit working papers. For these, audit working papers are the assets of the company and they can retain it.

On the other hand, the logic behind the preservation of working papers by the auditor is that he is doing audit work on behalf of the Company but he prepares working papers for his benefits of work. Besides these, he should keep these working papers for any charges made against him by the company for negligence of duty or for misfeasance. Therefore, he is the real owner of the audit working papers.

Case Laws

(i) Stockkinsky vs. Bright Grahm & Company (1938): In this case it was held that working papers are the property of the auditor even after the payment of his audit fees. The judgment of the court was in favour of the auditors on the ground that during the performance of his duties, he acts as an independent contractor and not as an agent of his client.

(ii) Chantry Martion & Company vs. Martin: In this case, it was held that working papers for the purpose of producing Balance Sheet are the property of the auditor and the correspondence made between the auditor and the income tax department relating to tax liability of the client is the property of client.

Therefore, it can be concluded that the auditor is the owner of the working papers prepared by him so far as it relates to the examination of books of accounts.

Auditing In Depth- Its Scope And Objective

Auditing in depth: Auditing in depth is a technique of detailed examination of some selected transactions of each class to assure the accuracy of financial data's.

According to Taylor and Perry, "IT (Auditing in depth) implies the examination of the system applied within a business entailing the tracing of certain transactions from the origin to their conclusion investigating at each stage the record created and their appropriate authorization."

Scope or applicability of auditing in depth: Generally auditing in depth is applied in the organization which is large enough and there are huge transactions. If there is no internal control system in the organization or the system is inefficient, this technique is not applicable. In large organizations, if there is an efficient internal control system, the auditor can take help of auditing in depth because detailed examinations of all transactions and records are not possible. In this case, the auditor should determine the transactions on selective basis and should apply audit in depth from the beginning to the conclusion of some selected transactions of each class to assure the accuracy of financial data's.

Objective of auditing in depth: Auditing in depth has a great importance to the auditor for examination of books of accounts from the beginning to the conclusion of some selected transactions of each class to assure the accuracy of financial data's Routine checking is a checking of books of books of original entry and ledgers as a matter of routine work to determine the of final accounts. On the other hand, test checking is a technique the arithmetical accuracy and to detect errors and frauds and ensures the reliability of final accounts. On the other hand, test checking is a technique of intensive checking of some selected transactions on random basis out of huge transactions to avoid waste of time, Labour, inaccuracy and costs. To remove the demerits of both routine checking and test checking auditing in depth is applied. Auditing in depth is the detailed examination of some selected transactions of each class from the beginning to the conclusion to assure the accuracy of financial data's.

The following are the objective of auditing in depth:

(i) Detailed checking of selective transactions
(ii) Help for test checking
(iii) Useful for verification
(iv) Easy detection of frauds
(v) Verify accuracy

Advantage of Auditing in Depth:

The following are the advantage of auditing in depth:

(i) Detailed examinations of accounts on selective basis
(ii) Saving in time, labour and costs
(iii) Manipulation of accounts can be checked
(iv) Shareholders interest protected
(v) Moral pressure on client's staff
(vi) No monotony in work

Disadvantage of Auditing in Depth:

There are limitations of auditing in depth. These are discussed below:

(i) Not applicable in all cases:
(ii) Chances of risks
(iii) Not suitable for unskilled audit staff

AUDIT FILE AND ITS CONTENTS:

Audit file: The file which is used for preserving necessary papers and information obtained during the course of audit is known as audit file.

Classification of audit File: Audit file may be of two types: (a) Permanent audit file and (ii) current file.

Permanent Audit File: The document collected during the course of audit and are kept permanently in the audit and which is required in the future years is known as permanent audit file. The contents of permanent audit files are:

(i) Statement showing nature and objectives of the business, name of the management people and their functions, organization structure, nature of activities i.e. manufacturing or service, important contracts with the third parties etc.
(ii) The primary documents relating to organization i.e. Memorandum of Association, Articles, of Association in the case of company and partnership deed in the case of partnership firm.
(iii) List of books accounts maintained by the entry.
(iv) Check list of internal control system.
(v) Copy of correspondence between the auditors and debtors, creditors, bank, income tax, authority and with the other third parties.

(vi) Important points of minutes of board meetings and shareholders meetings.
(vii) Copy of previous audit report.
(viii) List of all fixed assets, debtors, creditors, investments etc.
(ix) Procedure and methods of accounting maintained by the organization etc.

Current Audit File: This file prepared for the current year under audit and according to the needs of the auditor. Generally this file is not required in the succeeding years. The contents of current audit file are:

(i) A statement of changes made in the organization during the year on the basis of internal control system
(ii) A statement of evaluation of internal control and internal check system.
(iii) Some important decisions taken by the auditor during the current year.
(iv) A statement of discussion with the management.
(v) A reconciliation statement of bank and petty cash account.
(vi) Relevant documents and explanatory statements during the audit period.
(vii) Copies of letter made between the organization and the third parties.

Advantage or Importance of maintaining Audit File

Maintaining audit file gives different advantages to the auditor. These are discussed below:

(i) Help to prepare subsequent audit file
(ii) Assist to help for comparison
(iii) Gives quick and ready information
(iv) increase in efficiency
(v) Saving in time, Labour and Costs
(vi) Continuity of work

TEST CHECKING

If the organization is large enough and there are huge transactions, it is very much impracticable and hard job for the auditor to examine and verify each transaction one by one. Detailed checking of transactions required time, effort and money. To overcome this situation, the technique of test checking is applied.

Test checking is a technique of intensive checking of some selected transactions on random basis out of huge transactions to avoid waste of time, Labour inaccuracy and costs.

According to professor **Meigs, "Testing and test checking means to select and examine a representative sample from a large number of similar items."**

In the opinion of **L.R,. Dicksee,, "the theoretical responsibility of the auditor extends ultimately to every entry in the books of accounts, but it does not follow that it is likely necessary possible to examine every entry in details."**

In case of large organizations, if there is a sound system of internal control system, the auditor can take help of test checking.

INTERNAL CONTROL INTERNAL CHECK AND INTERNAL AUDIT

Due to increase in size and nature of activities today's business worlds is most competitive. In this competitive business more and more control is required or smooth running of business.

Internal control is the total control of an organization financial and other wise to safeguard business assets, prevention and detection of errors and frauds, increase the efficiency of the management and good system of according records and includes internal check and internal audit.

According to Spicer and Pegler, "Internal Control is best regarded as the whole system of controls financial and otherwise, established by the management in the conduct of a business including internal check, internal audit and other forms of control. "
Features of Internal Control System:

A big organization having a sound internal control system has the following characteristics:

(i) Total System of control
(ii) Fixes authority and responsibility
(iii) Integrate other subsystem
(iv) Control also non-financial activities
(v) Effectiveness depends on employees
(vi) Minimizations of errors and frauds

Objective of Internal Control in relation to an according system

As per auditing Accounting Standard (AAS)-6 of the Institute of Chartered Accountants of India, the following are the objectives of Internal Control System in relation to an accounting system:

(i) Authorization
(ii) Accountability
(iii) Safeguarding of assets
(iv) Comparison

Advantage of Internal Control System:

Being a total control system, internal control has many advantages. These are:

(i) Entire system of control
(ii) Use different tools for control
(iii) Early detection of Errors and frauds
(iv) A Reliable System to the External Auditor
(v) True and Fair View of Accounting
(vi) To review the effectiveness of internal check and internal audit system
(vii) Brings overall Efficiency
(viii) Increase Overall Efficiency and Profitability

Disadvantages or Limitations of Internal Control System:

In spite of many advantages, internal control system Is not free form limitations. These are:

(i) High cost
(ii) Not Flexible
(iii) Chances of Errors and Frauds
(iv) A Routine matter

INTERNAL CHECK

Internal check system is a part of Internal Control System. To execute internal control system check is implemented. Internal Check system is such an arrangement of allocating tasks among the employees where work of one employee is automatically checked by others i.e. no one is allowed to do the total work of a transaction.

According to F.R.M de Paula "Internal Check means practically a continuous internal audit carried on by the staff itself, by means of which the work of each individual is independently checked by other members of the staff."

Internal check has been defined by the Institute of Chartered Accountant of England and Wales as "checks on day to day transactions which operate continuously as part of the routine system whereby the work of one person is proved independently or is complimentary to the work of another, the object the prevention of early detection of errors and fraud."

Principles or Features of Internal Check System

The following are the main principles of good system of internal check:

(i) **Allocation of Duties:** Under this system, duties are allocated in such a way that no one person can be allowed to access all the transactions of a financial matter.

(ii) **Checking of transactions:** The system are introduced in such a way that day to day transactions are checked and chances of errors and frauds are minimized.

(iii) **Continuous service:** This is a continuous built in device and a part of routine system i.e. the system is repetitive.

(iv) **Complementary:** Work is complementary i.e. the total job is allocated in such a way among the employees that the work of each person is checked by other.

(v) Encourage to take leave: To detect frauds every employees of the organization should be encouraged to go on leave at least once in a year.

(vi) **Separation of duties:** Those who are in charge of assets should not be permitted to deal books of accounts. AS a result chances of manipulation of accounts can be minimized.

(vii) Use of mechanical devices: Some mechanical devices e.g. Automatic Cash Register, Cheque Signing Machine etc may be employed to prevent misappropriation of cash.

(viii) **Sound accounting control:** A sound system of accounting control should be implemented for each important class of assets.

(ix) Sound budgetary control: A sound budgetary control system should be implemented for each important class of assets.

(x) **Rotation of jobs:** Transfer of employees from one job to another is to be made for detection of errors and frauds.

(xi) **Perpetual inventory system:** A good perpetual inventory system with accountability should be implemented.

(xii) **Deposit of cash:** Receipts of cash should be immediately deposited in the bank.

(xiii) **Effective control:** Effective control should be implemented over all purchases, sales, receipts and issue of goods.

(xiv) **Periodic verification:** There should be a system of periodical verification and testing go some accounting records.

(xv) **Periodical review:** Periodic review of accounting procedure is a part of internal check system.

(xvi) **Others:**

(a) Storekeeper giving charge of store should not be allowed to keep accounts relating to purchase.

(b) A good internal check system should be implemented regarding payment of wages (c) Accounting of credit sales and credit purchase should be strictly dealt with.

OBJECTIVES AND ADVANTAGES OF INTERNAL CHECK SYSTEM

Following are the objective and advantages of internal check system.

(i) Division of Work
(ii) Responsibility
(iii) Early detection of errors and frauds
(iv) Proper books of accounts.
(v) Timely preparation of Final Accounts
(vi) Dependence of Auditor
(vii) Exercising moral pressure
(vii) Increase Overall Efficiency
(viii) Overall Economy

DISADVANTAGE OR LIMITATIONS OF INTERNAL CHECK SYSTEM:

Though internal check system has numerous advantages still this is not free from limitations. These are

(i) Costly system
(ii) Not Applicable for small organization
(iii) Chances of collusion.
(iv) Monotonous for the workers
(v) Disorder in work

DISTINCTION BETWEEN INTERNAL CONTROL AND INTERNAL CHECK SYSTEM

Internal Control	Internal Check
1. Internal Control is a total control i.e. financial and otherwise to safeguard assets of the business.	1. Internal Check is a part of internal control system and is a set of rules that are the part of accounting system.
2. The object of internal control is not only to detect errors and frauds but also to formulate management policies with efficiency.	2. The main purpose is to maintain accounts in such a way that errors and frauds can easily be detected and prevented.
3. As internal control covers total control of the organization its scope is wider	3. As internal check covers accounting aspect and detection of frauds and errors, its scope is narrower.

Internal Control	Internal Check
4. AS internal control is a total system of control its principles are flexible and may change according to the need of the organization.	4. Generally, rules framed out for implementing internal check is not changed for a time period.
5. As internal control is a total control i.e. financial and otherwise, the total responsibility is of the directors.	5. As work is allocated among the employees in such a way the work of one person is automatically checked by others. So each employee performs his own work and the directions do not interfere on the job.

INTERNAL CHECK IN RESPECT OF PAYMENT OF WAGES EMPLOYING A LARGE NUMBER OF WORKERS

Internal check system is part of Internal Control System. To execute internal control system internal check is implemented. Internal check system is such an arrangement of allocating checked by others i.e. no one is allowed to do the total work of a transaction.

Internal check regarding payment of wages: A sound of internal check regarding payment of wages may avoid errors and frauds which may be revealed from time and piece wages records.

The following steps may be followed.

(i) There should be a separate Time and Pay Roll department.

(ii) A record card for each employee should be maintained where date of apportionment, terms of employment, rate of wages, should be written.

(iii) A good time keeping system should be introduced so that time of entering and leaving of each employee is recorded.

(iv) Actual time spent by each worker on the jobs should be properly recorded in the job card and signed by the departmental manager.

(v) In case of piece rated workers details by the departmental manager.

(vi) Those persons who prepares wages sheet does not have access with the preparation of attendance sheet.

(vii) There should be proper authority for grant of overtime work.

(viii) The person who is in charge for payment of wages should not have connection with the preparation of wages sheet.

(ix) While preparing wages sheet, number of workers shown in the wages sheet should be matched with the records of the personnel department, so that chance of inclusion of dummy workers can be detected.

(x) Incentives and production bonus given to the workers must be based on time saved or getting more output in standard time and the bases of calculating time saved should be checked.

(xi) Wages should be paid in the presence of a responsible person who can intently the employee.

(xii) Unclaimed wages should be deposited immediately into the bank.

INTERNAL CHECK WITH REGARD TO CREDIT PURCHASE OF A BIG BUSINESS ORGANIZATION

The following are the guidelines of a sound system of internal check with regard to credit Purchase of a big business organization.

(i) **Separate department for purchase:** In case of large organization there are huge transaction regarding purchase of different goods. For this purpose, a separate department for purchase should be established under an authorized person.

(ii) **Receiving purchase requisition:** Each departmental manager should prepare purchase requisition duly authorized and signed mentioning the quantity and quality of goods required and send it to the storekeeper or direct to the purchase department. After receiving purchase requisition the purchase manger should like initiative for purchase of goods.

(iii) **Verify the quantity of stock:** After receiving purchase requisitions the purchase department should verify the stock in hand of different goods and determine the quantity to be purchased.

(iv) **Inquiry for purchase:** After determining quantity t of goods to be purchased, the purchase manager gives tender for purchase or make inquiry from different supplier regarding price, quality, quantity, mode of transport, payment terms, facility of discount, time required, to supply etc.

(v) **Selection of supplier:** After considering all the factors mentioned above, the purchase department select the supplier who will supply goods at least cost with required quality.

(vi) **Giving purchase order:** After selecting supplier the purchase manager should place purchase order to the supplier. Generally five copies of purchase order are prepared and distributed as: (a) one copy sent to the selected supplier (b) one copy is retained by the purchase department (c) one copy is sent to the stores department (d) one copy is sent to the accounts department and (e) the last copy is sent to the department who gives purchase requisition.

(vii) **Receiving and inspecting goods:** When the supplier supplies goods that should be inspected at the factory gate by the responsible official and tested if regards quality and if satisfied then passes it for receiving the goods.

(viii) **Preparing goods received note:** After receiving inspection reports, the receiving department should records the details of goods received in a form known as "Goods Received Note". One copy of goods received note is to be sent to the storekeeper, one copy to the accounts department and the last copy to the purchase department.

(ix) **Return of goods purchased:** If goods received is not as per quantity ordered and of required quality or goods send by the supplier is defective then it is to be returned to the supplier along with a debit note.

(x) **Checking and passing of bill for payment:** After receiving goods the purchase manger will take initiative to make voucher for payment. The invoice must be serially numbered and entered in the Inward Invoice Register. A final voucher is prepared on the basis of invoice and other documents and payment is to be made as per terms of contract.

(xi) **Maintaining proper records:** All importance documents should be properly maintained i.e. purchase order, goods received note, inspection report, debit/ credit note, challens, voucher etc.

INTERNAL CHECK WITH REGARD TO CASH DEPARTMENT OF A LARGE DEPARTMENT STORE

A large departmental store generally has many departments with respect of various goods and services. There should be a separate cash department for receiving and handling of cash and cheques. A good system of internal check regarding cash department must have the following gaudiness:

(i) All incoming mails should be opened in presence of a responsible officer not connected with persons like cashier and administration department.

(ii) Receipts of all cheques and cash are to be immediately recorded in cash abstract.

(iii) All cash and cheque received should be immediately deposited into bank.

(iv) bank paying in slips should be prepared by person other than cashier.

(v) Printed receipt book with serial number to be used and all receipts must be issued to the depositors signed by the appropriate authority.

(vi) Any defective slip should be identified and market it as cancelled with proper initials.

(vii) There should be a regular check of counterfoils of the paying-in slips with the cash book recording the receipts of cash and cheque.

(viii) To get the better result of internal check system use of automatic cash register is preferred.

(ix) Unused cheques and receipt book should be kept in safe custody under a responsible person.

(x) Periodical bank reconciliation statement should be prepared to know the actual cash balance.

INTERNALAUDIT

A big organization has to maintain enormous books of accounts. Internal audit being a part of internal control system is a detailed review of the books of accounts throughout the accounting year by a specialist group of employed auditors independently within an organization to assure management that proper accounts has been maintained, and the system gives adequate safeguard to maintain revenue and protect misappropriation of assets and evaluated the effectiveness of other controls and confirms that the polices given by the management are being properly executed.

The institute of Charted Accountant of England and Wales defines internal audit as "as review of operations and records, sometimes continuous undertaking within a business by a special staff."

Features of Internal Audit:

Internal audit has some fundamental features. These are discuses below:

(i) **Separate identify:** A separate department must have to be established for conducting internal audit continuously monitors the accounting work throughout the accounting year.

(ii) **A sub-system of internal control:** Being a part of internal control system internal audit continuously monitors the accounting work throughout the accounting year.

(iii) Independent appraisal: Internal audit department with the help of its specialized group of auditors group of auditors protect misappropriation of assets and evaluated the effectiveness of other controls and confirms that the policies given by the management are being properly executed.

(iv) **Advisory function:** By caucusing the weak points in the accounting system, the internal auditor gives valuable suggestion to the top management for taking appropriate measures to rectify it.

(v) **Judge the effectiveness of internal check system:** The efficiency and effectiveness of internal check system can be verified by the internal auditor and he can inform to the appropriate authority if there is any drawback in the system.

(vi) **Review of accounting system:** Continuous review and monitoring of accounting system is the most important task of the internal audit department. For this purpose, internal auditor applies different analytical procedure.

Objective and Advantage or Importance of Internal Audit:

The following the objectives and importance of internal audit system:

(i) Accuracy in financial accounts
(ii) Maintaining standard accounting policies
(iii) Evaluation of internal check system
(iv) Judges overall financial efficiency
(v) Detect inefficiency in production
(vi) Examines proper authority
(v) Early detection of errors and frauds
(vi) Ensure proper safeguard of frauds:
(vii) Verifies different assets
(viii) Verify efficiency of fanatical system
(ix) Constructive suggestion.

Disadvantage or Limitations of Internal Audit:

In spite of many advantages the internal audit suffers from certain limitations. These are

(i) Expensive
(ii) Expertise needed:
(iii) Lack of impartial opinion

Distinction between Internal Audit and Statutory Audit

Internal Audit: Internal audit being a part of internal control system is a detailed review of the books of accounts throughout the accounting year by a specialist group of employed auditor independently within an o0rganization to assure management that proper accounts has been maintained, and the system gives adequate safeguard to maintain revenue and protect misappropriation of assets and evaluated the effectiveness of other controls and confirms the policies given by the management are being properly executed.

Statutory Audit: Statutory audit is compulsory audit for the companies conducted by the qualified independent auditor as per company's act 1956. The primary duty of a Statutory auditor is to give onion in his report that profit and loss account and balance sheet of the company have been drawn up as per law and whether the accounts shows a true and fair view of he state of affairs of the company or not.

Following are the difference between Internal Audit and Statutory

Internal Audit	Statutory Audit
1. Internal audit is n audit conducted by the employees of the company	1. Statutory audit is a compulsory audit for the companies conducted by the qualified independent auditor as per company's Act, 1956.
2. Internal auditors are appointed by the management of the organization.	2. Statutory auditor is generally appointed by the shareholders in the annual general meeting of the company.
3. No Statutory qualifications are prescribed in the company's act for internal auditor.	3. A Statutory auditor must have prescribed qualifications under Section 226 of the company's Act, 1956.
4. Generally internal audit is done continuously for the whole year,	4. Generally statutory audit is done after the preparation of final accounts and at the end of the financial year.
5. The scope, nature, rights and duties of work is determined by the management.	5. The scope, nature, rights and duties of statutory auditor are determined by the company's Act, 1956.
6. The Primary duty of Internal auditor is to find out the accuracy of the account and to detect any errors and frauds which have been committed.	6. The Primary duty of a Statutory auditor is to give opinion in his report that profit and loss account and balance sheet of the company have been drawn up as per law and whether the accounts shows a true and fair view of the state of affairs of the company or not.
7. Internal auditor has to submit his report to the management,	7. Statutory auditor has to give his report to the shareholders.
8. Internal auditor can be removed by the management.	8. Statutory auditor has to give his report to the shareholders.
9. Remuneration of internal auditor is fixed by the management.	9. Remuneration of statutory auditor is fixed by the shareholders in the annual general meeting.
10. Internal auditor gibes suggestion tot eh management regarding efficiency of business and how to prevent and frauds	10. Statutory auditor is not an advisor except specifically requested.
11.Each and every transaction is checked by internal auditor	11. Statutory auditor while auditing can take help of test checking.
12. Internal auditors have no right to attend general meeting.	12. Statutory auditors have a right to attend annual general meeting.

DISTINCTION BETWEEN INTERNAL AUDIT AND INTERNAL CHECK

Internal Audit	Internal Check
1. Internal audit being a part of internal control system is a detailed review of the books of accounts throughout the accounting year by a specialist group of employed auditors independently within an organization to assure management that proper accounts has been maintained and the system gibes adequate safeguards to maintain revenue and protect misappropriation of assets and evaluated the effectiveness of to other controls and confirms that the policies given by the management are being properly executed.	1. Internal Check system is such an arrangement of allocating tasks among the employees where work of one employee where work of one employee us automatically checked by others i.e. no one is allowed to do the total work of a transaction.
2. Internal audit is an audit conducted by a separate department and by the professionally qualified employees.	2. In case of internal check, work is so distributed that job done by one employee is automatically checked by others.
3. The primary duty of internal auditor is to find out the accuracy of the accounts and to detect any errors and frauds which have been committed.	3. Internal check is such an efficient tool which protects the organization for being committing errors and frauds.
4. Internal auditor gives suggestion to the management regarding efficiency of business and how to prevent errors and frauds.	4. Internal check is being used as an efficient system prevails in the organization and almost every employee is covered under this system. Hence this is not an advisory system.
5. Internal auditor had to submit his report to the management.	5. Under the system of internal check, day to-day transactions are being reported to the head of the department.

RELIANCE OF STATUTORY AUDITOR OR INTERNAL AUDIT SYSTEM

External Audit: Statutory audit is compulsory audit for the companies conducted by the qualified independent auditor as per company's act, 1956. The primary duty of a Statutory auditor is to give opinion in his report that profit and loss account and balance sheet of the company have been drawn up as per law and whether the accounts shows a true and fair view of the state of affairs of the company or not.

Internal Auditt: Internal audit being a part of internal control system is a detailed review of the books of accounts throughout the accounting year by a specialist group of employed auditors independently within an organization to assure management that proper accounts has been maintained, and the system gives adequate safeguards to maintain review and protect misappropriation of assets and evaluated the effectiveness of the other controls and confirms that the policies given by the management are being properly executed.

1. Routine checking is a process of verification of arithmetical accuracy of transaction recorded in the books of accounts.	1. Vouching is the verification of accounting entries recorded in the books of accounts with documentary evidences such as vouchers, invoices, confirmation etc and to check the genuineness, relevance, validity, authenticity of the transactions through the help of inspection, observation, inquiries, confirmation etc.
2. The scope of routine checking is very limited i.e. checking of arithmetical accuracy, casting posting, totaling, carry, forward etc.	2. Vouching includes routine checking i.e. the scope is very large.
3. Routing checking includes casting, totaling and balancing of books of prime entry, checking of ledger balance, arithmetical of Trial balance etc.	3. Vouching includes verification of accounting entries with the vouchers, invoices, confirmation genuineness of the transactions with the help of inspection, observation, enquiries etc.
4. Only some minor errors can be detected.	4. Through the process of vouching major errors and frauds can be detected.
5. No expertise is required for conducting routine checking.	5. Expertise is required for the job of vouching.

CONTINGENT LIABILITY AND AUDITOR'S DUTY:

Contingent Liability: Contingent liability is not an actual liability at the end of the present year but may become liability in the future on the happenings on certain unpredictable contingencies. Examples are; (i) Liability for bill discounted with the bank yet to be matured. (ii) Liability for pending case before the court. (iii) Guarntee given on behalf of others (iv) Liability regarding party paid up shares (v) Arrear on Cumulative Preference Shares.

How it is shown in Balance Sheet? According to company's act 1956, contingent liability should be shown as a foot note in the Balance Sheet and state that

(i) Claims against the company not acknowledged as debts.
(ii) Uncalled liability on shares partly paid
(iii) Arrears on fixed cumulative dividend.
(iv) Estimated amount of contracts remaining to be executed on capital account and not provided for.
(v) Other money for which the company is contingently liable.

Auditors Duty: The following points should be considered for verification of contingent liability:

(i) Examine the minute book to ascertain the probable future contingent liability.
(ii) Examine, whether sufficient provision has been made for uncertain contingent liability.
(iii) Examine the Bill book and confirm the amount of bills discounted before the date of maturity;
(iv) Check the provision which has made for arrear cumulative preference dividend.
(v) Verify that all contingent liability should have correctly shown in the balance sheet as a foot note.

(vi) Disclosure about contingent liability is to be given in the financial statement as required by accounting standard (AS) 29.

Contingent Assets	Contingent Liability
1. Contingent assets are those assets the claim for which may depend on performance and activities of future period. Examples are (i) Uncalled share capital of a company (ii) a legal action taken by the company against another company for use of its patent.	1. Contingent liability is not an actual liability at the end of the present year but may become liability in the future on the happenings on certain unpredictable contingencies. Example are; (i) liability for bill discounted with the bank yet to be matured. (ii) Liability for pending case before the court.
2. Indian Company's Act does not prescribe any procedure to show contingent assets in the balance sheet.	2. Contingent Liabilities are shown as foot note in the balance sheet.

THE DEFFERENCE BETWEEN DEPRECIAIOTN AND OBSOLESCENCE ARE GIVEN BELOWS:

Depreciation	Obsolescence
1. Depreciation may be defined as gradual and permanent decline in the value of fixed assets as a result of wear and tear, obsolesce, efflux ion of time, market changes or for any other reasons.	1. When a new technology or technical know-how captures the market and on account of that, existing assets losses its value is known as obsolescence. l i k
2. Provision for depreciation can be estimated beforehand So that there is Lower risk for replacement of assets.	2. Provision for obsolesce can not be estimate Accurately obsolescence is a Type of loss which may occur within a Short time.
3. Generally depreciation on fixed assets is made in a uniform percentage over the years.	3. In case of obsolescence, a fixed amount not be determined accurately.

Provision or Specific Reserve	General Reserve
1. Provision is a specific reserve made out for the purpose of some uncertain liabilities or for a known loss expected at a future date.	1. A general reserve is a reserve which is created out of normal profit of the business for the purpose of meeting unknown future losses or for strengthening the financial position of the business.
2. Provision is created for meeting uncertain liabilities.	2. Reserve is created for providing further working capital and for strengthening the financial position of the business.
3. Provision is a charge against profit	3. Reserve is an appropriation of profit.
4. Provision is to be made to meet some known expenditure or loss e.g. provision for depreciation.	4. General reserve is created for meeting any purpose.

Provision or Specific Reserve	General Reserve
5. The amount of provision to be created does not depend on profit.	5. The amount of reserve to be created depends upon the availability of profits.
6. Provision may be shown in the liability side of the balances sheet or can be deducted from the respective assets on the asset side.	6. Reserve is shown in the liability side of the balance sheet under the head Reserve & Surplus.
7. The amount of provision which is created for meeting any particular liability cannot be used for distribution of dividend.	7. Dividend can be distributed out of free reserve as reserve is made out of distributable profit.
8. Some provisions made for specific purposes are a tax deductible item for the purpose of income tax e.g. provision for depreciation as per income tax act.	8. Amount transferred to general reserve out of distributable profit not admissible expenses as per income tax act.
9. If provision is not made for known losses or for future uncertain contingencies the auditor should clearly mentioned it in his audit report.	9. A certain percentage of profit is to be transferred to reserve account before declaring dividend. Except that an auditor has nothing to do if a company does create reserve out of distributable profit.
10. Income can not be accurately measured without making provision.	10. Reserve is made out of distributable profit. So, reserve has no direct role for measurement of income.

THE DIFFERENCE BETWEEN RESERVE AND RESERVE FUND ARE DISCUSSED BELOW:

Reserve	Reserve Fund
1. A general reserve is a reserve which is created out of normal profit of the business for the purpose of meeting unknown future losses or for streng thening the financial position of the business	1. Reserve fund is a part of profit created out of normal business activities for the purpose of investing the amount in outside securities and to earn profit.
2. Reserve is created for providing further working capital and for strengthening the financial position of the business.	2. The purpose of creating reserve fund is to invest the amount outside the business in profitable securities and to earn profit i.e. non – trading income.
3. Reserve is shown in the liability side of the balance sheet under the head 'Reserve & Surplus.'	3. Reserve fund is shown in the liability side of the balance sheet under the head 'Reserve & Surplus' and reserve fund investment is shown in the assets side of the balance sheet under the head 'Investment'.
4. Dividend can be distributed out of free	4. Reserve fund cannot be utilized for reserve as reserve is made out of distributable profit. payment of dividend except from 'Dividend Equalization Fund'.

Contd.

Reserve	Reserve Fund
5. A company must have to transfer a certain percentage of profit to general reserve before declaring dividend.	5. No amount of profit should be transferred to the reserve fund before declaring dividend.
6. Reserve is the base for providing additional working capital or for strengthens financial position of the business	6. Reserve fund is not a source of additional working capital of the business rather it is a source of non trading income.

DISTINCTION BETWEEN CAPITAL RESERVE AND REVENUE RESERVE

Capital Reserve	Revenue Reserve
1. The reserve which arises out of capital profit is known as capital reserve e.g. (i) Profit on revaluation of assets. (ii) Profit on revaluation of assets. (iii) Profit on re – issue of forfeited shares (iv) Shares or debentures are issued at a premium. (v) Profit prior to incorporation of a company (vi) Purchase of own debenture by redeeming at a discount in the open market etc.	1. A revenue reserve is a reserve which is created out of normal profit of the business for the purpose of meeting unknown future losses or for strengthening the financial position of the business.
2. Capital reserve is utilized for written off capital losses.	2. Revenue reserve is used for written of revenue losses and also for writing of capital losses.
3. Dividend can be declared out of this profit subject to some conditions.	3. Dividend can be distributed out of free reserve as reserve is made out of distributable profit.
4. Business assets increase out of capital reserve.	4. Revenue reserve is created for providing as reserve is made capital and for strengthening the financial position of the business.
5. Capital reserve can arises any time during the continuity of the business	5. Revenue reserve is created out revenue profit at the end of financial year.

Capital expenditure	Revenue expenditure
1. Capital expenditure are those which are made for the purchase or acquisition of assets for earning revenue and the benefit is obtained for a number of years. Purchase of land and building, plant and machinery, patent, furniture etc are the examples of capital expenditure.	1. Revenue expenditure is those which are incurred for day to day operating activities of the business and whose benefits are exhausted within the current accounting year. Expenses on material, labour and overheads etc are the examples of revenue expenditure.
2. The benefit from capital expenditure is not exhausted within the current accounting year but also extended for some future years. Capital expenditure is unexpired cost.	2. The benefits from revenue expenditure are exhausted within the current accounting year. Revenue expenditure is expired costs.

Contd.

Capital expenditure	Revenue expenditure
3. A large sum of money is to be paid for capital expenditure.	3. Amount of revenue expenditure is comparatively lower than capital expenditure.
4. Depreciation on capital expenditure is charged against revenue and is treated as expenses.	4. Revenue expenses are fully charged against revenue as expired costs.
5. Fixed assets made out of capital expenditure can be sold out or transferred.	5. Here, goods or services made from revenue expenditure can be sold not.
6. Through capital expenditure inflow of assets arises.	6. Through revenue expenditure income generated.

SECRET RESERVE

Secret Reserve: A Secret Reserve is a reserve, the existence of which is not disclosed on the face of the balance sheet. Secret reserve indicates+ concealment of profit either by means of understatement of assets or overstating its liabilities. When a company makes secret reserve, it indicates that the actual financial position is better than what it has been shown in the books of accounts.

According to Spicer and Pegler, "Secret reserve is a reserve, the existence and / or amount of which is not disclosed on the face of the Balance Sheet".

Methods of creating Secret Reserve: Secret reserve may be created in the following ways: .

(i) By showing capital expenditure as revenue.
(ii) By showing fewer amounts on fixed assets.
(iii) By showing undervaluation of stock.
(iv) By recording fictitious expenditure in the books of accounts
(v) By making more provision for bad debt and for outstanding liabilities.
(vi) *By* showing the liabilities of the business at more amounts.
(vii) By showing more amount of purchase and fewer amounts of sales in the books of accounts.
(viii) By showing excess depreciation on fixed assets.
(ix) By not considering the increase in the value of assets.
(x) By recording contingent liability as real liability.

Merits or Advantages or Benefits of creating Secret Reserve: There are some benefits or advantages of creating secret reserve for the business because it strengths the financial position of the company and this reserve can be utilized when situation and needs demands. The benefits of creating secret reserve are discussed below.

(i) Sound financial structure:
(ii) To protect unexpected future losses:
(iii) Not to disclose actual financial position to the competitors:
(iv) To give lower dividend
(v) Maintaining stable rate of dividend

Auditor's duties regarding Secret Reserve:

Secret reserve is legally prohibited as per companies act except certain companies who may create secret reserve i.e. banking, investment, insurance and electricity companies. The duties of an auditor regarding secret reserve are given below:

(i) The auditor should carefully examine the books of accounts and verify the assets and liabilities to find out the existence and the amount of secret reserve if any.

(ii) The auditor should enquire the Articles of Association and find that whether any clause has been given for creation of secret reserve.

(iii) The auditor should verify the purposes for which secret reserve has been utilized and give his opinion regarding this in the audit report.

(iv) If excess provision has been made for bad and doubtful debt in the books of accounts that should be clearly mentioned by him in his audit report.

(v) He should examine whether proper valuation of assets and liabilities have been made..

(vi) He should confirm that secret reserve created is not used by the managerial personnel for their personal purposes.

CAPITAL RESERVE AND RESERVE CAPITAL: DISTINCTION

The difference between capital reserve and reserve capital are given below:

Capital reserve	Reserve capital
1. The reserve which arises out of capital profit is known as capital reserve. e.g. (i) Profit on revaluation of assets. (ii) Profit on sale of assets (iii) Profit on re-issue of forfeited shares (iv) Shares or debentures are issued at a premium.(v) Profit prior to incorporation of a company.(vi) Purchase of own debenture by redeeming at a discount in the open market etc.	1. This is a part of authorized capital which is not called except in case of liquidation of company is known as reserve capital.
2. Capital reserve is utilized for Written off capital /	2. Reserve capital cannot be utilized for any purposes except in cases of winding up of a company.
3. Capital reserve is treated as internal liability and is shown in the Balance Sheet under the head 'Reserve and Surplus.'	3. Capital reserve is not treated as liability and is not shown in the Balance Sheet.
4. This reserve is created out of capital profit .	4. This reserve is created out of authorized capital.
5. Dividend can be declared out of this profit subject to some Conditions.	5. There is no relation between reserve Capital and dividend.
6. Business assets increase 'out of capital reserve.	6 Reserve capital does not increase the liability of the business.
7. Capital reserve can arises any time during the continuity of the business.	7 In case of winding up of a company reserve capital is required.

London Oil Storage Company Ltd. vs. Seear Hasluck and Company (1904): In this case the auditor was negligent to verify the existence of cash in hand. The auditor was liable for branch of duty for not taking proper steps to verify the existence of assets shown in the balance sheet.

Arthur E. Green & company vs. The Central Advance And Discount Corporation Ltd. (1920): In this case the auditor was guilty for negligence for not considering huge amount of bad debt which remains unpaid for a long time and the company was not made sufficient provision for bad debt. As a result, profit was inflated and dividend was paid on the basis of this profit.

Irish Woolen Company vs. Tyson and Others (1900): In this case, the auditor was liable for damages of the company by reason of falsification and manipulation of accounts which might have been discovered if he exercise reasonable care and skill during the course of his audit.

Therefore, it can be concluded that an auditor must verify the truth regarding financial transaction and assets and liabilities which are shown in the balance sheet. He must exercise reasonable care and skill to disclose the falsification of accounts.

The Kingston Cotton Mill Company Ltd. (1896).

Justice Lindsay told it is no part of the auditor's duty to take stock. No one contends that it is. He must rely on other people for details of the stock- in – trade in hand, if there are no suspicious circumstances.

Westminister Road Construction and Engineering Company Ltd. (1932)

In this case, it was held that an auditor must take the fullest use of all materials available to him and although he is neither a stock taker and nor a valuer of work – in – progress. He will be guilty of misfeasance if he fails to take notice of all available evidence from which it could be reasonable concluded that the work – in – progress was overvalued.

Le Lievere and Dennes vs. Gould (1893): In this case it was held that as there is no contractual relationship between the auditor and the third party, the auditor is not liable.

Distinction between Audit and Investigation:

Investigation of accounts: Investigation of the accounts of business means special examination of the books of accounts and records for some special purpose e.g. checking of books of accounts of an existing business intended to purchase by a person or a company may conduct investigation of audited accounts of their business:

EDP AUDIT OR AUDITING FOR COMPUTERIZED ACCOUNTING:

ITs FEATURES AND ADVANTAGES:

EDP audit or auditing for computerized accounting: EDP audit. is a process of collection where evidences are collected and evaluated to assure that the system properly safeguards assets, maintains data integrity, reliability and efficiency of the information system, uses resources of the organization in an efficient manner and gives a sound reporting structure.

Features/Principles/objectives/advantages benefits of EDP audit: The following are the advantages or principles of EDP audit:

(i) EDP audit evaluates that proper and sufficient data control, data integrating and efficiency of the information system. .

(ii) It properly safeguards the assets and uses and also includes hardware, software, system documentation, data files etc.

(iii) This system of audit ensures the utilization of resources in an efficient manner and within the minimum costs.

(iv) Under this audit, proper administration and procedural controls are created and implemented.

(v) It, ensures that data processing of different application system are accurate.

(vi) It ensures that there is a proper system of reporting structure.

(vii) Under this system of audit, rules, regulations and statutory laws are maintained and ensure compliance of statutory rules.

(viii) It reviews the system of scope of the organization data processing method and the system efficiency and effectiveness and also asses the fulfillment of need of the users.

(ix) By maintaining managerial control over the data processing system, it reduces the chances of errors and frauds.

(x) Through the help of EDP audit, areas· can be detected where more work is to be performed. Security programme and overall control for the risk associated with the information system can be found out.

LIMITATIONS OF EDP OR COMPUTERIZED ACCOUNTING:

Though EDP audit has many advantages to the auditor, it is not free of limitations. The difficulties which arise during EDP audit are discussed below:

(i) Problems to get supporting vouchers: In case of manual auditing system every transaction has a supporting voucher and with proper authorization. But in case of computerized accounting many transactions are directly put in to the computer without the record of authorization e.g. purchase invoice, sales invoice, discount allowed etc. This creates a problem to. the auditor regarding authenticity of transactions because of non-existence of input documents. Output reports may not give supporting details e.g. printed reports which may contain only transactions details and total.

(ii) Easy way to fraud and manipulation of data: Accounting through computer system may give chances of huge fraud and manipulation of data's in different ways. If there is easy access and lack of security, frauds may leads to loss of substantial amount.

(iii) Deficiency of visible audit trail: In conventional accounting there is a system of in depth checking and verification of transactions from the beginning to the end through a series of process and it is possible to get necessary documents and supporting vouchers. But in a computerized accounting system, there is' no series of process followed for recording of transactions as input. Therefore, there is a lack of audit trail and as a result there is a huge chance of manipulation.

(iv) Problem of codification: In conventional accounting system transactions are classified according to the different accounting heads. But in computerized accounting different codes are used for the transactions which creates problem for the auditor except expertise in this field.

(v) Effect of computer virus: This is a serious problem for computerized accounting. This is a preplanned programme applied to destroy the area of different accounting data, for the purpose of the employee's personal gain. The auditor has to be very cautious regarding computer virus while auditing through computer.

MAJOR AREAS ON INTERNAL CONTROL SYSTEM IN AN EDP ENVIRONMENT:

The main objective of EDP audit is to proper data control, data integrity, system efficiency and safeguarding of assets. But the objective of EDP audit would fail to get result if there is not a sound internal control system in the organization. The major areas of internal control system are discussed below:

A big organization having a sound internal control system covers the following major areas:

(i) Total system of control: Internal control system is a whole system of control financial and otherwise.

(ii) Integrate other subsystem: To execute the proper functioning of internal control, internal check and internal audit are implemented.

(iii) Control all aspects: Internal control system is such a control which exercises control over assets, . liabilities, revenue and expenses.

(iv) Control also non-financial activities: Internal control exercises not only internal check and internal audit but also perform non-financial activities for smooth running of business.

COMPUTER INFORMATION SYSTEM AND INTERNAL CONTROL:

Internal control is the total control of an organization financial and otherwise to safeguard business assets, prevention and detection of errors and frauds, increase the efficiency of the management and good system of accounting records and includes internal check and internal audit."

Some of the important internal control system for computer information system is:

(i) Creation of Password: There should be a system of password for authentication of the person for processing the task. In other words, data fed into the system and processing done by the computer is authorized.

(ii) Process of Edit Test: Financial Control and Edit Control test help in accurate data entry and the accurate processing of computer information system.

(iii) File Libraries: This is a system which can be used as an internal control technique to protect the computer information system from destruction anti corruption.

(iv) Audit Trails: This system helps to preserve all those records within the system from which financial statement can be obtained.

(v) Batch Cancellation Stamp: This control helps repetition of processing of data and only one time processing is required.

(vi) General Control: This control helps to implement overall control on all the activities of computer information system. The sub-system of this control is (a) Organization Control (b) System and Documentation control (c) Hardware Control (d) Procedural Control etc.

(vii) Application Control: In addition to general control, control of application of the computer information system is also important. The sub- system of this control is (a) Input Control (b) Output Control and (c) Processing control.

CHARACTERISTICSOF AN EFFECTIVE SYSTEM OF COMPUTER AUDIT PROGRAMME

The characteristics of compute~ audit programme are:

(i) The system must be simple enough for being use so that it can remember countless details normally required in writing or changing computer programme.

(ii) The system of computer audit programme would be such so that it is easily understandable to all.

(iii) It has the capacity for being used with different configuration of computers.

(iv) The staff should be sufficiently trained and the package must-have adequate support at the time of installation. There should be enough flexibility for future revision of. the programme.

(v) The package must have statistical sampling capability.

(vi) The programme should frame in such a way so that it can process different types of applications. .

(vii) The system should be such that it can be easily executed by all users and can be compared with the existing system.

(viii) The program must have function of report writing and is capable to prepare multiple reports in a single program run and also can generate output report format which is flexible as per requirement.

Steps for Auditing of Computerized Accounting:

The following steps should require before audit of computerized accounting:

(i) Examine the fundamental features of computerized accounting. This includes:
   - (a) System and methods of keeping accounting (b) Management information system
   - (c) Documentation of input
   - (d) Procedure and system of control
   - (e) Methods of segmentation of duties.

(ii) Evaluate the system of documentation. This includes:
   - (a) Contents of data
   - (b) Internal controlsystem
   - (c) Coding procedure
   - (d) Formats of input
   - (e) System flow chart
   - (f) Documentation of new system software
   - (g) Access to system documentation.

(iii) Control over inputs. This includes:
   (a) Authorization of transactions
   (b) Is there any missing transactions or transactions are changed or duplicated.
   (c) Rejection of incorrect transactions.

(iv) Designing of test procedure. This consists of:
   (a) Choice of testing technique
   (b) Processing of testing operations.

(v) Audit tools through computer. This includes:
   (a) Construction of general audit programme
   (b) Test dect
   (c) Recovery procedure of data and computer programme.

(vi) Preparing audit programme.

(vii) Compliance audit procedure

(viii) Review of output

(ix) Timely submission of report to the management.

DISTINCTION BETWEEN FINANCIAL AUDIT AND COST AUDIT

Financial Audit	Cost Audit
1. Financial audit is the audit of financial accounts of an organization, at the end of the financial year to reflect true and fair view of accounts.	1. Cost audit is the audit of cost accounting records of an organization to reflect true cost of a product or service and pricing.
2. Financial audit is compulsory for every company as per company's act, 1956.	2. Cost audit is not compulsory except in certain' cases i.e. companies' carrying. on business of manufacturing or mining and where the Central government has directed to maintain cost accounts in certain industries under Section 209(d) and compulsory cost audit under Section 233B.
3. The purpose of financial audit are to find out whether financial accounts are properly maintained and whether reflects true and fair view of the state of affairs of the company.	3. The objects of cost audit are to examine the cost accounting records, verify it and to give report regarding efficiency or inefficiency in cost of production and detailed analysis of cost data's.
4. In this audit all types of financial transactions are examined.	4. In case of cost audit, only expenses related to costs i.e. material, labour, overheads, and stores are thoroughly checked.
5. Financial audit is primarily conducted to protect the interest of the shareholders.	5. Cost audit is primarily conducted to protect the interest of the management, customers, government and of the society.
6. The first auditor of a company is appointed by the board of directors and subsequent auditors are appointed by' the shareholders in the annual general meeting in certain cases.	6. Cost auditors are always appointed by the board of directors with the previous approval of the Central government.
7. The financial auditor has to verify the value of stock and ensure that it has been correctly valued and shown in the balance sheet and can	7. In addition to valuation of stock a cost auditor has to determine the quantity of stock and has to see it is excessive or inadequate.
8. A financial auditor does not check the cost records in detail where manipulation can be made.	8. A cost auditor examines the cost records in detail to find the errors and also to find manipulations in the cost accounts.
9. Audited financial accounts are required to give return of income to	9. Audited cost audit is not generally acceptable to the income tax department.

10. The Financier auditor gives his opinion regarding true and fair view of accounts and do act as an advisor.	10. The cost auditor gives his opinion regarding true position of cost accounting records and also gives advice regarding increase in efficiency and profit in the
11. At the end of audit work the financial auditor sends his audit report to the management of the company.	II. At the end of cost audit the cost auditor sends his audit report to the company as well as to the Company Law Board.

MANAGEMENT AUDIT - ITs SCOPE AND OBJECTIYES

Management Audit: Management audit is a method of independent and systematic evaluation of the management activities at .all levels of management to ascertain the functions, efficiency and achievement of' the management (i.e. policies) as compared to standards set by the company.

According to L. R. Howard, "Management audit is an investigation of business from the highest level downward in order to ascertain whether sound management prevails throughout, thus facilitating the most effective relationship with outside world and smooth running of internal organization."

As per Taylor and Perry; "Management auditing is a method to evaluate the efficiency of management at all levels throughout the organization, or more specifically, it comprises the investigation of a business by an independent body from the highest executive level downwards, in order to ascertain whether sound management prevails through and to report as to its efficiency or otherwise with recommendations to ensure its effectiveness where such is not the case."

Scope of management audit: The scope of management audit is much wider than financial audit because management audit evaluates not only financial audit but also other aspects of the business. It is the method of evaluating the total efficiency of the management from the top level to the lowest level.

Therefore, the main scope of management audit is:

(i) Evaluate the efficiency of the management: Management· audit evaluates and appraise the efficiency of the management at all levels.

(ii) Implementation of principles and policies of the management: Management audit review whether principles and policies formulated by the management have been successfully implemented or not.

(iii) Find variances: It detects the variances in efficiency with the standards set by the management. .

(iv) Analyze the reasons for variances: Management audit analyze the reasons for inefficiencies of the management for not fulfilling the targets.

(v) Recommend suggestions for improvement: It gives suggestions for improvement in the areas e.g. production, sales, purchase, finance, human resources, administration etc.

Objectives of management audit: Management audit is the total audit of the management i.e. reviews how the policies of the management have been implemented and its efficiency to execute the policy. Therefore, the scope is much greater than financial audit, as it examines the all aspects of the management. Management audit has some objectives. These are discussed below:

(i) Verifying the efficiency: Management audit aims at to asses the efficiency at all levels of management and implementation of policies.

(ii) Gives suggestion for increase in efficiency: Management audit highlights the inefficiencies in different areas of management and gives his valuable suggestions and means to improve the efficiencies.

(iii) Asses the effectiveness of Planning and policies: Management audit examine and evaluates the plans and policies and judge whether planning and policies are properly implemented.

(iv) Helps to increase profitability: Management audit helps the management to increase profitability by giving remedies to maximize the organization's resources in an efficient way.

(v) Helps to co-ordinate activities: Management audit detects the interrelationship among the activities, evaluates the authority and responsibility and gives valuable suggestions for improvement of co- ordination among the activities and the employees. .

(vi) Gives valuable advice: By scanning the management efficiency and detecting the weak spots of different levels of management, the management auditor gives valuable advice to the top management regarding different policies and future course of action

DISTINCTION BETWEEN FINANCIAL AUDIT AND MANAGEMENT AUDIT

Financial Audit: Financial audit is the systematic examination of the books of accounts to give opinion regarding true and fair view of the financial position. Management audit is the evaluation of the efficiency of the management at all levels' i.e. financial and otherwise. Therefore, management audit is a total audit of the business and financial audit is a part of it.

Management audit: Management audit is a method of independent and systematic evaluation of the management activities at all levels of management to ascertain the functions, efficiency and achievement of the management (i.e. policies) as compared to standards set by the company.

The difference between financial audit and management audit are discussed below.

Financial Audit	Management Audit
1. Financial audit is the scientific and systematic examination of the books, accounts, vouchers and other financial records that will help the auditor to give opinion regarding true and fair view of the state of affairs of the business and to verify that profit and loss account reflects a true and fair view of profit or loss for the financial year.	1. Management audit is a method of indepen dent and systematic evaluation of the man agement activities at all levels of manage ment to ascertain the functions, efficiency . and achievement of the management (i.e. policies) as compared to standards set by the company.
2. The scope of financial audit is given in the company's act, 1956. This audit is only relating to financial transactions, so its scope is limited.	2. The scope of management audit is to asses the efficiency of the employees at all levers of management which is related to produc tion, marketing, finance, human resources, sales etc, so its scope is larger than finan-cial audit.
3. The person who conducts financial audit must have professional qualification, knowledge, skill, ability and expertise in the field of financial accounting except in some cases where he may not be a Chartered Accountant.	3. The person who . conducts management audit should have a strong background in different l subjects and expertise in differ ent fields in addition to financial matters.
4. Financial' audit generally starts after the close of the financial year and after' making all accounts ready.	4. Management audit may be conducted at any time depends on the needs and circumstances.
5. Financial audit is the historical examination of books of accounts of an organization by an auditor to assure that the books of accounts reflects a true and fair view of state of affairs and profit and loss for the vear.	5. Review and appraisal of implementation of policies and assessment of overall efficiency is the main task of the management auditor.
6. Financial auditor gives opinion regarding true and fair view of the financial position of the organization.	6. Management auditor makes assessment of the overall efficiency at all levels of management and gives suggestions for
7. The task of financial auditor ends when he gives his report and gives his opinion on it.	7. When the financial audit ends, management audit starts and ends when they give a report and makes outcome of assessment and gives suggestions for
8. Financial audit is compulsory in case of companies as per Companies act, Company.	8. Management audit is not compulsory as per companies act, 1956. This depends on the needs of the 0> o
9. Financial audit report is to be given to the members of the company.	9. Management audit report is to be given to the appointing authority.

ADVANTAGES OR IMPORTANCE OF MANAGEM'ENT AUDIT:

There are several advantages of conducting management audit of an organization. When an organization grows in its volume and activities, there is a need for management audit for evaluating efficiency and effectiveness of the management at all levels of the organization. The advantages and importance of management audit are discussed below:

(i) Evaluates efficiency *of* the management: Management audit is a method of independent and 'systematic evaluation of the management activities at all levels of management to ascertain the functions, efficiency and achievement of the management (i.e. policies) as compared to standards set by the company.

(ii) Scrutiny of the plans, policies and procedure: Management audit helps to determine how the management has implemented their plans, policies and procedure to reach the organizations goal.

(iii) Helps for correction of plans, policies and procedure: Through management audit, it is possible to change or revise the plans, policies and procedure as per needs of the company.

(iv) Aids for decision making: Management audit asses the ability of the managers to take important decisions and helps them to rectify the defects.

(v) Helps to get loan: Financial institutions who gives huge loan to the organizations are interested to know the efficiency of the management and the profitability. Management audit certainly gives a guide to them.

(vi) Helps to get subsidy: Before granting subsidy by the government, to any entity they are interested to know the efficiency and functioning of the management. Management audit helps in this matter.

(vii) Helps to increase profitability: Management audit helps the management to increase profitability by giving remedies to maximize the organization's resources in an efficient way.

(viii) Gives valuable advice: By scanning the management efficiency and detecting the weak spots of different levels of management, the management auditor gives valuable advice to the top management regarding different policies and future course of action.

Limitation or disadvantages of Management Audit:

Though management audit has a high value for the organization to evaluate overall efficiency of the management, still there are some limitations of this audit. These are discussed below:

(i) Reluctant to accept: The management people are not very interested to conduct such audit because of their weaknesses and inefficiency which may be revealed.

(ii) High costs: Conducting management audit of a company is a costly matter. Therefore, except large organizations small businesses can-not afford the cost of doing management audit.

(iii) Unavailability of experienced auditor: Management audit is a complex task because of its nature and large scope. The person who conducts such audit must have professional qualifications, expertise, skill, ability, and other qualities. But there are scare human resources in this field.

(iv) Not a regular audit: As management audit is conducted according to needs and circumstances of the management and is not a regular audit, the benefit of this audit can be achieved for short period.

PROPRIETY AUDIT .... ITs SCOPE AND OBJECTIVES

Propriety audit: Propriety audit is a method of audit which verifies the reasonableness of expenditure incurred by an organization and is not detrimental to public interest. This audit is generally applicable to the government organizations.

According to E. L. Kohler, " Propriety means that which meets the test of public interest, commonly accepted customs and standards of conduct. Propriety audit is an audit in which various actions and decisions are examined to find out whether they agree in public interest and whether they meet the standards of conduct."

Scope and objectives: Propriety audit not only determines the accuracy of books of accounts but also justify the expenditure in term of propriety and reasonableness. Therefore, this audit tests the public interest and evaluates its financial propriety in relation to standards or commonly accepted customs. Propriety audit is generally applicable to the government organizations as it involves a huge public money. So, public accountability is the main criteria of propriety audit. It evaluates the efficiency and prudence of government department and its propriety in relation to public money. The scope and objectives are:

(i) Confirm collection of revenue: Propriety audit helps to assess whether revenue are properly collected and recorded in the books of accounts.

(ii) Helps to detect fraud and misrepresentation: This audit helps to judge whether there is any fraud and misrepresentation of funds.

(iii) Wastage of funds: With the help of propriety audit wastage of public funds can be determined and also its utilization can be verified.

(iv) Verify justification of expenditure: Verify Justification of expenditure in relation to generally accepted standards and customs.

(v) Not detrimental: It verifies that the contracts made by the organization with the third parties are not detrimental to the public interest.

(vi) Finds misuse of power: Whether there is any misuse of power at the top level of management regarding appropriation of funds.

(vii) Evaluates internal control system: This audit evaluates whether internal control system is effective and well performing.

ADVANTAGES OF PROPRIETY AUDIT

There are many advantages of conducting propriety audit. These are discussed below:

(i) Review of plans, policies and procedure: Propriety audit helps to determine how the management has implemented their plans, policies and procedure regarding utilization of funds.

(ii) Scanning of activities of the directors: Propriety audit helps to measure the efficiency of the directors regarding justification and propriety of expenditure made by them.

(iii) Evaluates internal control system: This audit evaluates whether internal control system is effective and "Yell performing. If there is any weaknesses in the system that may be located and remedial measures can be taken.

"AN AUDITOR IS A WATCH DOG BUT NOT A BLOOD HOUND".

The remark was made by Justice Lopes in a famous case law, The Kingston Cotton Mill Company Ltd (1896). The contents of the case are given below.

Facts of the case: Stock was overvalued for several years fraudulently '0 inflate profit and dividend was paid out of that profit which results in erosion of capital. The auditor took the value of stock certified by the manager and the value was agreed by the auditor without applying reasonable care and skill and entered in the balance sheet with a note "as per manager's certificate."

Judgment: In this case Justice Lopes observed, "It is the duty of an auditor to bring to bear on the work he has to perform that skill, care and caution which a reasonably competent, careful and cautious auditor would use. What is reasonable skill, care and caution must depend on the particular circumstances of each case. An auditor is not bound to be a detective, or, as was said, to approach his work with suspicion or with a foregone conclusion that there is something wrong. He is a watch-dog but not a bloodhound. He is justified in believing tried servants of the company in whom confidence is placed by the company. He is entitled to assume that they are honest, and to rely upon their representations, provided he takes reasonable care. If there is anything calculated to excite suspicion he should prove it to the bottom, but in the absence of anything of that kind, he is only bound to be reasonably cautious and careful.

Q. What is Pre and Post audit?

Ans. Pre-Audit: Before payments are made by the business entities, proper verification should be made. This is known as pre-audit. For example, payments made for salaries, medical bills, conveyance expenses etc. In this case payment should be made after proper scrutiny of the expenses by the employees of the organization.

Post-Audit: The payments which are incurred within a very short period and it is not possible to scrutiny of the payments by the employees of the organization e.g. festival bonus is to be paid by a large organization to their employees within a day, then payment is made immediately. After making payment, verification can be made. This is known as post-audit.

Q. Give two point of difference between continuous audit and periodical audit.

Ans.

Continuous Audit	Periodical Audit
1. In this audit detailed examination of books of accounts are continuously made throughout the whole year.	1. This audit starts after completing books of a accounts and after the close of the financial year.
2. More expensive and applicable for large organization.	2. Less expensive and applicable for all organization.

Q. What is audit risk?

Ans. Audit risk is the risk of giving inappropriate opinion on financial information given by the auditor in his audit report. Therefore, before giving opinion regarding any matters the auditor should consider risk at each level of activity.

Q. What are collateral vouchers? .

Ans. A voucher which is produced instead of original voucher is called collateral voucher.

Q. What is cut-off procedure?

Ans. Cut-off procedure is a process of examination of transactions of a particular period and that would be separate from those in the forthcoming period. In other words, Cut-off procedure means separation of transactions of on period from other period.

Q. State the sources of payment of dividend in case of a company limited by shares.

Ans. As per Section 205 of the company's Act, 1956, the sources of payment of dividend are: (i) Out of current years distributable profit (ii) Undistributed profit of the past years (ii) Moneys provided by the Central or State Government under guarantee

Q. What do you mean by Audit Trail?

Ans. Audit trail refers to a system of designing of an information system in a manner that the previous data and information may be find out at any stage to verify the source, correctness, authenticity, flow and destination including the stages of security procedures for establishment of integrity of data and information.

Q. What is Fictitious Assets?

Ans. Fictitious assets are those assets which has no real physical existence i.e. assets having any realized value but whose benefit may be extended for some years. E.g. preliminary expense, profit and loss (Dr.), discount on issue of shares etc.

Q. Why Auditing is called a dynamic Social Science?

Ans. Like a social science audit has also some social objectives and social responsibilities toward the business and to the society. With the passage of time complexities and volume of business has increased substantially and increased. As a result there is a major change in its scope and responsibility Audited accounts protect the interest of the business owners, employees, customers, creditors, financial institutions, Debenture holders, Preference shareholder, Tax department, government and the others. For this auditing is called a dynamic social science.

Q. Can dividend be paid out of pre – incorporation profit?

Ans. Legally, a company has no existence before incorporation. So the profit earned at that time is not a legal profit. Therefore, a company can not declare dividend out of profit made prior to incorporation.

Q. Give the meaning of capital profit. Give examples.

Ans. Profit which should not arise normal business activities or day to day activity is known as capital profit. In other words profit arises out of non – trading activity is capital profit.

Q. What is operational audit?

Ans. Operational audit is the audit of examination of all operations and activities of an organization. It evaluates the efficiency of the departments which are in conformity with standards set by the entity and also determine how much economy and efficiency has been achieved.

Q. What is inherent risk with reference to the relevant Auditing and Assurance Standard?

Ans. As per AAS 6 inherent risk is the susceptibility of an account balance or class of transactions to misstatement that could be material either individually or, when aggregated with misstatements in other balances or classes, assuming there were no related internal controls.

Q. Distinguish between Audit and Investigation. (give two points).

Ans.

Audit	Investigation
1. Audit is the scientific and systematic examination of the books, accounts, vouchers and other financial records that will help the auditor to give opinion regarding true and fair view of the state of affairs of the business and to verify that profit and loss account reflects a true and fair view of profit or loss for the financial year.	1. Investigation is a process through which an investigator on behalf of his client investigates different matters as per need of the client and gives report to him.
2. A person must be Charted Accountant for conducting audit of a company.	2. There is no prescribed qualification in the company's act for conducting investigation.

Q. What is Surprise Check?

Ans. Some times the auditor makes a surprise check to ascertain the effectiveness of Internal Control system and to examine whether transactions are promptly recorded in the books of accounts. E.g. verification of cash balance, stock etc.

Q. Is there any distinction between Intangible assets and Fictitious assets?

Ans.

Intangible Assets	Fictitious Assets
1. Intangible assets are those assets which can not be touched or seen but whose existence can be realized through some producing ability e.g. Patent, Trade Mark, and Goodwill etc.	1. Fictitious assets are those assets which has no real physical existence i.e. assets having any realized value but whose benefit may be extended for some years. E.g. preliminary expenses, profit and loss (Dr.) discount on issue of shares etc.
2. These assets are generally shown in the Balance Sheet at cost price.	2. These assets are written off over the years and unadjusted amount is shown in the assets side of the Balance Sheet.

Q. Distinguish between Net Profit and Divisible profit.

Ans.

Net Profit	Divisible Profit
1. The excess of current income over current expenditure is net profit.	1. The part of profit which can be legally distributed as dividend among the shareholders is known as divisible profit.
2. As per companies act 1956, a company can not distribute its whole net profit as dividend among the shareholders without providing depreciation of the current years and also the previous year or years and without setting aside ascertain percentage of profit to the reserve	2. The company is not bound to give the whole net profit (after making depreciation and amount set aside for reserve) if the directors thinks it prudent to use profit for the development of the company.

Q. Give two advantages of Statistical Sampling in Auditing.

Ans. The advantages of statistical sampling are (i) This method helps to estimate the minimum sample size considering the risk and precision and (ii) It gives a good description of a large population of data than a detailed examination of all the data.

Q. Give two example of deferred revenue expenditure.

Ans. Examples are: (i) Preliminary expenses for formation of Company (ii) Discount on issue of Debentures.

Q. Distinguish between Depreciation and Fluctuation in Value.

Ans.

Depreciation	Fluctuation in Value
1. Depreciation may be defined as gradual and permanent decline in the value of fixed assets as a result of wear and tear, obsolesce, efflux ion of time, market\ changes or for any other reasons.	1. Fluctuation is a temporary decrease and increase in the value of an asset due to rise and fall in market price of an asset.
2. Provision for depreciation can be estimated beforehand so that there is lower risk for replacement of assets.	2. No depreciation is provided for fluctuation of assets because earning capacity or working life of assets does not affected due to fluctuation in value of assets.
3. Generally, depreciation is made on fixed assets.	3. Fluctuation in value may be on fixed assets or current assets.

Q. Is valuation included in verification?

Ans. Verification means checking of physical existence of assets and liabilities and confirmation and accuracy of actual ownership and liabilities shown in the balance sheet. The scope of verifications larger than valuation i.e. valuation is a part of verification. Therefore valuation is included in verification.

Q. What is meant by preliminary expenses?

Ans. When a company wants to form its business, some expenses are required for formation which is called preliminary expenses e.g. expenses relating to Memorandum and Articles of Association, Lawyers fees, expenses for preparing project report, prospectus etc.

Q. What is the meaning of window dressing?

Ans. Window dressing is a process of showing the state of affairs in a Balance Sheet in such a way that reflects a better position than its actual position to fulfill some objectives.

Q. Distinguish between Interest and Dividend.

Ans.

Interest	Dividend
1. Interest is paid on loan capital such as Debentures, loan from financial institution etc.	1. Dividend is calculated and paid on subscribed share capital such as equity share capital and Preference share capital.
2. Interest is treated as expenses of the company and charged to Profit and Loss account.	2. Dividend is treated as appropriation of profit and charged to Profit and Loss Appropriation account.
3. Payment of interest is a tax deductible item.	3. Payment of dividend is not a tax deductible item.
4. Irrespective of profit or losses of the entity interest has to be paid.	4. If there is no profit the question of payment of dividend does not arises subject to some exception.

Q. What is CRR?

Ans. Capital Redemption Reserve is a reserve which is created out of undistributed profit equal to the nominal vale of redemption of Preference Share out of profit.

Q. Give two example of asset, "Intangible but not fictitious assets."

Ans. Patent, Goodwill.

Q. What are wasting assets? Give examples.

Ans. Wasting assets are those assets which are continuously depleted and losses its value at the end of a particular time period for earning revenue. Examples are Oil Well, Quarry, Mines etc.

Q. Preksha, a member of the ICAI, does not hold a Certificate of practice. Is her appointment as an auditor valid?

Ans. To be an auditor a person must be chartered accountant of India within the meaning of the chartered Accountants Act, 1949 and also a member of the institute holding a certificate of practice. In the given case, Preksha does not have Certificate of Practice. Hence she is not eligible to be appointed as an auditor of a company.

Bibliography

1. Allen, Devin E., "Asian Contract Law", (1972), published by Cambridge University Press.
2. Anson, W.R., "Principles of the English Law of Contract and of Agency in its relation to contract", ed. 21st (1959), Oxford at the Clarendon Press, London.
3. Anand, R.L. & Iyer, Commentary on the Specific Relief Act, 1963 (Act No. 47 of 1963), ed.12th, (2011), Delhi Law House.
4. Atiyah P.S., "The Rise and fall of freedom of Contract", (1985), Clarendon, Press, London.
5. Atiyah, P.S., "Introduction to the Law of Contract",(1995), and ed.6th, (2005) published by Clarendon Press, Oxford.
6. Awasthi, S.K., "Digest on Indian Contract Act, 1872: with allied legislations", ed.1st, (1999), Dwivedi & Co., Allahabad.
7. Bangia, R.K. (Dr.), "Law of Contract & Specific Relief with Special emphasis on Law of Tender", 1994(1), reprint 2015.
8. Beatson, J., "Anson s Law of Contract", ed.27th, (1998), and ed.28th, (2002), published by Nairobi: Oxford University Press.
9. Bhadbhade, Neelima, "Contract Law in India", ed.2nd, (2012), published by Kluwer Law Intl.
10. Chawla, R.C. & Garg, K.C., "Business and Company Law", ed.1st, (1996), Kalyani Publishers, New Delhi.
11. Cheshire, Fifoot & Furmston, "Law of Contract", ed.14th, (2001), published by Lexis-Nexis, U.K.
12. Cheshire, Fifoot & Furmston, "Cases on the Law of Contract", ed.3rd, (1959) and ed.6th, (1973), Published by Oxford University Press.
13. Chitaley & Rao, "Indian Contract Act", ed.57th, (1956), Vol. I to V.
14. Chitty, "Contracts - General Principles", ed.26th, (1989), Vol. I.
15. Chitty, "Chitty on Contract", ed.28th, (1999), Volume-I, II and Supplementary, published by Sweet & Maxwell.
16. Chitty, "Mercantile Contracts", (2001), published by Universal Law Publishing Co. Pvt. Limited.
17. Chorley & Giles, "Slater s Mercantile Law", ed.15th, (1965), published by Pitman, London.

18. Curzon, L.B., "Contract Law", ed.2nd, (1995), published by Cavendish Publication, London.
19. Desai T.R., "Indian Contract Act Sale of Goods Act and Partnership Act", (2009) S.C. Sarkar & Sons Pvt. Ltd., Kolkata.
20. Dias R.W.B., Dias R.W.M., "Dias on Jurisprudence", ed.5th, (1985), published by Aditya Parkashan.
21. Furmston, M.P., "Law of Contract", ed.16th, (2012), published by Oxford University Press.
22. Furmston, M.P., Cheshire, Fifoot, "Law of Contract", ed.15th, (2007), published by OUP: Oxford.
23. Gandhi, B.M., "T.R. Desai on The Indian Contract Act and the Sale of Goods Act (With Notes Based on English and Indian Cases)", ed.20th, (2009), published by Lexis-Nexis Butterworth, Delhi.
24. Grubb, Andrew, "The Law of Contract (Butterworth s Common Law Series)", ed.3rd, (2007), published by Lexis-Nexis Butterworth.
25. Halsbury s Laws of England, ed.3rd, Vol.I. (1952), published by Lexis-Nexis Butterworth.
26. Nair, Krishnan, "Law of Contract ", (1995), published by S.Gogia & Co., Hyderabad.
27. Leake, S.M., "Principles of Law of Contract", (1911), published by Stevens & Sons Ltd., London.
28. Malik, Surendra & Malik Sudeep, "Supreme Court on Contract and Specific Relief - Since 1950 to 2014 (3 Volume Set)", ed.2nd, (2014), published by Eastern Book Company.
29. Mallick, M.R., "Commentaries on Indian Contract Act", (1999), published by Kamal Law House.
30. Markanda, P.C., "The Law of Contract (2 Volume Set)", ed.2nd, (2008), published by Lexis-Nexis Butterworths.
31. McGregor, "Damages", ed.16th, (1997), published by Sweet and Maxwell Ltd., London.
32. McKendrick, Ewan, "Contract Law - Text, Cases and Materials", (2005) Oxford University Press.
33. Peel, Edwin, "Treitel on The Law of Contract", ed. 1st, (South Asian), (2012), published by Sweet & Maxwell.
34. Pollock, Fredrick, "Indian Contract and Specific Relief Acts", ed.13th, (2006) edited by R.G. Padia, Lexis-Nexis Butterworths, Delhi.
35. Pollock & Mulla, "Indian Contract and Specific Relief Acts: with a commentary, critical and explanatory", ed.9th, (1972), by Jeevan Lal Kapur & N. M. Tripathi, Bombay.
36. Poole, Jill, "Textbook on Contract Law", (2012), published by OUP: Oxford.
37. Ramaswamy, B.S., "Contracts and Their Management", (2002), published by Lexis-Nexis Butterworths, Delhi.
38. Rao, C. Kameshwar, "Law of Damages & Compensation", ed.6th, (2005), Law Publishers (India) Pvt. Ltd. Allahabad.
39. Rao, V. Kesava, "Contracts I - Cases and Materials", (2004), published by Lexis-Nexis Butterworths, Delhi.
40. Richards, Paul, "Law of Contract", ed.9th, (2009), published by Pearson, London.
41. Saharay, H.K., "Dutt on Contract – The Indian Contract Act, 1872", ed.11th, (2013), published byEastern Law House.

42. Salzedo, Simson, "Brief Cases on Contract Law", (1995), published byCavendish Press, London.

43. Sanjiva Row, "Commentary on The Indian Contract Act, 1872 and Tenders", ed.13th, (2014), published byDelhi Law House.

44. Sen, G.M., "Case Book on the Law of Contract", ed.1st, (1970), published by Metropolitan Book Co., Delhi.

45. Simpson, A.W.B., "A History of the Common Law of Contract", (1975), published by Oxford University Press, New York.

46. Singh, Avtar. (Dr.), "Indian Contract Act", ed.9th, (2005), and "Law of Contract & Specific Relief", ed.11th, (2013), Eastern Book Company, Lucknow.

47. Singh, Nagendra, "Commercial Law of India", (1975),published by Thomson Press, New Delhi.

48. Singhal & Subbaramanium, (1999), 4th Edition, Vol. I and II, Indian Contract Act, the Law Book Company.

49. Smith,J.C. and Thomson, J.A.C., "A Case Book on Contract", ed.3rd, (1966), published by Sweet & Maxwell, London.

50. Subba Rao, G.C.V. "Law of Contract",(1995), published by S.Gogia & Co., Hyderabad.

51. Taylor, Richards. D., "Law of Contract", ed.3rd, (1989), published by Blackstone, London.

52. Treitel, G.H., "The Law of Contract", ed. 9th, (1995) published bySweet& Maxwell, London.

53. Venkata Iyer, T.S., "The Law of Contracts", ed.7th, (1999),Vol. I and II,published by Gogia & Company.

54. Weeramantry, C.G., "The Law of Contract" vol.2, (1998), Lawman (India) Pvt. Ltd. New Delhi.

Index

E

F

G

H

I

J

K

L

M

N

O

P

U

V

W